POSTCOLONIALISM AND THE HEBREW BIBLE

Society of Biblical Literature

Semeia Studies

Gerald O. West, General Editor

Editorial Board:
Pablo Andiñach
Fiona Black
Denise K. Buell
Gay L. Byron
Jione Havea
Jennifer L. Koosed
Jeremy Punt
Yak-Hwee Tan

Number 70

POSTCOLONIALISM AND THE HEBREW BIBLE
The Next Step

POSTCOLONIALISM AND THE HEBREW BIBLE

The Next Step

Edited by
Roland Boer

Society of Biblical Literature
Atlanta

POSTCOLONIALISM AND THE HEBREW BIBLE
The Next Step

Copyright © 2013 by the Society of Biblical Literature

All rights reserved. No part of this work may be reproduced or transmitted in any form or by any means, electronic or mechanical, including photocopying and recording, or by means of any information storage or retrieval system, except as may be expressly permitted by the 1976 Copyright Act or in writing from the publisher. Requests for permission should be addressed in writing to the Rights and Permissions Office, Society of Biblical Literature, 825 Houston Mill Road, Atlanta, GA 30329 USA.

Library of Congress Cataloging-in-Publication Data

Postcolonialism and the Hebrew Bible : the next step / edited by Roland Boer.
    p. cm. — (Society of Biblical Literature. Semeia studies ; number 70)
  Includes bibliographical references.
  ISBN 978-1-58983-770-6 (paper binding : alk. paper) — ISBN 978-1-58983-771-3 (hardcover binding : alk. paper) — ISBN 978-1-58983-772-0 (electronic format)
  1. Bible. O.T.—Postcolonial criticism. 2. Bible. O.T.—Criticism, interpretation, etc. I. Boer, Roland, 1961– editor of compilation.
  BS1178.H4P67 2013
  221.6—dc23   2013004125

Printed on acid-free, recycled paper conforming to
ANSI/NISO Z39.48-1992 (R1997) and ISO 9706:1994
standards for paper permanence.

Contents

Abbreviations vii

Introduction
   Roland Boer 1

Essays

Playing an Aotearoa Counterpoint: The Daughters of Zelophehad
and Edward Gibbon Wakefield
   Judith McKinlay 11

Rethinking Orality for Biblical Studies
   Althea Spencer-Miller..35

Gazing (at) Native Women: Rahab and Jael in Imperializing
and Postcolonial Discourses
   Steed Vernyl Davidson 69

"Nothing Like It Was Ever Made in Any Kingdom":
The Hunt for Solomon's Throne
   Christina Petterson 93

Is There an "Anticonquest" Ideology in the Book of Judges?
   Uriah Y. Kim 109

The "Enemy Within": Refracting Colonizing Rhetoric in
Narratives of Gibeonite and Japanese Identity
   Johnny Miles 129

Hosea and the Empire
   Leo Perdue...169

African Culture as *Praeparatio Evangelica*: The Old Testament
as Preparation of the African Post-colonial
Gerald West 193

Thus I Cleansed Them from Everything Foreign:
The Search for Subjectivity in Ezra–Nehemiah
Roland Boer 221

Essays

"It Is More Complicated": Reflections on Some Suggestive Essays
Richard Horsley 241

Responses to Miles, Perdue, West, and Boer
Joerg Rieger 261

Contributors 273
Index of Ancient Texts 277
Index of Modern Authors 285

Abbreviations

AB	Anchor Bible
ATD	Das Alte Testament Deutsch
AcT	*Acta Theologica*
ANET	*Ancient Near Eastern Texts Relating to the Old Testament.* Edited by James B. Pritchard. 3rd ed. Princeton: Princeton University Press, 1969
BA	*Biblical Archeologist*
BASOR	*Bulletin of the American Schools of Oriental Research*
BBC	Blackwell Bible Commentaries
BCT	*The Bible and Critical Theory*
BibInt	*Biblical Intertpretation*
BMW	Bible in the Modern World
BTB	*Biblical Theology Bulletin*
BTIJ	*Black Theology: An International Journal*
BZAW	Beihefte zur Zeitschrift für die alttestamentliche Wissenschaft
BZMT	Beiträge zur mimetischen Theorie
CS	Christian Scriptures
CSSH	*Comparative Studies in Society and History*
EJA	*European Journal of Archaeology*
ExpTim	*Expository Times*
FRLANT	Forschungen zur Religion und Literatur des Alten und Neuen Testaments
Gesenius	Gesenius, Wilhelm. *Thesaurus philologicus criticus linguae hebraeae et chaldaeae Veteris Testamenti*. Vols. 1–3. Leipzig: Vogel, 1829–1842.
HBT	*Horizons in Biblical Theology*
HLS	*Holy Land Studies: A Multidisciplinary Journal*
IBMR	*International Bulletin of Missionary Research*
ICC	International Critical Commentary
IRM	*International Review of Mission*

ISR	*International Socialist Review*
JAH	*Journal of African History*
JAOS	*Journal of the American Oriental Society*
JBL	*Journal of Biblical Literature*
JBQ	*Jewish Bible Quarterly*
JETS	*Journal of the Evangelical Theological Society*
JEtS	*Journal of Ethnic Studies*
JIH	*Journal of Israeli History: Politics, Society, Culture*
JRA	*Journal of Religion in Africa*
JSOT	*Journal for the Study of the Old Testament*
JSOTSup	Journal for the Study of the Old Testament Supplement Series
JSS	*Journal of Semitic Studies*
JTSA	*Journal of Theology for Southern Africa*
KTU	*Die keilalphabetischen Texte aus Ugarit*. Edited by Manfried Dietrich, Oswald Loretz, and J. Sanmartín. Neukirchen-Vluyn: Neukirchener, 1976. 2nd enlarged ed. of *KTU: The Cuneiform Alphabetic Texts from Ugarit, Ras Ibn Hani, and Other Places*. Edited by Manfried Dietrich, Oswald Loretz, and J. Sanmartín. Münster: Ugarit-Verlag, 1995.
LHBOTS	Library of Hebrew Bible/Old Testament Studies
Neot	Neotestamentica
NICOT	New International Commentary on the Old Testament
OTE	*Old Testament Essays*
OTL	Old Testament Library
OTS	*Old Testament Studies*
PEQ	*Palestine Exploration Quarterly*
ScrHier	*Scripta Hierosolymitana*
SHBC	Smyth & Helwys Bible Commentary
SJOT	*Scandinavian Journal of the Old Testament*
SocT	*Social Text*
SWC	*Studies in World Christianity*
UQR	*Union Quarterly Review*
VT	*Vetus Testamentum*
VTSup	Supplements to Vetus Testamentum
WBC	Word Bible Commentary
ZAW	*Zeitschrift für die Alttestamentliche Wissenschaft*

INTRODUCTION

Roland Boer

Although postcolonial approaches to the Bible were first broached by Hebrew Bible scholars, it has been some time since a volume of collected essays on the Hebrew Bible has been produced. In the hypermarket of academic fashions, a decade seems like an eternity. So when one writes "in the early days" of postcolonial criticism, it designates barely more than a decade and a half, yet within that time and in the vast swirl of possible approaches to biblical interpretation, let alone the wider field of literary criticism, postcolonial criticism has established itself as a major approach in biblical studies. Two other streams have combined to cement postcolonial criticism in such a dominant position. The first is the older stream of liberation readings, emerging during the 1960s but actually deriving from a millennia-long tradition of popular revolutionary engagements with the Bible, among the marginalized poor in Latin America, African Americans in the United States, women, and queers in many parts of the world. The second is the development of anti-imperial readings, in which various subtle codes and subthemes are read as counters to the dominance of empires, right through from the Assyrians to the Romans. Postcolonial, liberation, and anti-imperial—these then have mutually encouraged one another to speak up and not hold their many tongues.

As the essays and books on postcolonial analysis began to flow, as more and more texts came under analysis, as scholars from Sweden to the Sudan, from Botswana to Buenos Aires became interested in postcolonial approaches, the initiative has clearly been taken up by New Testament scholars. In this light and in the most comradely of gestures, in this volume scholars of the Hebrew Bible have taken up the challenge and gathered together a collection of essays in order to take the debate a step or two forward. That the time is right for such an intervention may be signaled by the fact that in 2011 a new program unit at the SBL began its work, called

Postcolonialism and Biblical Studies and chaired by Christopher Stanley and Yak-Hwee Tan. Up until now, papers have been presented in a variety of sessions, from African Biblical Hermeneutics, through Ezra–Nehemiah, to Ideological Criticism. At least now we have an umbrella section where all the potentialities of the intersections between biblical criticism and postcolonialism may be explored.

Before proceeding, a word of definition: it is an old point but worth repeating, that the "post" in postcolonial has a dual reference, the one temporal and the other critical. Temporally, *post*colonialism refers both to a period of time after the era of capitalist colonialism that came to an untidy end with the final wave of anticolonial revolutions in the 1950s and 1960s, and to new, more subtle and often more brutal forms of neocolonialism. Critically, *post*colonialism designates a renewed and very different mode of assessing colonial eras. Initially, the focus was very much the era of capitalist colonialism that seemed to be passing, with much attention given to the British Empire. But postcolonial criticism also developed tools for analyzing all manner of colonial endeavors, whether in the dim and distant past or very much in the present (such as the fading US empire).

For the remainder of the introduction, I offer the generically expected survey of the contributions gathered here, so that readers may gain an overview and dip in where interest is piqued. Authors for the volume were given a good deal of room to move, either focusing on a biblical text with postcolonial methodology, or exploring the interactions between the Bible and a (post)colonial context.

We begin with Judith McKinlay's "Playing an Aotearoa Counterpoint: The Daughters of Zelophehad and Edward Gibbon Wakefield," in which she takes the brief double narrative concerning the daughters of Zelophehad in the book of Numbers (chs. 27 and 36), and follows the postcolonial strategy, advocated by Musa Dube and others, of setting together texts from different times and contexts in such a way that their colonizing ideologies may be seen in sharper focus. McKinlay follows Tat-siong Benny Liew's description of "using race/ethnicity and/or postcolonialism as an interpretative category" in such a way that it leads to "an extensive and intensive detour, that takes one to and through a different literary land(scape)," so that on return to the biblical text "what and how one sees" will be changed by the encounters (146). The issue in the Zelophehad daughters' narrative is clearly a matter both of gender and of land. Viewed through a postcolonial lens, it concerns the distribution of land by those who have not yet arrived but who are already allotting property that is not theirs. In McKinlay's contribution, the different textual landscape through which a detour is made is that of nineteenth-century Aotearoa New Zealand. A contrapuntal reading sets the Numbers passages with texts concerning Edward Gibbon Wakefield and his New Zealand Company, and their settlement of Port Nicholson, planned from their base in London. The feminist turn in this postcolonial reading follows a strategy of imaginative conversation with the daughters, which unsettles the view of the daughters as five women who daringly challenge the ruling of the day, namely that only sons may inherit, as they are now seen demanding land that was not theirs, but other peoples' land. The question always to be asked and explored is whether viewing such texts together, biblical and nonbiblical, through a postcolonial lens brings a more acute awareness of the ways colonizing powers claim and maintain their dominance. Feminist and postcolonial readings are both inherently political, so it is McKinlay's contention that these texts do not remain isolated in the past, but face us with ourselves in all the complexities of our lives. This contribution is written in Aotearoa, a country still living with its colonial past, where the inhabitants currently live with the complexities of the consequences of the colonizers' land deals and settlements, and with their complicity, as *Pakeha* (non-Maori) in a politics that is still largely one of dominance.

There follows Althea Spencer-Miller's "Rethinking Orality for Biblical Studies," in which she draws deeply on the nature of orality in the Caribbean to propose some fundamental recastings of the treatments of orality and literacy in biblical criticism and wider afield. As she points out, Werner Kelber, Richard Horsley, and others have revitalized debates on the relationship between orality and early Christian literature. Subsequent discussions include themes of orality in conjunction with literacy, memory, performance, rhetoric, aurality, discourse, and even silence. Yet, in these discussions, orality remains an inferior in the conjoining but also a category that is not self-sufficient. This essay responds to orality's deprecation by arguing that orality is a substantive and independent communicative modality that functions alongside literacy with mundane regularity. This idea provides the basis for further exploration of hermeneutical and translation possibilities when orality is considered as a potent integrative force.

Also from the Caribbean is Steed Davidson and his "Gazing (at) Native Women: Rahab and Jael in Imperializing and Postcolonial Discourses." Davidson begins by pointing out that the position of Native Woman is an ambiguous one within postcolonial discourse. Given that the figure of the

Native Woman tends to be used by imperializing discourses as justification for conquest and other civilizing missions, anti-imperial discourses tend to gather around this figure as a means of preventing incursions into the homeland. Caught in the intersections of race, gender, and imperial power, the Native Woman hardly appears to possess any agency or liberatory potential. While not the subaltern that stands outside the frame, the challenge to construct/locate agency for the Native Woman remains a gap in postcolonial discourse. Davidson's contribution explores this dilemma with respect to Rahab and Jael in the books of Joshua and Judges respectively. He explores the limits in the work of various scholars that have treated these two figures from imperializing and anti-imperial perspectives. This lays the foundation for evaluating and proposing alternative positions for reading native women from a postcolonial perspective.

From Rahab and Jael as native women, we move to a very different but no less colonial situation in the Danish Empire, especially the period of the absolute monarchy from 1660 to 1848. In this context, Christina Petterson's "'Nothing Like It Was Ever Made in Any Kingdom': The Hunt for Solomon's Throne" explores the way the story of Solomon's throne in 1 Kings may be read alongside the appropriation of King Solomon by the kings of the absolute monarchy. Petterson focuses specifically on the actual throne used in the Danish royal anointment rituals from 1671 through to 1840. The throne itself was modeled on the ivory throne of Solomon, whose equal was not to be found in any kingdom (1 Kgs 10:18–20). The skeleton of the chair is wood—not just any kind of wood, but ebony, letterwood, and kingwood, veneered with narwhale tusk, and flanked by columns of turned tusk. Eight gilded allegorical figures decorate the corners and the throne is crowned with a massive amethyst. The throne presents itself as a striking piece of craftsmanship, an opulent display of wealth. It has endless symbolic value, drawing on a vast number of intertexts that present it as the seat of absolute potency. Petterson's chapter places both thrones in their imperial and biblical contexts and through these lenses provides an analysis of the materials used and the symbolism conveyed.

Uriah Kim follows with "Is There an 'Anticonquest' Ideology in the Book of Judges?" Kim deals with the use of anticonquest ideology in the book of Judges in general and Judg 10–12 in particular. This ideology allows ancient Israelites to claim foreign lands while securing their innocence and depicts the people of the land negatively in order to validate the conquest and annihilation of the land and its people. Jephthah's speech to the king of Ammonites (Judg 11:12–28) is fraught with rhetorical strategies and assumptions that reflect the politics of God, land, and identity in ancient Israel. When Jephthah's anticonquest rhetoric is viewed from Josiah's reign, one of the three likely imperial contexts (the Neo-Assyrian, Neo-Babylonian, and Persian Empires) from which Judges was edited, it mimics the Neo-Assyrian imperial ideology of conquest, imitating the empire while at the same time undermining its authority. Thus the ancient Israelites' stance toward the empire is ambivalent, as is their view of women (11:1–11, 29–40) and relationship to one another (10:6–18; 12:1–7). Moreover, in spite of chapters 10–12 being framed by the proper judges (10:1–5 and 12:8–15), ancient Israel's conflict with others (10:6–18) and within its various peoples (12:1–7) reveal that its effort to formulate a coherent God–land–identity narrative was filled with irregularities and interruptions.

In similar territory—the companion book of Joshua—but with a very different focus is Johnny Miles's "The 'Enemy Within': Refracting Colonizing Rhetoric in Narratives of Gibeonite and Japanese Identity." Miles's concern is the treatment of Japanese Americans during the Second World War, read through an intersection with Josh 9 and the Gibeonites. In both cases, one may formulate the following thesis: only when threatened by the "alien" perceived as an enemy among the colonizer does the colonizer act in such a manner as to remove the enemy within. In order to explore this thesis, Miles analyzes the rhetoric of Josh 9 and juxtaposes it to that of twentieth-century American anti-Japanese sentiments. He uncovers numerous parallels between both groups' colonization experiences, parallels that simultaneously contributed to the identity construction process for each ethnic group. In addition to language naturally fueling prejudicial attitudes manifested in the exploitation of the "other" for the benefit of "self," language circumscribes a social space, within both the residential and labor sectors, and creates a narrative that altogether establishes ethnic boundary markers and reinforces ethnic identity. Miles's contribution refracts that rhetoric of a process which marks an ethnic group's status as subservient and colonized so as ultimately to reveal the true "enemy within."

Leo Perdue turns postcolonial analysis to historical concerns with his study, "Hosea and the Empire." Perdue draws upon the work of both Meindert Dijkstra (regarding the Babylonian crisis confronting Judah) and Homi Bhabha (concerning hybridity) in order to focus on what he calls the "neo-Babylonian metanarrative" in order to understand Second Isaiah as a hidden transcript. Perdue finds Bhabha's discussion of hybridity helpful in presenting a thick description of Jewish resistance to Babylonian rule, especially among some of the exiles. For Bhabha the symbiosis of new events and discourse through hybridity leads to necessary cultural adaptations expressed through evolving tradition. Yet it is not merely adaption with a view to assimilation that occurs. Rather, hybridity becomes a subversive tool designed to deconstruct the metanarrative of the empire. The objectives of the altered, past traditions in Second Isaiah were to subvert the influence of Babylonian rule on the exiles and to construct for themselves a new language and means of living that viewed Yahweh in monotheistic terms and the exiled community as the chosen people of the universal creator and director of history. This theology became the expression of a "revolutionary monotheism" that reshaped Judah's theology and cultural hermeneutics and sought to subvert the influence of the empire on their religious identity and faith.

Our penultimate contribution has a distinctly South African focus—Gerald West's "African Culture as *Praeparitio Evangelica*: The Old Testament as Preparation of the African Postcolonial." West begins by pointing out that a strand within African theology has long argued that African culture is Africa's Old Testament and therefore Africans have had their own preparation for the gospel (that is, the New Testament). This argument is a direct response to missionary-colonialism and its denigration and demonization of African religion and culture. This theological strand in Africa has pointed to the many similarities between the Old Testament (West uses this designation deliberately) and African religio-cultures. Indeed, a comparative approach, pointing to and probing the similarities between African religio-cultural contexts and the Old Testament, has been and remains the dominant form of African biblical scholarship across the African continent. As Justin Ukpong has argued, though the comparative paradigm arises as a reaction to missionary-colonialism, it has also developed a substantive proactive orientation. West's chapter explores ways in which the Old Testament has made a substantive contribution to the formation of the African subaltern, both religio-culturally and sociopolitically. For while African religio-cultural systems have functioned as African "Old Testaments," this has never meant that Africans have moved directly to the New Testament, bypassing the Old Testament because they already have their own equivalent. Quite the opposite is the case. The Old Testament has assumed a massive presence in all forms of African Christianity, even those minimally affected by missionaries. West uses as a specific example the use of the Old Testament in Ibandla lamaNazaretha (The Congregation/Community of the Nazarites), the

African Independent/Initiated Church founded by Isaiah Shembe in the early 1900s in South Africa, and thriving today in postliberation South Africa. In particular, West's contribution probes the role of the Old Testament in the formation of Isaiah Shembe himself and in his formation of his community. West draws extensively on the primary material produced by Isaiah Shembe himself, and relates this to a re-appraisal of the work of subaltern studies (a return to which is long overdue in biblical studies versions of postcolonialism).

Finally, in "Thus I Cleansed Them from Everything Foreign: The Search for Subjectivity in Ezra–Nehemiah" I offer a sustained example of ideological suspicion that seeks to return class to a significant place in postcolonial analysis. I do so by focusing on the issue of subjectivity, a key feature of postcolonial analyses of colonial identity. How is a person constituted as a subject? What are the specific processes that produce subjects? Barely recognized in the ongoing debates concerning subjectivity (from Althusser to Butler) is that the problem itself arose in response to colonialism and anticolonial struggles from the nineteenth century onwards. The urgent issue was how colonial powers should view colonized peoples, whether they had the full status of citizen-subjects or were, in another use of the term, "subjected" peoples. In light of this background, I argue three points. First, subjectivity is a conservative question, for it postulates a universality of exclusion and not inclusion, a universal subject based on the exclusion of certain criteria and people (I make this point fully aware of the list of credentialed "left" thinkers, however mild or sharp, who have broached the matter of the subject). Second, these patterns of exclusion and identity are codes for class, which slips out of the picture too quickly. Third, in the case of Ezra–Nehemiah we find not only an effort at producing distinct subjects in a colonial matrix, but also a vicious pattern of subject-class formation that, while giving the impression of an inclusive universal, actually operates via an exclusive universal.

The respondents, Richard Horsley and Joerg Rieger, agreed to split the chapters between them, thereby offering cross-pollinating responses. The advantages both bring are due not merely from their respective wealths of experience and reflection, but also because they come from outside Hebrew Bible studies—one is a New Testament scholar, the other a theologian.

Essays

Playing an Aotearoa Counterpoint: The Daughters of Zelophehad and Edward Gibbon Wakefield

Judith McKinlay

> Then the daughters of Zelophehad came forward ... Mahlah, Noah, Hoglah, Milcah, and Tirzah. They stood before Moses, Eleazar the priest, the leaders, and all the congregation, at the entrance of the tent of meeting, and they said... (Num 27:1–2)

What is happening here and what am I to make of it? That double question, of wonderment and a critical curiosity. Others, of course, have been there before me. In 1988 Katharine Doob Sakenfeld gave an inaugural lecture titled "In the Wilderness, Awaiting the Land: The Daughters of Zelophehad and Feminist Interpretation."[1] That was over twenty years ago, a time when feminist scholars were still, in her words, "in the wilderness," so presenting three different readings of the passages in Numbers 27 and 36, using three different methodologies—all of them feminist, and, most significantly, all presented as viable even as they differed—was a strongly political move. The published version is now part of the history of feminist biblical interpretation. In the paper she quoted Letty Russell, suggesting that the "midas touch" of feminist studies turned everything "not to gold but to questions of authority" (Russell 1987, 12). Rereading her paper has led me to think once again about agendas and interests. Feminist scholars are now mostly out of the wilderness and part of a much larger group of scholars whose "midas touch" tends these days to

---

1. Published in *The Princeton Seminary Bulletin* 9.3 (1988a). A slightly modified version was reprinted in *Theology Today* in the following year as "Feminist Biblical Interpretation." These followed a previous paper, "Zelophehad's Daughters," published in *Perspectives in Religious Studies* (1988b).

turn everything to questions of power rather than authority, although, as Dennis Tucker reminds us, it is not so much a case of either/or but an awareness of the "triangulation between authority, power and justice" that is "critical" (2008, 483). We are perhaps even more aware that the process of unraveling, revealing and exposing ideological interests involves asking questions not only of texts but of ourselves. It is twelve years since Daniel Patte's challenging call, "regarding each of our individual interpretations, the question 'Why did we choose this interpretation rather than another one?' can no longer be avoided by pretending that it was demanded by the text" (1998, 22).

There should now be nothing new in this. We know that readers and contexts make a difference, that readers always read from somewhere, and that we all bring our interests and considerable baggage with us. I read as a woman, a biblical reader, and a *Pakeha*, that is, nonindigenous New Zealander. All three aspects contribute to my identity, which is further formed by the stories of women, both within and outside the biblical texts, and by the history of the land in which I live, Aotearoa New Zealand, to give it both its Maori and *Pakeha* names. As a woman, I want to champion these five daughters of Zelophehad, who so daringly challenge the system. I read their narrative in considerable wonderment. Where did they find the courage to stand there, in full view, speaking not only coherently but so radically? How was it that they got away with it? I am in some awe of these five, Mahlah, Noah, Hoglah, Milcah and Tirzah, whose action in stepping forward to present their case opens chapter 27. Not only did the tradition remember them, setting the names of all five of them on the scroll, even prefaced with their genealogy, but, as Tamara Eskenazi notes, their story "forms a counterpoint to stories about the five women in Exodus 1 and 2," which together "create a symbolic symmetry" that frames Israel's journey, from Egypt to those years in the wilderness (2008, 1025). I am indeed in awe of them.

I return to the text and read it again, watching these five who so daringly challenge the ruling of the day that only sons may inherit, a ruling that comes with the full weight of divine warrant. There is no indication of fear or knee-shaking anxiety, although they must surely have been aware of the possible consequences of such a challenge. They simply step up and present the facts of their case. "Give us," they demand, not softening it with any polite niceties. Nor do they do this privately, but at the entrance of the tent of meeting, challenging Moses in full view and hearing of the whole assembly, including Eleazar, the priest, and their leaders. The reaction is immediate: no words but action. In a move that links his action with that of the daughters, signaled by the repeated verb *qrb*, Moses takes the challenge to his God, who is also their God, who, seemingly without hesitation, declares this to be a just case and orders, with full doubly weighted verb, that they be given their due inheritance rights. One does wonder why this was not the ruling in the first place, considering that, according to Zafrira Ben-Barak (1980), in at least some of the earlier ancient Near Eastern societies daughters did have such rights, in order to save a family's patrimony. As a woman, I want to agree with Yael Shemesh, that "It is the tale of a personal victory by five intelligent women, whose initiative bettered the legal status of a particular category of women" (2007, 82), and to say with Katharine Sakenfeld, "those with the least power and the most to lose dare to challenge the epitome of authority, God's own spokesperson Moses, and even implicitly to suggest that God's own decrees may have overlooked an important point" (1988b, 40). I want to clap them and say, well done! You are indeed heroic foremothers.

Yet it is always more complicated than this, and, in any case, there is something a little naïve in wanting to make such whole-hearted claims. I reread the text once more, and find myself asking what it is that I am reading. Is this fact or fiction? Did these daughters ever exist, or is their story simply a narrative introduced—perhaps even written—by the scribes to enliven, as well as explain, an otherwise inexplicable legal ruling? Perhaps they are no more than a fictional element in a haggadah, explaining a changing halakah. But would any scribes have acted so independently of tradition? Could these five daughters really be no more than the figments of scribal imagination? Surely they must have existed somewhere in Israel's remembered past. Scholars who study social and cultural memory note that while "the construction of social memory can involve direct connections to ancestors in a remembered past," it can also "involve more general links to a vague mythological antiquity," and, more significantly, that so-called memories of the past may include "re-interpretation(s) of monuments or landscapes" (Van Dyke and Alcock 2003, 3). The archaeological findings of Noah and Hoglah listed as the names of towns on clay fragments of the eighth-century B.C.E. Samaria Ostraca would seem to hint of this. Tirzah and Mahlah also appear as names or variants of names of towns or regions in other biblical texts (1 Kgs 14:17; Cant 6:4; 1 Kgs 19:16), while Milcah is thought to refer to the region between Noah and Hoglah. Tamara Eskenazi, who lists these findings, suggests that "It is conceivable that the five sisters are among the ancestors whose names became toponymns (place names)" (2008, 972–73).[2] But could it not be the other way round, that the narratives grew from the place names? I imagine the five saying to me,

> Why are you raising all these problems? Did you not see that even before our story begins, our names—the names of all five of us—appear in the long list of the second census in Num 26:33—that we are there in Israel, among all the sons?
> Oh yes, I say, bypassing the matter of historicity, but you are only there because Zelophehad had no sons. The text makes that very clear: *Zelophehad had no sons but only* (*ki 'im*) *daughters*. You are the lamentable substitute. Your genealogy in chapter 27 even begins with a listing of sons, five sons, before the substitute five daughters.
> But they insist: we *are* there and that's the point. We're a memory important to Israel.

That, of course, is the key. As Van Dyke and Alcock note, "people remember or forget the past according to the needs of the present" (2003, 3). Further, as Baruch Levine notes, the passage does appear to meet a need, for "[o]n the face of it," the function of Num 27 "is to introduce innovative legislation" (2000, 342). This apparently groundbreaking legislation is, however, not quite so innovative when we reach its revision in chapter 36. As Sue Levi Elwell comments,

> given that biblical culture was based on a binary understanding of sexuality, and that all women were potential brides and mothers, it seems odd that these women are initially dealt with solely as inheritors and not as sources of land and wealth for their eventual, inevitable husbands. Chapter 36 rectifies this oversight. (2006, 118–19)

Not surprisingly, considering this oversight, the elders are not happy with the ruling of chapter 27: they are indeed concerned about their tribal

---

2. Eskenazi adds, with acknowledgement of the input of Carol Meyers, "this conclusion is strengthened by the fact that many of the fragments from Samaria also mention other names from Joshua 17, referring to individuals who appear elsewhere as clan names as well as territory names" (2008, 973). This is also noted by Ben-Barak (1980, 27).

property rights and land possession, which, for them, is *the* pressing concern rather than the more particular matter of the daughters' case, namely, Zelophehad's name or respected memory. Theirs is a more clandestine approach, not public, not at the entrance to the tent of meeting, not in the presence of Eleazar the priest, but simply to Moses and the heads of the ancestral houses. Nor does Moses physically take it to God, but simply delivers the new verdict *according to the word of YHWH*. The daughters are not even present. As Sakenfeld writes, they seem to have been "little more than pawns in a potential land dispute" (1988a, 184).

Or is there more to this double narrative? Whether or not these two chapters were written at different times, by different authors or inserted by different redactors, all of which have been suggested by various commentators, placed as they are now, they form an inclusio, "fram[ing] the deliberately unfinished story of the second generation" (Ulrich 1998, 538).[3] It is a significant piece among the many preserved as Israel's cultural memory. The teasing question, however, is, What was it that the tradition shapers wanted remembered? What present arrangement was to be legitimated by such a narrative? Was the role of the daughters' tale to answer any querying of women's inheritance? In this preview of life in the land, Israel's literary mock-up, was there, as Roland Boer suggests, a need to counter this possibility and to reassert the primary place of the male line in all its aspects, including inheritance? So that what this double narrative opens up is a "glimpse of something denied or repressed ... specifically the threat of women with inheritance *not* attached to a man," but not entirely denied, for in "a subtle ideological move" the text declares, narratively, "that female inheritance is perfectly understandable within a pattern of male inheritance" (2009, 55–56). There is something chilling about the cleverness of this ploy that both opens up and closes in women's lives.

Yet the combination of women and land hints at more at stake than simply inheritance and women's place in that, for, as Carol Delaney observes, "women *are* land.... fields and daughters are tended and the fruits of this labour are to be kept within the group" (Delaney 1991, 102; quoted by Carden 2006, 437).[4] For the tribal elders there is to be no question: naturally, the daughters must marry within the clan, for these are

---

3. Noted also by Milgrom (1990, 512) and Olson (1996, 165).
4. See, regarding the Deuteronomic law, Tal Ilan: "The basic assumption of the law is that women, rather than owning property, are in themselves a form of property" (2000, 176).

their women and their land, and so the narrative concludes, "*the daughters of Zelophehad did as YHWH had commanded Moses, they married sons of the father's brothers ... and their inheritance remained in the tribe of their father's clan*" (Num 36:10–12). And, of course, as Sakenfeld comments, the ruling is weighted more heavily by the theological theme that permeates the book, for not only does the story conclude with "the women's compliance.... the entire book ends with an illustration of the narrator's overarching theme of the perfect faithfulness of the second generation" (1992, 50).

Widen the focus, however, and there may be a yet more earthy realpolitik involved. For the Book of Numbers has its sight firmly set on the land, the prize gifted by YHWH, to which Israel determinedly moves in spurts and stages. Snaith's suggestion in his 1966 reading, noting Josh 16:1–6, that this double inheritance tale was a way of "account[ing] for the fact that the tribe of Manasseh held land to the west of the Jordan," as well as "the lands of Gilead and Bashan on the east," may still hold (1966, 126). Baruch Levine, too, writes,

> Clearly the episode of Zelophehad's daughters is related to the anomalous situation of the tribe of Manasseh, the only one that settled both to the east and to the west of the Jordan. This, then, is the historiographic agenda that was ultimately of greater significance than the legal exception involved. The function of the episode was to legitimate Manassite claims in Canaan proper. (2000, 342; see, similarly, Simkins 2004, 12)

However, according to the narrative, the land remains largely to be entered! They have not got there yet! Certainly there are skirmishes and some inroads, such as the capture of Gilead by the sons of Machir in Num 32:39–40, where *Moses gave Gilead to Machir, son of Manasseh, and he settled there*. Interestingly, as Levine points out, in Num 32:33 Moses gives the half-tribe of Manasseh the lands of kings Sihon and Og "before there is any mention of that group at all!" (2000, 500–501). Significantly, too, there is no mention of any divine command to capture the land of Transjordan, and even more interestingly, the land the daughters are requesting as their right, is not captured land, but an *ăḥuzzâ*, land acquired through grant or purchase.[5] Yet Moses is distributing this land from outside its boundaries.

---

5. Levine (2000, 346) notes that "Later priestly authors often used *ăḥuzzâ* as a synonym for *naḥălâ*, leveling the primary distinction between the two terms." This

All this negotiating and reconsidering is taking place on the fields of Moab. Moses is marking out and handing over other peoples' land, from Moab. I am reminded again by those who work in this field that "memories are not ready-made reflections of the past, but eclectic, selective, reconstructions." Not only can such reconstructed memory "symbolically smooth over ruptures, creating the appearance of a seamless social whole," but typically "is often used to naturalize or legitimate authority" (Van Dyke and Alcock 2003, 3). There is, of course, the added factor here: Moses is the servant of YHWH, the go-between. This is allocation by the deity, part of Israel's projected "theo-economics," to use Boer's term (2009, 111). Once written down, such ancient constructed memory, bolstered by its divine warrant, is seen and understood as "secure and reliable" (Van Dyke and Alcock 2003, 3–4). I need to remember, however, that this is the reconstruction of those who won Others' land, that it is their scribal representatives who recorded and preserved it to be a part of their sacred scriptural tradition.

So I turn again to the daughters of Zelophehad and say to them, much as I would like to honor you for your initiative and the risk you took, as disenfranchised women, in "successfully confront[ing] an unjust system and propos[ing] a more equitable law" (Eskenazi 2008, 971), I find I cannot overlook the fact that the land you were demanding, as your right, was not yours at all, but other peoples' land. You were part and parcel of Israel's planned settlement of Canaan. Your so-called promised land was Canaan's milk and honey land. You are part of Canaan's story just as much as Israel's.

They reply that it is now part of their sacred history, and in any case, the point I am making is my own particular interpretation. Can I not leave them in peace, and respect a past ordained by YHWH?

I begin to wonder what I am doing, conversing with textual figures, who, as I have argued, are likely fictional elements of an ideologically

---

is how the term *'ăḥuzzâ* is being used here in the general sense of "territory, land." He cites v. 7, where *'ăḥuzzâ naḥălâ* is used rather than *'ăḥuzzâ* alone as in v. 4. This distinctive use of *'ăḥuzzâ* in v. 4 does, however, seem significant in a postcolonial reading. The addition of *naḥălâ* would seem to be an extension rather than a synonymous addition: YHWH is decreeing that the *'ăḥuzzâ* is to be an inheritance, i.e. it is theirs to be handed on to their inheritors after their death.

composed scroll. I ask myself, Does this matter? Postcolonial critics, however, answer strongly that it does: we need critical approaches, such as the postcolonial lens, to reveal the ideological manipulating that lies behind these carefully crafted narratives. For, as R. S. Sugirtharajah describes it, the postcolonial lens functions as "an interventionist instrument which refuses to take the dominant reading as an uncomplicated representation of the past" (2005, 3). It is this postcolonial optic that helps us see and appreciate, in Sugirtharajah's term, the "lopsidedness" of Israel's so-called remembered history (1998, 93), for, as I have noted above, "people remember or forget the past according to the needs of the present." The complication is that "the needs of the present" are frequently obscured and kept well out of view. Following the storyteller's scenario in its twists and turns through the book of Numbers, our eye has been firmly fixed on these homeless Israelites. We have watched and felt for them. Now, as they are on the last leg of their long trek, we are persuaded to sympathize in turn with the daughters, with Moses and these tribal elders, all concerned for their future, albeit still poised there on the plains of Moab. The politics of a much later Israel or Yehud are well hidden. The drama of the story draws us in, and would have us accept that these rulings are indeed delivered by God, rather than having been written on the scroll by some later exilic or postexilic hand. In any case, uncovering the particular agenda is difficult. Was it the issue of justifying the holdings of the Manasseh tribe, as Snaith and Levine have proposed? Or is Simkins right, suggesting that the amended version in chapter 36 represents the need of a postexilic Yehud, that it is an attempt by the Yehud leadership to reassert the rights of the extended family in a return to a domestic mode of production (2004, 12)?[6]

Postcolonial criticism is not, however, only concerned with (re)reading the past. It has an equal, and urgent, interest in the present, aware, with the memory theorists, that "social memory is an active and ongoing

---

6. Simkins understands the daughters' arresting win in ch. 27 to have been an early tradition, but "by the time of the compilation of the book of Numbers in the post-exilic period, the precedent set by the daughters of Zelophehad raised concerns for the extended family, now living under a new mode of production—the resurgence of the domestic mode. Therefore a new story was added as an addendum" (2004, 12). See also Budd 1984, 389. See Römer 2005, among others, who understands the final form of the Deuteronomistic History taking shape in Yehud during the Persian period.

process," intruding into the consciousness of the present (Van Dyke and Alcock 2003, 3). It typically refuses the option of studying the past or documents of the past, as if they are hermetically sealed from the present, for it recognizes that, as David Lowenthal writes, "The past is everywhere. All around us lie features which, like ourselves and our thoughts, have more or less recognizable antecedents.... Whether it is celebrated or rejected, attended to or ignored, the past is omnipresent."[7] What is equally true is that the details of our own, today's, past are also frequently hidden. For colonizers and their descendants take care in shaping their answers to the question that all settler peoples have to answer: "By what authority and on what grounds can they justify to themselves either their own moves or those of their parents, grandparents or great-grandparents to gain and preserve authority over land and the people of the land" (Fleras and Spoonley 1999, 14)?

It is their careful crafting, if not manipulation, of a country's memory that the postcolonial lens probes, with its sharp "realization of the problematic of domination and subordination" (Segovia 2005, 65). The "problematic" of this section of the book of Numbers is clear: the distribution of land by those who do not own it, yet are allotting its sections from beyond its borders. What is equally clear is that while the scribes responsible may have been hard at their work in postexilic Yehud, retrospectively claiming the legitimacy of their land, features of their so-called history are certainly not unique to Israel or Yehud. Outsiders' distribution of land that takes little or no account of the rights of people already living there, with their own history of settlement, immediately links this ancient biblical text with the colonizing pasts of countries such as Aotearoa New Zealand. For the distribution of land by intruding colonizers is a problematic feature from an omnipresent past that continues to haunt us in the twenty-first century, however much we might wish to ignore and erase it from our memory.

The critical question is how to explore the connection in a way that allows us to recognize the "lopsidedness" of our own understanding of our past. For while postcolonial criticism provides a lens or framework, it is, as Sugirtharajah writes, "a reading posture" and not a methodology (1998, 93). The challenge is to choose an analytical tool that is capable of highlighting similar or shared agendas or ideologies that are part of these

---

7. Lowenthal (1985, xv), quoted by Van Dyke and Alcock 2003, 3. See Sugirtharajah's statement that postcolonialism's "insight lies in understanding how the past informs the present" (2001, 11).

histories, both Israel's and my own. Edward Said has suggested a contrapuntal reading, a rereading of the cultural archive "with a simultaneous awareness both of the metropolitan history that is narrated and of those other histories against which (and together with which) the dominating discourse acts" (1993, 51). The past of Aotearoa New Zealand is, of course, far removed both from the histories claimed in the book of Numbers and those experienced by its writers and/or editors. Musa Dube's programmer of "reading sacred and secular texts, ancient and contemporary texts ... side by side," to highlight "imperializing or decolonizing" ideologies, does, however, provide the possibility of a cross-cultural, cross-time counterpoint (2000, 199–200). Even if Aotearoa New Zealand is a largely secular society, the book of Numbers remains part of our cultural archive—the Bible is part of our heritage, brought here through different historical routes. Maori received it from the missionaries, in that ambivalent and ambiguous colonizing move. For those of us descended from settlers it traveled on the ships with our forebears. So Israel's narrative of origins, as well as our own, is part of this country's cultural archive, even if both lie half-forgotten beneath our skin.

It is not difficult to find a partner for my contrapuntal reading, for just as Moses distributed land from the plains of Moab, so Edward Gibbon Wakefield, sitting in his London office, set his sights on Aotearoa. So I now turn to these other texts, for here, too, there are written records as well as present-day assessments and reassessments. The parallels immediately catch my eye: just as Moses sent out Caleb to look over the land in chapter 14 and in chapter 34 appointed him, as one of the tribal commissioners, to apportion it, so Wakefield, from his London-based New Zealand Company, on the other side of the world, sent out William Mein Smith, the appointed Surveyor-General. In his case, with a carefully detailed plan "for the splendid town of Britannia, with 1100 acre sections laid out in a strict geometry" (Temple 2002, 267). The fact that his blueprint bore little relation to the geography of the land is no surprise.[8] That was, however, of no consequence to the planners, for the prospectus drawn up in London for the projected immigrants "emphasized that, by the time the first immigrant vessels arrived, both a town and extensive country estates would have been laid out" (Patterson 1990, 61).

---

8. As Patterson writes (1990, 64), the survey designed in London "was inappropriate to the conditions. Based on the creation of a regular 'chessboard' of rectangles, it had been most extensively used previously on relatively flatlands."

If Numbers is largely a historical fiction, Wakefield's writings, *A Letter from Sydney* (1829) and *A View of the Art of Colonization* (1849), have also been rightly described as "works of fiction" (Wevers 1997, 180), in that his vision was equally utopian.[9] Where Moses planned an Israelite settlement in Canaan, Wakefield's strategy was a very English plan, albeit for a land occupied by Maori. There was, of course, an underlying reality: Britain, as well as Moses, needed land. For nineteenth-century England, as Philip Temple writes, "New Zealand seemed Eden's most likely location" (2002, 233). Wakefield himself writes in *A Letter from Sydney*, "the emigrants are to "regard the colonies as the land of promise" (in Temple 2002, 128). Both writers appear to have the Bible in mind.

While Wakefield's was no militaristic conquest, his assumption, like that of the narrated Moses, was that the land was there for the taking. Certainly there were inhabitants, but much of the country was "wilderness land ... worth nothing to its native owners" (in Temple 2002, 230–31).[10] If this does, at least, recognize that this was not *terra nullius*, the term "wilderness" carries other echoes, not least the wilderness passage through which the Israelites had made their long trek to the so-called promised land. Later New Zealand Company documents use the term "waste lands," in the quite specific sense of "land which was utilised in a way different from the norm in English society.... The land should be fenced, ploughed, replanted in a neat, controlled, English manner," the point being that, in the eyes of the New Zealand Company colonizers, "this unfenced, ecologically controlled structure looked peopleless and unplanned" (Love 1997, 6).[11] Yet, like Canaan, the land was peopled, and so the argument: this

---

9. As Wevers explains, "They express in narrative form ... the project of colonization" (1997, 180). Temple (2002, 127) describes *A Letter from Sydney* as "a racy account of life in the penal Antipodes, mixed with economics, political puffery and moral purpose leading to the explication of a theory of planned colonisation.... There was also a certain romance to conjuring up utopias in the sun."

10. Referring to a twenty-four-page pamphlet, *Instructions from the New Zealand Land Company to Colonel Wakefield* (i.e., William), dated 1838.

11. As Rosemarie Tonks notes (1990, 35), Governor Hobson was to use the term "waste lands" in his Land Titles Validity Proclamation issued in January 1840, restricting land sales to "waste lands" which Maori could sell "without distress or inconvenience to themselves." In 1853 Governor Grey issued a proclamation regulating "the Sale, Disposal ... Letting ... and Occupation of the Waste Lands in New Zealand," which Moon (2009, 55) describes as "the single most aggressive act against Maori that the colonial Government had yet perpetrated." The Waste Lands Act of 1854 moved

British settlement would be of considerable benefit to Maori for "instead of a barren possession with which they have parted," they would "have property in land intermixed with the property of civilized and industrious settlers, and made really valuable by that circumstance" (Temple 2002, 230–31).[12] But, crucially, this would not be their land. As late as 1853 Wakefield was continuing to advocate that native title be extinguished "either by confiscation or by the gentler process of purchase."[13]

The ideology is clear, and chilling. Just as Israel was YHWH's chosen, so, in Wakefield's view, as he writes in *A Letter From Sydney*, "any people, no doubt, must be the better for communication with the most civilised people in the world" (in Temple 2002, 141). For, as he writes to his brother-in-law, Charles Torlesse, in 1837, "the New Zealanders are not savages, but a people capable of civilization. A main object will be to do all that can be done for inducing them to embrace the language, customs, religion, & social ties of the superior race" (in Temple 2002, 190). The picture that the New Zealand Company "blazoned over the British press" was "of the Maori people longing so greatly for Europeans to come and 'civilise' them that they gladly signed away all their lands" (Burns 1989, 119). The reality was, of course, a little different: Maori "were astonished and bewildered to find Pakeha tramping over their homes, gardens and cemeteries, and in place sticking pegs in the ground," and, in fact, "took the obvious action and quietly removed the surveyor's pegs" (151–52).

The "art of colonisation," in Wakefield's terms, was "the art of finding yourself, wherever you were, 'at home' and not in exile from home," a version "of the theme of 'natural occupancy,'" which, as Linda Hardy writes, is "one of the dreams of empire," the dream both of Israel and the Wakefields (1997, 190–91). So, for example, William Wakefield, Edward's brother, who had been sent out to New Zealand to oversee the distribution of land, started by "claiming title in a symbolic way that made

---

this power from the governor to parliament and the provincial councils. See Moon (2009, 114).

12. According to the pamphlet *Instructions from the New Zealand Land Company to Colonel Wakefield*. A significant feature of the plan was to set aside one-tenth of the Company's lands as reserves for Maori. However, as Tonks (1990, 50) notes, these were ill-chosen, "as many were too far from the pa and too hilly for good potato grounds."

13. Wakefield, in *The New Zealand Spectator and Cook Strait Guardian*, April 2, 1853, quoted by Moon (2009, 53), who comments that Wakefield's "visions of acquiring cheap land had previously done a great deal to blight race relations in the country."

the land British in imagination. He renamed all the main features of the harbour. The Heretaunga River became the Hutt; Matiu Island became Somes" (Temple 2002, 251). As Philip Temple states (251-52), "This obliterating of Maori names, this possessive naming, could be described as a terrible arrogance but it was the natural and unconscious act of people confident in their own superiority." This was no longer a dream of empire, but a sign of its reality.

Ian Wedde's fictionalized tale has William Wakefield

> flapping his arms, his head jerking about as if he expected to see a populous town rise out of the ground before his very eyes, English gardens of droopy elms on the outskirts with pretty English women in them, green veins in their necks, and further out post-and-rail enclosures and the squire knocking dung from his riding boot by the stables ... those word pictures of drooping elms and workers' houses and English farmyards, and never even a mention of a Maori—where were *they* in all these fancy plans? (1986, 191-93)

There are resounding echoes here of Deuteronomy's vision of entering a land of fine cities and houses filled with every good thing, vineyards and olive groves already planted and cisterns already prepared (Deut 6:10-11).

But imagined utopias do not turn so easily into reality. Despite the rulings delivered in Numbers, once they arrive in the land, the daughters do not immediately gain the land due to them. They have to speak up for themselves and appeal once again (Josh 17:3-6), this time to Eleazar and Joshua, and the leaders, although it seems from the preceding verses that male descendants gained their land as promised, without further ado. For the daughters, as Ankie Sterring comments, "apparently the presence of so many witnesses ... including Eleazar the priest, is in itself not sufficient to let the procedure run smoothly" (1994, 95). And where, one might ask, considering the concern of the elders that these daughters marry, are their husbands? Once again, they are on their own. Nor is there any mention of how the daughters viewed the land itself once they had arrived there. Were they happy with what they saw? Perhaps this is an understandable silence considering the risk they had taken in challenging in the first instance, and also considering the fact that YHWH is the gift-giver providing the warrant for their claim. Yet, in the same chapter, Joshua is heard dealing with the complaints of the sons of Joseph, who are not happy with their allotment, just as William Wakefield found himself fielding complaints from immigrants who, having signed up for "country sections," found on their arrival in 1842 that their allotments were considerably more countrified and much further away from the urban center of Wellington than they had been led to believe (Temple 2002, 303).

Levine's suggestion (2000, 360–61) that "questions about some of the holdings of Manasseh west of the Jordan" may be lying behind the daughters' tale, and that the priestly historiography served to establish, "at least temporarily … the integrity of this territory," also finds some parallel in Aotearoa, where questions over the validity of the New Zealand Company's land sales had serious and long-ranging legal consequences.[14] In both cases such questioning was deemed unacceptable. William Wakefield writes home to England, "if the 'real and good conscience' of the case rather than legal forms were considered, the Company's titles were 'unimpeachable', with the bargains made with the Maori conducted in a spirit of justice and openness" (in Tonks 1990, 49).[15] As Temple writes (2002, 302), "for William, Jerningham and their many supporters in Wellington, putting Maori rights before theirs was a betrayal of British race and civilization," this despite the fact that "one of the company's grand aims had been precisely to bring civilized law and society to the Maori."[16] Does one ask of the rights of the Canaanites?

Behind both histories, with their judicial accounts of land title and legal appeals, there also lies the shadow of violence. As Boer comments, while Israel attempts to set out a blueprint for life in the land, the irony is that the imaged peace and prosperity "relies on the covert violence of a series of repressions" (2009, 140).[17] The daughters' insistence that their father's death in the wilderness was not in any way connected with the Korah insurrection of Num 16 is a reminder of this, but as the narrative

---

14. Temple also notes (2002, 367) that "William's disputes and poor relations with Maori, Crown officials and his own surveyors meant that clarity over colonists' land titles was interminably delayed, causing frustration and conflict within the settlements."

15. Re a letter written May 30, 1842. As Tonks notes (1990, 39), the task was firstly "to establish the title of the sellers to the property which had been sold—a difficult task since the Maori often disputed among themselves as to their respective rights—and then find out whether the sale was legitimate."

16. In the end, after many delaying tactics, compensation became, to quote Tonks (1990, 58), "the cure-all for a faulty title."

17. Suggesting further (Boer 2009, 124) that "the ideal of a peaceful Israel is a fantasy since it necessarily hides the fantasmatic kernel of structural violence on which that ideal is based."

moves on towards their challenge, it is the Baal-peor episode of chapter 25 that leaves "a profound tension" yet to be resolved (Grossmann 2007, 56–57). The echo of 25:6 in the daughters' narrative in chapter 27 is chilling: in both the act is "before a similar audience ... in the same location ... presented openly and publicly" (65). Further violence follows in chapter 31, waged with divine warrant and cloaked under the pretext of obedient vengeance. For the Wakefields and the New Zealand Company it is the Wairau Massacre of 1843, following their claim of the rich Wairau valley, land not only in Maori possession but in Te Rauparaha's, a skilled and fearsome warrior, chief of the Ngati-Toa. To survey and claim his highly valued land was not only provocative and illegal, but foolish in the extreme, and the consequences both dire and predictable.[18] While there is no sense at all of any divine justification in the Wakefields' actions, in both cases a gap in the narrated histories is suddenly opened: we see the ruthlessness and cost of a confronting dominance that so often, and perhaps inevitably, threatens the political utopian dream.[19]

At this point, the daughters interrupt, claiming they seem to have become invisible. Besides, they say, this has been wholly an account of male Wakefields. Were there no women? I hesitate, remembering Kwok Pui-lan's statement that it is "the intricate relationship between colonialism and patriarchy" that sets the task for feminist postcolonial critics, in

---

18. As the inquiries about the legalities of the company's claims were still proceeding, the survey had no legal warrant. The Company, however, was running short of land, 70,000 acres short, so despite Te Rauparaha's appeal to the Land Commissioner, it proceeded. Misunderstandings and misjudgments were to follow. Burns (1989, 238) quotes from Commissioner Spain's first report, dated September 12, 1843, that the New Zealand Company had attempted "to set British law at defiance. It really appears that the Company having put into their deeds such a description of the property alleged to have been purchased as to comprise one-third of New Zealand, have afterwards selected the most available districts within their imaginary boundaries, without the slightest reference as to whether they had purchased them of the aborigines or not."

19. See Boer (2009, 115) regarding the Hexateuch: "the perpetual effort to close down the unending rebellion against the state-in-waiting is also the mark of the impossibility of this myth's realization"; see also his comment regarding "a deeper logic at the heart of political myths that is still with us today. Each system operates in terms of an ideal or utopian projection of what it might be. The key to realizing that ideal is overcoming some obstruction or other. The catch is that the obstruction or limit is precisely what makes the system work, its necessary limit."

that "the analysis of one without the other is incomplete" (2006, 48). So I turn to them again.

> Are you really so concerned about women's rights? Certainly your challenge brought about a surprising flexibility in the godhead, so that gender justice might seem to have ruled, but was it not the case that your main concern was preserving your father's name? Your case was not "a demand for justice for women in general," but "his name and memory" (Shemesh, 86). Once the elders intervened, the world of sons and fathers remained firmly in place. After that second ruling you only get to own your land for your lifetime. Once you die, it belongs solely to your husbands, and heirs, who will only include daughters if you have no sons. Besides, I say, why this collective fivesome? Is it to downplay your power—it needed five of you rather than just one memorable woman?

As Cheryl Exum writes, "One way of dealing with women's power is to diffuse it" (1994, 83). She was writing of Exod 1–2, but the point is the same.

And yes, there was a gender concern for Wakefield. As Raewyn Dalziel notes, *A Letter from Sydney* indicates "he was concerned about sexuality and reproduction, setting down the principle (which he never abandoned), that the ideal emigrants were young married couples" for "without women colonisation could not succeed." And it is women who bring religion into view, for he writes in *the Art of Colonization* that "the best sort of woman to be a colonist was she for 'whom religion is a rule, a stay and a comfort'" (Dalziel 1997, 78, 83). And yes, there was a female member of the Wakefield family who comes into the Wakefields' New Zealand story, William's daughter Emily. She, too, loved her father, although she predeceased him. In fact, a letter from a cousin, Francis Dillon Bell, records that her "affections from childhood were so thoroughly centred on *him*, that kindness of others, & separation from him, could never attach her to any one else!" (in Temple 2002, 410). Was this the case with Zelophehad's daughters, who were clearly all unmarried in chapter 27? Marriage, of course, is the issue in chapter 36. Much of Emily's story also revolves around marriage. Soon after she arrived in the country she became engaged and all seemed happiness, until her fiancé fractured his skull in a fall. Despite being sent to London for treatment he did not recover. As Temple describes it, "Emily loitered palely in the house above the port, waiting news of the man to whom she was inextricably betrothed" (2002,

371). The man she did marry, shortly after the earlier fiancé's death, was Edward Stafford, who was later to become a significant figure in New Zealand's early history.[20] Here, too, there were political benefits: "William had no wealth, but he had influence and Stafford could return to Nelson with the 'Colonel in one pocket and the Company in the other" (Temple 2002, 402). So, I tell the daughters,

> Sakenfeld's statement about your being "little more than pawns" (1988a, 184) describes both you and Emily. All of you are pawns in the arrangements of your patriarchal societies, your marriages as political as your colonialist complicity.
>
> Oh yes, they say, those terms "patriarchal" and "colonialist"— so very twenty-first century—so very anachronistic, so cleverly imposed upon our world, by your "so-called" scholarship.

Do I argue back and justify myself? Should I say to them that I am indeed reading and writing their story from my twenty-first-century perspective? Do I tell them that I cannot do other than read through my own viewpoint? For, as Aichele, Miscall, and Walsh have recently written, we can understand the past "only in terms of who/what we are now." History, even as recent a history as The New Zealand Company project, "as a story of the past, must always be constructed in the present—a present that is itself not a given, objective 'reality', but also a construct produced in the fluid tension between numerous desires, interests, thoughts, memories ... and so on" (2009, 400–401). This is why every reading is a rereading. This is why even in the case of the New Zealand Company, where there are official documents as well as personal writings and letters, these will continue to be reread, reinterpreted and reassessed, as one collection of essays I have used indicates in its title, *Edward Gibbon Wakefield and the Colonial Dream: A Reconsideration*. I decide, however, that this conversation has now served its purpose.

As in any counterpoint, there are themes and counter-themes, some heard more strongly than others. I have chosen those I wished to highlight, leaving others to be heard more faintly, if at all. It is clear that Moses is the key character in the book of Numbers, and perhaps a more fitting partner

---

20. Edward Stafford was elected prime minister on June 2, 1856, the first significant holder of the office, the previous two having lasted only a matter of days.

here for Edward Gibbon Wakefield, but then Moses, as I have indicated, is the God/Israel go-between, a feature that Wakefield certainly does not share or claim. And, despite Moses' prominence, it was the daughters that led me to attempt this exercise in counterpoint, who provided the opening chord, as it were. Besides, to quote Kwok Pui-lan, postcolonial feminist critics are to "pay special attention to the biblical women in the contact zone," defining the "contact zone" as "the space of colonial encounters" (2006, 48). Although the point I am emphasizing here is that these biblical women are involved in land matters before they even reach the contact zone. It is, however, their legal challenge and its restricting amendment that point to the complexities and tensions that are part of any colonizing history that would present its people as having rightful possession of a desired and coveted land.

While, as I have noted, the book of Numbers is most likely not a recording of factual history at all, it does, however, present itself as such. In any case, it is not history per se that concerns me here but the ideology underlying both the Numbers narrative and the Wakefields' project. To quote Colleen Conway,

> methods such as postcolonial studies may well be concerned with what happened in the past, but typically only insofar as a view of the past informs a particular reading of the text in the present. Indeed, it is this latter point that distinguishes the place of history in these postcolonial readings. (2008, 86)

In the same way, it is not whether something actually took place that matters, so much as the effect of the narratives that recount the supposed events. For it is these that form our collective memory, which has been described as "one of the great stakes of developed and developing societies, of dominated and dominating classes, all of them struggling for power or for survival and advancement."[21] We, in twenty-first-century Aotearoa New Zealand, are a people still grappling with a legacy of issues of power from our colonial past, including the divide of "dominated and dominating classes," as is attested in so many of our statistics. We have a very real need to hold up these documents of "collective memory," both from the Bible and our own historical past, for close scrutiny, by whichever critical

---

21. Le Goff 1992, 97–98, quoted by Van Dyke and Alcock 2003, 3.

means. For, as Richard Bradley notes, "Even the falsest of memories can have enormous implications" (2003, 226).

The postcolonial lens is one way of exploring such implications and effects. Colleen Conway, using the analogy of stage productions, writes of John's Gospel as "a cultural token [that] lends itself to wide-ranging productions as we try to work out who we are in the twenty-first century" (2002, 492). It seems to me that a contrapuntal postcolonial reading is one such production. Although as I have been pursuing my contrapuntal weaving of these two narratives, far apart in time and genre, I have been very aware of Tat-siong Benny Liew's observation that "at the end one cannot be sure if race/ethnicity and/or postcolonialism is a lens through which one interprets the Bible, or whether the Bible is a lens through which one investigates race/ethnicity and/or postcolonialism" (2005, 146). The daughters' narrative has, of course, allowed me to add gender/patriarchy. He is writing specifically of the postcolonial lens, but it applies even more aptly to a postcolonial counterpoint.

So, finally, what have I achieved in setting these two narratives together? I am well aware that there are inherent problems in weaving together two such different "histories." David Jobling, for example, warns against drawing simplistic analogies between societies far apart in time and mode of production (2005, 194). I recognize, too, that interweaving a narrative where Moses, the servant of God, and YHWH are key figures, with a notably nondivinely sanctioned history, runs the risk of an ideological gulf that is too wide, that the result may be an inherently unbalanced and dissonant counterpoint. In response, I would simply quote Liew's description of the gains of a postcolonial approach (2005, 146):

> Using race/ethnicity and/or postcolonialism as an interpretive category should lead to an extensive and intensive detour that takes one to and through a different land(scape). This different place is one filled with different names, texts, concerns, traditions, and procedures. By the time one (re)turns to the biblical text, what and how one sees will also have become different because of all the differences that one has encountered along the way.

My detour has taken me through two landscapes where I have watched both Zelophehad's daughters and the Wakefields, all playing their parts. Certainly I now read the daughters differently, but I also read my own context differently. I frequently walk along beside Wellington harbor, Wakefield's Port Nicholson, drawing in and delighting in its beauty. It is so easy to forget Canaan and Te Whanganui a Tara, Wellington's original name.[22] Yet such forgetfulness is an erasure of profound injustice. I have been reading and writing as a *Pakeha* New Zealander, but the first essay in *Edward Gibbon Wakefield and the Colonial Dream: A Reconsideration* is written by Ngatata Love, of Te Āti Awa descent, who, after asking the effect of Wakefield's settlement on his people, continues: "The short answer is that the people living within these shores lost everything. They lost their lands, their laws, their language, their livelihood, their very reason for being. It was total devastation" (1997, 5). I imagine those silenced Canaanites nodding in agreement. In response to the question posed by Daniel Patte, "Why did I choose this interpretation rather than another one?," for me, as the daughter of settlers, embedded and complicit as I am in the politics of a postcolonial society, it has, quite simply, been a personal matter of ethics.[23]

Yet at the end, I still find myself wanting to say, with Yael Shemesh, that Zelophehad's daughters were "five intelligent women" whose "personal victory" did "benefit women" (2007, 82). I still want to agree with Katharine Sakenfeld, that "those with the least power and the most to lose" did show considerable courage in daring "to challenge the epitome of authority, God's own spokesperson Moses, and even implicitly to suggest that God's own decrees may have overlooked an important point" (1998b, 40). I realize that I need more than one production as I work out who I am in this twenty-first century in Aotearoa New Zealand. For myself, I shall continue to hold these readings in tension.

REFERENCES

Aichele, George, Peter Miscall, and Richard Walsh. 2009. An Elephant in the Room: Historical-Critical and Postmodern Interpretations of the Bible. *JBL* 128.2:383–404.

---

22. The English translation is The Great Harbor of Tara, named after the founder of the first Maori settlement, who first built a pa at Matiu Island, renamed Somes by Wakefield, before shifting to the mainland.

23. See Aichele, Miscall, and Walsh 2009, 386: "These hermeneutical strategies (i.e. feminist and postcolonial) have consistently led the way in raising the question of the ethics or politics of interpretation, an issue very near to the heart of postmodern hermeneutics."

Ben-Barak, Zafrira. 1980. Inheritance by Daughters in the Ancient Near East. *JSS* 25.1:22–33.
Boer, Roland. 2009. *Political Myth: On the Use and Abuse of Biblical Themes*. Durham and London: Duke University Press.
Budd, Philip J. 1984. *Numbers*. WBC 5. Waco: Word Books.
Burns, Patricia. 1989. *Fatal Success: A History of the New Zealand Company*. Auckland: Heinemann Reed.
Carden, Michael. 2006. The Book of the Twelve Minor Prophets. Pages 432–455 in *The Queer Bible Commentary*. Edited by Deryn Guest, Robert E. Goss, Mona West, and Thomas Bohache. London: SCM.
Conway, Colleen M. 2002. The Production of the Johannine Community: A New Historicist Perspective. *JBL* 121.3:479–95.
———. 2008. There and Back Again: Johannine History on the Other Side of Literary Criticism. Pages 77–91 in *Anatomies of Narrative Criticism: The Past, Present and Future of the Fourth Gospel as Literature*. Edited by Tom Thatcher and Stephen D. Moore. Atlanta: Society of Biblical Literature.
Dalziel, Raewyn. 1997. Men, Women and Wakefield. Pages 77–86 in *Edward Gibbon Wakefield and the Colonial Dream: A Reconsideration*. Edited by the Friends of the Turnbull Library. Wellington: GP Publications.
Delaney, Carol. 1991. *The Seed and the Soil: Gender and Cosmology in Turkish Village Society*. Berkeley: University of California Press.
Dube, Musa W. 2000. *Postcolonial Feminist Interpretation of the Bible*. St. Louis: Chalice.
Elwell, Sue Levi. 2006. Numbers. Pages 105–21 in *The Queer Bible Commentary*. Edited by Deryn Guest et al. London: SCM.
Eskenazi, Tamara C. 2008. Numbers. Pages 787–1029 in *The Torah: A Women's Commentary*. Edited by Tamara Cohn Eskenazi and Andrea L. Weiss. New York: URJ Press and Women of Reformed Judaism.
Exum, J. Cheryl. 1994. Second Thoughts about Secondary Characters: Women in Exodus 1.8–2.10. Pages 75–87 in *A Feminist Companion to Exodus to Deuteronomy*. Edited by Athalya Brenner. Sheffield: Sheffield Academic Press.
Fleras, Augie, and Paul Spoonley. 1999. *Recalling Aotearoa: Indigenous Politics and Ethnic Relations in New Zealand*. Auckland: Oxford University Press.
Grossmann, Jonathan. 2007. Divine Command and Human Initiative: A Literary View on Numbers 25–31. *BibInt* 15:54–79.

Hardy, Linda. 1997. Unnatural Occupancy: The Wakefields versus James Heberley in *Symmes Hole*. Pages 186–94 in *Edward Gibbon Wakefield and the Colonial Dream: A Reconsideration*. Edited by the Friends of the Turnbull Library. Wellington: GP Publications.

Ilan, Tal. 2000. The Daughters of Zelophehad and Women's Inheritance: The Biblical Injunction and Its Outcome. Pages 176–86 in *Exodus to Deuteronomy*. Edited by Athalya Brenner. Feminist Companion to the Bible, Second Series. Sheffield: Sheffield Academic Press.

Jobling, David. 2005. "Very Limited Ideological Options": Marxism and Biblical Studies in Postcolonial Scenes. Pages 184–201 in *Postcolonial Biblical Criticism: Interdisciplinary Intersections*. Edited by Stephen D. Moore and Fernando F. Segovia. London: T&T Clark International.

Kwok Pui-lan. 2006. Making the Connections: Postcolonial Studies and Feminist Biblical Interpretation. Pages 45–63 in *The Postcolonial Biblical Reader*. Edited by R. S. Sugirtharajah. Oxford: Blackwell.

Le Goff, Jacques. 1992. *History and Memory*. Translated by S. Rendall and E. Clemen. New York: Columbia University Press.

Levine, Baruch A. 2000. *Numbers 21–36*. AB. New York: Doubleday.

Liew, Tat-siong Benny. 2005. Margins and (Cutting-)Edges: On the (Il)Legitimacy and Intersections of Race, Ethnicity, and (Post)Colonialism. Pages 114–65 in *Postcolonial Biblical Criticism: Interdisciplinary Intersections*. Edited by Stephen D. Moore and Fernando F. Segovia. London: T&T Clark International.

Love, Ngatata. 1997. Edward Gibbon Wakefield: A Maori Perspective. Pages 3–10 in *Edward Gibbon Wakefield and the Colonial Dream: A Reconsideration*. Edited by the Friends of the Turnbull Library. Wellington: GP Publications.

Lowenthal, David. 1985. *The Past Is a Foreign Country*. Cambridge: Cambridge University Press.

Milgrom, Jacob. 1990. *Numbers*. Philadelphia: Jewish Publication Society of America.

Moon, Paul. 2009. *The Edges of Empires: New Zealand in the Middle of the Nineteenth Century*. Auckland: David Ling.

Olson, Dennis T. 1996. *Numbers*. Louisville: John Knox.

Patte, Daniel. 1998. Critical Biblical Studies from a Semiotics Perspective. *Semeia* 81:3–26.

Patterson, Brad. 1990. "A Queer Cantankerous Lot": The Human Factor in the Conduct of the New Zealand Company's Wellington Surveys.

Pages 61–87 in *The Making of Wellington 1800–1914*. Edited by David Hamer and Roberta Nicholls. Wellington: Victoria University Press.

Römer, Thomas. 2005. *The So-Called Deuteronomistic History: A Sociological, Historical and Literary Introduction*. London and New York: T&T Clark International.

Russell, Letty. 1987. *Household of Freedom: Authority in Feminist Theology*. Philadelphia: Westminster.

Said, Edward W. 1993. *Culture and Imperialism*. London: Chatto & Windsor.

Sakenfeld, Katharine Doob. 1988a. In the Wilderness, Awaiting the Land: The Daughters of Zelophehad and Feminist Interpretation. *The Princeton Seminary Bulletin* 9.3:179–96.

———. 1988b. Zelophehad's Daughters. *Perspectives in Religious Studies* 15.4: 37–47.

———. 1992. Numbers. Pages 45–51 in *The Women's Bible Commentary*. Edited by Carol A. Newsom and Sharon H. Ringe. Louisville: Westminster John Knox.

Segovia, Fernando F. 2005. Mapping the Postcolonial Optic in Biblical Criticism: Meaning and Scope. Pages 23–78 in *Postcolonial Biblical Criticism: Interdisciplinary Intersections*. Edited by Stephen D. Moore and Fernando F. Segovia. London: T&T Clark International.

Shemesh, Yael. 2007. A Gender Perspective on the Daughters of Zelophehad: Bible, Talmudic Midrash, and Modern Feminist Midrash. *BibInt* 15:80–109.

Simkins, Ronald A. 2004. Family in the Political Economy of Monarchic Israel. *BCT* 1:6–17.

Snaith, N. H. 1966. The Daughters of Zelophehad. *VT* 16.1:124–27.

Sugirtharajah, R. S. 1998. A Postcolonial Exploration of Collusion and Construction in Biblical Interpretation. Pages 91–116 in *The Postcolonial Bible*. Edited by R. S. Sugirtharajah. Sheffield: Sheffield Academic Press.

———. 2001. *Postcolonial Criticism and Biblical Interpretation*. Oxford and New York: Oxford University Press.

———. 2005. *The Bible as Empire: Postcolonial Explorations*. Cambridge: Cambridge University Press.

Temple, Philip. 2002. *A Sort of Conscience: The Wakefields*. Auckland: Auckland University Press.

Tonks, Rosemarie. 1990. "A Difficult and Complicated Question": The New Zealand Company's Wellington, Port Nicholson, Claim. Pages 35–59 in *The Making of Wellington 1800-1914*. Edited by David Hamer and Roberta Nicholls. Wellington: Victoria University Press.

Tucker, W. Dennis, Jr. 2008. Women in the Old Testament: Issues of Authority, Power and Justice. *ExpTim* 119.10:481-86.

Ulrich, Dean R. 1998. The Framing Function of the Narratives about Zelophehad's Daughters. *Journal of the Evangelical Theological Society* 41.4:529-38.

Van Dyke, Ruth M., and Susan E. Alcock. 2003. Archaeologies of Memory: An Introduction. Pages 1-13 in *Archaeologies of Memory*. Edited by Ruth M. Van Dyke and Susan E. Alcock. Oxford: Blackwell.

Wedde, Ian. 1986. *Symmes Hole*. Auckland: Penguin.

Wevers, Lydia. 1997. My Mrs Harris. Pages 179-85 in *Edward Gibbon Wakefield and the Colonial Dream: A Reconsideration*. Edited by the Friends of the Turnbull Library. Wellington: GP Publications.

Rethinking Orality for Biblical Studies

Althea Spencer-Miller

Nations could have only one linguistic or cultural future—either this seclusion within a restrictive particularity or, conversely, dilution within a generalizing universal. This is a formidable construction, and the "oral genius" of peoples of the world urges us to burst our way out of it. (Èdouard Glissant 1997, 105)

1. Introduction

The relationship between orality and biblical literature already had a long history in scholarship when Walter Ong, S.J., gave it new impetus in 1982. He was not the first biblical scholar to venture into this territory. Before Ong, Hermann Gunkel (1907) provided the initial impulse for biblical scholars' attention to orality.[1] Werner Kelber followed Ong in 1983, applying his orality theories to form critical approaches within Christian Scriptures (CS)[2] scholarship. From the early 1980s through to the end of the first decade of the twenty-first century, work on orality and literacy in CS continued in earnest. The development of new media introduced exciting new frontiers within biblical scholarship. Building on Gunkel's heritage, Hebrew Bible (HB) scholar Susan Niditch (1996), in applying oral theories to the ancient Israelite biblical canon, develops and expands the understanding of the oral cultural matrix of the HB. In common with early oral biblical scholars, she focuses on identifying varieties of oral structures

---

1. Gunkel's confidence that writing belongs to civilization and orality to uncivilized races (1) is precursor to Ong's evolutionary approach to the orality/literacy relationship.
2. Although the terms Hebrew Bible and Christian Scriptures do not solve all the issues that adhere to the Old Testament and the New Testament, I use them here instead with the acronyms HB and CS.

within ancient texts. Orality, then, has perdured in the scholarship on the HB and on the CS, the latter being the canon that concerns this essay.

Ong deepened our understanding of orality by exploring its psychodynamics (2002, 37–76)[3] in a framework that distinguishes between oral and literate mentalities. Within CS studies, Werner Kelber (1983), and others such as Joanna Dewey (1995a, 1995b), Jonathan Draper (2003, 2004), and Richard Horsley (2006a), utilized Ong's base to explore its implications for Synoptic and Pauline studies.[4] Ong's psychodynamics provide a sturdy foundation of dimensions, categories, and descriptors of orality with which to launch into unexplored aspects of biblical culture. Yet, this short list of scholars is a litany of predominantly literary thinkers whose works trek along the boundaries of orality and literacy. Their works bear the stamp of a literary orientation and consequently there are lacunae in their depictions of orality. Scholars with an oral-literate self-consciousness that is as strong as their literary orientation can elect to work from an autobiographically styled cultural resource base. Self-conscious, oral-literate scholars can engage, adjust, and supplement the fundamental dimensions, categories, and descriptors of orality with auto-ethnographic[5] breadth and depth. Doing so can reduce the number of lacunae, expand this facet of biblical scholarship, and extend the use of orality theory to other areas of

---

3. In his chapter on the psychodynamics of orality Ong offers additive, aggregation, redundancy, conservative, concrete, agonistic, empathetic/communal, homeostatic, as some oral characteristics.

4. The anniversary publication edited by Tom Thatcher in 2008 is a tribute to Kelber's (1983) impact.

5. With this assertion, I enter contested space. First, the Caribbean itself is rife with intra-regional identity contestations. The relationship of members of the Caribbean Diaspora to those contestations is also moot. I do not intend to avoid contestations against this claim. To Caribbean resident and diaspora readers, I offer this as an effort to reflect from a self-conscious posture of Caribbean orality rather than solely as an attuned and directed Western academic. Belinda Edmonson (1999) offers essays that reflect in various ways on this issue. Also, it is inconceivable that there are Western scholars who derive from purely literate cultures or that there are no oral-literate predecessors among biblical scholars. It is not possible to make assured comments about that derivation as autobiography is not a common practice within this group. Stephen Moore describes "personal criticism [as] a form of self-disclosure" (2010, 130) in a discussion of autobiographical/autochirographic criticism. I choose to write auto-ethnographically rather than autobiographically. This is an oral posture in which a cultural and we/I co-exist in a dynamic relationship, a kind of autobiographical metonymy.

biblical studies. This essay offers such an approach and discusses hermeneutics and translation as two such areas.

An auto-ethnographic, anticolonial influence and interest pervades this essay's reaction to biblical orality studies with a primary focus on Walter Ong. However, Ong's confident declaration (2002, 2) that "readers of books such as this—are so literate that it is very difficult for *us* to conceive of an oral universe of communication or thought except as a variant of a literate universe" evokes in me a resistant shudder that eschews this exclusionary statement (emphasis mine). The curious statement does not appear to imagine oral-literate cultures. In addition, it seems to assume that oral-literate cultures lack the signatures of orality. Further, there may be another assumption that even if oral-literate cultures and individuals retained orality's signatures, they would not read Ong's book. In other words, Ong neither imagines nor includes the existence of this reader who has both oral and literate signatures. Because I am responding from an auto-ethnographic position, I must explicate my relationship to orality, CS orality studies, and to the exclusionary "us" that is explicit in Ong and implicit in the assumptions that inform statements about oral consciousness found in the work of other similar scholars (e.g., Hyldahl 2008, 42–43).

I am a product of only one small island's culture, Jamaica. I also think and act under the influence of the larger Caribbean region and its diverse cultures.[6] As such, Ong's grating assumption confirms my experience that aspects of those cultures are excluded from the presuppositions, history, and deployment of traditional exegetical methods and theories within biblical scholarship. That exclusion requires that as a scholar within the Western epistemological framework I must contain instincts cultivated in the nurturance of my island and regional heritage. Western biblical scholarship, as a cerebral-cognitive universe, constrains the holism of communication events in the Caribbean context, which is oral in its cultural orientation. A Western orientation implicitly requires that scholars adopt a voyeuristic, literary posture in relation to oral cultures. However, voyeurism cannot penetrate to the generative sources driving the complex, throbbing dynamic that is under observation. Neither can

---

6. The Caribbean is home to a diversity of cultures and that includes religious diversity. Christianity is the largest religion in the region and is highly influential in all territories. Biblical quotations enjoy proverbial status and their use is often a rhetorical strategy in folk argumentation.

it satisfy the oral-literate consciousness. Ong points to this voyeuristic inadequacy when he observes with respect to mastering the Latin language, "Although it was tied in to a residually oral mentality, it provided no access to the unconscious of the sort that a mother tongue provides" (Ong 2002, 160). Those missing instincts, the inaccessible unconscious, arguably are the lacunae in the fabric of biblical interpretation and in its subset, orality studies. The insiders' understanding of orality as a mode of being is the missing subjectivity, which is a fundamental lacuna. Within that fundament rests implications for biblical hermeneutics and translation. This essay, founded in auto-ethnography, proffers one insider's understanding of orality from a Jamaican/Caribbean perspective.[7]

There are substantive and substantial differences between my interests and investments in orality and that of the general canonical and extracanonical discussion. Hitherto, orality has gained validity from its relevance for text-based studies (cf. Bauckham, 240–63). Ong's concerns furthered that relevance because the relationship between literacy and orality focused his research. I have an ideological interest in expanding the cultural imaginations that are available for understanding orality in antiquity. These imaginations would derive from cultures that provide insider rather than voyeuristic perspectives. Ong's descriptions of the psychodynamics of orality are compelling and are not to be excluded. However, my intention is to provide insights that are complementary and supplemental to the operative theories and to introduce other investigatory trajectories within biblical studies based on Caribbean experiential orality. The purpose of my auto-ethnographic posture is to revise the exclusionary "us" by offering an expanded understanding of orality and utilizing it differently within biblical studies. Therefore, I will proffer a multidimensional understanding of orality that is holistic and quotidian. I will also explore trajectories of hermeneutics, language, and culture for their oral ramifications.

This essay is ovulatory, definitely not yet a zygote, the beginning of an effort to articulate the difference an auto-ethnographic oral perspective makes to both textual hermeneutics and translation as art. It suggests contours for a collage, a tapestry of epistemological mechanisms that represent the oral modalities of reception and comprehension within com-

---

7. Later presentations of facets of orality are grounded in an auto-ethnographic study of Caribbean orality that was conducted in Antigua, Barbados, Jamaica, and Trinidad. The results of that study are still being tabulated at the time of writing.

munication events. Therefore, I favor articulating the cultural texture that an oral awareness can contribute to a liberatory approach to orality. This texture, in turn, can significantly nuance our understanding of textual reception in antiquity whether read quietly or aloud. The first step, then, is to substantiate the claim that there are lacunae in the current paradigm. Next, I explore different ways of understanding orality that anticipate discussions of textual analysis and translation. Finally, I offer the challenge of engaging alternative cultural imaginations as viable and necessary for the tasks of reconstructing ancient cultural epistemologies.

2. The Genealogy's Lacunae

To recognize lacunae within biblical scholarship's oral genealogy requires reassessing its orality theory. That orality persists as a cultural modality despite the development and advancement of literacy is the base of my critique. A binary framing of the relationship between literacy and orality, along with a focus on epic performance, mnemonics, and the literary orientation of scholars serve to occlude orality's cultural continuity and texturing. These also prevent a fuller understanding of orality's potential for biblical hermeneutics. This essay focuses on Ong, but the articulation of a sharp distinction between orality and literacy began with Gunkel. This sharp distinction permits the assertion that literacy displaces orality, its inferior, to function as a truism in Ong's psychodynamics.

Ong asserts, "A more positive understanding of earlier states of consciousness has replaced" (2002, 171) earlier designators of orality as primitive, savage, and inferior. Yet even he does not find orality ever to have been an ideal. It should not be a permanent state for any culture (171). Ironically, he attributes Homer's *Odyssey* to oral cultures and asserts that such a production is beyond the reach of literates (171–72).[8] This assertion accompanies Ong's understanding that literacy eradicates orality and its peculiar pre-literate skills (115–23, esp. 117). He does not discard orality altogether, but eventually relocates it at the foreground of the text. "Reading a text," Ong says, "oralizes it" (172). Reading aloud invokes a particular reception context. Richard Horsley describes the reception arena of early

---

8. Oddly, Ong may have an ally in Édouard Glissant on this point. Glissant, having observed that oral languages (by which, unfortunately, he means non-chirographic) have been crudded by literary disdain, calls for those "oral languages to create" (1997, 105). His is a call to poetics.

Christian literature as one of performance. He says, "If a text was usually recited orally before a group, then it must be understood less as an artifact in the abstract and more as communication of a message by performer to audiences in their historical-social context. Performance was 'always already' a dynamic communication situated in a social context" (Horsley 2006a, 1; cf. Draper 2006, 71–107, esp. 72).[9] Like Horsley, Werner Kelber (2006, 25–42) thinks of Q as an orally derived text and as an instance of oral performance that should be understood in terms of the techniques of oral performance. Oral motility relocates to textual performance and regains its voice in vocalized reading. The movement of orality from precursor to after-act and the imposed pseudo-locational restraint treats of orality as though it were a clastic topography like unto a Lego set (Ong 2002, 8).[10] The idea that orality is disposable in one stage of human evolution only to morph mercurially at a point mediated by writing is a vulnerable articulation. Yet, this articulation invisibly flavors discussions of oral influence within biblical studies. Oral epic performance roots the articulation and abets, along with biblical textual interests, the orality–literacy binary framing of the analysis. The agonistic presentation of the orality-literacy relationship is produced by and reinforces a binary conceptualization of the relationship. Lost in translation, and thus a lacuna, is the awareness that an oral mentality remains as the matrix of communication and of performance as communication. Orality is so much more than speech. The reading and performance of texts is oral first, because reception is an oral mentality, and only secondarily, because it is spoken.

In classical studies, the focus on epic oral performance begins with the works of Albert B. Lord and Milman Parry (see Parry 1971).[11] That led biblical scholars to explore, nuance, and refine the function, goals, and mechanisms of memory that preoccupy much of the literature (cf. Ong 2002; Crossan 1999, 59–84; Horsley, Draper, and Foley 2006; Kelber and Byrskog 2009). Advances beyond this basic level occurred as orality studies included more cultures, and covered more diverse oral cultural mani-

---

9. Draper demonstrates the clearest understanding that orality continues apace with literacy.

10. Ong connects orality to vocalization (2002, 8). This, too, is a limitation on orality. As I will argue later, orality is a composite approach to life and, as such, is more than speech and illiteracy.

11. Adam Parry names Walter Ong among those whose works were influenced by Milman Parry (1971, xliii).

festations and activities. The cultural and institutional roles for memory grew in importance and eventually superseded mnemonic structures in importance (see Alexander 2009, 113–54; Kirk 2009, 155–72; McIver 2011). Yet, the interest in oral literature[12] that accompanied these developments understood this body of material as performance works. The analysis of performance works required an understanding of Greco-Roman oral culture and epic performance continued to provide the template and the terms for understanding oral literature in its performance. A very thin, unstable, line divides discussions of oral performance and oral reception. At that line, Kelber (2006), for example, returns to the written text in his discussion of Q: "Understood orally, the speeches in Q encapsulate a world of words, phrases, ideas, images that resonate with a map of experiences and associations shared by speakers and hearers. In short, Q as an oral derived text relies heavily on extra-textual factors, shifting meaning from production to performance" (2006, 36). The emphasis remains on orality as functional in performance and texts though not in reception as a subjective process. A description of orality as a cultural modality is missing, hence the absence of orality reception theories. Orality, as a cultural mode, encompasses all of that moment when the written is performed and the unspoken codes and experiences of the community determine the specific textual meaning in the particular performance. Devoid of that aspect, it is logical that biblical scholars' interest in orality, which begins as an effort to solve a historical critical dilemma, proceeds to technological/media discussions, and advances in oral technology—a different arena for the production of performance orality (Ong 2002, 157). Eventually, orality as a cultural modality with a peculiar and discoverable subjectivity in relation to structures of power, politics, social organization, and ethnic/cultural communication disintegrates within the discussion. Hence, there is a lacuna.

Once we note that reliance on the oral performance of cultural epics is foundational to oral theorizing, it is possible to recognize that reliance

---

12. Ong finds it fortunate that the term is "losing ground." He says, "For most literates, to think of words as totally dissociated from writing is simply too arduous a task to undertake, even when specialized linguistic or anthropological work may demand it" (2002, 14). Contra Brathwaite, who affirms oral literature as "our oldest form of literature … in the Caribbean, our novelists have always been conscious of these native resources, but the critics and academics have, as is kinda often the case, lagged far behind" (14).

as fundamental to limiting orality. Memorized performances of cultural epics are, admittedly, phenomenal. However, epic performances cannot be the sole or primary mediators of orality. The performance is an instant in time, a choreographed moment with unwritten but understood cultural requisites. It is possible that sometimes a performer learns these requisites by enculturation and recalls them or acts upon them by instinct. It is also possible that some of these will never be articulated because they are part of the performer's naturalness. The reliance on excavating oral characteristics or psychodynamics from the performance of epics can be both occlusive and rigidly circumscriptive because the voyeur cannot readily access the performances tacit requisites. Thus, she or he girdles the complexity of orality's cartography and domesticates orality in the service of an orderly and manageable discussion. Orality, domesticated within the literacy girdle, loses the multifurcation and polydimensionality of its particular epistemological substance as enhanced by the dynamics of physical presence and embodiment (see Silberman 1987, 3–4). Within the girdle, literacy is allowed to bind orality. In those conditions, it is possible to reduce orality to a pre-literate mentality (Ong 2002, 172). The epic's foundational girdle provides and legitimizes a negative and diminishing attitude to orality.

As already noted, another derivative of epic performances, as database for orality, is the mnemonic focus. Epic performances provide a resource for assessing the efficiency and teleology of memory in oral cultures. Of course, the control materials in memory experiments are written records of the performed epics. Therefore, both oral performances of epics and the written records provide examples for assessing the qualitative relationship between orality and literacy. Therein is another vulnerability. Mnemonic discourse exposes the limits of Ong's definition of oral cultures as "cultures with no knowledge at all of writing" (2002, 1). The textual bias in the analyses invisibly and instinctively subordinates orality to chirography and assesses its memorization capacities by recourse to literate chirographic standards. It is established that in the performance of epics there is a formulaic approach to memorization that involves stock *topoi*, tropes, and repetition (22–27, 33–35, 136–48). While performers tend to recall the *topoi* and tropes with accuracy, variations in associated details may occur. Therefore, oral performances that are memory-based are rarely verbatim replications. Chirography is one of the signs of literacy. Chirographic recordings promote verbatim recall where verbatim requires word-for-word correlation (contra Bauckham

2006, 240).¹³ Verbatim replication is the standard that indicates orality's inferiority to literacy. The focus on efficacious memory results from the importance of establishing the reliability of biblical textual transmission, given its oral beginnings. If oral recitation does not reproduce with chirographic verbatim reliability, then the derivative biblical texts need either to be understood differently or approached with other criteria. Therefore, scholars after Gunkel introduced oral mnemonics into biblical studies, and expended much thought on and critical analysis of memory mechanisms and their efficacy as manifested in epic performance. In the ensuing years, the inferiority of orality in this regard was affirmed repeatedly and its subsuming into the literary mindset became common sense.

According to Ong and John Dominic Crossan, even illiterate (and therefore oral) performers preferred the written record for its mnemonical superiority and other reasons (Ong 2002, 14–15).¹⁴ Crossan describes one instance when an illiterate epic performer was impressed by his epic in print. Crossan interpreted this as surrender to texts as superior memorization. He clearly articulates the implication: "Finally, writing triumphs, and even oral creativity defends itself as verbatim exactitude. There is something terribly sad about Avdo Međedović's pride in recounting a compliment that dooms his craft to inevitable irrelevance" (Crossan 1999, 78). Ong locates a more tenacious endurance before orality finally surrenders in the Middle Ages (2002, 113–14). According to Ong, this marks orality as pre-literate and sometimes transitional, or residual (113, 159). Orality, as a psychodynamic impulse, "diminishes with writing and print" (156). It seems inevitable that orality will secede to chirography. In this scheme, any overlap of orality and chirography is temporary. Chirography defines the outer perimeter of Ong's oral psychodynamics insofar as he holds that it eventually exterminates their usefulness and existence. This reduction of

---

13. Bauckham argues for faithful, oral preservation of the traditions. He cites Kenneth Bailey, who worked for more than 30 years in the Middle East. According to Bauckham, Bailey argues for a typology of formal control over the transmission of certain traditions. "In the case of proverbs and poems, verbatim reproduction is mandatory. A mistake of even a single word by the person reciting will be emphatically corrected by the listeners in general" (Bauckham 2006, 255–56, citing Bailey 1995, 7).

14. On the other hand, Ong recognizes that sometimes cultures in transition to literacy do not immediately value writing (2002, 95, 113). Nonetheless, Ong does not retreat from the theory that literacy eventually erases orality.

orality faces an accusation of "oraturecide."[15] The insistence of this essay is that orality never dies. It is too intrinsic to the fabric of human existence to disappear.

In the binary opposition of orality and literacy, both orality and its versicular signifier, the epic, disappear. According to Ong, in the history of literature, "Eventually, the epic loses even imaginary credibility: its roots in the noetic economy of oral culture are dried up" (2002, 156). The literary agon between orality and chirography is a binary construction conceived in the imagination of a chirographic occlusion. The literary imprisonment by Johannes Gutenberg's invention of the printing press hinders an alternative imagination for orality. As Kelber indicates (2006, 35), biblical scholars are products

> of a print-based education and as scholars actively participating in print culture, [operating] within the framework of typographical conventions that have dominated Western civilization roughly from the fifteenth century to the present [and] structured our scholarly consciousness and created the media conditions in which biblical scholars have analyzed, dissected and interpreted texts.

Apparently, chirographic-typographic media also structure our capacity to imagine orality. Within that structure, writing is orality's perduring mnemonic, the fullness to orality's lack. Overly neat discussions of the impact of orality that rest on this bedrock may be replete with functional oral illiteracy and thus anti-oral in their very flavor. There, orality is understood only as an honorable but lowly pedestal to chirography and its technological heirs. This betrays both a literary orientation and a truncated understanding of orality.

Ong's work is so fundamental for biblical thinkers on orality that we should note, also, his value for the understanding of orality that this essay offers. His work proffers an agenda for scholarship (2002, 153–76), furnishes a rich vocabulary for discrete categories, and for understanding categorical subtleties as he has done with memory and the psychodynamics of orality. Ong's guiding theory that chirography and orality construct distinguishable mental structures is fundamentally indisputable (3). He identifies specific facets that establish the contrast between

---

15. "Oraturecide" is a neologism peculiar to this essay. It means to infer the killing of orality.

the two. Ong manifests profound and advanced understandings of orality when he discusses the teleology of mnemonics in terms of cultural memory and identifies the somatic content (67). He leads his readers to orality's portal when he suggests that "Primary orality fosters personality structures that in certain ways are more communal" and "Oral communication unites people in groups" (68; cf. Kelber 2003, xxiii). In between those two observations, Ong overreaches by generalizing that oral personality is more externalized and less introspective than the writing person (104, 173–75; cf. Hyldahl 2008, 44). The absolute certainty with which such platitudes are asserted bespeaks the methodological absence of the oral-literate scholar who chooses to write from within that orientation. Nonetheless, those terms are pertinent to understanding orality and require future discussion.

The lacunae remain, however. Discussions of memory need to incorporate informed understandings of the role of epic as common history and collective memory, the interactions between the performer and the audience, the community expectations that influence the performance, and the relationship between the past and the present as mediated by the performance. The connective tissue between all these aspects of the performance determines the moment's authenticity. Verbatim, as faithfulness, is determined by authenticity in the performer's relationship to all those facets. Mnemonic fidelity is living, dynamic, and not an exacting preservative. The assignation that the overlap between orality and literacy is a temporary, transitional situation is untenable. Additionally, the fact that literacy does not readily displace an oral mentality would be more discernible were there a more comprehensive focalizer than epic performance and frames other than the orality/chirography and orality/literacy binaries.

Despite the advent of writing, signs of orality remain in communication events other than epic performance and reading aloud for an audience. Aurality, optics, tactility, collectivity, presence, embodiment, are all terms that relate to an oral modality. They continue to be behaviors that individuals activate in communication events even when they have developed literacy. Ong repeatedly notes the tenaciousness of orality (2002, 76–114).[16] So it is surprising that his discussion climaxes in orality's erasure. He traces

---

16. Douglas Burton-Christie notes that oral cultures tended to treat writing with suspicion. Burton-Christie suggests that "This resistance reflects not only a certain natural conservatism, but an acute sense of the potential loss in a transition from orality to literacy" (1997, 419).

that tenaciousness until the development of rhetoric (113–14). Eventually, rhetoric "migrated from the oral to the chirographic world" (114). Ultimately, the development of the three Rs in education represented the complete displacement of orally grounded rhetorical education (114). Rhetoric, the core of formal education may have been displaced but orality as a life orientation certainly was not. Orality is an epistemological orientation that infuses peoples from the individual through to the very structures of empire. The British school uniform, for example, is part of a school system that is constructed upon units of belonging from the classroom to the entirety of a particular school. The uniform symbolizes the whole formed by those units of belonging. It structures the holistic sense of a unified community from the classroom to the school. This is a form of communal orality enacted upon the body accessorized. The uniform is a non-chirographic/non-typographic text. This communal oral orientation to education is the matrix and teleology of literacy. Contra Ong, orality did not disappear in England. Jamaica is a former British colony. We retained the school uniform as a mechanism of community formation, school pride, and for the maintenance of inter-generational solidarities. The institutions that produce literate individuals and cultures also construct this communal orality.

Strands in orality theories and practice hitherto assume a displacement relationship between orality and literacy where oral theory is informed by oral performance, mnemonics, and orality as the reading of written texts. What would emerge should we consider orality independent of all these assumptions? Orality as a mode of being does not disappear when literacy appears (see Draper 2006, 71–72). It remains as the matrix of literacy, the conduit of communication, and the disrupter of the written. Any approach to orality that only seeks to excavate its petrified remains in the written text or its post-chirographic appearance will miss its omnipresence in each communicative event.

3. Moving toward an Expanded Understanding of Orality

I return for a moment to my autobiography. Earlier, I described my cultural background as Jamaican and Caribbean. By accretion, the United States of America and the Western-styled academy are adopted cultural backgrounds. The patterns of my inherited and my adopted cultures are very similar but also amply distinct. The distinctions separate postcolonial islander from imperial continental inhabitants in enculturation and epistemology. Orality is one way of thinking about the differences. Thus the questions: What is orality? Does the acknowledgment of epistemological orality enhance, alter, or affect biblical criticism with distinctiveness? Oral performance differs from the print-based, post-Gutenberg, silent, individual reading so common to scholarship. Analogous to music, the movement from cognitive, disembodied lenses to oral, embodied lenses requires a transposition, a changing of key, en route to understanding orality as an epistemology, a perspective, a modality, and a condition of interpretation. The transposition allows the embrace of oral cultural elements such as embodiment, opticality, aurality, tactility, vocality, and tacit cultural codes as interrelated and necessary accessories in holistic communication. The exploration of these in an ovulatory essay is an invitation to explore the possibilities in reciprocal insemination between oral and literary epistemologies.

Orality subjectivity as epistemology is a messy chowder. It is thick and its categories are ill-fitting lumps that resist fixity. How antithetical, then, the tendency to reduce it to neatly defined terminology as though orality could ever only be a well-tuned tool or method or an exigency of illiteracy. I have posited that orality is a cultural mode. To that I add that it is a way of being in the world, in life, and in communications, a fundamental subjectivity. Subjectivity is a stigmatized concept in traditional biblical scholarship. There it bears the stigma of bias, prejudice, and the accusation of an inability to objectify oneself in separation from the textual material, a regnant value. Yet, biblical critics have normalized their cultural subjectivity into invisibility and normativeness with the illusion that auto-ethnographic invisibility equals objectivity. On the other hand, Michael Jackson offers a definition of radical empirical ethnography[17] that emphasizes participatory experience. He says, "Unlike traditional empiricism, which draws a definite boundary between observer and observed, between method and object, radical empiricism denies the validity of such cuts and makes the *interplay* between these domains the focus of its interest" (1989, 3–5). Experiential subjectivity is, in the view of radical empiricists, an indispensable database in ethnographic research. There is no objectivity without subjectivity.[18] Margarita Suárez categorizes her

---

17. Jackson does not address methodologies for auto-ethnography. However, by addressing the role of the subjectivity in data gathering, radical empiricism opens methodological space for the legitimacy of the auto-ethnographic approach.

18. Contra Ong (2002, 45), for whom objectivity is achieved through separation from the subject. Writing enables that separation.

auto-ethnography as "reflexive ethnography." She declares, "Reflexive ethnography presumes a passion for the people under investigation. There is no room for the detached observer in this schema" (2002, 175). To acknowledge subjectivity is to elevate the cultural self as a meaningful, participatory, and functional existent, present and potentially active in any area of endeavor. It indicates an understanding that particular sociocultural, geographical, and climatological factors and human positionalities in relation to these factors shape our ways of existing in the world. In addition, subjectivity represents a habituated norm and normalcy that provides unseen and unacknowledged accustomedness to and information for our behaviors and responses. These three aspects of subjectivity are omnipresent and influential. To be objective means, then, to be aware of subjectivity's presence, scope, and limits. For the purposes of this project, I seek to bring oral subjectivity into visibility for increased understanding and refinement, and to explore its usefulness in a heuristic intent.

Oral subjectivity refers to the tenor of a society's mode of communication and orientation to reality. Edward C. Stewart and Milton J. Bennett (1991, 6–12), found the nineteenth-century work of Ferdinand Tönnies (1957) helpful for understanding the characteristics of custom and tradition-based societies (cf. Draper 2006, 71). Tönnies identified and designated clusters of characteristics as belonging to either a *Gemeinschaft* or a *Gesellschaft* state. According to Tönnies, *Gemeinschaft* society is largely custom and tradition based upon common language, race, religion, and ethnicity with political and economic power restricted by the group's geographical location. Stewart and Bennett organize Tönnies's two categories into a number of elements. *Gemeinschaft* elements include interpersonal relational sensibilities such as a communal sense of social belonging, community-oriented goals, informal tradition-based ascriptions, opinions, and beliefs that are private only in their relationship to community custom, and personal identity that is associated with belonging to the community (1957, 7). Ong's psychodynamic descriptors, empathy and participation, are commensurate with *Gemeinschaft* elements. He recognizes the communal as integral to learning and knowing (esp. 2002, 45–46).[19]

---

19. Empathy is more than the ability to feel with someone else. It is a blurring of the boundaries in a way that the individuality of each person is imbricated (not enmeshed) in all the individuals within a group and the group's gestalt dynamics. Individuals know themselves and can distinguish themselves from the group. In a *Gemeinschaft* society, individuation develops within the communal imbricating process.

Ong implies that empathy and participation are incommensurate with literacy. Therefore, *Gemeinschaft* attributes contrast with *Gesellschaft* societies. Tönnies describes *Gesellschaft* societies as based on an objective reality that is external to the individual. Stewart and Bennett's (1991, 7) expanded description includes social ties based on: rational agreement and self-interest; social ties regulated by law; groups forming for specific purposes with membership based on special interest or technical; educational or professional attainments; identity as separate from belonging; individual citizenship and state membership taking precedence over membership in groups; individual status as a product of achievement (Spencer-Miller 2007, 173–77). The terms *Gemeinschaft* and *Gesellschaft* stand as basic reminders of a fundamental difference in life orientations. *Gemeinschaft* and *Gesellschaft* can be synecdoches respectively for narrative/mythic/oral and scientific/empirical/literate epistemologies.

Gemeinschaft and *Gesellschaft* societies roughly correspond to oral and literate subjectivities as modes of being. These subjectivities are not dispensable modalities. They signify distinctive ways of defining co-existence, belonging, and community formation. According to Stewart and Bennett, the distinction "parallels in a historical frame the contrasts of Western versus non-Western and colonizer versus colonized, and it provides insights into subjective modalities in *Gemeinschaft* and *Gesellschaft* societies" (1991, 8). *Gemeinschaft*, as a category, provides entrance into the worldview and ways of an oral culture but without employing illiteracy as an essential criterion. The categories are useful for conversation but do not suggest absolute mutual exclusiveness in the social realities. As societies unfold both categories overlap and find expression. One or the other may predominate as markers of societal norms. The societies that are useful for biblical studies are those that retain predominantly oral markers or are oral in cultural orientation (cf. Draper 2004, 2). In this regard, I maintain that Caribbean territories provide examples of oral predominance. More Caribbean scholars are thinking in this vein, among them Edward Brathwaite (1984), Catherine John (2003),[20] Heather Russell (2009),[21] and Mau-

---

20. John is one of the few Caribbean writers who understand orality as encompassing a cultural largesse that is not defined by literacy or chirographic profligacy. Contra Michael Jagessar, who repeatedly identifies Caribbean ecumenical hero Philip Potter as oral because he has not written much (1997, 16).

21. Similar to John, Heather Russell works with an expanded understanding of orality. See her allusion to the quilting code as a form of oral history (2009, 19).

reen Warner-Lewis (1996). Our predecessors include Aime Césaire and Èdouard Glissant. Describing Glissant's and Césaire's thought, J. Michael Dash writes, "The written word was seen as a degenerate outgrowth of speech" (1992, xxi). Moreover, of Césaire, in particular, Dash presses, "To Césaire ... the rationally censored world of the written had to yield to something more intuitive, more verbose, and less restrained ... the watchwords were opacity and orality" (xxi). The oral auto-ethnographic consciousness is aware of a way of being oral that breaks the bounds of the oral–literate binary.

To *Gemeinschaft*, sight and sound, I add embodiment. The oral way is intimate and flamboyant in gesticulation. Rolling of the eyes, mouth twitches, pouts are action intonations when accompanying words. Sometimes, they are the word. In Jamaica, flashing of the skirt hem by a flick of the fingers intensifies disdainful statements. The body, as it moves, placing the hand a kimbo, hand over the mouth in laughter, holding the waist in jocularity, different styles of walking, the tactile maneuver that betokens attentiveness, dramatized conversations, and myriad others are indispensable to meaning making. All these enhance, transform, and explicate the meaning of words. Thus, Judith Soares describes them as accessories to language.[22] And thus, polysemy has dimensions beyond the lexical when communication is corporeal in its entirety. When I think of communication in antiquity, all this information occupies my imagination. It matters to interpretation that interactive embodiment and presence are missing from the chirographic/typographic medium, often even when it is read aloud. Orality is a quotidian performance. It is not a staged moment. Orality's wholeness is a way of being in the world, a modality of existence that is normal, normative, and productive of particular communal mores and social understandings that have specific, diverse communication expressions and layers of meaning.

With that understanding of orality's wholeness, it is possible to assert that oral subjectivity is a discernible and articulable way of being that has recognizable modalities in communication that include transmission, reception, and comprehension. Further, it is a feature of Caribbean island life. Caribbean cultures are oral/literate hybrids. A prerequisite for disentangling the peculiar psychodynamics of each modality is the recogni-

---

22. Comment made in an interview in Barbados, August 20, 2010. Dr. Judith C. Soares is Coordinator of the Women's Development Unit and Tutor at the University of the West Indies, Cave Hill Campus, Barbados.

tion that they are imbricate mentalities and that orality is the matrix of literacy. Although the historical relationship between orality and writing seems sequential, orality remains a cultural fundament. Writing is orality's artifice. Interpretation of the written should proceed with a sense of orality as culture's very fabric rather than as literacy's precursor or as writing brought to speech.

Summarily, then, oral subjectivities communicate with communal awareness, an orientation to communal well-being, prioritize community in meaning making, are narrative in logic, and include holistic, sensory embodiment as necessary elements of communication. With this and Tönnies's categories in mind, we are clarifying that a post-Gutenberg literary orientation is very incomplete for understanding texts from a world that we describe as oral. It is inadequate to understand orality only as the absence of literacy or writing oralized. It is much more than a lexical command and the ability to vocalize. There is promise for further progress in understanding ancient oral cultures where we understand orality as a quotidian performance that accompanies literacy and numeracy, and in which communication and comprehension tends toward emphatic holism and communal empathies. Communal empathy is the case with the Caribbean. As George Mulrain notes,

> In Black culture—and the Caribbean is no exception—when one speaks of the reader's context, it must be realized that it is the "reader writ large" being referred to. One should read the text from the point of view of the community.... The communitarian approach is a response to the individualistic approach which Western interpreters delight in. (122)

Finally, I infer that awareness of orality's capabilities and capacities renders it available and accessible for translation and hermeneutical methodologies.

4. From Orality to Orality

Among orality scholars, there is consensus that the ancient Mediterranean culture was an oral culture and texts produced in that milieu are to be treated as orally derived. As Werner Kelber notes,

> despite its resolutely text-centered habits, historical criticism has by no means been unaware of orality's role in the formation of biblical texts. The impact of form criticism, the method devised to deal with oral

tradition, on biblical scholarship of both the Hebrew Bible/Old Testament and the New Testament has been immense. Today, form criticism is besieged with multiple problems, the most significant of which is its complicity with post-Gutenberg assumptions about ancient dynamics of communication. (2003, 40)

Therefore, a major shift in the approach to form criticism was needed and this occurred among some Q/Gospel of Thomas scholars. Their conversation, first collectively published in *Oral Performance, Popular Tradition, and Hidden Transcript in Q* (Horsley 2006a), takes issue with Kloppenborg's chirographic orientation to Q analysis in *The Formation of Q: Trajectories in Ancient Wisdom Collections* (2007, orig. 1987), discussing Q as an orally derived text. This has implications for understanding its genre and interpreting Q.[23] In that conversation, three issues emerge that suggest areas to which an experiential understanding of orality could contribute. They are the relationship between orality and composition, orality and literacy, and orality and performance. The three issues are interrelated and raise critical issues for the analysis of orally derived texts.

Jonathan Draper (2006) finds that a "rhythmographic presentation of the text" is a way of understanding the relationship between the text and orality. Textual rhythmography, according to Draper, is a literary ritualization of oral mnemonic aids. Thus, the text displays oral patterning (2006, 80–89, esp. 87–89). His uncovering of textual rhythm manifests kinship with oral performance and oral modalities. Draper is persuasive because there is a clear logic to his point. He is disproving Kloppenborg's argument that there are no signs of oral character in Q. Draper wishes to "demonstrate that, on the contrary, the units of the covenantal discourse of Jesus in Q show a clear oral patterning and structure" (2006, 77). Draper's argument is cognitively and corporeally persuasive. As an oral-literate person, I find that his explanation and layout of the Lukan Covenant Discourse on the Plain connects to the musculature for dance in the oral body and evokes the rhythms that my body holds as individual and cultural memory. In

---

23. Despite the copious output on orality studies in the years following the 1987 publication of *The Formation of Q: Trajectories in Ancient Wisdom Collection*, the second edition (2007) fails to engage developments in this area. Consequently, Kloppenborg reiterates the erroneous understandings of orality that the 1987 edition presents. This is an example of the ongoing marginalization, if not exclusion, of alternative epistemes by traditional historical-critical scholars.

other words, his examination made cognitive and corporeal sense. Mine is a deep oral subjective response to a textual claim that affirms Draper's sense of the oral rhythm in the text.

On the other hand, Horsley's refutation of Kloppenborg's Q stratification theories points to limited literacy in Galilee and Roman Palestine in general. Horsley insists that the inscriptions attesting the functions of local village leaders "do not appear to provide evidence for scribes sufficiently educated that they could compose instructional literature" (2006a, 10). The implication is that an illiterate culture cannot produce written concatenated texts. Joanna Dewey supports Horsley's conclusion: "A more important argument against the oral concatenation of the discourses into a whole is that oral cultures do not tend to gather oral material formally into coherent wholes" (Dewey 2006, 105). By this criterion, both Draper's rhythmography and my embodied response should be fallible, but not all is lost. Dewey's summation of the tendencies of all oral cultures through all temporalities and regions has a solitary basis in her essay. One African storyteller, Candi Rureke, identified by name and by tribal tradition, Nyanga, refused to concatenate particular hero narratives at the request of Westerners. Dewey borrows this example from Ong (Ong 2002, 143), but diverges from his use of it. Ong contextualizes this example in an affirmation that a wider scope of cultural references would improve our understanding of orality. Dewey's usage lifts Rureke to the status of an eponym for all oral cultures. She concludes with Rureke that concatenation is never done. For Dewey (2006, 105), Rureke's comment was a reflection on every oral culture's inability to concatenate. Moreover, an implication of Ong's discussion (2002, 143) is that Rureke's response was to a request for a sequential narration. Rureke had no interest in sequential narration. It was not his or her Nyanga tradition. The unwillingness to depart from traditional storytelling methods to sequential narration has no obvious relevance to the capacity to concatenate. Contrarily, I consider that Draper's and my oral sensibilities indicate that antiquity's concatenating literati preserved their own orality in their texts (cf. Foley 2006, 134–35). They may even have preserved the concatenating achievements of their illiterate associates. I continue, therefore, to press for auto-ethnographic impulses and self-awareness as supplements to more or less voyeuristic orality studies. Other examples that are closer to oral sources suggest that illiterate, and by dint of current working definitions, oral, peoples concatenate.

Contrary to Dewey's position on concatenation, Lalla and D'Costa provide a written record of slave concatenation. In *Language in Exile*, Lalla and D'Costa republish a Cumina Chant. Cumina is a religious ceremony that predates "the African indentured migrants who came to Jamaica between 1845 and 1861 and who helped to revive African customs and religion wherever they settled" (Lalla and D'Costa 1990, 207). This example suggests a pre-emancipation, possibly eighteenth-century memory. Interestingly, the chant appears to combine three or more languages: Ewe, Twi, and Gã with a Yoruba overlay (208). More to the point here is that the chant is a religious document attesting the oral capacity to ritualize, organize, and chant aspects of their belief system in a complex way, despite illiteracy. Clearly, literate persons recorded the chant. Nonetheless, it is a product of illiterate people. It is erroneous to limit the compositional capacities of illiterate peoples, especially where literacy/illiteracy is critical to analyzing orally derived texts.

When scholars equate orality with illiteracy,[24] they obscure orality as a mode of communication and being, thus erroneously limiting its capacities. They obscure the reality that writing is orality scaled down. Orality co-exists with both literacy and illiteracy as a way of being and an orientation to life. As such, the markers of orality exceed the tendency to associate it with and restrict it to performance events. Horsley describes Galilee as a culture that was not "truly oral" (2006b, 73). He understands that "oral tradition continues to be performed even where it exists already in written form as an *aide memoire*" (73). Nonetheless, it seems that Horsley has in mind orality as a moment of staged performance. We must expand the notion of oral environment beyond the staged or ritual performance context. It will be useful to understand orality as a mode of being and an epistemology that governs every aspect of communication events, from the quotidian to the staged. Thus, the oral subjective differential can gain traction in the hermeneutical arts and add deeper cultural dimensions to stark textual analysis.

I welcome the orality-motivated move away from individual logia analysis toward an oral-rhetorical approach despite orality's instability (cf. Horsley 2006b, 37). To my modern, orally enculturated and literate ears, meaning instability is music! Jonathan Draper infuses that note of textual

---

24. Illiteracy is the inability to read writing. In one sense, it represents the absence of writing and reading written texts in a person's life. It does not equate with intellectual incompetence and mental deficiencies for higher-order conceptualizations. Usually, nonreaders of writing would not be so rude as to forthrightly declare the stupidity of scholars who cannot read the corporeal texts of oral and oral-literate cultures.

instability into his assessment of Q. He understands that textual meaning does not reside in the written, but in the performance context. Performance is the source of meaning instability and that is the very nature of orality. Meaning making is neither systematic nor univocal (see Draper 2006; Hyldahl 2008, 44, 50–51). However, the relationship between performance and orality is loosely analogous to that between an entablature and the edifice it sits atop where the entablature is analogous to performance. Performance is truncated orality, a metonymic episode, almost an oral lollapalooza. Meaning instability is the reality of the texts we have inherited. It is an instability that typography camouflages but does not obliterate.

Orality, understood as cultural modality, is the matrix of performance. Performance derives from orality. The receiving community is apiece with its culture in the moment of reception and then returns to that culture and the performance re-enters community through the audience.[25] As Brathwaite describes, "Reading is an isolated, individualistic expression. The oral tradition on the other hand demands not only the griot but the audience to complete the community" (1984, 19). He continues that meaning resides in the creation of the community continuum. My sense of community extends beyond the group around the griot. Arguably, Brathwaite implies a sense of that extension in his discussion of the impact of the Mighty Sparrow's calypso, *Ten to One Is Murder* on the outcome of his shooting trial (25). This is a description of a palpable and mercurial cultural fabric but it also indicates the elusiveness of cultural subjectivities. It is easier, then, to focus, as Kelber and others do, on the performed text and apply the implications of meaning instability as he does with Q (Kelber 2006). However, that turn disengages us from the oral matrix and from engaging the text with fulsome and present orality. It thus removes com-

---

25. This insight emerges in the context of the annual pantomime in Jamaica. The pantomime is usually an engaging, humorous, fictionalized, romantic, and staged musical commentary on the political and social foibles of the preceding year. It is a hyperbolic satire in which real events and leading personalities are recognizable. Clearly, audience members who best understand the nuances would have been aware of the year's events, ensuing conversations, and patterns of behavior. What is not visible is the way in which appropriations of the caricatures feed into the analyses, reflections, and verifications. The techniques of pantomime production are important to the artists. For the audience the important questions focus on the pantomime's interpretation of civic realities, its aptness, authenticity, and insightfulness.

munity and culture from textual analysis.[26] The restoration of meaning possibilities, with respect to culture and community, will arise from the interiority/subjectivity of the auto-ethnographic scholar. That would be a hermeneutical contribution.

Translation and hermeneutics via textual analysis are convenient arenas for connecting oral subjectivities to academic biblical studies. Scholars with conscious oral sensibilities and an autoptic viewpoint can articulate the movement from subjectivity to phenomenon. Such scholars are not supplementary resources to enable historical critical scholars to better exercise their expertise. The ultimate goal is to establish the necessity of foregrounding auto-ethnographic oral subjectivity as the preferred modality for understanding writing processes, performance, communication, and, especially, reception in oral antiquity. It would be irresponsible to suggest that scholars aware of their oral narrative culture will perfectly remove all lacunae or reduce them to imperceptibility. My imagined auto-ethnographic scholars and I are anachronistic in our relation to ancient Mediterranean history. We are of profoundly entangled oral-literate subjectivities. However, it would be irresponsible to act out the Westernized belief that the post-Gutenberg perspective naturally and necessarily can do a better job than can an oral epistemology and subjectivity. The challenge is to demonstrate that oral subjectivity can enhance our understanding of antiquity's modalities for biblical studies. Including orality as a cultural modality in the tool kit of the biblical scholar increases the foundational epistemological postures and imaginaries that gird our textual analyses, interpretations, and translations. The next section addresses translation possibilities.

5. Language and Translation

It is not possible to translate the plenitude of embodied communication into words. The verbal gaps that a body fills or the unspoken gestures that inflect the spoken are missing from the written script. Also missing are the clicks, kiss teeth,[27] and garment-to-body expressions that commu-

---

26. The turn is also a point at which oral and orally oriented cultures are vulnerable to exclusion from the reservoir of available cultural imaginaries for biblical interpretation. The discussion is at risk of returning to controlled formulae for scientific-oriented applications to oral texts.

27. Kiss teeth is an elongated gurgling hiss formed by the interaction of tongue,

nicate mood and emotion. It is fair to assume that the biblical authors could no more communicate, on papyri, the meanings that depended on the multiple mechanisms of oral communication and complete their communicative intent than can we. Is this why prepositions and untranslatable particles in Greek confound?[28] Every phoneme means something. That untranslatable particles confound me is a sign that my language orientation is determined by Western rationalism rather than by my oral cultural orientation. Paradoxically, that it confounds me is also a sign that my language orientation was formed by an oral orientation. I cannot believe that there is an untranslatable phoneme. Some phonemes may have translations that are embodied culturally, for example, the Jamaican kiss teeth. I imagine oral communication events as verbal, sensory, and embodied. Speech includes intonated words, sentences with gaps, culturally loaded innuendos, eyes, hands, clothing, and body; filled with aposiopeses and asyndeta that need bodies for explication. It remains for readers to fill the gaps with their own enculturation—the gaps indicated by untranslatable particles, odd prepositions, incomplete sentences, run-on sentences, wildly unwieldy sentences, and missing conjunctions. A fulsome description of oral communicative modalities must include vocality, tactility, aurality, opticality, and gesticulations, that is, a holistic embodiment theory of communication. The dominant literate modality for translation with its *Gesellschaft* orientation needs an alternative imagination in order to proximate the plenitude that is lost in chirographic translation.

Differing cultural imaginations suggest there are problems to be associated with biblical translation into the official languages of former Christian empires: British, French, Dutch, Spanish, and, because of biblical scholarship's intellectual history, I include German.[29] The criteria for prioritizing manuscripts and understanding the meaning of emendations,

---

teeth, and saliva. It has a range of meanings that include frustration, disgust, impatience, disappointment, and surrender. The intensity of any of these can be communicated by lengthening or intensifying the sound.

28. I am using untranslatable particles as metonyms that evoke a sense of translation as an inexact art.

29. Édouard Glissant (1997) calls these vehicular languages and identifies them as essential to maintain colonial power. Of French he says, "Because it lacks an anchor in areas of concrete and undisguised domination ... for some time now some people have pledged the French language to establishing a sort of semiconceptual dominance. It would thus maintain its transparency and *contain the increasing opacity of the world within the limits of a well-phrased classicism*" (111, emphasis added).

lacunae, and relationships between manuscripts are formed and bound by the subjectivities of these countries' educated elite. Acceptable academic translation proceeds from manuscripts to formal and vehicular languages. Mitigating cultural myopia as it affects translation matters. Translation can also proceed from manuscripts to nation languages (see Brathwaite 1984, 5)[30] and be both acceptable and edifying.

Orality exposes the dearth, within biblical scholarship, of cognate cultures that ought to be requisite contributions to our understanding ancient oral cultures. The introduction of auto-ethnographic orality reduces the violence of anachronistic historical reconstructions by utilizing the imaginations of proximate cultures. This thought is not new, clearly. New is the possibility of auto-ethnographic subjective information in reconstructing ancient cultures. Its applicability to biblical translation is a wide-open frontier. Biblical translation beckons because it promises collaboration among scholars from Africa and the African Diaspora who can develop certain auto-ethnographic insights in the application of orally oriented cultures to biblical translation. This section furthers the ovulatory exploration in the direction of biblical studies. It begins with reflection on Edwina Wright's essay, "The Relationship between Hebrew and African Languages." In it she describes a linguistic land bridge, the Afro-Asiatic phylum that connects the African continent to ancient Middle Eastern languages. Her survey opens space in which to question the arrogated and naturalized right of colonizing languages, Dutch, English, French, German, and Spanish, in their elite manifestations, as appropriate vehicles of biblical translation. In addition, by foraging through Jamaican[31] for vestigial connections to the Afro-Asiatic phylum, I begin the challenge to regnant translation claims that are implicit in the paradigmatic "naturalness" of translating into the aforementioned languages.

Wright notes that there is a fundamental linguistic connection between Hebrew and African languages. This connection, she says, "is demon-

---

30. Nation languages are the languages developed by slaves and laborers whom the colonizers introduced into the colonies.

31. Jamaican is the current designation for the language spoken by the majority of Jamaicans. This development is associated with the Bible Translation Project hosted by the Bible Society of the West Indies. Rev. Courtney Stewart has overseen this project for approximately twenty years. During that time the language's name changed from Jamaican Patois to Jamaican English and finally to the current term, Jamaican. Jamaican is the term I will continue to use when referring to the language of Jamaicans.

strated by the fact that the Semitic language family, inclusive of Hebrew, Aramaic, Ugaritic, and Akkadian, is part of a larger language super family (phylum) known as Afro-Asiatic" (1999, 89). Further, Wright identifies some contours for comparison among the Afro-Asiatic languages as "significant similarities ... have been found among various branches in vocabulary, in some sound patterns, and in some grammatical forms (especially in some verbal forms, pronouns, and gender referents)" (94). The Afro-Asiatic phylum includes "Semitic, Berber, Egyptian, and the distinctly Black African language groups: Chadic and Cushite" (85). Wright lays a foundation for tracing the connection between African and Semitic language groups.

The promise of this connection is still inchoate and the relevance of these to New Testament studies, except for Coptic language and culture, is not yet self-evident. Nonetheless, the ancient connection between the African continent and the Middle East is an irresistible site of investigation for post/anticolonial linguistics. Certainly, the connection to island inhabitants remains opaque. In 1984, Brathwaite already opined that no one had as "yet made a study of the influence of Asiatic languages on the contemporary Caribbean" (1984, 6 n. 1). Encouragingly, for this essay, he notes that the nation languages, as they developed in colonial times, influenced "the way in which the English, French, Dutch, and Spaniards spoke their own languages" (7–8). Encouraged and enthusiastic, I construct two hypothetical bridges, linguistic and cultural, that connect both New Testament studies and island culture to the Afro-Asiatic phylum. The former is the more difficult of the two, based as it is in little-studied linguistic subtleties, at least in relation to biblical studies.

The foundation linguistic blocks that Wright provides are part of the Afro-Asiatic phylum. At this construction site, some geographic regions are prioritized. These are Egyptian Coptic, the Berber dialectics found in Libya, Algeria, Tunisia, Mauritania, and Senegal, and the Western Chadic dialects found in Nigeria, Cameroon, and possibly Togo. Maureen Warner-Lewis, a Caribbean comparative linguist, includes small Togo and the Benin Republic (formerly Dahomey) along with Nigeria, Ghana, and Libya in her linguistic analysis of Trinidadian Yoruba (1999, 17–19; cf. Brathwaite 1984, 7). On a map of Africa, the westward direction of Wright's selected languages begins in Egypt, that is, northeastern Africa, and ends in west central and northwestern Africa. There are assumptions in this depiction of a march across the African continent that requires further research. The primary assumption is that these dialects can bear the weight of similarity suggested by Wright, the intimated similarity that this essay's bridge-building quest finds necessary. The second assumption is that these dialects will display sufficiently strong connections to Egyptian Coptic, the linchpin language that connects the island colonies and their sociolinguistic heritage to Coptic literature in New Testament studies, to the sociolinguistic realities of the Mediterranean and then, by extension, to Greco-Roman culture. These are four discrete elements, each with its peculiar web of intra-connections of sufficient complexity to question the viability of the tenuous connection within the quadratic. These foundation blocks, the similarity of African tongues within the Afro-Asiatic phylum and the quadratic relationship should be the primary sites of research.[32] The route of this potential phylum's influence flows from the Mediterranean world, through continental Africa, to the Caribbean and the Americas.

The more challenging bridge is the detailed establishment of oral cultural mechanisms' relevance for biblical translation. Alongside this is the difficulty of proposing African and African Diaspora languages as edifying for biblical translation. Paradoxically, oral semiotic instability that increases the risks in translation is the feature that also promises to improve the integrity of translation outcomes. I began this project with weighty uncertainty that oral mechanisms can make a difference in translation. They must. The similarities are not only linguistic, they also reside in African religious, artistic, musical, proverbial, folk lore survivals in the Caribbean. Therefore, shored by these survivals, Wright's introductory survey, Brathwaite's yearnings, and Warner-Lewis's Yoruba efforts, we can chart a prospective path that includes language and culture. It should not be necessary to create such a chart. German, French, Spanish, or English translators do not justify their presumptive right to translate into their languages. That one should translate the Bible into these regnant dialects is such a naturalized presumption! It is aggrieving that translation into the nation languages, those that abut, neighbor, and extend the Mediterranean reach, requires justification! The colonial past's and present's weighty certitudes and self-assuredness are an overbearing load to move en route to the establishment of oral culture's relevance for translation and hermeneutics. There are fragile signs that the load might be movable.

---

32. Also pertinent to this exploration is the linguistic relationship between the Caribbean and the United States of America vis-à-vis the Gullah peoples of the continental United States. The Gullah peoples are also island people and bear significant language similarities to some Caribbean territories, e.g., Jamaica, Barbados, and Trinidad.

6. Envisaging the Linguistic Future

With consideration given to Wright's work and a nod toward the importance of cognate cultural understandings for translation, it is no longer self-evident that the dominant dialects of majority cultures are natural heirs to ancient Greek, Coptic, and Hebrew. The map of the linguist terrain flows through the tribal dialects of Africa, from the west coastal peoples, through north central Africa and eventually to the northeastern corners of that continent. This map is, of course, incomplete. There is no reason, other than the Western slave connection to the selected regions of Africa, for excluding the remaining dialects of Africa. Yet, the African continent is not the only region with a stake in this translation project. Island descendants of the African slaves and descendants of those who came as indentured workers share a dialect tradition that emerged from the deft language acquisitions and adaptations of their ancestors. There are reminiscences and hints of Africa's tongues in those dialects. Including these dialects in biblical translation, I suggest, would provide an enlightening enhancement. We should peer into that possibility, at least. The galvanizing force that drives the map's highlights is the potential that sociolinguistic commonalities hold for translation. Given the oral modalities of these cultures, should we find sufficient commonalities across the map, their oral sensibilities can recognize more polysemic possibilities and fill untranslatable particles with meaning. They can enhance translation possibilities with additional tonalities that are integral to orality. As de Waard and Nida indicate about functional equivalence, "There is no way in which translation can be isolated from the total communication act" (de Waard and Nida 1986, 46). Although de Waard and Nida are not addressing orality, their expansiveness in the observation that "one must be concerned with the accuracy with which the content is presented rather than the number of words which may be employed to accomplish this" (46–47) gestures toward the plenitude that translation from oral tongues requires. Moreover, oral communication mechanisms are integral to the "total communication act," including oral performance.

The linguistic map is an effort to establish grammatical and syntactical similarities between Jamaican English and Coptic.[33] This, too, is an

---

33. Other Caribbean languages are also creolizations of the colonizer's languages. Barbadian English, Trinidadian and Tobagonian English, Curaçao's Papiamentu, Haitian French, also should be explored for their relevance. Suriname provides a wider

ovulatory moment. It is presented as a suggestion of unexplored possibilities, a beginning rather than a formation. There are some clues such as L. Emilie Adams's bold claim:

> Amazing as it may seem, traditional Jamaican patois has actually preserved a method of plural formation the roots of which stretch back to the Meroitic language spoken in the first millennium B.C. ... its pattern of forming noun plurals is clear: the third person plural pronoun, *abe*, functions as the plural suffix. (1991, 14)

She reflects that Jamaican pluralizes by adding the pronoun "them" to the noun (see Singler 1991, 545). Adams notes the possible association of this grammatical structure with the Mandingo ancestors of the Mali Empire in the medieval period. She speculates that the "Mali people may have preserved important cultural and linguistic traditions dating back two thousand years to the ancient Nilotic empire of Kush, whose capital city, Meroe, was near modern Khartoum in the Sudan" (1991, 14). Throughout her grammar Adams consistently compares Jamaican English to African languages. The latitudinal lines run from Jamaica to Cameroon, Central Africa, Ghana, Nigeria, and Togo. These countries accounted for 63 percent of the slaves brought to Jamaica (28–29). These countries represent the majority sub-phyla of the Afro-Asiatic phylum, including Berber, Egyptic (Coptic), Chadic, and Cushitic. Egyptic, or Coptic as it is identified in New Testament studies, as the language of the Nag Hammadi texts, is the logical choice for beginning to make connections. Although this map centers Jamaica, my hope is that these continental nations and more Caribbean territories develop skilled scholars to tackle the task of biblical translation.

From my first language, Jamaican, my awareness of possible comparisons began with the recognition of slim similarities between Jamaican English and Coptic.[34] The following sampling of similarities between Jamaican and Coptic is very limited. The similarities are invitations to further research. They are not comprehensive, and certainly they are not exhaustive. The samples represent findings in this early stage of explo-

---

variety of languages. Notable among them for inclusion here are Sranam Tongo, Saramaccan, and Ndyuka.

34. This comparison is also an indication of possibilities for comparison with other Caribbean languages, the Gullah people of the United States, and Coptic.

ration. Adams's Jamaican grammar, Thomas Russell's *The Etymology of Jamaican Grammar* (1868), and Thomas Lambdin's *Introduction to Sahidic Coptic* (1983) are instrumental to this comparison. Syntactic structures provide substantial indications of linguistic memory and heritage. Simple similarities include genitive constructions, compound demonstrative pronouns, and direct speech. One way Sahidic Coptic constructs genitives is by inserting the possessive marker, preposition, "*N*" (*en*) between the related nouns. Jamaican English marks the genitive with the preposition, "*a fi* + possessor." The genitive in both languages is a prepositional, compound, construction. However, the noun or pronoun possessed may follow the genitive marker. Demonstrative pronouns in Jamaican English are generally compounded as "*dis ya*" (this here, this one), "*dat deh*" (that there, that one), and pluralized as "*dem ya*" (lit. them here, these) or "*dem deh*" (lit. them there, those), similar to the "*et Mmau*" (*et emmaw*, lit. that one there or that) of Coptic. Lastly, both languages demonstrate variable articles in both the definite and indefinite constructions. In each of these areas, there are several points of nuance and finesse of construction, usage, and function within sentences. These points await further comparison and analysis but note that they are not standard to formal English. This small group of similarities raises the possibility of other, more complex similarities, an indication of possible research trajectories.

Of the comparative grammatical areas, direct speech is the strongest. In English, the introduction of a direct quote, in speech and writing, consists simply of a noun or pronoun preceding a speech or emotive verb such as "she spoke," or "they lamented," and others. The insertion of the demonstrative pronoun, "that," indicates an indirect quote. Jamaican and Coptic construct direct speech similarly and together are different from formal English. In his Coptic grammar Lambdin instructs, "When introducing a direct quotation, the verb *jw* (*jō* to say, speak to) requires a 'dummy' object, *Mmos*, (*emmos*) or the suffix *-s* followed by the conjunction *je*" (1983, 44). In Jamaican English a direct quote may be introduced by "*Im seh dat seh...*,"[35] for which "he said that say" provides a literal translation. There is an underlying communication pattern to both constructions though the vocabulary differs. The pattern may be described, from a Jamaican perspective, as articulating a need to underscore the earnestness, authenticity, or

---

35. Sometimes "seh (say)" is used as the demonstrative pronoun, "that." I include this, although the grammatical form may now be obsolete.

sincerity of a verbatim representation of another's speech though it may not be fulsomely verbatim in a literary sense. These observations, as hypotheses, betoken the urgency of further exploration and analysis of connections. They indicate vestiges of linguistic and cultural memory. With more linguistic research and subjective cultural understanding, there will be opportunities to substantiate and refine the idea that dialects of Africa and the African Diaspora, may be closer to the Mediterranean orality, ancient and modern, than are the formalized dialects of English, French, German, and Spanish.[36]

7. Conclusion

Ovulation, as a metaphor for this essay, hints at the possibility of fecundity. Identifying possibility is the modest aspiration of this essay. Despite the irony of using the written medium to persuade post-Gutenberg thinkers that orality transcends and fulsomely contextualizes writing, its intricacies indicate the inadequacies of writing for this project. This effort aligns with advances in biblical orality studies that call for the inclusion of more cultures. Edwina Wright's finger points to the African continent's linguistic heritage as an area requiring further research. Similarly, Edward Kamau Brathwaite and Maureen Werner-Lewis, and others enflesh linguistic similarities with cultural vestiges. The inclusion of Jamaican indicates other potential sources for oral and linguistic cultures that are closer to the Western world. Altogether, these suggest that an exploration of sociolinguistic bridging of the African Diaspora to northeastern Africa, east Africa, and the Middle East is a worthy undertaking. A renewed and expanded focus on orality suggests, further, that there are vast unexplored cultural terrains in biblical studies awaiting auto-ethnographic research. These indicate directions that lend themselves to anticolonial developments in biblical studies. They are worthy of study because there is an unexamined history and there are unincorporated cultures that offer legitimate alternative cultural imaginations for biblical studies. Moreover, they are worthy of study because they can inform us about cross-cultural synchronic and diachronic sociolinguistic evolutions to the benefit of biblical translation. Finally, an auto-ethnograph-

---

36. The closest cognate cultures are, of course, the contemporary peoples of Mediterranean nations.

ically informed orality is available for deeper exploration and analysis because auto-ethnographic, anticolonial, orally oriented biblical scholars exist and we can read.

REFERENCES

Adams, L. Emilie. 1991. *Understanding Jamaican Patois: An Introduction to Afro-Jamaican Grammar*. Kingston: LMH Publishing.
Alexander, Loveday. 2009. Memory and Tradition in the Hellenistic Schools. Pages 113–54 in *Jesus in Memory: Traditions in Oral and Scribal Perspectives*. Edited by Werner H. Kelber and Samuel Byrskog. Waco: Baylor University Press.
Bailey, Kenneth. 1995. Informal Controlled Oral Tradition and the Synoptic Gospels. *Themelios* 20:4–11.
Bauckham, Richard. 2006. *Jesus and the Eyewitnesses: The Gospels as Eyewitness Testimony*. Grand Rapids: Eerdmans.
Brathwaite, Edward Kamau. 1984. *History of the Voice: The Development of Nation Language in Anglophone Caribbean Poetry*. Port of Spain: New Beacon.
Burton-Christie, Douglas. 1997. Oral Culture, Biblical Interpretation, and Spirituality in Early Christian Monasticism. Pages 415–40 in *The Bible in Greek Christian Antiquity*. Edited and translated by Paul M. Blowers. Notre Dame: University of Notre Dame Press.
Crossan, John Dominic. 1999. *The Birth of Christianity: Discovering What Happened in the Years Immediately after the Execution of Jesus*. New York: HarperCollins.
Dash, J. Michael. 1992. Introduction. Pages i–xxii in *Caribbean Discourse: Selected Essays by Eduard Glissant*. Translated by J. Michael Dash. Charlottesville: University Press of Virginia.
Dewey, Joanna, ed. 1995a. *Orality and Textuality in Early Christian Literature*. Semeia 65. Atlanta: Scholars Press.
———. 1995b. Textuality in Oral Culture: A Survey of the Pauline Traditions. *Semeia* 65:37–65.
———. 2006. Response to Kelber, Horsley, and Draper. Pages 101–107 in *Oral Performance, Popular Tradition, and Hidden Transcript in Q*. Edited by Richard Horsley. SemeiaSt 60. Atlanta: Society of Biblical Literature.
Draper, Jonathan, ed. 2003. *Orality, Literacy, and Colonialism in Southern Africa*. SemeiaSt 46. Atlanta: Society of Biblical Literature.

———, ed. 2004. *Orality, Literacy, and Colonialism in Antiquity*. SemeiaSt 47. Atlanta: Society of Biblical Literature.

———. 2006. Jesus' "Covenantal Discourse" on the Plain (Luke 6:12–7:17) as Oral Performance: Pointers to "Q" as Multiple Oral Performance. Pages 71–98 in *Oral Performance, Popular Tradition, and Hidden Transcript in Q*. Edited by Richard Horsley. SemeiaSt 60. Atlanta: Society of Biblical Literature.

Edmonson, Belinda, ed. 1999 *Caribbean Romances: The Politics of Regional Representation*. Charlottesville: University Press of Virginia.

Foley, John Miles. 2006. The Riddle of Q: Oral Ancestor, Textual Precedent, or Ideological Creation? Pages 123–40 in *Oral Performance, Popular Tradition, and Hidden Transcript in Q*. Edited by Richard Horsley. SemeiaSt 60. Atlanta: Society of Biblical Literature.

Glissant, Édouard. 1997. *Poetics of Relation*. Translated by Betsy Wing. Ann Arbor: University of Michigan Press.

Horsley, Richard A., ed. 2006a. *Oral Performance, Popular Tradition, and Hidden Transcript in Q*. SemeiaSt 60. Atlanta: Society of Biblical Literature.

———. 2006b. Performance and Tradition. Pp. 43–70 in *Oral Performance, Popular Tradition, and Hidden Transcript in Q*. Edited by Richard A. Horsley. SemeiaSt 60. Atlanta: Society of Biblical Literature.

Horsley, Richard, Jonathan Draper, and John Miles Foley. 2006. *Performing the Gospel: Orality, Memory, and Mark*. Minneapolis: Fortress.

Hyldahl, Jesper. 2008. Normativity and the Dynamic of Mutual Authorisation: The Relationship between "Canonical" and "Non-Canonical" Writings. Pages 42–52 in *Matthew, James and Didache: Three Related Documents in Their Jewish and Christian Settings*. Edited by Huub van de Sandl and Jürgen K. Zangenberg. Atlanta: Society of Biblical Literature.

Jackson, Michael. 1989. *Paths toward a Clearing: Radical Empiricism and Ethnographic Inquiry*. Bloomington: Indiana University Press.

Jagessar, Michael N. 1996. *Full Life for All: The Work and Theology of Philip A. Potter: A Historical Survey and Systematic Analysis of Major Themes*. Zoetermeer: Uitgeverij Boekencentrum.

John, Catherine A. 2003. *Clear Word and Third Sight: Folk Groundings and Diasporic Consciousness in African Caribbean Writing*. Durham: Duke University Press.

Kelber, Werner. 1983. *The Oral and the Written Gospel: The Hermeneutics *of Speaking and Writing in the Synoptic Tradition, Mark, Paul, and Q.* Philadelphia: Fortress.

———. 2003. Oral Tradition in Bible and New Testament Studies. *Oral Tradition* 18.1:40–42.

———. 2006. The Verbal Art in Q and Thomas: A Question of Epistemology. Pages 25–42 in *Oral Performance, Popular Tradition and Hidden Transcript in Q.* Edited by Richard Horsley. Atlanta: Society of Biblical Literature.

Kelber, Werner H., and Samuel Byrskog, eds. 2009. *Jesus in Memory: Traditions in Oral and Scribal Perspectives.* Waco: Baylor University Press.

Kirk, Alan. 2009. Memory. Pages 155–72 in *Jesus in Memory: Traditions in Oral and Scribal Perspectives.* Edited by Werner H. Kelber and Samuel Byrskog. Waco: Baylor University Press.

Kloppenborg, John S. 2007. *The Formation of Q.* 2nd ed. Philadelphia: Fortress.

Lalla, Barbara, and Jean D'Costa. 1990. *Language in Exile: Three Hundred Years of Jamaican Creole.* Tuscaloosa: University of Alabama Press.

Lambdin, Thomas O. 1983. *Introduction to Sahidic Coptic.* Macon, Ga.: Mercer University Press.

McIver, Robert K. 2011. *Memory, Jesus, and the Synoptic Gospels.* Atlanta: Society of Biblical Literature.

Moore, Stephen D. 2010. *The Bible in Theory: Critical and Postcritical Essays.* Atlanta: Society of Biblical Literature.

Mulrain, George. 1999. Hermeneutics within a Caribbean Context. Pages 116–32 in *The Bible and Postcolonialism, 2.* Edited by R. S. Sugirtharajah. Sheffield: Academic Press.

Niditch, Susan. 1996. *Oral World and Written Word: Ancient Israelite Literature.* Louisville: Westminster John Knox.

Ong, Walter. 2002. *Orality and Literacy: The Technologizing of the Word.* 2nd ed. New York: Routledge.

Parry, Adam, ed. 1971. *The Making of Homeric Verse: The Collected Papers of Milman Parry.* Oxford: Clarendon.

Russell, Heather. 2009. *Legba's Crossing: Narratology in the African Atlantic.* Athens: University of Georgia Press.

Russell, Thomas. 1868. *The Etymology of Jamaican Grammar.* Kingston: DeCordova MacDougall.

Silberman, Lou H. 1987. Introduction: Reflections on Orality, Aurality and Perhaps More. Pages 1–6 in *Orality, Aurality and Biblical Nar-*

rative. Edited by Lou H. Silberman. SemeiaSt 39. Atlanta: Society of Biblical Literature.

Singler, John Victor. 1991. Social and Linguistic Constraints on Plural Marking in Liberian English. Pages 545–62 in *English around the World: Sociolinguistic Perspectives.* Edited by Jenny Cheshire. Cambridge: Cambridge University Press.

Spencer-Miller, Althea. 2007. Orality and the Narrative Techniques of the Acts of the Apostles, the Homeric Epics, Greco-Roman Novels, and Greco-Roman Historiography: A Comparative Approach. Doctoral thesis, Claremont Graduate University.

Stewart, Edward C., and Milton J. Bennett. 1991. *American Cultural Patterns: A Cross-Cultural Perspective.* Yarmouth, Maine: Intercultural Press.

Suárez, Margarita M. W. 2002. Across the Kitchen Table: Cuban Women Pastors and Theology. Pages 173–93 in *Gender, Ethnicity, and Religion: Views from the Other Side.* Edited by Rosemary Radford Ruether. Minneapolis: Augsburg.

Thatcher, Tom, ed. 2008. *Jesus, the Voice, and the Text: Beyond the Oral and the Written Gospel.* Waco, Tex.: Baylor University Press.

Tönnies, Ferdinand. 1957. *Community and Society.* East Lansing: Michigan State University Press.

Waard, Jan de, and Eugene A. Nida. 1986. *Functional Equivalence in Bible Translating: From One Language to Another.* Nashville: Thomas Nelson.

Warner-Lewis, Maureen. 1996. *Trinidad Yoruba: From Mother Tongue to Memory.* Tuscaloosa: University of Alabama Press.

Wright, Edwina M. 1999. The Relationship between Hebrew and African Languages. Pages 89–96 in *Holy Bible: African American Jubilee Edition.* New York: American Bible Society.

Gazing (at) Native Women: Rahab and Jael in Imperializing and Postcolonial Discourses

Steed Vernyl Davidson

Postcolonial theory challenges the expectations that neat divisions occur in the Hebrew Bible. As the product of a beleaguered and ultimately landless people, the application of strict binary categories of colonizer/colonized, oppressor/oppressed, or even center/margin to the Hebrew Bible faces the complexities of historical exactitude versus historiography, realism versus fantasy, survival versus resistance, among other things. Recognizing the complexities of the colonial context makes simple categorizations difficult. To the extent that we agree that the Hebrew Bible stands as a product of empire while also being produced in the midst of empire, then the seemingly contradictory discourses of imperialism and anti-imperialism will emerge in the same text, and vexingly so, at the wrong times and places. On the issue of the native woman, imperial and anti-imperial discourses engage in a shared battle since they both produce the native woman as a site of conflict. Consequently, the easy identification of oppressive imperializing discourses and liberatory anti-imperializing discourses remains elusive. The peculiarities of the figure of the native woman, located at the intersections of gender, race, and imperial power, raises a conundrum that exposes the limits of postcolonial theory. While the exposed limits hardly point to the inadequacy of postcolonial theory, both the partial exploration and the imbalanced attention to this issue among biblical scholars suggest the need for further reflection. This essay explores the difficulties inherent in imperial and anti-imperial discourses with respect to the native woman, in biblical texts, and offers tentative proposals for thinking through this problem.

The figure Native Woman invokes the ambiguity and slipperiness inherent in both terms. By Native, I foreground here the resistance inherent in the term as used by indigenous people to press their original claims to their homelands. In the process of doing so, the term also invokes histories of conquest, settlement and colonization, and thereby conjures up notions of exoticism and primitivism. The term Woman here represents the set of gendered performances that attempt to reduce female bodies in all their varieties to a single entity. Woman stands as a signifier of an artificial construct. Therefore, while the essential concerns of this essay seek to address issues faced by indigenous and Third World women, I use the term Native Woman here as a disruptive discursive to show that these flesh and blood women do not turn up in these discourses.[1] The representation that appears, the Native Woman, an object of fascination, functions as an image that, as Rey Chow points out, serves as "the place where battles are fought and strategies of resistance negotiated" (Chow 1994, 127). Chow notes that the tendency to invest this image with subjectivity, as a form of resistance, fails to deal with the image itself and that the real issue for postcolonial discourse lies not in rehabilitating the image but in locating authentic representations of the image.

My concern in this essay goes beyond a postcolonial reading of the Native Woman that describes her as the pawn in imperializing discourses or recovers for her agency that shows resistance to colonizing tendencies. While I pay attention to those issues, I am more interested in how a postcolonial perspective deals with the representation of women in the Bible, particularly those that may be triply oppressed, as Gayatri Spivak formulates it (Spivak 1994, 90). I wish to open a conversation that engages the figure Native Woman as a constructed image and also the power of the figure, Native Woman. For while on one level the figure can be dismissed as a textual representation, on another level, given the power of texts to define and name reality, this figure participates in the reality of indigenous and Third World women. Beneath the seemingly stable figure/image, Native Woman, lies an unstable mass of social reproductions. Yet at the same time Third World women transcend, even though not able to fully escape, the simplicities inherent in the representation of the Native

---

1. I choose to indicate the literary representation Native Woman by capitalizing the term as a way of avoiding the use of quotation marks and suggesting something peculiar. In referring to what may be real and actual women I use the lowercase form of the term. I do the same with regard to men.

Woman. As Hazel Carby suggests, representation often times can be worse than being left out, since these images fail to capture the full dimensions of women and their relationships with power (Carby 2000, 389). Following on the rethinking of the assumptions of power advocated by Chandra Talpade Mohanty that avoids thinking of power simply as "power relations [that] are structured in terms of a unilateral and undifferentiated source of power and a cumulative reaction to power" (Mohanty 1994, 213), the space that I wish to carve out explores the interplay of race, gender, and imperial power and the location of the subject Native Woman at those intersections.

The choice of Rahab and Jael as the focus of this essay arises out of convenience to limit the scope of exploration but also to respond to the pairing of these two women as united in the betrayal of their own people to serve the interests of an invading group. Elie Assis in his article, "The Choice to Serve God and Assist His People: Rahab and Yael" connects these women as "gentile woman assisting an Israelite man" (Assis 2004, 82). While he narrates clearly the common structures in the respective narratives, Assis inscribes an imperializing interpretation that accepts the superiority of Israel and automatically the inferiority of the cultures from which Rahab and Jael emerge. Among the common elements of both narratives, Assis finds sexual connotations and representation of the Native Men as weak in both narratives. While not a unique observation about these narratives, the confluence of invasion, gender, sexuality, and cultural superiority appears not merely in the pairing of Rahab and Jael but more so in Assis's contrast of these two women with Delilah. Assis finds common paths among the three women; however, Delilah's exceptionalism lies in the fact that she acts contrary to the interests of her lover, the Israelite man Samson (2004, 87). The troubling conclusion that Delilah makes for a less than desirable character because she serves the interests of her people, while Rahab and Jael can stand as role models precisely because they go against the interests of their own people troubles nativist sentiments. Even more than this, the value of these three women, all Native Women involved in various levels of sexual congress with a Foreign Man, rests upon their ability to abandon their culture and homeland. The obvious imperializing nature of Assis's work calls forth the postcolonial impulse to rescue the Native Woman from this discourse and equip her with an agency that resists imperialist tendencies.

As natural as this impulse may be to the postcolonial reader, its effects are illusory since the image still stands. Further, this "rescue mission" most likely involves a male response that conscripts the Native Woman's nationalist allegiances. In what follows, I explore and assess the treatment of Rahab and Jael for imperializing and anti-imperializing discourses. In the process I am making a distinction between anti-imperializing/colonizing and postcolonial discourse since, as Robert Young points out, the term postcolonial "specifies a transformed historical situation" (Young 2001, 57) that produces new formations in response to changed political circumstances. I use postcolonial here to denote the need to move beyond and think beyond the experiences of colonialism while retaining the resistant character of the anti-imperializing moment. To the extent that the image Native Woman emerges as a colonial product and maintains some staying power, I am interested in moving to a space that goes beyond the mere repudiation of the image. But first, I need to narrate and explore the field of thinking in relation to Rahab and Jael. In the end, I offer some tentative solutions of what a postcolonial response to the image may look like.

The narratives of Rahab and Jael, in Joshua and Judges respectively, resemble the script that surfaces quite often in conquest narratives. Louis Montrose observes that from the 1570s feminized and nude depictions of the Americas begin to appear in Western Europe. He also points to the "sexualizing of [European] exploration, conquest and settlement" (Montrose 1991, 2).[2] Citing the work of Rene Maunier, Musa Dube notes that the general tendency to feminize lands and cultures takes a turn in imperialist contexts where women serve as the first point of contact with the representatives of the invading empire, exclusively men. Dube shows that this contact then sets the stage for "the tragic romance" tale between the Native Woman and the white European male as featured in the Disney movie *Pocahontas* (2000, 73).[3] The gendered language of conquest, therefore, quickly transfers onto the bodies of women, thereby replacing the land with a body and reducing the territory to a single individual in the imperialist imagination. This substitution and replacement offers what

---

2. Much of Montrose's study focuses on Sir Walter Raleigh's published work, *The Discoverie of the Large, Rich, and Beautifull Empire of Guiana* (1596) and Raleigh's relationship with Queen Elizabeth I. While Montrose locates a connection between Elizabeth's reputed virginity, the alleged sexual relationship between Elizabeth and Raleigh, and the highly sexualized language in Raleigh's work, he does not view Raleigh's portrayal as an isolated case (Montrose 1991, 3).

3. Lori Rowlett offers useful correctives to the misrepresentations of historical facts in the Disney portrayal of *Pocahontas* (Rowlett 2000, 67).

Montrose, following Michel de Certeau, sees as a "historied body" (Montrose 1991, 6) rather than a flesh and blood depiction of the Native Woman or the indigenous people whose lands are being conquered, and thereby produces "writing that conquers."[4]

Biblical narratives of conquest appear to follow similar paths to those seen in modern European colonial expansion. Lori Rowlett locates the trope of the hypersexualized Native Woman as applied to Native Americans in the way the Bible talks about Canaanites. Building on the work of Frederick Pike, Rowlett identifies four elements shared in common by the stories of Rahab and Disney's Pocahontas. These four elements include: woman falls in love/has sex/marries conqueror; woman saves conquerors by going against her own people; woman embraces the conqueror's culture as the first step of conversion and "moving up"; woman, especially her body, is co-opted by the conquerors culture (Rowlett 2000, 68). Dube reminds us that not every narrative that involves the meeting of a Woman, particularly an indigenous Woman, in the Bible results in conquest since it depends upon whether the Woman is a colonizing and colonized Woman. She cites the cases of Pharaoh's daughter and Zipporah as instances where the social location of the woman, in the case of Pharaoh's daughter, a princess, and the Woman's denial of affection, in the case of Zipporah who offers Moses the cold shoulder, do not lead to conquest. She argues that these Women differ from Rahab whose "story ... is a script about the domestication of the promised land" (Dube 2000, 76–77).[5]

Unlike the Rahab story, the story of Jael does not follow the tidy script that categorizes it as an imperializing text. The historical circumstances that the book of Judges invokes reflect more of the realities of what are known as settler colonies should we pay attention to theories other than the conquest theory regarding Israel's origins in the land.[6] Nonetheless the

---

4. Montrose draws this term from the work of Michel de Certeau (Montrose 1991, 6).

5. Dube believes that the story of Dinah's rape may also be considered an imperializing text (2000, 77 n. 40).

6. Theories such as the peasant revolt as refined by Norman Gottwald (1979), the pioneer settlement theory of Robert Coote and Keith Whitelam (Coote and Whitelam 1987, 19–20), as well as Lawrence Stager's ruralization model (Stager 1998, 141–42) offer different conceptions of how the book of Judges discusses the relationship between Israel and other groups in the land. These help orient a postcolonial reading of the book of Judges that pays attention to the settler colony phenomenon in modern colonial experience by omitting the aspects of ties to a "mother country."

meeting between Sisera and Jael and their subsequent interactions produce a counter-effect to the romantic storyline that Rowlett and Dube assign to the Rahab story. Johanna Bos views the Jael story as a reversal of the male narrative "betrothal type-scene" that involves a man with a failing quest rescued by a woman. She lists the main elements of this type-scene as: travel to a foreign land; an encounter most often initiated by the woman but not at a well, a site of fertility; deception; a gift; and on the departure of the woman an announcement of success (Bos 1988, 39). Although naming foreign travel as a critical element in this type-scene, Bos pays little attention to the imperial implications in the examples that she analyzes. Arguably, the stories of Tamar and Ruth, which Bos includes in her analysis, lead to the co-optation of these women into the genealogy of David and alienation from their indigenous culture and, to this extent, can be seen as replicas of the Rahab story. The same case can be offered for Jael, though to a different degree since neither the prose account in Judg 4 nor its poetic counterpart in Judg 5 offers an indication of Jael's fate and future. This gap need not disqualify this story from consideration, since both 4:23–24 and 5:31 celebrate Jael's actions as a crucial step in Israel gaining the upper hand over their enemies in the quest to stabilize their hold on the land of Canaan. The ambiguities about Jael's ethnic identity and therefore ethnic loyalties, as well as the fact that this narrative does not deal with Israel's first contact with the indigenes of the land notwithstanding,[7] several ele-

---

7. Judges 4–5 may not stand as a conquest story in the way that Josh 2 does, given that the book of Judges presumes a division of the land already given to the tribal groups though not occupied by these groups (Judg 1:1). The book of Judges appears focused on occupation rather than conquest as it narrates the tenuous hold the various tribal groups have on their allotted portion of the land (Judg 1). I read Judges as describing a failed or at best a failing occupation of the land that requires constant military engagement with the Canaanite tribes, akin to the measures needed for a swift and decisive conquest of the land as narrated in Joshua. Richard Nelson suggests that Judges presents "an incomplete conquest," a reality that results from divine punishment for disobedience in contrast to the "complete" conquest in Joshua. From this perspective, I view Judg 4–5 as a story of conquest (2002, 96). In contrast, Susan Niditch positions the book of Judges as dealing with Israel's quest to "achieve liberation from oppressors and to gain political and geographic control of the land" (2008, 1). Although Niditch observes that most of the wars in the book take place between "Israelite and non-Israelite enemies," and although she offers a good summary of theories relating Israel's origins in the land as preparation for a disclaimer not to match "narrative details with specific historical events" (5), thereby positioning her to pay attention to "the stories and the variegated threads in Israelite culture" (8), she largely

ments tie the Rahab and Jael stories together. The common bonds of the Native Woman, affection/sexuality, and land occur in both stories to varying degrees and in different directions. Yet still both stories contribute to imperializing and anti-imperializing discourses in similar ways. To this extent, they both offer opportunities for engaging the image of the Native Woman and the postcolonial reflection upon this representation.

The role of gender in imperializing discourses foregrounds the Native Woman but implies weakness and inadequacies on the part of the Native Man. The preference for representing the first contact as taking place with the Native Woman occurs not because the Woman is a point of weakness in the defenses that can be exploited, but rather that Woman serves as a signifier for territory. Partha Chatterjee remarks that "the figure of woman often acts as a sign in discursive formations, standing for concepts or entities that have little to do with women in actuality" (Chatterjee 1993, 68). In fact, Frantz Fanon sees these struggles occurring around women precisely because of the proximity of fantasies of violence and eroticism (1965, 45). These discourses rather than representing weak and retiring Women present robust and militarized Women that occupy the social spaces normally reserved for Men. This representation of Women thereby feminizes the Native Man as the basis for notions of the inferiority and weakness of indigenous cultures. The construction of weak Native Man serves to emasculate the native men and can also be accomplished by emphasizing the masculinity of the colonial male. Chatterjee notes how "the 'hypermasculinity' of imperialist ideology made the figure of the weak, irresolute, effeminate babu a special target of contempt and ridicule" (1993, 69).

Imperializing discourses about the Native Woman, therefore, hold out the promise of female gender empowerment to the Native Woman on the presumption that she lacks power and other benefits denied her by the Native Man. Fanon describes the European preoccupation with veiled Algerian women as a desire to "defend this woman, pictured as humiliated, sequestered, cloistered … inert, demonetized, indeed dehumanized object" (1965, 38). The separation of the Native Woman from her culture in order to offer her an improved status serves as part of the seduction of the Native Woman. In this regard, the sexual implications of the transac-

---

ignores how the book describes a script of dispossession of land from other occupants whether indigenes or not. Admittedly, like Niditch, I am not concerned at this point about the historical accuracy of the text. My purpose here lies in following the rhetoric of conquest and dispossession that lies in the texts.

tion between the Foreign Man and the Native Woman become clear. The involvement of sex in facilitating this improvement of female power in the discourse operates as a form of violence against the indigenous people and their territories. Montrose views the instances of sex, forced or otherwise, in the written historical accounts of European colonizers, taken together with the feminization of conquered lands, as not simply an expression of male lust but rather "an ideologically meaningful (and overdetermined) act of violence" (1991, 19). Sex with native women becomes the means, therefore, for acting out forms of violence perpetrated upon conquered lands and the men who form a barrier of resistance to conquest. Further, writing these accounts blurs the distinctions between event and text, between woman and land, between sex and war, and so forth. Ultimately, these issues form the background against which the image Native Woman gets reproduced.

Interpretations of the Rahab and Jael stories most often note the elements of sex, gender, and the celebration of these women as deserving a place in Israelite society, whether through actual membership (Josh 6:25) or memorialization in cultural lore (Judg 5:24). Unlike Dube's and Rowlett's readings of Rahab, standard interpretations remain content to keep these elements apart by highlighting the ambiguity of the spies' contact with Rahab and emphasizing Rahab's profession as the evidence of her transformation and the value of Israelite conquest (Robinson 2009, 257).[8] Despite her presentation as a sex worker in Joshua, Rahab morphs into a figure of respectability in later Jewish and Christian traditions. Rahab appears in Jewish legend as Joshua's wife (Lerner 2000, 52), and the ancestress of prophets and priests like Huldah and Jeremiah (Robinson 2009, 258). Similarly, Christian interpretations, as seen in Heb 11:31 and Jas 2:25, emphasize Rahab's sexual deviance, prophetic activity and, naturally, her conversion (258).[9]

---

8. Robinson observes how the rabbis concentrate on Rahab as a loose woman in their readings of the text as the means of emphasizing her transformation. Rabbi Isaac's view that the mere mention of the name Rahab results in spontaneous ejaculation represents this hypersexualized reading of Rahab (Robinson 2009, 257). Phyllis Kramer traces Jewish interpretations that valorize Rahab while accenting her status as a sex worker (Kramer 2000, 158–61).

9. David Gunn reports of Martin Luther's typological reading that sees Jael as the Church offering Sisera "the milk of gentler doctrine to calm him and then pierces his spirit with the strong word of the Gospel as representative of Christian readings of Jael." Gunn further observes that both Catholics and Protestants associate Jael with

Different dynamics exist in the Jael story where the male–female interaction between Sisera and Jael is not one of the colonial male and native female. Jael's role in assisting with Israel's dominance of the land casts her as sympathetic to those colonialist aspirations.[10] Here as in the Rahab story the issue revolves around the hypersexuality of the Native Woman. Most interpreters understand Jael's brutal slaying of Sisera as occurring after some form of sexual congress. The level of sexual interaction varies from interpreter to interpreter and so too the degree of initiative taken by Jael. Ellen van Wolde notes five actions taken by Jael in Judg 4:18–19 in relation to Sisera that "bear a strong resemblance to the sexual act."[11] Van Wolde further raises the issue that Jael's name in the Hebrew represents a masculine rather than a feminine form and that her name may be "symbolic of the nature of her actions."[12] Pamela Reis goes further to suggest that Jael has sex twice with Sisera in the "female superior-position" and possibly for a third time with Barak.[13] Reis pushes the issue of Jael's

---

Mary as an early warrior in the fight against sin, the enemies of God, and evil as a descendant of Eve, in keeping with Gen 3:15 (Gunn 2005, 71–75).

10. Yairah Amit's analysis of Judg 4 structures the chapter units and scenes. She identifies the Jael story as the third scene and fifth unit, which she titles "the solution scene." Amit suggests that the narrative slows at this portion of the chapter and supplies a greater level of detail (Amit 1987, 96). It appears to me that this is a culmination of the battle for control of the land started by Barak and won for him by Jael, the Native Woman. However, in this instance Barak only encounters Jael at the end of the battle. Given the portrayal of Jael as hypersexual and bloodthirsty, separating her from Barak works not only for his safety but also to invest the Native Woman with the stigma as one to be avoided.

11. Van Wolde lists the five assertive actions taken by Jael as: coming out to call Sisera; taking the mallet in her hand; going in to Sisera with sexual overtones; driving a peg into his throat; and driving the peg into the ground (van Wolde 1995, 245). Meike Bal disagrees that Jael's invitation to Sisera or her offering of milk instead of water should be viewed as sexual overtures. She justifies her refusal to place Jael in the role of the seductress based upon a reading of the anthropological code. Further, she reads Jael's actions as more related to mothering (1988a, 26; 1988b, 63).

12. Van Wolde argues that the feminine form of the name should be תאל and not יאל (1995, 245).

13. Reis constructs her argument based upon the rarity of the word שמיכה in Judg 4:18 which, contrary to other translators who render this as "rug," she reads as Jael's body. Her argument also rests on the variability of ש and ס thereby making the word שמיכה a cognate of סמך, meaning to lean; likely a reference to Jael leaning her body as the covering upon Sisera. The repetition of the verb כסה in 4:19 leads Reis to conclude a second sexual encounter. However, while שמיכה is missing in this verse its

sexuality because she believes the text constructs a sexually promiscuous woman in keeping with what she regards as the "xenophobic nature of the Bible; non-Israelite woman are, ipso facto, immoral" (Reis 2005, 36).[14]

Gender and sexual conduct stand as two of the legs on which the platform of otherness is constructed in imperializing texts. In these two narratives, the Native Woman is not only sexually active but also readily available. Rahab as a sex worker is available to all comers for a fee. The effortlessness with which the spies encounter her indicates her easy availability. Jael readily offers sex to strangers, without pay, on multiple occasions in a short time span. Thus both Native Women appear as prostitutes. Montrose observes the occurrence of the idea of self-prostitution in the 1596 work of Raleigh's lieutenant Laurence Keymis, *A Relation of the Second Voyage to Guiana*, as justification for the sexual (ab)use of indigenous women and ultimately the exploitation of the land. Montrose also points out that this discourse serves as an affront to the indigenous males, given that their women are "their most valued and most intimate possession" (Montrose 1991, 19). Second, the discourse also implies that sex with the sexually forward indigenous women stands not as an act of aggression on the part of the colonizing men but rather appears as taking advantage of opportunities offered. In this regard, Montrose concludes from Keymis's statement, "Fruitfull rich grounds, lying now waste for want of people, do prostitute themselves unto us, like a faire and beautifull woman," that "Englishmen [are] not … territorial aggressors but rather as passive beneficiaries of the animated land's own desire to be possessed" (1991, 19).[15] The image of the sexually forward Native Woman stands in the foreground

---

mention in 4:18 implies it in 4:19. Reading יבא אליה ("he went in to her") in 4:22 as a sexual reference as it occurs in other places, Reis suggests that a sexual encounter takes place between Jael and Sisera (2005, 29–30, 35).

14. As part of this portrayal of Jael, Reis argues that when she raises the possibility that Jael has sex with Barak that this occurs in the tent with the corpse and that the text wishes to indicate this (2005, 36).

15. David Marcus comments that the name Rahab means wide or broad and that if used in a proleptic sense in the passage suggests "the wide-open woman who is 'the wide-open door to Canaan.'" Marcus, however, does not think that the name is being deployed as sexually suggestive, since Rahab is presented as a heroine and not as a "traditional prostitute" (Marcus 2007, 152). The extent to which intentionality can be assigned to the choice of the name Rahab remains uncertain. Nonetheless, the meaning of the name in the context of this narrative appears striking and raises interesting connotations on the perception of the sexual availability of native women.

of an equally emasculated Native Man, who remains inadequate to meet the insatiable appetite of his Woman. The idea of male inadequacies holds more than sexual implications. This idea also speaks to the Native Man's inability to militarily defend his territory.

Both of these biblical texts represent males as weak and ineffective, particularly in their military prowess. Outplayed, outsmarted, and deceived by the females, male military failures appear inevitable. Apart from the common element of betraying their own people to aid Israel, Assis observes the presence of weak men as a further connection in the Rahab and Jael stories (2004, 85). While no instances of Rahab's sexuality explicitly surface in the text, the ready contact between Rahab and the king of Jericho implies a level of familiarity (Josh 2:2–4). In fact, Richard Nelson observes a playfulness in the interaction between Rahab and the king he characterizes as "ambiguous sexual innuendo" (1997, 43). From this perspective Nelson reads Rahab as effectively using her sexuality as a means to deceive the king, or as he puts it, "she uses her prostitution as protective coloring to claim innocence and, repeatedly, ignorance" (1997, 49). The view of the Native Man being undone by the hypersexuality of the Native Woman persists in the Jael story. Following the logic of the text, Gale Yee notes that the author in Judg 4:21 inverts the sexual identity of Jael and Sisera in what she regards as a reversed rape scene: "The man becomes the woman; the rapist becomes the victim; the penetrator becomes the penetrated. The tent peg in Jael's hand becomes synecdochically the raging phallus" (1993, 116). The Native Woman image in imperializing discourses exists as a reproduction that has in view the emasculation of the Native Man as the pretext to territorial occupation.

Should the postcolonial reading of these texts bracket and ignore their sexual implications, the picture of the heroic Native Woman still poses troubling suggestions. The selective portrayal of the empowered Native Woman places her in the role of the victim of patriarchy who with sufficient impetus from outside forces, successfully flees her Native oppression. The binary of Native Man/Native Woman imposes power assumptions unto Third World societies that are at times false and at other times inadequate to serve as liberatory paths.[16] This dichotomy reinforces the

---

16. Carby questions whether patriarchy should be defined in a uniformed way across cultures, since her observations of female-headed households in immigrant communities, the long tradition of women working outside of the home whether as domestic workers or sex workers to support families, and the structural emascula-

selective deployment of the subject status to the Native Woman. At whatever level the Native Woman functions as a subject in the discourse she always appears in need of rescuing, or serves as the scapegoat in Freud's voicing of "the hysterical woman" as a subject that leads Spivak to coin the sentence, "White men are saving brown women from brown men" (Spivak 1994, 92). Regrettably, the image of the empowered, autonomous, self-affirming Native Women is only a mirage, and an ironic production at that, as Carolyn Sharp suggests: "Femaleness can be marginalized even in texts in which particular women are valorized as strong, clever, or obedient in whatever ways the androcentric norms of that particular context requires" (2009, 86).

Dissatisfaction with imperializing discourses normally opens the space for anti-imperial discourses to rescue the Native Woman from co-optation and therefore to deploy that image as an asset against colonizing tendencies. In the case of Rahab and Jael, given the impossibility of rewriting the biblical texts or adjusting centuries of the history of interpretation, the anti-imperial reaction requires distancing the stories as too complicit in colonizing tendencies to be of value for postcolonial readers. This move not only parodies the Native Woman as a tool of colonialist mimicry in the way Homi Bhabha describes it, but also places a demand upon native women to clarify their loyalties in the way Fanon advocates (1965, 48). In the process, the Native Woman emerges as a further contested site. At this point, I use Bhabha and Fanon as two sides of the same issue to frame the analysis of the postcolonial reflection on the representation of the Native Woman. Bhabha's notion of mimicry calls attention to ways in which the image Native Woman destabilizes norms yet in the process casts native women in a grotesque light as an image and reality to be avoided. Evidently, I am using Bhabha to read these reproductions as directed to a colonialist audience. On the other hand, Fanon's examination of gender and colonial dynamics that also involve race helps to expose the myth of Rahab's and Jael's integration into Israelite community. Fanon's perspective offers the view of these texts from the vantage point of the colonized.

Bhabha bases his conception of mimicry on the duplicitous nature of colonial discourse, "a tongue that is forked, not false" (Bhabha 1994, 85). Mimicry operates as a colonial strategy to incorporate the colonized sub-

---

tion of men in colonialist and racist contexts realign traditional conceptions of gender hierarchy (Carby 2000, 391).

ject within the culture and control of the colonizer while at the same time maintaining the distinctions between the two. Colonial discourse needs to use signifiers, language, and images to represent the colonized that can make them recognizable to a colonial reader. This representation results in what Bhabha describes as "*a subject of a difference that is almost the same, but not quite*" (1994, 86, emphasis original). The representation of both Rahab and Jael are subject to mimicry in different ways. The text represents Rahab as a viable candidate for membership in Israelite society, or what Susanne Gillmayr-Bucher refers to as "an example of a 'good' stranger" (Gillmayr-Bucher 2007, 147) and Robinson sees as a "model convert" (Robinson 2009, 258). Rahab's eagerness to assist the spies, the readiness with which she betrays her people, and the facility with which she understands the political and theological implications of the presence of the Israelite camp on the doorsteps of her country all stand out as remarkable aspects of a narrative that portrays her as a useful tool for the completion of the conquest. Gillmayr-Bucher suggests that as Rahab speaks in the narrative she does not appear as a Canaanite woman since her "real otherness is repressed." She sees Rahab instead as "an Israelite theologian disguised as the 'other'" (2007, 147). Bhabha's mimicry or some similar notion appears to be influencing how Gillmayr-Bucher views Rahab. And while I find mimicry useful in understanding this representation, we can mistake Rahab for an Israelite if we listen only to her voice in the narrative. However, paying attention to what is said about Rahab provides an unflattering portrait of this newly found convert. The narrator's and Joshua's voices constantly undercut any resemblance between Rahab and Israelite culture. The spies never directly address Rahab as a subject and apart from the biographical introduction in Josh 2:1 the narrator only names her in the story as a subject in relation to the king of Jericho (Josh 2:3). Rahab's only other mention is as "the woman" in Josh 2:4. In the narrative scenes for the battle of Jericho when Joshua reminds his soldiers to spare Rahab, she is referred to as "Rahab the prostitute" (Josh 6:17), and again in speaking to the two spies he simply calls her "the prostitute" (Josh 6:22). The notice of her settlement in Israel repeats her identity as a sex worker (Josh 6:25). Additionally, the notice that Rahab and her family were rescued from the city even though her name is mentioned and she interacts with the same men she hid as spies, this notice emphatically points to Rahab's family being outside of the camp (Josh 6:23). The hiphil form of נוח (essentially, deposit or leave) used in this verse states that this location outside of the camp would be their permanent place. If the text performs mimicry on Rahab it does a poor job, since she remains the Canaanite sex worker unable to be transformed into anything other than her assigned role. As Bird points out, the only way up for Rahab is "to become a good harlot, a righteous outcast, a noble-hearted courtesan, the exception that proves the rule" (Bird, 131).

Bhabha allows that the effectiveness of mimicry lies in the production of "its slippage, its excess, its difference" (Bhabha 1994, 86). Certainly, the Rahab of Josh 2 and 6 provides enough difference for her foreignness, the threat of her sexuality, and the ambiguities of her profession to be acknowledged as not suitable for full entry into Israel. While Bhabha views mimicry as an unstable position that produces a "partial representation" (88) that operates as both "resemblance and menace" (86), I find that the narrative in Josh 2 and 6 presents a destabilized Rahab, already marked and excluded. Like Sharp and Bird, I view the representation of Rahab as a resistant and empowered figure to be somewhat of a stretch.[17] For Sharp, Rahab represents an ironic twist in a normally transparent xenophobic reaction to foreign women, given that Rahab is precisely the type of Woman that Israel fears, yet she is spared as a rare exception (Sharp 2009, 99–100). Similarly, Bird attributes Rahab's usefulness in the narrative to a profession that locates her on the edge of society. And at the same time, Bird notes that as a result of this marginalized position Rahab is forever marked and explained by this narrative of "harlot's loyalty" (Bird 1989, 130). Seemingly, Rahab as the representation of the Native Woman hardly progresses beyond the space afforded to the "noble savage."

Bhabha's mimicry does not fully capture the representation that is Rahab in this narrative. If mimicry operates at all here it remains at the level of the idea that a Native Woman could be converted and incorporated into the colonizers' culture, let alone one as colorful as Rahab. The text seduces readers, I would dare say here postcolonial readers, with this possibility but never actualizes it. To the extent that the book of Joshua exists as a discourse by Israelite writers about Canaanite cultures and peo-

---

17. Fanon's description of the unveiled Algerian woman, a creation of European attacks upon Algerian culture of veiling, that in part influences Bhabha, functions as a sort of Trojan horse. This emancipated Algerian woman, now "radically transformed into a European woman, poised and unconstrained, whom no one would suspect, [is] completely at home in the environment," and can perform military operations (1965, 57). The application of this idea to Rahab encounters several obstacles, among them that Rahab enters the narrative already marked as the outsider.

ples directed to Israelite audiences is the extent to which Rahab as a reproduction of the Native Woman never approaches the place where she fully enters the culture as an insider. That Rahab could qualify for entry into Israel given the first brush strokes that paint her appearance in the narrative stands only as wish. In fact, what Bhabha describes as the devolving of mimicry into menace seems more applicable to Rahab who stands more as "a difference that is almost total but not quite" (Bhabha 1994, 91).

If Bhabha's mimicry addresses the colonialist discourse that reproduces a partial image of the Native Woman in the guise of the colonizer, Fanon offers a searing warning to the colonized about the seductions of becoming like the colonizer. Fanon speaks of this from the perspective of romantic relationships between "the woman of color and the white man." He describes the attraction to white culture as an escape path: "whitening oneself magically as a way of salvation" (2008, 27). The desire to become white, Fanon thinks, stems from learned self-hate and expresses itself in a more noble desire of "saving the race" (2008, 37). Rahab's portrayal fits quite easily into an anti-imperialist discourse, making her a quick target as a sellout. Her willingness to aid the spies is matched only by her desire to become one with the Israelites through speaking their language and honoring their god (Josh 2:9–13). Remembering that Fanon examines these issues with the question of authentic love in the face of social inequalities releases Fanon's analysis, as used here in the case of Rahab, from being reduced to simplicities. Fanon raises the issue that the decision of the colonized woman to become a part of the colonizer's culture, whether that be through marriage, cultural assimilation, or even conversion as with Rahab, is no simple and smooth movement. The loss for the colonized woman is easily blurred by the fantasy of gain that she achieves by being accepted into colonial culture. Echoing Fanon, Marcella Althaus-Reid points to the danger of oversimplifying Rahab as a sellout: "Rahab's betrayal is not only a betrayal of her nation, it is the betrayal of her friends and compatriots, her culture and her traditional spirituality" (Althaus-Reid 2007, 137). That the text represents Rahab as making this choice to side with spies as a simple matter suggests a low view of Canaanite culture.

Jael's story presents greater levels of complexity since Jael serves as an extension of Deborah in this narrative. Deborah appears as a leader at the start of Judg 4, bearing titles such as prophetess and performing functions such as judging (Judg 4:4). Her military skill also receives mention when she discusses military strategy with Barak, indicating a plan to draw out and deliver Sisera (Judg 4:7). The text takes a turn into dramatic irony at

4:9 when it leaves open for Barak the name of the woman who would gain glory from the battle. Without offering any explanation as to why Sisera eludes both Barak and Deborah, Jael enters the narrative at the point that Deborah exits (Judg 4:17). The implication that Deborah would deal the deathblow to Sisera is resolved by Jael's act of violence against him. In effect, Jael becomes the murderous violent extension of Deborah without Deborah having to perform any unseemly actions. The framing of these female figures in the story, one an Israelite the other possibly a Canaanite, allows us to see the operations of mimicry. Insofar as Sisera stands as Israel's enemy and Jael kills him, she resembles Deborah. To the extent that she embodies the military prowess needed for the fight, Jael models the type of leadership that Deborah offers in Israel. The point of slippage for this image arises precisely where Jael acts in ways that Deborah does not act. The emphasis on the difference between the two female characters appears more pointed in the poetic parallel of Judg 5. In the song Deborah is named as a "mother" in Israel (Judg 5:7) and is represented as offering moral support for the battle in contrast to the figure of Jael constructed around a succession of violent verbs: struck, crushed, shattered, pierced (Judg 5:26).

Prior to Jael's introduction in the narrative the text paves the way with several hints of mimicry. The intrusive detail in Judg 4:11 of the extended biography of Heber sets the stage for Jael to enter the narrative rather than Heber who never appears in the narrative. The details of the genealogical links between the Kenites and Moses' father-in-law draw Jael into the Israelite orbit even while it distances her husband Heber from any connections with Israel. The later indication in Judg 4:17 that Heber's clan made peace with the king of Hazor and would potentially harbor a fugitive, Sisera, adds even more motivation for thinking of Jael as being at one with Deborah's cause and following through narratively with action started by Deborah. Jael acts independently of her husband even to the point of breaching the peace that his clan made with the king of Hazor. Like Deborah who acts without reference to an unseen husband, Jael acts in opposition to an unseen husband. Like Deborah, Jael simply deems Sisera a threat without any indication of how this information is collected. Like Deborah, Jael sets out on her own and directs a man's movement. As a Kenite, though possibly a near kin of the Israelites, Jael remains "almost the same but not quite" in Bhabha's terms. The ode of Deborah memorializes Deborah as a member of Israel (Judg 5:7) but keeps Jael as a member of her own clan and more particularly culturally situated among the tent dwellers (Judg 5:24).

As is the case with Rahab, the motivations for Jael's actions remain hidden in the text. The two times the text mentions Jael, she appears as the wife of Heber. This notice provides more than a simple connection with her husband; it ties her to the representation of her husband in the text. Heber stands as the exceptional Kenite, living at the furthest distance possible from the rest of his kin (Judg 4:11) and making peace with the king of Hazor, Israel's enemy (Judg 4:17). Therefore, Heber, the absent cuckolded Native Man, deserves his fate. Whatever initiative Jael takes in relation to Sisera she not only acts towards him but against her husband. By supplying these few details and omitting mention of Jael's real motivation for involvement in Deborah's battle, the text produces Heber and consequently his clan's amity with Sisera as Jael's real problem. The violence against Sisera empowers Jael in relation to her husband, and forestalls the fate that Sisera's mother imagines can come to women (Judg 5:30). The implication of Jael as a victim of the Native Man resembles Fanon's notions of the European demand for the unveiling of Algerian women as a way to "save" them (1965, 42). Fanon points out that while the demand for the removal of the veil implies that a hidden beauty lies behind it, European culture already constructs an image of the Algerian woman that does not always conform with European standards of beauty. As Fanon offers, the veiled Algerian woman "had to look so much like a 'fatma.'"[18] As already pointed out, the focus on the Native Woman operates not so much in her interests but as access to the land. The narrative ends without any mention of Jael's fate or future but instead focuses on the domination of the indigenous people (Judg 4:24; 5:31). This ending indicates where the real interests lie. The representation of Jael as violent, calculating and cold-hearted serves as the point of slippage where she is almost the same as Deborah but not quite. However, rather than this revelation serving as the threat to the colonizing discourse, I find that it supports that discourse by using Jael as the emblem of a violent and amoral culture that needs to be either avoided, suppressed or transformed.

The anti-imperial discourse in relation to portrayals like Rahab and Jael reduces these images to pictures of, at worst, oppressed women or at best complicit in their own exploitation. The discourses of imperialism

---

18. Fanon makes the observation in the context where Algerian women were involved in the military struggle and would hide weapons under their veils. As a security measure soldiers needed to assess which women were potential threats and therefore readily judge her to be a "harmless" Algerian woman (1965, 61).

and anti-imperialism distort not only the image of the Native Woman but the body of the native woman. Fanon admits to this when he describes the experiences of the unveiled Algerian woman having "an impression of her body being cut up into bits, put adrift."[19] Equally, he sees the Algerian woman who adopts the veil after being without it as encountering a body "made shapeless and even ridiculous."[20] Without expecting that the representation of the Native Woman by the discourse of colonialism would produce a perfect copy of indigenous women or even one that actually resembles real women, postcolonial readers face the truth that recuperating agency for this Woman, investing her with resistant notes, or even locating in her actions the source of liberations, all reach limits too easily.

To dispense with these images especially when for the postcolonial reader of the Bible they are the only ones available also becomes an untenable response. In this regard Rey Chow's acceptance of the untranslatability of the Native Woman proves a useful starting point. Chow suggests that if granting agency to the Native Woman stands as the postcolonial project then it requires filling out her context and providing evidence of this, and in the process serving the purposes of the imperial discourse which as she says "achieves hegemony precisely by its capacity to convert, recode, make transparent, and thus represent even those experiences that resist it with a stubborn opacity" (1994, 133). This means, therefore, that the postcolonial reading of the Native Woman neither dispenses with the image nor seeks to rehabilitate it. Either move further distorts the image but more particularly confers a false value upon the native woman that suggests her worth far in excess of what either the colonizer or colonized males would grant her.

In general, the reproduction of the Native Woman accompanies the imperial urge to view, travel, and conquer. The image Native Woman represents the imperial gaze writ large. Rahab immediately enters the story of the spies in response to Joshua's command to "view the land" (Josh 2:1). Similarly, Jael enters the narrative without any clear prompt for her to emerge into the scene (Judg 4:18). The swift production of the Native Woman in these biblical narratives suggests the strong link between

---

19. Fanon goes further to speak of the unveiled woman as naked and in "conflict with her body (1965, 59).

20. Explaining the movement back into the veil for the Algerian woman no longer on the frontlines of the battle, Fanon refers to the bodily deformations needed to adjust back into the veil (1965, 62).

gender and imperialism. Interrupting the imperial gaze, as Fanon articulates, serves as a critical point of resistance. Fanon shows that the European fascination with the veiled Algerian woman lies in uncovering that which is hidden in order to control it: "Unveiling this woman is revealing her beauty; it is baring her secret, breaking her resistance, making her available for adventure" (1965, 43). He goes on to note that the veil serves as the Algerian woman's resistance to European desire, since in hindering the attempts to be seen, she likewise disturbs efforts to possess her. Fanon invests the veiled woman with power as one "who sees without being seen" (1965, 44). It is precisely in the production of Rahab and Jael as characters that can be seen and surveyed that they become malleable to imperializing purposes. Remaining hidden, staying veiled, resisting representation may well be the obvious response to interrupting the imperial gaze. Remembering that we speak here of literary characters makes it all the more important to operationalize such resistance to the imperial gaze.

Although, Fanon advances that the veiled woman retains "a cultural, hence national, originality" (1965, 42), this too stands as an image and a reproduction. Fanon's idea of cultural purity suggests too easily the preservation of male privilege in relation to native women and offers little scope for critical examination of the power of native women within their own cultural contexts. Understanding that, as Mohanty suggests, power may not always be expressed as undifferentiated sources, transformation or even recognition of the power position of native women in their societies can function as a point of resistance to colonialism. Reflecting on the power available to the colonized, Chatterjee locates resistant power in what he calls the spiritual or inner domains as distinct from the outward domains. He places the family as one of the elements in the inner domain that, once transformed, serves as resistance to colonial intrusion (Chatterjee 1993, 9). Chatterjee notes how in the Indian context colonial resistance addressed the modernizing demands of colonial culture not by dismissing these demands but rather by making "modernity consistent with the nationalist project" (121). This response produced a "new woman" alongside a "new patriarchy" that offered women a different status in accord with the goal of nationhood. To be clear, Chatterjee recognizes this as patriarchy but notes that in this context women were "bound ... to a new, and yet entirely legitimate, subordination" (130). Fanon already admits to the power of the native woman in her subject position as one who can gaze and one conscripted in the fight against the colonizer. Images like those of Rahab and Jael gesture imperfectly to stronger forms of resistance narrated elsewhere and textualized in the lives of women and therefore serve as the basis for engaging the place of women in Third World societies. The preoccupation with the colonial project, as Dube points out (1999, 215), all too often suggests that the "women's question" receives a lower priority. Images of the Native Woman also require a postcolonial conversation of gender in the native context in the way Andrea Smith makes the call to move away from representation to imagining spaces of freedom for all persons (Smith 2010, 82).

Postcolonial reflection on the image Native Woman can shift the focus away from the imperial gaze and on to the resistant view of the native woman. While these narratives will not yield for us detailed description of this resistant view, the image itself serves as the form of resistance. Its reproduction points to its failure to capture the reality of the native woman. As Bhabha offers, the point of slippage in mimicry disrupts the authority of the colonial discourse (Bhabha 1994, 88). From another perspective, Chow reflects upon the ability of technology to achieve cultural displacement and the moral issues this raises given that "'false' images are going to remain with us whether or not we like it" (Chow 1994, 142). The moral questions in this regard persist as long as the image lives, and this becomes particularly troubling with a technology of recording and reproduction such as the Bible. However, that which the technology of the text captures at best stands as a border figure. The image exists at the intersection of text and reality, between literary character and flesh and blood woman, between domination and resistance, between the captured and the one that gazes back. The postcolonial response requires destabilizing the power of the text, in this case the Bible, as the final arbiter of reality, especially the reality of the native context. Even more pertinent this destabilization needs to interrupt the ability of the text to pass off historied bodies, as Montrose terms it, as real bodies. The text and image exist in the borderlands, no doubt a place of uncertainty, but the place where the native context thrives and exists. The postcolonial move requires the removal of the text from the certainty of the colonizer's world in this ambiguous space where it gets treated as a border figure.

Admittedly both Rahab and Jael are represented in the narratives as border figures. Althaus-Reid sees this in the location of Rahab's home situated in the city wall with windows facing away from the city. So too Kah-Jin Jeffrey Kuan and Mai-Anh Le Tran position Rahab as physically in an "in-between space, between the inside and the outside" (Kuan and Le Tran 2009, 33). Althaus-Reid reads Rahab in her position as a sex worker as already defying the demand by a "sacralized imperial ideology which thrusts forward to acquire a definite political, social and sexual identity" (Althaus-Reid 2007, 132). Additionally, the constant descriptor of Rahab as a זנה (prostitute) places her in the borderlands between the public and domestic. Whether זנה should be seen as an innkeeper, as K. M. Campbell suggests (1972, 243), or as "a woman who sells a variety of foods," as Rashi reads it, according to Lerner (2000, 52), these activities blur the distinction between work and home. Essentially, whatever trade Rahab participates in her space defies capture since it functions variously as workspace and living quarters with little to demarcate one from the other. Equally, Jael too appears as a border figure on the edges of the narrative at first, then as a central character toward the end. She lives with her husband in the far reaches of the Kenite territory. The text uses the idiom of Heber stretching out his tent until Elon-bezaanaim (ויט אהלו עד־אלון בצענים, Judg 4:11) to emphasize the remoteness of their location. This location appears to be removed from the fighting but still close enough as a site of refuge. Heber and Jael are removed from their Kenite kin but still identified as Kenites. Kenites are variously seen as friends of Israelites and enemies.[21] On her own Jael possesses these border qualities when she engages and invites Sisera into her tent. Preferring to read שמיכה in Judg 4:18 as "curtain" that divides the tent into separate quarters for the women, Bal suggests that Jael's invitation to Sisera puts him at a place that "represents the suspension of limits between the sexes." Accepting that Jael covers Sisera with the "curtain," Bal points to the ability of Jael to suspend the division between the sections of the tent, and further the division between sexes and thereby making sense of Sisera's order to Jael to answer "there is no man here" in response to an enquiry about the presence of a man (Josh 4:20) (1988b, 122).

The engagement with these intersecting and perhaps conflicting issues of race, gender, and colonial power requires attention to the complexity of each of these constituent parts. No doubt the varieties of gender and race expressions in Third World communities, as well as the varied experiences of colonial power point the postcolonial reaction away from simple reductive statements and more toward what Althaus-Reid would offer as a "bisexual epistemology" (2007, 132). Attention to the queerness of

---

21. Niditch notes that Kenites can be seen as conquered people in Gen 15:19, enemies in 1 Sam 27:10, kinsfolk and military partners in Judg 1; 16 and 1 Sam 15:16 (2008, 66).

gender and race identity and even of colonial power offers a different starting point for dealing with the image Native Woman. In coming to terms with the image as ambivalent the postcolonial response does not operate as a deconstructive turn to the text to shore up the agency of the native woman. Rather the postcolonial response assumes the text as already fractured given the reality of the native woman. In this regard I want to end with Bhabha's idea that the menace implicit in colonial mimicry inevitably means that these reproductions would break under their own weight. Precisely in the tension between text and reality, between woman and Woman, the image shatters because real women read these texts.

> In the ambivalent world of the "not quite/not white," on the margins of metropolitan desire, the *founding objects* of the Western world become the erratic, eccentric, accidental *objets trouvés* of the colonial discourse—the part-objects of presence. It is then that the body and the book lose their part-object's presence. It is then that the body and the book lose their representational authority. Black skin splits under the racist gaze, displaced into signs of bestiality, genitalia, grotesquerie, which reveal the phobic myth of the undifferentiated whole white body. And the holiest of books—the Bible—bearing both the standard of the cross and the standard of empire finds itself strangely dismembered. (Bhabha 1994, 92)

REFERENCES

Althaus-Reid, Marcella María. 2007. Searching for a Queer Sophia-Wisdom: The Post-Colonial Rahab. Pages 128–140 in *Patriarchs, Prophets and Other Villains*. Edited by Lisa Isherwood. London: Equinox.
Amit, Yairah. 1987. Judges 4: Its Content and Form. *JSOT* 39:89–111.
Assis, Elie. 2004. The Choice to Serve God and Assist His People: Rahab and Yael. *Biblica* 85:82–90.
Bal, Mieke.1988a. *Death and Dissymmetry: The Politics of Coherence in the Book of Judges*. Chicago: Chicago University Press.
———. 1988b. *Murder and Difference: Gender, Genre and Scholarship on Sisera's Death*. Bloomington: Indiana University Press.
Bhabha, Homi. 1994. *The Location of Culture*. London: Routledge.
Bird, Phyllis. 1989. The Harlot as Heroine: Narrative Art and Social Presupposition in Three Old Testament Texts. *Semeia* 46:119–39.
Bos, Johanna W. H. 1988. Out of the Shadows: Genesis 38; Judges 4:17–22 and Ruth 3. *Semeia* 42:37–67.

Campbell, K. M. 1972. Rahab's Covenant: A Short Note on Joshua ii 9–21. *VT* 22:243–44.
Carby, Hazel V. 2000. White Woman Listen! Black Feminism and the Boundaries of Sisterhood. Pages 389–403 in *Theories of Race and Racism: A Reader*. Edited by Les Back and John Solomos. London: Routledge.
Chatterjee, Partha. 1993. *The Nation and Its Fragments: Colonial and Postcolonial Histories*. Princeton: Princeton University Press.
Chow, Rey. 1994. Where Have All the Natives Gone? Pages 125–51 in *Displacements: Cultural Identities in Question*. Edited by Angelika Bammer. Bloomington,: University of Indiana Press.
Coote, Robert B., and Keith W. Whitelam. 1987. *The Emergence of Early Israel in Historical Perspective*. Sheffield: Almond.
Dube, Musa W. 1999. Searching for the Lost Needle: Double Colonization and Postcolonial African Feminism. *SWC* 5:213–28.
———. 2000. *Postcolonial Feminist Interpretation of the Bible*. St. Louis: Chalice.
Fanon, Frantz. 1965. *A Dying Colonialism*. Translated by Haakon Chevalier. New York: Grove.
———. 2008. *Black Skin, White Masks*. Translated by Richard Philcox. New York: Grove.
Gillmayr-Bucher, Susanne. 2007. "She Came to Test Him with Hard Questions": Foreign Women and Their View on Israel. *BibInt* 15:135–50.
Gottwald, Norman. 1979. *The Tribes of Yahweh: Sociology for the Religion of Liberated Israel 1250–1050 BC*. Maryknoll, N.Y.: Orbis.
Gunn, David M. 2005. *Judges*. BBC. Malden: Blackwell.
Kramer, Phyllis Silverman. 2000. Rahab: From Peshat to Pedagogy, or: The Many Faces of a Heroine. Pages 156–72 in *Culture, Entertainment and the Bible*. Edited by George Aichele. Sheffield: Sheffield Academic Press.
Kuan, Kah-Jin Jeffrey, and Mai-Anh Le Tran. 2009. Reading Race Reading Rahab: A "Broad" Asian American Reading of a "Broad" Other. Pages 27–44 in *Postcolonial Interventions: Essays in Honor of R. S. Sugirtharajah*. Edited by Tat-siong Benny Liew. Sheffield: Sheffield Phoenix Press.
Lerner, Berel Dov. 2000. Rahab the Harlot and Other Philosophers of Religion. *JBQ* 28:52–55.
Marcus, David. 2007. Prolepsis in the Story of Rahab and the Spies (Joshua 2). Pages 149–62 in *Bringing Hidden to Light: The Process of Interpreta-*

tion: *Studies in Honor of Stephen A. Geller*. Edited by Kathryn F. Kravitz and Diane M. Sharon. Winona Lake: Eisenbrauns.

Mohanty, Chandra Talpade. 1994. Under Western Eyes: Feminist Scholarship and Colonial Discourses. Pages 196–220 in *Colonial Discourse and Post-Colonial Theory: A Reader*. Edited by Patrick Williams and Laura Chrisman. New York: Columbia University Press.

Montrose, Louis. 1991. The Work of Gender in the Discourse of Discovery. *Representations* 33:1–41.

Nelson, Richard D. 1997. *Joshua: A Commentary*. OTL. Louisville: Westminster John Knox.

———. 2002. *The Historical Books*. Nashville: Abingdon.

Niditch, Susan. 2008. *Judges: A Commentary*. OTL. Louisville: Wesminster John Knox.

Reis, Pamela Tamarkin. 2005. Uncovering Jael and Sisera: A New Reading. *SJOT* 19:24–47.

Robinson, Bernard P. 2009. Rahab of Canaan and Israel. *SJOT* 23:257–73.

Rowlett, Lori. 2000. Disney's Pocahontas and Joshua's Rahab in Postcolonial Perspective. Pages 66–75 in *Culture, Entertainment and the Bible*. Edited by George Aichele. Sheffield: Sheffield Academic Press.

Sharp, Carolyn J. 2009. *Irony and Meaning in the Hebrew Bible*. Bloomington: Indiana University Press.

Smith, Andrea. 2010. Dismantling the Master's House with the Master's Tools. Pages 72–85 in *Hope Abundant: Third World and Indigenous Women's Theology*. Edited by Kwok Pui-lan. Maryknoll: Orbis.

Spivak, Gayatri Chakravorty. 1994. Can the Subaltern Speak? Pages 66–111 in *Colonial Discourse and Post-colonial Theory: A Reader*. Edited by Patrick Williams and Laura Chrisman. Hertfordshire: Harvester Wheatsheaf.

Stager, Lawrence E. 1998. Forging an Identity: The Emergence of Ancient Israel. Pages 123–75 in *The Oxford History of the Biblical World*. Edited by Michael D. Coogan. New York: Oxford University Press.

Wolde, Ellen van. 1995. Ya'el in Judges 4. *ZAW* 107:240–46.

Yee, Gale A. 1993. By the Hand of a Woman: The Metaphor of the Woman Warrior. *Semeia* 61:99–132.

Young, Robert J. C. 2001. *Postcolonialism: An Historical Introduction*. Malden: Blackwell.

"Nothing Like It Was Ever Made in Any Kingdom": The Hunt for Solomon's Throne

Christina Petterson

The rise and fall of King Solomon is narrated in 1 Kgs 1–11 and 1 Chr 28–2 Chr 9. In both narratives there is an account of Solomon's riches after the visit of the Queen of Sheba (1 Kgs 10:14–29; 2 Chr 9:13–28). Within these displays of wealth we find a couple of verses dedicated to the construction of the ivory throne (1 Kgs 10:18–20; 2 Chr 9:17–19). The throne is made of ivory overlaid with gold with a rounded back and armrests. Next to each armrest there was a lion, and on the six steps of the throne there was a lion on each end of the step. It is particularly the golden overlay that seems to connect it with the context, since 1 Kgs 10:14–22 and 2 Chr 9:13–21 are particularly obsessive about the amounts of gold available to the king, where it came from and what it was used for. The gold came from the fleet of ships of Tarshish, as well as from the traders and the business of the merchants (1 Kgs 10:15 and 2 Chr 9:14).

In his chapter dealing with 1 Kgs 10, Walter Brueggemann claims that the account of Solomon in 1 Kgs 10 parallels "what we of late have come to call 'the global economy'" (2000, 138) and that Solomon is "at the center of a huge commercial enterprise in which wealth from every transaction comes to Jerusalem from every direction" (135). I agree with Brueggemann that the narrative is constructed so as to place Solomon at the center; the disagreement concerns at the center of what? It is clear that we are to understand that Solomon has endless resources of wood, gemstones, and gold at his fingertips. And that these resources in the text function to construct a kingship of international renown.

However, is it possible to speak of Solomon's appropriations of resources in terms such as "global economy" or "commercial enterprise"? Roland Boer notes that biblical scholars who deal with social and economic questions have a tendency to deploy a capitalist nomenclature when dealing with ancient texts (2007, 35). He sees this as perpetuating the myth that capitalism is everywhere "in various stages of its long path to maturity" (35). Brueggemann, while using this terminology to critique the "uncaring massive force" of global economy (2000, 138), ends up constructing it as this ubiquitous force. But translations also reinforce this presumption. For example, in the verse mentioned above (1 Kgs 10:15 and 2 Chr 9:14), "traders" is used to translate 'nšy htrym only in these two verses (Koehler and Baumgartner 2001, 1708). Elsewhere the verb twr it is translated by "seek," thus producing a translation, for example, as "men who seek." Instead of reproducing capitalist terminology, Boer argues that we should look toward different economic models to conceptualize the economic relations of the ancient Near East. One example is that put forth by the so-called "substantivist" position, which argues for a precapitalist economic model that emphasizes the embedded nature of a given economy within the physical environment and social groups (see Nam 2011). One spokesperson for the substantivist position is the economic historian Karl Polanyi (1886–1964), who published *The Great Transformation* in 1944.[1] In Polanyi's view, the Industrial Revolution (i.e., the "great transformation") created an economy that was socially disembedded (Nam 2011). Based on contemporary historical and anthropological research,[2] Polanyi notes that "man's economy, as a rule, is submerged in his social relationships. He does not act so as to safeguard his individual interest in the possession of material goods; he acts so as to safeguard his social standing, his social claim, his social assets" (2001, 48). Thus the economic system runs on noneconomic motives (i.e., *not* for financial gain or the accumulation of monetary wealth) but serves social interests, such as gaining or retaining prestige (48).

Despite Brueggemann's noble efforts, I find it important to acknowledge the difference between the economic situation then and now, following in the footsteps of David Jobling (1991) and his analysis of the Solomon narrative within a tributary mode of production. And I believe distinguishing between different economic conditions will bring neocolonial issues into sharper relief.

---

1. Thanks to Roland Boer for this reference.
2. Polanyi's use of this research to construct an economic model should also be subjected to critical analysis. One of Polanyi's great inspirations was Bronislav Malinowski, and it is his work on the Trobriand Islands that Polanyi uses to construct a precapitalist economic model.

So how does Polanyi's substantivist approach sit with the Solomon narrative? The acquisition (no, capitalist word), the accumulation (no, capitalist word), the drawing in of the materials for the various constructions came from various connections, especially the connection with King Hiram of Tyre, a connection established by David (1 Kgs 5:15). Note how the agreement between Solomon and Hiram is reciprocal in terms of wish or desire (ḥpṣ).³ While Hiram would fulfill Solomon's wishes in terms of cedar and cypress wood, Solomon would fulfill Hiram's wishes in terms of food for his household. Furthermore, many of the riches which arrived in the courts came from royalty elsewhere. Thus the queen of Sheba brought gold, spices, and precious stones (1 Kgs 10:10), and likewise the whole world, who seeks Solomon in 10:25, brings presents, contributing to the accumulation (no, capitalist word), surplus (*no, very capitalist word*), gathering of riches in the court of Solomon.

Within all this, the construction of Solomon's throne is a very small, but interconnected part of the larger narrative. The materials for the throne are also connected with Hiram, namely the Tarshish ships, which are out with Hiram's ships. And once every three years the Tarshish fleet would arrive, carrying gold and silver, ivories, apes, and peacocks (1 Kgs 10:22).⁴ Thus, the way the narrative is constructed has the effect of placing Solomon at the center of a flow of endless resources of wood, gemstones, and gold, all in the service of constructing a kingship of international renown. David Jobling calls this the sphere of ideal external economics, which means that "the nations of the world are glad to increase the wealth of Solomon, with no indication that this is a hardship or a diminution of their own wealth" (1991, 62), and notes that this is the thrust of chapter 10. This sphere corresponds to the ideal internal economics, where all of Israel benefits and prospers from Solomon's wealth. Both of these ideal spheres are a fictional world generated by the narrative, a world which is undermined by the spheres of real economics, external and internal. The real external economics is indicated by the trade agreement with Hiram, and the exchanging of cedar for food. The real internal economics comes

---

3. The queen of Sheba uses the same root, ḥpṣ, to articulate the action of Yahweh placing Solomon on the throne (1 Kgs 10:9). Furthermore, in 1 Kgs 10:13, Solomon tends to the queen's wishes.

4. Ivory is not a prevalent item in the Hebrew Bible. Apart from its appearances in the texts discussed above, it appears in Ps 45:8; Cant 5:14; 7:4; Ezra 27:6, 15; Amos 3:15; 6:4. In the New Testament it appears only in Rev 18:12.

to the fore in Solomon's administration apparatus (4:1–19) and the forced labor (5:13–18), all of which indicate that the wealth comes at a cost.[5]

Brueggemann also draws attention to the world behind the opulent display of wealth in the Solomon narrative. He brings out the oppressed labor behind the temple and its materials, the taxes used to finance the temple and the palace, the contrast between royal affluence and peasant subsistence, all in all the all-consuming enterprise of Solomon's building activities, impinging on every aspect of Israelite economy. In a sense, Brueggemann is connecting the dots with 1 Sam 8:11–18, and Samuel's prophetic threats about the nature of kings—to which I shall return. Would Brueggemann's points of social indignation be more forcefully stated with a different economic model? First of all, the use of the noun *ḥpṣ* indicates a social stratification. As mentioned above, the reciprocal nature of the fulfillment of desire occurs only between the royalty, namely, Solomon-Hiram and Solomon-Sheba—although we do not explicitly hear which of Solomon's desires Sheba fulfills. In the case of Hiram and Solomon, however, Solomon provides food for Hiram's household "year after year," while Hiram provides Solomon with timber, which was used to construct the temple, the house of the forest of Lebanon, and his own house. One might therefore characterize the nature of kingship ideally envisioned in the narrative as centrifugal, as a massive pit being filled with the earth's resources. Such a nature of kingship—as one for whom the world is an open-cut mine—served as ready source and legitimates later (precapitalist) practices of centrifugal swallowing. It is to such a practice we now turn.

1. An Afterlife of King Solomon

"Here sits our Solomon, Frederik, a son in his father's place." This was the proclamation issued by the bishop of Copenhagen during the anointment of Frederik IV in 1699. In the following anointment ceremonies of six of the absolute monarchs in Denmark, Solomon was the central figure brought forth as a favored role model. While Henry VIII of England favored King David as his personal royal ideal, Solomon was popular with the Danish kings because he inherited his kingship and his kingdom from his father. Thus the bishops tirelessly repeated the handing over of the kingdom from

---

5. The sex work that is present through the prostitutes in ch. 3 should also be included in the real internal economic sphere. See Ipsen 2008 and 2009.

father to son, and how blessed God was to provide the Danish kingdom with such an impressive bloodline.

Another applicable Solomon motif was his wisdom and just nature.[6] The favored source for emphasizing this aspect of Solomon's persona was Ecclesiastes, a text attributed to Solomon, and as such appears within the anointment ceremonies. Finally Solomon's peaceful reign was connected to the reign of the anointed Danish king. Already Luther had established a connection between the name Frederik and Solomon in *Temporal Authority: To What Extent It Should be Obeyed*: "Solomon, whose name in German means 'Frederich' or 'peaceful' ... had a peaceful kingdom, by which the truly peaceful kingdom of Christ, the real Frederich and Solomon, could be represented."[7] These three characteristics of Solomon (his bloodline to David, his wisdom, and his peaceful reign), which were expounded in the anointment ceremonies of the Danish king, were governed by two intertexts. The first is the Psalms, which serve to emphasize the status of the king as God's chosen one. The application of the features of the Davidic figure to the Danish king blurs the boundaries between the two kingships. The second text is Rom 13 and its emphasis on the divine origin of authorities and the subjects' duty to obedience. This text thoroughly governs the interpretations of Solomon as the Danish king and leaves the listener with the impression that the Danish king sitting before us is a descendant of David and Solomon, half god–half man, handpicked by God to govern in divine righteousness. Solomon's wealth, which I have dwelt on above, also comes to play a role, most blatantly through the reconstruction of the throne.

However, what happens with Samuel's warning to the Israelites concerning a king in 1 Sam 8? How is this text, with its negative image of the king, interpreted? Christian V was the first king to be anointed, in 1681, as absolute monarch. In his sermon on Rom 13, Bishop Wandall drew in 1 Sam 8:9–17 and Israel's demands for a king. In the narrative, God sees this demand as a rejection of his kingship, and tells Samuel to warn the people with a description of how kings behave (1 Sam 8:9). Samuel iterates a long series of royal misdeeds: a king will use the people's sons as chariot

---

6. As exemplified in the narrative of the two prostitutes in 1 Kgs 3:16–28. This was a favored motif at the Danish court, which saw the arrival of Rubens's painting *Judgement of Solomon* in 1640 as a gift to Frederik III. Furthermore the small gilded mirror with a replica of this painting belonged to his queen, Sophie Amalie (Hein 2006, 41).

7. Written in 1523 when Luther was under the protection of Frederick (The Wise) III of Saxony.

runners and grooms, peasants and workers; he will take their daughters to perfumers, cooks, and bakers; he will take their best fields, vineyards, and orchards and give them to his courtiers; and he will take the tenth of their crop and give it to his courtiers and officers. Finally, he will take the best slaves and the best cattle to do his work. In Wandall's sermon these threats become "Samuelitiske Kongelov," Samuel's Royal Law, and thus a testimony to the king's rights and the people's duty to serve the king with their bodies and fruits of their labor—a somewhat surprising interpretation of 1 Sam 8. So, purely in terms of household management the king is entitled to anything within his local realm to serve his needs. That this self-perception also needs overseas resources becomes clear in the narwhal throne—one of the concrete items which emphasizes this divine kingship.

2. The Narwhal Throne

In Rosenborg Castle in Copenhagen, where the crown jewels are on display, stands the hideously magnificent narwhal throne. The throne was produced in the workshop of turner Bendix Grodtschilling, who was commissioned by the king (Frederik III) in 1662 to produce a throne fit for an absolute monarch. In 1671 it was more or less completed and subsequently used at the anointment ceremonies of the kings from 1671 to 1840. The throne was allegedly modeled on the ivory throne of Solomon, whose equal was not to be found in any kingdom (1 Kgs 10:18–20).[8]

When I was researching this paper, the throne was being restored. So I was so fortunate to have seen it broken down in pieces and was given a detailed description of its components. So, in the stables of the current dwelling of the Danish monarch, which have been made into a workshop for cabinet makers working on restoring the riches of the Danish crown, I was taken around boxes and crates full of pieces of narwhal tusk and the throne taken apart and broken down into its various units. The skeleton of the throne is wood, overlaid with a veneer of narwhal tusk. However, the skeleton is not just any kind of wood, but ebony, letter (or snake) wood, and kingwood from South America. Next we have the veneer material, which is narwhal tusk. Narwhal tusk is not usually used for veneer, nor is

---

8. The Danish king was not the only one to make use of the Solomon narrative to glorify himself. See Weiss for discussion of the use of the throne and the figure of Solomon in Bible manuscripts, art, and architecture to link various kings (Henry VI and Louis IX) with Solomon.

it a particularly suitable for this type of decoration. First of all, it is a naturally twisted material, which must be turned in order to produce plates. The tooth is hollow and not covered with enamel, which means that it loses color and becomes grey.[9] The pieces of the tusk fitted on the throne twist off and lose their color over time, which makes the throne a high-maintenance object. Ivory, which is not twisted and has enamel, would have been a far more practical material to use and would have lasted much longer (Bøge). Apart from the narwhal tusk, eight gilded allegorical figures decorate the corners, and finally the throne is crowned with an enormous amethyst. Today the amethyst is kept in the vault with the crown jewels, while a glass plate is in its place.

The throne is a striking piece of craftsmanship, as well as an opulent display of wealth and resources, not to mention its endless symbolic value, drawing on a vast number of symbolic structures that present it as the seat of absolute potency. Most significant in this context is the biblical throne imagery[10] and the narwhal tusk. Being a symbol of power the throne is most often connected with Yahweh, or a king under his protection. Thus Nathan prophesies in the promise to David that one of David's bloodline will sit on the throne and build Yahweh a house, and that Yahweh will establish his throne forever (2 Sam 7:13, 16). This son is Solomon, who in addition to building Yahweh a temple also builds himself a gold-covered ivory throne (1 Kgs 10:18–20). The grounded throne is thus a metaphor for a line of kings, which in the narrative of Solomon is materialized in an ivory seat. The narwhal throne, which is inspired by Solomon's throne, is a manifestation of wealth and riches, while it also seeks to represent eternity, in that it is the seat for the absolute monarch, who is divinely ordained through the bloodline. The throne thus constitutes what Kantorowicz calls the "super body," as distinct from the natural and mortal body (1957, 272). This aspect is strengthened by the bishops' emphasis on the throne as one made of the horn of unicorns,[11] which symbolizes immortality, power,

---

9. Stina Bøge, interview, Copenhagen, October 29, 2007.

10. However, there are other thrones in the Bible. Since the throne is a symbol of power, the idea of a throne is also frequently connected with God or Yahweh. Of particular interest to us would be God's throne in Revelation, which is white (20:11), and the final reality, when heaven and earth have disappeared. The white throne in Revelation thus signifies eternity and transcendence (Moore 1996, 122 n. 196).

11. Wandal, *Christian 5.*, s. 4; Bornemann, *Frederik 4.*, s. 12 og 138ff.; Worm, *Christian 6.*, s. 8–9; Hersleb, *Frederik 5.*, s. 8 all refer to a unicorn throne.

and a powerful antidote to poison.[12] As such it was a much sought after commodity in Europe (Pluskowski 2004), and both Frederik III and the Duke of Gottorp had narwhal horns in their collections. We must also bear in mind that the geographical provenance of the narwhal in the arctic regions makes it a valuable and uncommon article (MacGregor 1985, 41).[13]

From a postcolonial perspective, the materials used for the throne are very interesting, because they mark the beginnings of the Danish mercantile empire. If we begin with the narwhal tusk, then it is highly likely that this came from Greenland.[14] In the middle of the seventeenth century, several trading expeditions went forth to Greenland and came back with, among other things, a large amount of narwhal tusk (Gad 1967, 284, 289, 302, 310). At this point in time the mission to and colonization of Greenland had not yet begun, but the king, Frederik III, most certainly saw Greenland as his inheritance and possession, and laid a strong claim to sovereignty over Greenland. This showed up in assigning Greenland the symbol of a polar bear and including it in the Danish coat of arms (Gad 1967, 286). As far as the other materials are concerned, it is difficult to say precisely how they ended up in the turner's workshop. Gold was one of the primary commodities of the time, and through the Danish African

---

12. In England fabulous animals were also used to represent the king and his immortality and uniqueness. Kantorowicz shows how medieval law used the myth of Phoenix and its dual nature, comprising the immortality of the species, and the mortality of the individual (1957, 389). The Phoenix myth was also used to illustrate various seats of power (bishop, pope, and king). Interestingly, the French heir was sometimes called *Le petit Phénix* (394). See also Marin, who uses the myth to demonstrate "the desire for the absolute of all holders of power" (100).

13. Historian Finn Gad mentions several times that it is a valuable and desired trade item among Danes, English, and Dutch in Greenland (Gad 1967, 289, 310). In von Weber's biography on Christian III's daughter, Anna, he mentions that Antonius Pigafetta offered a large piece of unicorn horn for 50,000 daler-coins and a small piece for 10,000 daler-coins (1865, 476). Countess Palatine Elisabeth also had a horn for sale at the sum of 25,000 crowns of the sun (*Ecu d'or au soleil*). Unicorn horn was seen as one of the most effective medicines of its time, and Anna's medicinal abilities would have branded her a witch had she not been daughter of the Danish king. Instead of buying it at the price listed above, she asked her father for a piece in order to prepare her *aquae vitae* (477).

14. A Danish newspaper article discussing the restoration of the throne mentions that the king sent an expedition to Greenland to "acquire" unicorn horns for the throne and that the expedition returned with fifteen horns. I have not been able to confirm this information in the sources at hand (Jensen 2007).

trading company in Gluckstadt, Denmark, also had its own import of gold from the African gold coast from around 1659 (Justesen 2005, viii). This fact may be gleaned from the lists that indicate the losses that the Danish trading company suffered under the Dutch, who boarded several Danish ships and confiscated trading goods of several thousands of rix-dollars, in which gold is mentioned explicitly (Justesen 2005, 22).

Tracing the wood is a little more complicated. Ebony was a popular luxury item in Europe and had been well known in Europe since the sixteenth century (Russell-Wood 1992, 127; Boston 1997, 196), primarily imported from the East Indies and West Africa, but it is not possible to confirm it as a regularly "imported" item to Denmark.[15] Kingwood and snake-wood are easier to pinpoint geographically, since both species only grow on the South American continent. Kingwood, or violet-wood, is one of the Brazilian products Portugal resold in Europe (Arruda 1991, table 10.5). Snake-wood, which is extremely precious and rare, is not listed as a Portuguese item of trade in either Arruda or Russell-Wood. It grows in Surinam, Panama, Guyana, and Brazilian Amazon, the last of which is a former Portuguese colony. However, most analyses of the trade between Europe and South America in these centuries focus only on the competition between the European states, slave trade, and sugar production. If wood export is mentioned, it is only brazil-wood.[16] This downplays the one-sided exploitation of the resources of the colonies, the destabilization of ecosystems, and focuses solely on production and competition. According to Jose Arruda, the difference between the export of brazil-wood and the sugar factories is that while the sugar factories actually contributed to build the country and through slavery to stimulate growth, the wood trade was one-sided and did not contribute to any development or improvement of the economy. There was no investment, only trade (Arruda 1991, 375).

Returning to the narwhal throne, we now see that it is assembled from Greenlandic narwhal tusk, African ivory, and rare Brazilian wood. A further element of this decadence is that these precious wood-types

---

15. But see Asta Bredsdorff (2009, 177), who indicates that ivory did come to Denmark through the Danish East India Company from East India. See also Feldbæk and Justesen (1980, 65), where it appears that admiral Gjedde had a ship loaded with ivory and sent it to Denmark in 1620.

16. An exception is Russell-Wood, who notes in one of his tables that wood is one of the commodities between Brazil and Portugal (1992, xxxii).

only serve as the skeleton of the chair, and are thus veneered with narwhal. Veneering, which is overlaying one less expensive wood-type with a thin layer of another, more expensive, and beautiful wood-type, as well as inlays of several types of expensive woods within each other, became extremely popular in cabinet work in the second half of the seventeenth century, especially in France and the Netherlands (Green 2007, xxi; Boger 1966, 100). But in this case we are not looking at veneering a less expensive material with something more costly. Here we are dealing with a number of rare, costly, and reasonably inaccessible materials being overlaid with another precious material.

Since we are in the seventeenth century, and thus not yet in the throes of the industrial revolution, we have not yet moved into the self-regulating market, separate from the social order, which Polanyi sees as the prime characteristic of capitalism. External trade was less a matter of import and export, and more a question of "adventure, exploration, hunting [and] piracy," of war rather than of barter (2001, 62). Colonial pillaging is hardly an exception to this. As noted above, the gathering and display of wealth serves social interests, and for the Danish king, the narwhal or unicorn throne was a direct attempt in that direction.

3. Accountability and Solomon as an Example

> Next there came into sight, stored one on the other to the arch of the roof, a splendid collection of elephant tusks. How many of them there were, we did not know, for of course we could not see to what depth they went back, but there could not have been less than the ends of 4 or 500 tusks of the first quality visible to our eyes. There, alone, was enough ivory before us to make a man wealthy for life. Perhaps, I thought, it was from this very store that Solomon drew the raw material for his great throne of ivory, of which there was not the like made in any kingdom. (Haggard 1933, 238)

The narwhal throne of the Danish king is, however, not the only tusk throne in postbiblical times. Three other extant examples are: Archbishop Maximian at Ravenna's ivory throne from ca. 550 (Reeve, 137); the ivory throne of Ivan the Terrible from the mid-sixteenth century; and the ivory throne presented to Queen Victoria by the Rajah of Travancore, which was exhibited at the Great Exhibition in London in 1851 (Ellis 1851, 929; image 243 on previous page). Furthermore, there are the remains of an ivory throne from the sixth or seventh century in the Grado Cathedral

(Hahn 2005, 4), and, finally, an oak throne inlaid with ivory stands in the Vatican.

What all these thrones indicate is that the narrative of Solomon, with its disregard for resources and labor, as well as its desire to glorify the centerpiece of its story at all costs, can be seen as a significant link in the chain of the consumption of ivory, which has led to a serious decimation in the elephant and narwhal populations of the world. Both animals are now covered by the Convention for International Trade in Endangered Species (CITES).

In 1989 a trade ban on ivory was implemented by moving the African elephant to appendix 1 under CITES, which means a total trading ban on raw and worked ivory (Stiles and Martin 2005, 78). The narwhal is listed under appendix 2, which means that trade is permitted but must be documented with permits issued by the exporting country (Reeves and Heide-Jørgensen 1994, 130).

While arguments persist over the ivory ban, and whether it encourages poaching and illegal trade or whether it actually works, the focus is very rarely on the colonial history and the economic and social consequences for the exporting nations.[17] For example, if we look at the import in Europe of ivory prior to the ban according to Stiles and Martin's research (2005, 78–81), the Federal Republic of Germany imported, between 1952 and 1974, 25 tonnes of raw ivory per annum on average and, between 1979 and 1987, 19.8 tonnes per annum. The UK's import was, between 1970 and 1977, 20.3 tonnes per annum on average and, between 1980 and 1987, 21.8 tonnes per annum. France imported, between 1966 and 1977, 317 tonnes of ivory and, between 1979 and 1988, 141 tonnes—14 tonnes per annum on average. Spain imported, between 1969 and 1977, 106 tonnes of raw ivory, with no information on post-1977 imports. And Italy, between 1970 and 1977, imported 55 tonnes of raw ivory and very small amounts (measured only in kilograms) after 1977.[18]

---

17. However, in their article on the ivory trade ban, Jyoti Khanna and Jon Harford (1996) include the dilemmas that the various African nations face, such as enforcing the ban and upholding conservation with no financial support, as well as relinquishing a valuable income.

18. Stiles and Martin (2005) do not note why 1977 is a significant statistical date. One suggestion could be that in 1978 the elephant was placed under appendix 2, thus regulating trade and demanding a CITES certificate from the exporting country.

At an average price of US $140 per pound in 1989 (Khanna and Harford 1996, 148), elephant ivory was a significant income for the African countries delivering the ivory—for instance, Kenya, South Africa, Sudan, Namibia, Zimbabwe, Tanzania, DRC, Somalia, Burundi, Gabon, Equatorial Guinea, and the Central African Republic.

However, in 1989, prior to the revision of the CITES index, France, the United States, West Germany, and the European community had suspended all ivory imports (Khanna and Harford 1996, 149). This, along with Kenya's president Moi setting 2,500 tusks on fire to advocate a moratorium on ivory, eventually led to the upgrading of the elephant to appendix 1.

Khanna and Harford note that the "African nations, burdened with the responsibility to enforce the ban without much help from the most ardent proponents of the ban in the west, are increasingly feeling the strain of such a conservation strategy [i.e., the ban]" (1996, 147). Apart from the increase in expenses to enforce the ban, there is an estimated and growing stockpile (in 1997) of 462.5 tonnes of legal ivory[19] in Africa (Bulte and van Kooten 1999, 172 n. 1). The CITES Conference has twice voted to allow certain African countries to auction off 50 tonnes (1999) and 60 tonnes (2004) of government ivory (Stiles, 310).

While I am certainly not advocating a withdrawal of the ban, it is nevertheless necessary to consider how the elephant (and narwhal) populations became so decimated in the first place. Of the five European nations considered by Stiles and Martin above, Germany, the United Kingdom, and France have long and distinguished traditions for the craft of ivory carving. Incidentally, these nations were also significant colonial powers in Africa. The ivory carving centers in Germany flourished in the late nineteenth century (Beachey 1967, 269) and the main European trading firms in Africa in the nineteenth century, which dealt in ivory, were either German (Hansing and Company, Oswald and Company, and Meyer and Company, a branch of the largest ivory dealers in the world), English (Wiseman and Company), or French (Roux Frassinet and Company) (Beachey 1967, 278). During the colonial era, colonies were plundered and mined for their natural resources, which helped created some of the wealthiest states in the world. These wealthy states are now imposing

---

19. Legal ivory is ivory that results from confiscation from poachers, natural mortality, culling, and the destruction of problem animals (Bulte and van Kooten 1999, 172 n. 1, citing Milliken).

trade bans and environmental restrictions on the countries, whose natural wealth is unusable due to modern Western moral standards. Greenland, for example, is caught between the IWC's (International Whaling Commission) restrictions on whaling and being denied an increase in carbon emissions to develop industries. And several African nations are requested to relinquish a highly profitable resource in ivory, while simultaneously policing a ban on ivory hunting and trading that is both difficult and costly. We thus have a situation where developing economies continue to suffer a double burden: the consequences of a history of exploitation and a present situation of ecological restrictions imposed by the same suspects that have exploited them in the past.

In conclusion, to an essay that began with Solomon in the Bible and ended up—via Greenland—in Africa, it must be said that, while the throne plays a relatively small and to all appearances insignificant part of the narrative, it has fired the imaginations of kings, bishops, and treasure hunters. Its afterlives, in other words, have been disproportionately significant. The Solomon narrative's emphasis on gross exploitation of resources and of labor has legitimated subsequent pillaging, slaughter, oppressive absolutist regimes, and wasteful monarchies, all of which have repercussions for global economies today. Western Europe sits on the corpses of hundreds of thousands of whales and elephants, who have shed their lives to supply ivory for pianos and thrones, bones for hoop skirts and corsets, and oil for fuel and lights, while dictating apocalyptic scenarios and moral superiority.[20]

REFERENCES

Arruda, José Jobson de Andrade. 1991. Colonies as Mercantile Investments: The Luso-Brazilian Empire 1500–1808. Pages 360–420 in *The Political Economy of Merchant Empires*. Edited by James D. Tracy. Cambridge: Cambridge University Press.

Beachey, R.W. 1967. The East African Ivory Trade in the Nineteenth Century. *JAH* 8:269–90.

Boer, Roland. 2007. The Sacred Economy of Ancient "Israel." *SJOT* 21:29–48.

---

20. For helpful comments and suggestions to earlier versions of this essay I would like to thank David Jobling, Anne Elvey, Gillian Townsley, and Roland Boer.

Boger, Louis A. 1966. *Furniture Past and Present.* New York: Doubleday.
Boston, Thomas D. 1997. The East African Coast in the Age of Exploration. Pages 189–205 in *A Different Vision: Race and Public Policy.* Edited by Thomas D. Boston. London: Routledge.
Bredsdorff, Asta. 2009. *The Trials and Travels of Willem Leyel: An Account of the Danish East India Company in Tranquebar, 1639–48.* Copenhagen: Museum Tusculanum.
Brueggemann, Walter. 2000. *1 and 2 Kings.* SHBC. Macon: Smyth & Helwys.
Bulte, Erwin H., and G. Cornelis van Kooten. 1999. Economic Efficiency, Resource Conservation and the Ivory Trade Ban. *Ecological Economics* 28:171–81.
Ellis, Robert. 1851. *Official Descriptive and Illustrated Catalogue of the Great Exhibition of the Works of Industry of all Nations, 1851.* London: Spicer Brothers.
Feldbæk, Ole, and Ole Justesen. 1980. *Kolonierne i Asien og Danmark.* Copenhagen: Politikens Forlag.
Gad, Finn. 1967. *Grønlands historie I: Indtil 1700.* København: Nyt Nordisk Forlag.
Green, Harvey. 2007. *Wood: Craft, Culture, History.* London: Penguin.
Haggard, H. Rider. 1933. *King Solomon's Mines.* London: Cassell.
Hahn, Cynthia. 2005. The Meaning of Early Medieval Treasures. Pages 1–20 in *Reliquiare im Mittelalter. Hamburger Forschungen zur Kunstgeschichte,* V. Edited by Reudenbach, Bruno and Gia Toussaint. Berlin: Akademie Verlag.
Hein, Jørgen. 2006. En Trone af Enhjørningehorn og Løver af Sølv. *Siden Saxo* 2:39–45.
Ipsen, Avaren. 2008. Solomon and the Two Prostitutes. Pages 134–50 in *Marxist Feminist Criticism of the Bible.* Edited by Roland Boer and Jorunn Økland. Sheffield: Sheffield Phoenix Press.
———. 2009. *Sex Working and the Bible.* London: Equinox.
Jensen, Maria Lund. 2007. Kongens Tronstol og Klimaforandringerne. *Politiken-Videnskab,* July 15:7.
Jobling, David. 1991. "Forced Labor": Solomon's Golden Age and the Question of Literary Representation. *Semeia* 54:57–76.
Justesen, Ole, ed. 2005. *Danish Sources for the History of Ghana 1657–1754.* Vol. 1:1657–1735. Copenhagen: Royal Danish Academy of Sciences and Letters.

Kantorowicz, Ernst H. 1957. *The King's Two Bodies: A Study in Medieval Political Theology*. Princeton: Princeton University Press.
Khanna, Jyoti, and Jon Harford. 1996. The Ivory Trade Ban: Is it Effective? *Ecological Economics* 19:147–55.
Koehler, Ludwig, and Walter Baumgartner. 2001. *The Hebrew and Aramaic Lexicon of the Old Testament, Study Edition*. Leiden: Brill.
Macgregor, Arthur. 1985. *Bone, Antler, Ivory and Horn: The Technologies of Skeletal Materials since the Roman Period*. London: Croom Helm.
Marin, Louis. 1988. *Portrait of the King*. Minneapolis: University of Minnesota Press.
Nam, Roger S. 2011. *Portrayals of Economic Exchange in the Book of Kings*. Leiden: Brill.
Pluskowski, Aleksander. 2004. Narwhals or Unicorns? Exotic Animals as Material Culture in Medieval Europe. *European Journal of Archaeology* 7:291–313.
Polanyi, Karl. 2001 (1944). *The Great Transformation: The Political and Economic Origins of our Time*. Boston: Beacon.
Reeves, Randall R., and Mads P. Heide-Jørgensen. 1994. Commercial Aspects of the Exploitation of Narwhals (*Monodon monoceros*) in Greenland, with Emphasis on Tusk Exports. Pages 119–34 in *Studies of White Whales (*Delphinapterus leucas*) and Narwhals (*Momdon monoceros*) in Greenland and Adjacent Waters*. Edited by E. W. Born, R. Dietz, and R. R. Reeves. Copenhagen: Danish Polar Center.
Russell-Wood, Anthony J. R. 1992. *The Portuguese Empire 1415–1808: A World on the Move*. Baltimore: Johns Hopkins University Press.
Stiles, Daniel, and Esmond Martin. 2005. The African and Asian Ivory Markets in Europe: A Survey of Five Countries. *Pachyderm* 39 (July–December).
Weber, Karl von. 1865. *Anna Churfürstin zu Sachsen geboren as Königlichem Stamm zu Dänemark. Ein Lebens- und Sittenbild aus dem sechzehnten Jahrhundert*. Leipzig: Bernhard Tauchnitz.

Is There an "Anticonquest" Ideology in the Book of Judges?

Uriah Y. Kim

1. Jephthah's Speech and "Anticonquest" Ideology

There is an unusually long speech in the book of Judges, namely, that of Jephthah in Judges 11:12–28. Jephthah, the newly elected leader of the Gileadites, and the king of the Ammonites argue over a territory east of the Jordan and, in the process, the speech reflects a central ideology in the book of Judges. Jephthah sends messengers with this claim: "What is to me and you that you have come to me to fight against *my land*" (11:12).[1] The king of the Ammonites replies with the counterclaim, "For Israel took *my land* when he came up from Egypt, from the Arnon to the Jabbok and to the Jordan. Now return them in peace" (11:13). Both men assert that the land is his land. It is a bit confusing as to whether the land in question originally belonged to the Moabites (11:15, 18) or to the Amorites (11:21–22). But why does the king of the Ammonites argue that he has the right over this territory when it didn't belong to them in the first place? The passage does not consider this issue. We don't get to hear the Ammonite king's reasoning for his ultimatum.

But we do get to hear Jephthah's argument, a history lesson of sorts. He makes it clear that Israel is a peaceful people who prefer diplomacy over military conflicts and "did not take the land of Moab and the land of the sons of Ammon" (11:15). As if to demonstrate Israel's preference for peaceful resolutions, Jephthah sends messengers twice to the Ammonite king (11:12, 14) and in his speech Israel sends messengers three times to three kings the Israelites encounter in their journey (11:17, 19). According

---

1. All Bible translations in this essay are mine.

to Jephthah, Israel sent messengers to the king of Edom for permission to "cross over" (עבר) his land (11:17). When the king of Edom refused, Israel asked the king of Moab, only to receive the same answer (11:17). The text is careful to show that the Israelites did not enter any territory they did not have consent to do so. It is emphatic that Israel camped on "the other side" (עבר) of the border in question and "did not enter the territory of Moab" (11:18). But when Israel sent messengers to Sihon, the king of the Amorites, for license to "cross over [עבר] your land to my place" (11:19), he not only denied them to cross over (עבר) his land but gathered all his people and attacked Israel (11:20). Sihon was the aggressor who threatened to destroy Israel but was defeated, and Israel occupied all of his land (11:21). The kings of Edom, Moab, and the Amorites may have been right after all to suspect Israel's innocent request to "cross over" their lands.²

It is evident that Yahweh is behind Israel's victory over Sihon and the occupation of his land: "Then Yahweh God of Israel gave Sihon and all his people into the hand of Israel and they struck them. So Israel occupied all the land of the Amorites who had inhabited that land" (11:21). But Jephthah continues to bring God into his argument, overstressing God's involvement: "So now Yahweh the God of Israel has conquered the Amorites for the sake of his people Israel. Should you occupy it?" (11:23). Jephthah sounds fair and reasonable when he makes the following point in 11:24: "Should you not possess what Chemosh your god intends you to possess? Everything Yahweh our God gives to possess for our sake, should we not possess it?" Jephthah's theological argument is a simple one: the conquest and possession of a land is legitimate when God authorizes it. But then Jephthah throws in another basis for not relinquishing Israel's rights to the land: Israel had lived in that land for three hundred years. Jephthah asks, "Why didn't you recover them during that time?" (11:26), declaring that the Ammonites' title to the land has expired, having been washed away in the tides of history. Therefore, Jephthah is confident that he is in the right and ends his speech with the following challenge: "Let Yahweh, the judge, adjudicate today between the sons of Israel and the

---

2. The word עבר also appears six times in the introduction of (10:6–11:11) and the conclusion to (11:29–33) the Ammonite conflict. The text identifies the land in question as "beyond [עבר] the Jordan" (10:8), but the Ammonites "crossed over" to the west side (10:9), suggesting that they encroached Israel's territory first. After the speech the text notes that Jephthah "crossed over" three times (11:29) to get to the Ammonites and then repeats the word once more (11:32).

sons of Ammon" (11:27). The Ammonite king has been lectured to and does not say a word (11:28), implying that Jephthah (and the Israelites) is correct.

Jephthah's speech contains elements of "anticonquest" ideology,[3] which designates, according to Musa W. Dube, "the literary strategies of representation by which the colonizers secure their innocence while asserting their right to travel to, enter, and possess resources and lands that belong to foreign nations" (2000, 58).[4] Dube lists four literary-rhetorical representations of anticonquest ideology: first, a method of authorizing travel from one land to another, often with divine claims; second, a method of constructing the image of the targeted land and its people, usually representing the targeted land positively but its people negatively; third, a method of constructing the identity of the people who colonize distant lands, representing them as superior and exceptionally favored by divine powers; fourth, a method of employing genders to articulate relations of domination and subjugation, representing the colonizer as man and the colonized as woman.

Dube identifies these elements in the Exodus–Joshua narrative. In Exodus it is clear that God is the originator who sanctions the Israelites to travel to and take possession of a distant land, demanding the Pharaoh, "Let my people go!" Dube argues that moral discomfort over the divine command to travel to and to possess a land that does not belong to Israel is eased by the fact that the Israelites are escaping from Egyptian slavery. God's authorization to travel is seen as part of God's deliverance of Israel from slavery. Then Dube claims that "the literary method used to represent a land to be colonized, like those used to justify traveling, also revolve

---

3. When I shared this essay with my colleagues at Hartford Seminary, they were in agreement that the term "anticonquest" was confusing and misleading. That is, it sounds like this ideology is against conquest or colonialism, which is not the case. This ideology in fact masks and justifies the colonizer's actions and therefore presents de facto conquest as its benign opposite ("unconquest"). It would have been clear if it was called "conquest-denial" or "conquest-masking" ideology.

4. Dube's understanding of anticonquest ideology is based on Mary Louis Pratt's work (1992). Pratt analyzes particular genres of travel and exploration writing to South America and Africa in the eighteenth and nineteenth centuries by Europeans and concludes that the writings portrayed the colonizers/travelers as "seeing-man" whose "imperial eyes" passively gaze and possess and rule, ignoring violence, suffering, and unjust systems that surround him, which made his travel and observation possible.

around God, characterizing it as a God-promised land, a rich land, an inhabited land" (2000, 62). In the Exodus–Joshua account the God-promised land is represented positively, "a land flowing with milk and honey," and its people negatively. The inhabitants of the land are characterized in opposition to the Israelites. Even their cultures and gods are construed as sinful and inferior. These negative traits are described in the Exodus–Joshua narrative in order to justify Israel's domination and dispossession of the inhabitants and their land. Dube concludes, "Basically, the narrative casts the people of the targeted land negatively in order to validate the annihilation of all the inhabitants" (2000, 66).

In the anticonquest discourse, the identity of the colonizer is critical because "those who have the right to travel to, enter, possess, and control distant and inhabited lands must be shown to be exceptionally different and well-deserving above their victims" (Dube 2000, 66). Dube shows that in the Exodus–Joshua account the Israelites become a chosen race, a holy people, set apart and different from the inhabitants. Furthermore, she argues that patriarchy cannot be separated from imperialism when trying to understand the anticonquest ideology because it employs patriarchal gender relations to articulate the relationship between the colonizer (man) and the colonized (woman). She notes that the Exodus–Joshua narrative singles out the foreign women as the biggest threat to the purity of the sons of Israel and uses them to represent the status of the land (75–76).

I agree with Dube that the Exodus–Joshua account contains these elements of anticonquest ideology, which makes it fair to say that this narrative can be characterized as a colonial/imperial discourse. Therefore, it is not surprising that the West had used the Exodus-Conquest account, among other texts in the Bible, to justify its subjugation of the Rest, as Dube argues in her book, focusing on Europe's colonization of Africa. In Marc C. Brett's work (2008), he also acknowledges that there were favorite biblical texts that appeared regularly and were embedded in the discourse of colonialism to support the colonization of Australia and its people. However, he argues that colonial interpretations of the Bible have inverted the anti-imperial message of biblical texts written by ancient Israelites who were subject to the empires. He points out throughout his work that most of biblical texts were produced by those who suffered under "the shifting tides of ancient empires" rather than by those who colonized others. In Brett's analysis, the Bible provokes anti-imperial sentiments rather than warrant for colonialism. In conclusion, he maintains that because the Bible has been improperly used to support imperialism/colonialism, there is a need to re-examine the Bible in order to appropriate the constantly repeated theme of "resistance to empire" within it.

I agree with Brett that the biblical narratives, if read from their historical contexts, can be interpreted as anti-imperial rather than supporting imperial interests. There are, however, elements of colonial/imperial discourse in the Bible that support imperialism/colonialism, which cannot be discounted or dismissed. Dube, on the other hand, sees the Exodus–Joshua account as an imperializing text without considering the imperial/colonial contexts from which the narrative emerged. What is reflected in the biblical narratives then is a sense of ambivalence toward Israel's use of imperial ideologies to justify their domination of others. There is a sense of uneasiness about using anticonquest ideology to sanction Israel's attempts to subjugate others since they themselves were repeat victims of empires.

It is difficult to date Jephthah's speech in particular and different editorial layers in the book of Judges, which is viewed as part of the Deuteronomistic History.[5] But it is easier to talk about general contexts from which the Deuteronomistic History was produced. Thomas C. Römer (2005) offers a workable theory by presenting a three-stage development of the Deuteronomistic History from three successive sociohistorical contexts, that is, three imperial contexts: the Neo-Assyrian period, the Neo-Babylonian period, and the Persian period. In all three contexts, Israel was a victim, a petty kingdom or community in the shadow of successive empires, and its desire to claim a rightful ownership of the land is strong but contested. Josiah aspired to recover the northern kingdom and the land beyond the Jordan during the waning years of the Neo-Assyrian Empire; the community in the Babylonian exile, located at the heart of the Babylonian Empire, desired to return to the God-promised land while trying to maintain their group identity outside their homeland; and the community under the auspice of the Persian Empire tried to stake their claims on the land in competition with those who had already made home

---

5. Philippe Guillaume (2004), for example, proposes seven different historical contexts in which Judges was edited and attributes Jephthah's speech to the latest layer, ca. 150 B.C.E. Robert Polzin (1980), on the other hand, accepts Martin Noth's idea of the Babylonian exile as the context in which the Deuteronomistic History was produced but reads it as a work of an author rather than of an editor. Most scholars fall between these two positions. Some follow the double-redaction theory of Frank M. Cross. Others follow the multiple exilic editions of Rudolf Smend.

in it. This is to say, it makes sense to understand Jephthah's speech in particular and Judges in general from colonial/imperial contexts.

In the end, Jephthah's speech is not really addressed to the Ammonite king and may have not been part of the original story.[6] It probably was intended for or articulated the sentiments of the people situated in colonial/imperial contexts. We need to ask then, Why does Jephthah justify Israel's conquest and occupation of a foreign land when they are merely following the common ideology of the day? Empires conquered lands belonging to others with no more than lip service to divine powers. They hardly needed justification for their conquest. I have noted elsewhere that every king of the Neo-Assyrian Empire, for example, was expected to conquer and expand his land. In fact, it was consider every Assyrian king's primary duty (Kim 2005, 206–21). If Israel is able to conquer a land with divine support, then there is no further validation needed to occupy that land. But Jephthah's speech emphasizes God's role and presents Israel as a peaceful people who prefer diplomacy over military engagements and who have historical rights to the land. It overstresses God's role and Israel's innocence. Those who have added this speech to the book of Judges perhaps felt ambivalent about mimicking the empire, using anticonquest ideology to pursue their interests when they themselves were victims of imperial powers. I would like to explore whether such ambiguities are reflected in the book of Judges.

2. Anticonquest Ideology in Judges?

2.1. Divine Authorization to Travel, Conquer, and Occupy

How do the Israelites justify their conquest and possession of the land since they themselves acknowledge that they are "outsiders" and do not have the "natural" link to it? They make a connection to the land through divine authorization. In the great narrative that runs from Genesis to 2 Kings, God promises the land to their ancestors (Genesis), gives the authority to the Israelites to travel to Canaan (Exodus to Numbers), and commands the Israelites to conquer the land (Deuteronomy to Joshua). When we come to Judges, there is no warrant needed to travel to, conquer, and occupy the

---

6. The speech does not avert the war and makes no difference to the story, which suggests, as many commentators have argued, that it is a later addition. Elie Assis (2005), however, argues that the speech is integral to Jephthah's story because it functions to change God's mind about not delivering Israel ever again.

land since it has been established in the previous books. Judges, however, continues to reiterate some elements of divine authorization in its own ways. First, in the core section of Judges (3:7 to 16:31) God's role is limited to individual judges' successes and failures in relation to enemies rather than to the land itself. That is, God gives individual opponents rather than the land. Ehud says to the Israelites, for example, "Follow after me; for the Lord has given [נתן] your enemies the Moabites into your hand" (3:28). Deborah says to Barack, "For this is the day on which the Lord has given [נתן] Sisera into your hand" (4:14). God gives (נתן) the Ammonites into Jephthah's hands (11:32; 12:3). Second, most clear instances of divine authorization appear in passages that are considered later additions to the core section, which reflect the concerns and anxiety of being located in imperial/colonial contexts: Prologue One (1:1–2:5); Prologue Two (2:6–3:6); Addition One (6:7–10); Addition Two (10:6–16); Jephthah's Speech (11:12–28), and Epilogue (17:1–21:25).

In Prologue One (1:1–2:5) the issue of divine authorization to conquer and occupy the land is clearly evident from the very first verse: the Israelites ask for permission from Yahweh to wage war against the Canaanites. Yahweh sanctions Judah to go first—"Behold, I give [נתן] the land into his hand" (1:2). Each parcel of the land is referred to as an "allotment" (גורל, 1:3). Yahweh is the landlord and the land is Yahweh's property that can be divided among the sons of Israel. The sons of Judah capture Jerusalem and put it "to the sword and set the city on fire" (1:8), continuing a holy war begun in Joshua. In fact another city, Zephat, is placed under חרם ("ban"), based on the note that "they devoted it for destruction" (ויחרימו) and called the city Hormah (חרמה, 1:17). Yahweh is "with" Judah (1:19) and the house of Joseph (1:22) in their wars against the Canaanites, which indicates divine support to wage war against the inhabitants. Hebron is given (נתן) to Caleb "as Moses promised" (1:20), which is equivalent to God endorsing the transaction. Moreover, Caleb is analogous to Yahweh in that Caleb has the right to give his daughter to Othniel (1:12–15) just as God has the authority to give his land to Israel. Prologue One ends with a reiteration of God's permission to travel to and settle the God-promised land: "I brought you up from Egypt and brought you into the land that I had promised to your fathers" (2:1).

Prologue Two (2:6–3:6) begins with God's sanction to occupy the land: "When Joshua dismissed the people, the Israelites all went to their own inheritance to take possession of the land" (2:6). The term נחלה ("inheritance") is used synonymously with the term גורל ("allotment"), indicating that the settlement and division of the land has God's blessing. It reminds the Israelites again that it is "Yahweh the God of their fathers who brought them forth from the land of Egypt" (2:12), recapitulating God's mandate to travel to a distant land.

Addition One (6:7–10), a prophet's speech to Gideon, summarizes the exodus and conquest traditions: "I (Yahweh) brought you up from Egypt and brought you out of the house of slavery. And I delivered you from the hand of the Egyptians and from the hand of all who oppressed you. I drove them out before you and gave [נתן] you *their land*" (6:8–9). This speech clearly acknowledges that the land once belonged to another people and without God's support the conquest and occupation of the land would have been unthinkable. God reminds the Israelites that "You shall not revere the gods of the Amorites *in whose land you reside*" (6:10). Again, it is with God's permission that the Israelites are allowed to live in the land that once did not belong to them.

Addition Two (10:6–16) also acknowledges that the land beyond Jordan once belonged to some other people: "all the Israelites who live beyond the Jordan, *in the land of the Amorites*, that is, in Gilead" (10:8). This section lists Yahweh's repeated deliverances of the Israelites from multiple enemies and clearly indicates that they cannot continue to dwell in the land if not for Yahweh's support. In 11:12–28, Jephthah retraces Israel's journey from Egypt to the Transjordan where the Israelites defeat Sihon and end up occupying his land. He defends Israel's right to occupy the land which once belonged to another people, relying on divine claims to rebuff the Ammonite king's demand (11:23).

In the Epilogue the migration of the Danites also contains some elements of divine authorization to possess a foreign land (ch. 18). The narrative begins with the note that "in those days the tribe of Dan was searching for its inheritance (נחלה) to settle since until that time an inheritance (נחלה) did not fall to it amongst the tribes of Israel" (18:1). The tribe of Dan sends spies to look for a land far away from its original allotment to conquer (18:2; see also 1:34). The spies ask Micah's young Levite to discern God's will: "Please inquire of God so that we may know whether our path that we are going will be successful" (18:5). They want to know whether God approves and, therefore, authorizes their travel to a land that is not their own. The Levite gives a favorable reply: "Go in peace. Yahweh is in front of the path you are on" (18:6). Sure enough, they come to Laish, an isolated city, which will serve as the northern border of Israel, which is perfect for conquering (18:7) and spacious and lacking nothing

(18:10). The spies return to their brothers and claim that God has given them permission to conquer the city: "God has given [נתן] it into your hands" (18:10). The Danites burn down the city and put its inhabitants to the sword, as if the city and its people were under the "ban" (חרם). Then they rename and occupy it as their own city (18:27–29).[7]

It is clear that Judges reiterates or rather overstresses God's role in Israel's travel to and possession of a land that once belonged to the others. It is also hard to ignore the impression that this process came with much blood and violence, which was no different from the way empires conquer lands without the pretense of having divine permission to do so. Judges, however, portrays the Israelites as victims of violence, from slavery in Egypt to "foreign" oppressions in Canaan, perhaps to validate their use of violence in possessing the land that once did not belong to them and subjugating its people.

2.2. Representations of the Land and Its People

A second strategy used in anticonquest ideology is to represent the targeted land positively and its people negatively in order to argue that the inhabitants do not deserve to occupy the land and, therefore, the Israelites are vindicated in displacing them. There aren't many descriptions of physical features of the land since Judges is more interested in dealing with the inhabitants than the land itself. The land serves as a passive stage on which the drama of Israel's settlement unfolds, waiting to be occupied and reinscribed by the Israelites. They rename Canaanite cities as their own: Hebron was formerly Qiryah-Arba (1:10); Debir, Qiryat Sepher (1:11); Zephath, Hormah (1:17); Bethel, Luz (1:23); Dan, Laish (18:29); and Gilead was once the land of the Amorites (10:8). But when the narrative does comment on the land, it is represented positively. A general impression of Canaan in Judges is that the land is bountiful and good. The land is

---

7. Uwe F. W. Bauer, in contrast, does not see divine authorization in the Danites' conquest of Laish. Bauer argues that the Danite migration story contains some elements of the spy story genre and the Yahweh-war story genre, but these elements are used atypically to warn against changing "the heteronomous Israelite conquest with its corresponding God-given gift of land" into "an autonomous conquest, lacking a corresponding God-given gift of land, as it was carried out by the Danites (as the protagonists) and as it could be carried out again one day" (2000, 46). We will see below that there are indeed ambiguities in the Danite migration story.

fertile enough to support the Israelites, if not for the "outsiders" who take the bounty from them (6:3–6). The territory the Philistines occupy also seems to be fruitful, and they are successful in producing a variety of agricultural products (15:5). The Danite spies describe Laish as "very good" (18:9) and "wide and prosperous" (18:10).

I have noted elsewhere that the royal inscriptions of the Neo-Assyrian Empire portray the various kings and rebellious vassals as separate manifestations of the one common enemy who serves as the antagonist to the Assyrian king (Kim, 197–206). There is no genuine desire to know the others and their cultures and lands. They are inferior to the Assyrians in every way. They are senseless and wicked. The enemies are passive and incapable of military initiatives and are easily driven to panic and terror. Representations of Israel's co-inhabitants of the land follow such a scheme with important wrinkles.

Judges paints the people of the land with very broad brushes, uninterested in providing specific features of the inhabitants and their cultures, although there are a few instances of this. For example, in referring to the Midianites it says, "For they had golden earrings, because they were Ishmaelites" (8:24). Interestingly Ishmaelites and Midianites are lumped together as one people. From Israel's perspective, for all intents and purposes, there is no difference between them; they are interchangeable. Therefore, even though Judges names an assortment of people, they all play the same role, that of Israel's enemy. The most common word Judges uses to designate the others is אויב ("enemy," 2:14, 18; 3:28; 5:31; 8:34; 11:36, etc.). Israel's others are represented as being united in their enmity against Israel.[8] The Canaanites, the Hittites, the Amorites, the Perizzites, the Hivites, and the Jebusites, the stock peoples of Canaan according to the exodus tradition, are listed as the inhabitants of the land the Israelites have to displace (3:5). Thus, one expects the Israelites to be in conflict with these peoples. But

---

8. It is important to recognize that we may be dealing with the world of symbols rather than with the world of reality, as J. W. Rogers comments on similar texts that command the Israelites to utterly destroy the foreigners: "Clearly, we are not in the world of reality, but in a world where enemies have become symbols for wickedness, and utter destruction a symbol for the rooting out of evil" (1993, 292). J. Clinton McCann also makes a similar point that the references to the Canaanites and other peoples named in the book of Judges as enemies of Israel must be understood symbolically as "references to ways of organizing social life that perpetuate injustice and ultimately produce oppressive inequalities that threaten human life" (2002, 19).

what we see in Judges is that that they are in conflict with the Arameans (3:7–11), the Moabites (3:12–30), northern Canaanites (chs. 4 and 5), the Midianites, the Amalekites, and the "sons of the east" (chs. 6–8), the Ammonites (chs. 10–12), and the Philistines (chs. 13–16). There is no difference among them; differences exist only between Israelites and them. The narrative fixes the role of Israel's others as the enemies who are always scheming to plunder and oppress the Israelites, albeit with Yahweh's permission (3:8, 12; 4:2; 6:1; 10:7; 13:1).

In general Israel's enemies are described as formidable oppressors,[9] but they are also depicted as evil, foolish, or stupid in Judges. Even though the enemies are more powerful and numerous than the Israelites, they are easily defeated by the Israelites, in no small part due to their leaders' incompetence. The collection of stories of judges/saviors (3:7–16:31), which begins with Othniel (3:7–11), reflects this strategy. Othniel's victim is the king of Aram-Naharaim ("the Land with Two Rivers," referring to Mesopotamia), with a terrifying name, Cushan-Rishathaim, "double-evil," but he doesn't put up much of a fight and is easily defeated. In the Ehud story (3:12–30) we are introduced to King Eglon of Moab. Eglon's most salient characteristic is that he is a very fat man (3:17), and he is not very bright. He accepts Ehud's words at face value and dismisses his attendants and allows Ehud to enter his private (bath)room (3:19). He seems to pay respect to Ehud's god by getting out of his (toilet) seat (3:20). He is stabbed by Ehud, the fat of his belly engulfing Ehud's dagger while spewing out "dirt" (3:22). In the meantime, his servants patiently wait outside, embarrassed to interrupt the king during his "private" business. Ehud escapes while Eglon's servants were questioning one another about what to do (3:26).

In the Deborah and Barack story (4:1–5:31) Sisera has 900 chariots (4:2) and harshly oppresses Israelites (4:3). Sisera's army is described as "multitudes" (4:7). Clearly Sisera's army has superior military weapons and is greater in numbers but the Israelites defeat Sisera and his mighty army rather easily. Then Sisera is fooled and killed by a woman (4:17–22).

In the Gideon story (chs. 6–8) the Midianites, Amalekites, and the "sons of east" form an alliance (6:33, 7:12) and dominate Israel and take away Israel's sustenance (6:3–4). They and their camels gather on Israel's

---

9. Roger Ryan (2007) argues that the enemies' status and power were intentionally hyped to give greater credibility to the Israelites' victories.

land like locusts, far too many to count (6:5–6; 7:12), but Yahweh promises Gideon that "You'll strike Midian like you would one man" (6:16). Then Yahweh downsizes Gideon's army from 32,000 men to three hundred (7:1–7). Gideon's small troop defeats the vast army of the eastern alliance. In the middle of the night, the Midianites panic and are fooled into running for their lives (7:21–22). Even though they still outnumber Gideon's men, they are no match for them and are driven into terror (8:12).

In the Samson story (chs. 13–16) the narrative repeats the fact that Israel is under the oppression of the Philistines (by the narrator, 13:1; 14:4; 15:20; by the angel of God, 13:5; by the men of Judah, 15:11), only to learn that it is Samson who has ravaged the land of the Philistines for twenty years (16:24). Astonishingly the Philistines cannot control one man; they are out-muscled and outwitted by Samson. In 16:1–3, for example, the Philistines look foolish, setting up an ambush only to see Samson escape in the middle of the night. Ironically, almost comically, more Philistines are killed in Samson's death than all the Philistines killed during his lifetime (16:30).

Another way to depict negatively Israel's foes and their leaders is through bodily mutilation, which, according to T. M. Lemos, "served to bring shame upon the victim and their community by associating the victim with a lower-status group and/or by effecting an actual status change in the victim" (2006, 226). The first victim in Judges is Adoni-Bezek (1:4–7).[10] He flees (1:6) like other leaders of Israel's enemies throughout the core section of Judges. Moreover, after his big toes and thumbs are cut off, he is relegated to picking up scraps under the table for the rest of his life (1:6–7)—indeed a humiliating end to a king but a fitting end to Israel's enemy. The status of Adoni-Bezek (and his people) is lowered to that of a slave after the mutilation of his body and he must live at the mercy of the Israelites. Eglon is stabbed by Ehud in the belly and is discovered by his servants in a very humiliating position. Moreover, he becomes an object of the reader's gaze: "Behold, their lord, fallen toward the ground, dead" (3:25). Having collapsed face-first to the ground, Eglon's position/status was lowered through "mutilation" of his body and his people were "humbled [כנע] under the hand of Israel" (3:30; also 4:23–25; 8:28). Then Deborah predicts that Sisera will be sold to a woman (4:9). To add to an insult, he flees on his feet like a common soldier (4:15) even though he is the commander of 900 chari-

---

10. This story may not belong in Prologue One. It has characteristics closer to the core section of Judges.

ots. In the end, he is mutilated (his head shattered in 5:26) and becomes another object of the reader's gaze: "Look! Sisera is lying dead, and the tent peg is in his temple" (4:22; also 5:27). The men of Ephraim capture and kill Oreb and Zeeb, the two captains for Midian, and then sever their heads and carry them to Gideon (7:25). Gideon captures the two kings of Midian, who are draped in their purple garments, but he pays little respect to the men of royal status. He orders his firstborn Jether, a mere boy, to execute them (8:20). When Jether is unable to draw his sword, the kings demand some respect and Gideon obliges and kills them himself (8:21).

It is, however, the later additions that most clearly articulate the editors of Judges' attitude toward the others. In Prologue One (1:1–2:5), even though the Canaanites are willing to live with the Israelites (1:27–30), even as forced labor (1:28, 30, 33, 35), the message from Yahweh is clear: Do not mix with the indigenous people. Yahweh commands Israel not to make covenant with the inhabitants of the land and to destroy their altars (2:2). But the angel of Yahweh predicts that they will become adversaries and their gods a snare to the Israelites (2:3). In Prologue Two (2:6–3:6), it is the subsequent generations after Joshua's passing who lose sight of Yahweh and go after the gods of the people of the land (2:11, 12, 13, 17, 19), which is considered "evil in the eyes of Yahweh" (2:11; this phrase is repeated in 3:7, 12; 4:1; 6:1; 10:6; 13:1). By equating the worship of the gods of others with sin or evil, this section reaffirms the message not to mix with the others and reinforces the view that gods and cultures of the inhabitants are evil. It ends with the judgment that the new generations of Israelites failed because of their willingness to coexist with the others (3:6).

In Addition One (6:7–10), the others are the aggressors and oppressors (6:9). This passage reminds us again that Israel is not to worship the gods of Amorites in whose land they live (6:10). In Addition Two (10:6–16), Israel's foes וירעצו ורצצו ("crushed and oppressed") the Israelites (10:8; these words occur exactly at the mid-point of the book of Judges). The Ammonites are the aggressors who cross the Jordan to attack Judah, Benjamin, and Ephraim (10:9). Yahweh summarizes that multiple enemies have oppressed them (10:12). But the root cause of Israel's suffering is that the Israelites abandoned Yahweh and served the gods of their neighbors (10:13), that is, the foreign gods (10:16). In Jephthah's speech (11:12–28), Jephthah calls Chemosh (the god of the Moabites) the god of the Ammonites (Molech is their god). There is no difference between Chemosh and Molech to those who produced Jephthah's speech. The foreign gods, like Israel's multiple adversaries, played the role of enemies.

By portraying the inhabitants and their cultures or gods in this way the Israelites may have been simply following the common imperial ideology of their time, except to depict their enemies as formidable foes, which turns their victories into testimonies of their prowess. Ironically those who were victims of and depicted as inferior nobodies by the empires are using a similar strategy to denigrate and dominate their neighbors.

2.3. Representations of the Israelites

It is also important for an anticonquest ideology to establish the colonizing people as superior to the colonized people and favored by divine powers to defeat them. The narrative depicts the enemies as superior in military strength and in numbers (1:19; 4:3; 5:28) but the Israelites' military weapons are limited (5:8) and they are usually outnumbered. They are indeed underdogs. However, as Susan Niditch (2008) has argued, they are portrayed as tricksters who are able to defeat the enemies because they are smart and resourceful and, of course, God is on their side. Ehud is a good example of an underdog who defeats a more powerful enemy through trickery. He is a crafty, left-handed Benjaminite who fools and kills the much heavier Eglon with his "secret word" (3:19) and a sword "hidden" under his garment (3:21). Ehud defeats the Moabite soldiers who are described as "well fed and strong" (3:29), perhaps highlighting the imbalance between the Israelites and their oppressors. Shamgar uses whatever tool that was available, an ox goad in his case, to defeat six hundred Philistines (3:31), demonstrating his resourcefulness. Israel becomes very "weak" because of the Midianites (6:6). Even though Gideon is called "a mighty warrior" (גבור החיל, 6:12), he sees his clan as "the weakest") in Manasseh (6:15). Yet Yahweh downsizes Gideon's army from 32,000 to 300 soldiers (7:3–6). But this is not a problem for Israel. Gideon uses empty pots, trumpets, and torches to defeat the superior army of Midian. Jephthah is also called "a mighty warrior" (גבור החיל, 11:1), but he leads a band of "worthless men" (אנשים ריקים, 11:3). He is pressed into service when no one would take the lead against the Ammonites (10:17–18). He defeats the Ammonites rather easily because the spirit of Yahweh comes upon him (11:29) and gives the Ammonites into his hand (11:32). Yahweh's spirit also rushes upon Samson and he grabs a jawbone to defeat the Philistines (15:14–15). Such representations of Israel's heroes may reflect the Israelites' underdog or marginal status in imperial/colonial contexts where they have to rely on their cunning and God for their corporate survival.

There is an assumption in Judges, especially in the Epilogue, that the Israelites are morally superior to the others. The Levite bypasses Jebus because he was wary of "a city of foreigners, who do not belong to the people of Israel" (19:12). Instead, he chooses to spend the night in Gibeah, which belongs to Benjamin (19:14–15). The Levite and the Israelite readers expect more from their fellow Israelites. When the Levite's concubine is raped and eventually killed, he asks, "Has such a thing ever happened in Israel?" (19:30). This rhetorical question implies that such a "disgraceful folly" (נבלה, 20:6) does not happen in Israel because the Israelites are better than the others. But there is a mixed message on this matter. The Benjaminites in Gibeah betray the trust of a fellow Israelite (19:22–30) when the Levite placed his faith in them rather than in the foreigners. But it is the men of Gibeah who committed the "disgraceful folly" (נבלה, 19:23–24), behaving like foreigners. Then the Levite's behavior toward his concubine sends a shiver down the readers' spine. The Israelites act like the way the foreigners are alleged to behave. This is a startling admission of their moral failings and shows that they do not deserve the land more than the others, which undermines their anticonquest ideology.

To complicate the matter more, there are those who do not belong to Israel but act on behalf of the Israelites, blurring the border that distinguishes the Israelites and the others. There is the unnamed man of Luz who assisted the house of Joseph to conquer his own city (1:22–26; cf. Rahab's cooperation with the spies in Joshua 2). Is he Israel's enemy even though he helped Israel accomplish their mission? There is a Midianite soldier who interprets his dream in favor of Israel (7:13–14). Is he an enemy of Israel even though he prophesied Israel's victory? Shamgar son of Anath may have been a non-Israelite judge who delivered Israel from the Philistines (3:31). Jael is a wife of Heber the Kenite, who has a peace agreement with King Jabin of Hazor who is at war with Israel (4:17), and delivers the victory to the Israelites by killing Sisera, the captain of King Jabin. Where does she belong?

Moreover, Jephthah's speech tries to show that Israel is a peace-loving and fair-minded people who prefer diplomacy over military solutions. But this is the only time in Judges that a negotiation is used to diffuse a conflict with Israel's enemies (Assis 2005, 199). In fact the Israelites are not a peaceful people by any means.[11] In the core section of Judges, the Israelites

---

11. According to Mieke Bal (1988a), Judges is a book about violence and, more specifically, violence against women.

are oppressed by enemies all around and the narrative seems to suggest that if only enemies are destroyed, then Israel will be faithful to Yahweh and live happily ever after in God's promised land. Of course, this does not happen and the enemies may be the least of their problems. The Israelites spend more time and spill more blood fighting each other than their enemies. The Ephraimites were angry with Gideon and strongly contended with him (8:1). Gideon was able to diffuse the situation by flattering them, but Jephthah was undiplomatic when the Ephraimites confronted him in the same manner, killing 42,000 Ephraimites (12:1–6). Abimelech and the Shechemites form an alliance to overthrow the house of Gideon but then fight each other, resulting in many casualties (ch. 9). In the Epilogue the enemies do not make their appearance at all. Nevertheless, the Israelites are engulfed in violence and immorality. It is the people of Laish who are a peaceful people and the Danites behave like thugs. There is an all-out war between the Benjaminites and the rest of the Israelites in chapters 20–21, eventually killing the entire tribe of Benjamin save six hundred men.

In the end the Israelites need the enemies in order to sustain their identity as a people different from them. If they do get rid of their enemies, their ideology of "difference" would collapse.[12] How are the Israelites different from the others? Judges struggles to answer this question. Even though Judges continues to see the identity of Israel as a people set apart from the others, as a chosen or holy people who are called to follow Yahweh exclusively, the difference (therefore identity) between Israel and the others is not very apparent. The Israelites repeatedly go after the other gods and love the foreign women. Like Samson, Israel cannot seem to live without the women of whom Yahweh does not approve. Samson's parents plead with Samson, "Is there not a woman among the women of your brothers and among all my people that you insist to go to take a woman from the Philistines, the uncircumcised?" (14:3). These words echo Yahweh's frustration with the Israelites. The text simply acknowledges Israel's multiple failures in this matter. Israel is guilty as charged. They are no different from the others; they behave like their enemies they proclaim to

---

12. This observation is based on Roland Boer (2009), who examines the narrative that stretches from Genesis to Joshua as a political myth that constructs "rebels" (enemies in Judges) in order to imagine a state that can be set up if it wasn't for those pesky oppositions. The opposing forces (enemies in Judges), however, are part of a political myth even as it tries to eliminate them in order to fulfill its promise of what the world could be. But when those hindrances are removed, the myth also collapses as well.

loathe. Representations of the Israelites in Judges undermine their claim that the Israelites deserve the land more than the others because they are morally and religiously superior.

2.4. Gendering/Feminizing the Other

The anticonquest ideology employs female gender to represent the land and its people in order to show that they need to be dominated. Like the land that lays passive, waiting to be occupied, woman represents the Other who desires Israel and needs to be subjugated. The fact that the word for "city" in Hebrew is feminine and the term for "towns" is the Hebrew word "daughters" (בנות) facilitates the connection between the land (city/town) and woman. This is apparent when Caleb promises anyone who captures "it/her" (feminine demonstrative referring to the city of Qiryat-Sepher) that he will give him Achsah his daughter as wife (1:12). Yahweh gives a "daughter" to Israel as his city just as Caleb gives Achsah to Othniel as his wife (1:13).

The narrative asserts that the Israelites belong to one biological family. The Israelites are "the sons of Israel" (בני ישראל); they call their fellow Israelites "brothers" (אחים) and their ancestors "fathers" (אבות). The view is that the Israelites are united by blood relations, oddly connected through male bonds (that is, patrilineal kinship), and, therefore, Israel's identity is "natural."[13] Personal names include the formula *ben* X (son of X). A soldier is designated as איש ("man") or גובר ("warrior"). Yahweh is the "God of their fathers." Yahweh is a male god and Israel is his son. Such abundance of male terms to refer to the Israelites in general is used to draw one clear boundary that the narrative is desperate to maintain throughout the book of Judges, namely, the Israelites are not to marry the foreign women. The book of Judges sees non-Israelite women as a threat to the identity (or purity) of the sons of Israel. More specifically, the narrative warns that when the sons of Israel go after women outside of Israel, it inevitably leads to worshiping other gods. Israel's identity is tied to both sexual and divine

---

13. Regina M. Schwartz argues that kinship through blood relations is a social construct rather than a biological reality. She states, "After long and tortuous debates about the significance and forms of kinship systems, anthropologists are now telling us that there is virtually no such thing as kinship. There are *ideologies* of blood relations, *constructs* of brothers and sisters, but comparative cultural studies have shown us how diversely such notions are understood. There are no real blood relations" (1997, 78).

fidelity. They are repeatedly warned not to fornicate after other gods and marry women outside of Israel. But the sons of Israel take the daughters of the others and they give their daughters to the sons of the others and serve their gods (3:6).

Judges ends with two brutal stories of the Israelite men subjugating their women in order to give identity to the land and themselves. The Levite in ch. 19 sends the dismembered body of his concubine "throughout all the territory of Israel" (19:29), inscribing the land as one unified entity belonging to Israel as a whole. Then the text demarcates the territory of Israel, "From Dan to Beer-sheba, including the land of Gilead" (20:1). In the process of giving his version of why he dismembered his concubine's body, the Levite unifies the land once more with his words, "the entire land of the inheritance [נחלה] of Israel" (20:6). Then the Israelite men take by force four hundred women from Jabesh-Gilead and two hundred women from Shiloh to restock the Benjamin tribe (21:8–24). This was done in order for the Israelites to remain faithful to God (for they swore not to give their daughters to the Benjaminites) and to maintain the purity of the men of Benjamin (by not marrying women outside of Israel). This ending demonstrates the role of Israelite women in the identity of their men as well. They represent a way for the Israelite men to remain pure and be faithful to God. As Musa Dube observes, "Because the Israelite women belong to a jealous God, they can keep intact the identity of the nation as a chosen and treasured people of God over the rest of the earth. Thus, the women of the colonizer embody the status of colonizing men" (2000, 76).

Israel's identity is tied to maleness and the foreign women are a threat to this connection. The strongman Samson twice surrendered his secrets to the foreign women. In 14:15–17 Samson's wife nags him to tell the answer to his riddle and Delilah uses the same strategy to discover Samson's secret in ch. 16. It was the foreign women who neutralized his strength (manliness), something the foreign men couldn't do. He used to "ravage" the Philistines (16:24), but he "plays" for them (16:25–26) in the end. Such a reversal of gender role undermines the relationship between Israel and the Other. But it is not only the other women who unravel the Israelites' identity by humiliating their manhood. Women in general are a danger to Israel's identity and fidelity to Yahweh. Any woman can neuter Israel's maleness. Abimelech was humiliated when he was killed by an Israelite woman (9:53–54). Jephthah lamented that his daughter caused him to "bow down" (11:35) and sacrificed his daughter in order to keep his fidelity to God (11:34–40). The Levite pushed his concubine to the men of

Gibeah to save himself from being forced to perform as a woman. Then he told other Israelites that they intended to kill him (20:5) because he wanted to protect his manhood, that is, his identity as a son of Israel.

In the end, both Israelite and foreign women are sacrificed for the sake of the identity of the Israelite men. Women are victims of a competition among men in their game to determine who gets to rule over the land and its women. Therefore, imperialism cannot be separated from patriarchy, as Dube has observed. Judges does not protect the women of Israel. Instead, it sacrifices (Jephthah's daughter), kills (the concubine), and rapes (the women of Shiloh) Israel's daughters just as it does the foreign women in order to protect the identity of the sons of Israel.

3. Conclusion

There is clear evidence in Judges that the Israelites used some elements of anticonquest ideology to justify their travel to, conquest, and occupation of a foreign land. But the narrative also reflects some anxiety over using imperial ideologies since they themselves were victims of empires. The text overstresses the role of God in Israel's possession of a land that once belonged to the others. Even though Judges follows a common imperial logic of representing the others as incompetent and sinful, they are depicted as formidable oppressors and the Israelites as tricksters. This scheme reverses the imperial dichotomy of depicting "us" as strong and the others as weak. When Judges describes the Israelites, there are some ambiguities as to whether they are in fact morally and religiously superior to the others. They are as violent and immoral as the inhabitants they are supposed to displace. They are unfaithful to Yahweh by desiring the foreign women and going after their gods. The treatment and depiction of women reveals the inherent connection between imperialism and patriarchy. It is only by subjugating women, either Israelite or foreign, that the sons of Israel can recover their manhood (therefore their identity), which is lost when they are dominated by the other men of empires.

In the end some will see in Judges an imperializing text and others will hear a liberatory message. It can function as a warning against its oppressive ways or a call for empowering the oppressed. It is a double-edged sword that can cut either way. It uses imperial ideologies to resist the empire. However, to mimic the ways of empires for corporate survival is an ambivalent strategy. We should be careful not to swing too hard in either direction. We do not know who will fall by the s/word.

References

Assis, Elie. 2005. *Self-Interest or Communal Interest: An Ideology of Leadership in the Gideon, Abimelech and Jephthah Narratives (Judg 6–12)*. VTSup 109. Leiden: Brill.
Bal, Mieke. 1988. *Death and Dissymmetry: The Politics of Coherence in the Book of Judges*. Chicago: University of Chicago Press.
Bauer, Uwe F. W. 2000. Judges 18 as an Anti-Spy Story in the Context of an Anti-Conquest Story: The Creative Usage of Literary Genres. *JSOT* 88:37–47.
Boer, Roland. 2009. *Political Myth: On the Use and Abuse of Biblical Themes*. Durham, N.C.: Duke University Press.
Brett, Marc C. 2008. *Decolonizing God: The Bible in the Tides of Empire*. BMW 16. Sheffield: Sheffield Phoenix Press.
Dube, Musa W. 2000. *Postcolonial Feminist Interpretation of the Bible*. St. Louis: Chalice.
Guillaume, Philippe. 2004. *Waiting for Josiah: The Judges*. JSOTSup 385. London: T&T Clark.
Kim, Uriah Y. 2005. *Decolonizing Josiah: Toward a Postcolonial Reading of the Deuteronomistic History*. BMW 5. Sheffield: Sheffield Phoenix Press.
Lemos, T. M. 2006. Shame and Mutilation of Enemies in the Hebrew Bible. *JBL* 125:225–41.
McCann, J. Clinton. 2002. *Judges*. Interpretation. Louisville: John Knox.
Niditch, Susan. 2008. *Judges: A Commentary*. OTL. Louisville: John Knox.
Polzin, Robert. 1980. *Moses and the Deuteronomist: A Literary Study of the Deuteronomistic History*. New York: Seabury.
Pratt, Mary Louis. 1992. *Imperial Eyes: Travel Writing and Transculturation*. New York: Routledge.
Rogers, J. W. 1993. The Enemy in the Old Testament. Pages 284–93 in *Understanding Poets and Prophets: Essays in Honour of George Wishart Anderson*. Edited by A. Graeme Auld. JSOTSup 152. Sheffield: Sheffield Academic Press.
Römer, Thomas. 2005. *The So-Called Deuteronomistic History: A Sociological, Historical and Literary Introduction*. London: T&T Clark.
Ryan, Roger. 2007. *Judges*. Readings. Sheffield: Sheffield Phoenix Press.
Schwartz, Regina M. 1997. *The Curse of Cain: The Violent Legacy of Monotheism*. Chicago: University of Chicago Press.

The "Enemy Within": Refracting Colonizing Rhetoric in Narratives of Gibeonite and Japanese Identity

Johnny Miles

"What? The enemy lives among us?"
"Worse. The enemy resides within."

The first sight of the barbed wire enclosure with armed soldiers standing guard as our bus slowly turned in through the gate stunned us with the reality of this ordered evacuation. (Estelle Ishigo 1972, 6)

I hereby authorize and direct the Secretary of War, and the Military Commanders whom he may from time to time designate ... to prescribe military areas ... from which any or all persons may be excluded, and with respect to which, the right of any person to enter, remain in, or leave shall be subject to whatever restriction the Secretary of War or the appropriate Military Commander may impose in his discretion. The Secretary of War is hereby authorized to provide for residents of any such area who are excluded therefrom, such transportation, food, shelter, and other accommodations as may be necessary. (Executive Order 9066)

In a December 8, 1941, speech to the US Congress, President Franklin D. Roosevelt declared the Japanese bombing of Pearl Harbor on December 7, 1941 as "a date which will live in infamy." February 19, 1942, the date that President Roosevelt signed Executive Order 9066 (EO 9066) into effect, an act so few US citizens know about, is *the* date that *should* live in infamy. EO 9066 sanctioned the incarceration of more than 120,000 Japanese (two-thirds of whom were American citizens), an act that would have lasting effects, some subtle and silent, some not so, decades beyond the swirling politics of prejudice in 1942. For example, Helen Zia (2000, 24) recounts the following incident involving US Congressman Norman Mineta of

Hawai'i in 1984. Mineta, a second-generation Japanese American (*Nisei*) internee at Heart Mountain, Wyoming, who would later serve ten terms in the US House of Representatives, was invited to be the guest speaker at an automobile plant opening near San Jose, California in his district. After the ceremony, a senior vice president of General Motors and general manager of Chevrolet said to Congressman Mineta, "My, you speak English well. How long have you been in this country?"

The same subtle violence of a politics of prejudice manifests itself in a dark, forgotten part of Israelite history and Israelite relations with the further forgettable Gibeonites (so forgettable, in fact, that most people who have read the Bible know nothing about the Gibeonites). The rhetoric in the Gibeonite narrative of Josh 9 clearly circumscribes a social space for the alien Gibeonites within Israel, in part by linguistic deception that justified their colonization. Sociological insights from ethnic group processes will reveal the circumscribing effects of this rhetoric beyond simply establishing ethnic boundary markers to reinforcing an ever so subtle violent representation as ethnic identity. Only with the Japanese American experience does the politics of prejudice never remain silent with the overt, atrocious violence of their internment. Granted, there were no gas chambers or ovens that took lives, but lives were nonetheless unmistakably taken, and with them human rights and dignity. In an effort to refract the deceptive rhetoric of colonization, this essay traces those sociological factors in the identity construction of early twentieth-century Japanese Americans and their efforts at resistance in order to articulate the voiceless experience of the Gibeonites—a voice denied, an opportunity for resistance withheld, an identity not "other."

1. The Policy of Truth

"Jap Go Home!" "Goddamn Jap!" "Yellow Jap!" "Dirty Jap!" "Japs Go Away!" "Yellow Bastards!" "Yellow Monkeys." "Japs We Do not Want You." "No More Japs Wanted Here." "Keep California White!" These racial slurs and other ugly graffiti spewing anti-Japanese sentiments plastered across storefront windows and signs, sidewalks, railroad stations, and public restrooms heartily extended the American "Welcome!" to Japanese immigrants who would struggle with a restrictive social space. We can only imagine the kind of Israelite welcome extended to the Gibeonites. Although not warmly received by the general American public, Japanese immigrants were a welcome sight for the railroad and agricultural industries of the US mainland and the plantations of Hawai'i if only for the labor their bodies would provide. Even there, they could not escape the ethnic antagonism and racial prejudices that would ultimately come to a head in their confinement, *the* icon of their internal colonization. This section exposes the prejudicial politics contributing to, and the justifying rhetoric regarding, the Gibeonites' internal colonization juxtaposed with that of Japanese Americans.

1.1. INTERNAL COLONIZATION—PREJUDICIAL POLITICS

> After they had made a treaty with them, they heard that they were their neighbors and were living among them. (Josh 9:16)

Unlike the Chinese, the Japanese did not immigrate until after Commodore Matthew C. Perry's 1853 intrusion into Japan, which had successfully isolated itself from the West up to that point. When they did migrate, they did so in significant numbers, first to Hawai'i in the 1880s, and finally to the US mainland in the next decade. From 1891 to 1900 Japanese immigration increased to 24,326, with a population reaching 72,157 in the US by 1910. By 1924, 200,000 Japanese had arrived in Hawai'i and 180,000 to the mainland.[1] The majority of these immigrants early on, according to the 1910 US Census, were well-educated young men (40–60 percent in their 20s) with only 9.2 percent of those aged 10 years and older being illiterate in comparison to the 12.7 percent of their European counterparts.

---

1. Reasons sparking this immigration explosion vary, but two are prominent. First, farmers all over Japan encountered economic hardships. Farmers in the northern prefectures moved north to the island of Hokkaido for opportunities. And those in the southwestern prefectures had limited land per household resulting in a meager subsistence. Second, the contract-labor period (1885–1894) especially targeted Japanese farmers in the southwestern prefectures with opportunities for success. Beginning in 1884, the Japanese government allowed Hawaiian planters to recruit contract laborers, an initiative with a precedent set by the Hawaiian consul general in Japan who, in 1868, secretly recruited and transported 148 Japanese contract laborers to Hawai'i. The wage advantage enticing the Japanese to migrate was obvious. Higher wages and a favorable dollar–yen exchange meant that a Hawaiian plantation laborer could earn six times the daily wage than a laborer in Japan. The Immigration Act of 1924 stemmed the influx of Japanese immigrants by denying admittance to aliens ineligible for citizenship. The drop in population, however, would not be evidenced until between 1930 (138,834) and 1940 (126,947). See further population data in tables of Daniels (1981, 6, 21).

Mainland Japanese experienced an impersonal labor structure unlike that in Hawai'i. Labor conditions coupled with an intense racial discrimination contributed to the Issei ("first generation") ethnic economy and ethnic solidarity. After having left the railroads and mines, the Japanese increasingly entered the agricultural sector as farm laborers only to experience segregation within the labor market, itself a kind of boundary mechanism. Such boundary mechanisms, according to sociologists Stephen Cornell and Douglas Hartmann, function to establish social space, just one of many construction sites for defining ethnic identity (Cornell and Hartmann 2007, 182–85). Two factors are key to this particular function of establishing social space—boundedness and exhaustiveness—while simultaneously contributing to and reinforcing an ethnic or racial boundary,[2] including that of "self" (Spencer 2006, 176). Boundedness refers to "the extent to which the positions in the labor or residential markets available to group members are available only to them and not to nonmembers." A high degree of boundedness means an inordinate concentration of group members to the practical nonexistence of non-group members (e.g. diamond-selling Jews in New York City). Exhaustiveness refers to "the extent to which a particular position is the only opportunity available to group members" (Cornell and Hartmann 2007, 184–85). When considering the Japanese experience, we find that the large concentration of Japanese within the agricultural sector to their noticeable exclusion in other sectors of the labor market indicates high-boundedness and exhaustiveness factors. Though bound, the Issei did not want to remain field laborers. They had aspirations of becoming farmers, only natural since many were farmers in Japan.[3] Agriculture became central to the Japanese ethnic economy.[4]

---

2. Factors such as jobs, discrimination, pricing, and personal choice definitely play into residential space and ultimately the construction and reinforcement of ethnic identity. Migrants to a particular place tend to concentrate in one area, for example, the nineteenth-century Chinese of America residing in ghettos called "Chinatowns," generally because of limited opportunities available to them within the larger society.

3. In an effort to obtain land to farm, the Japanese utilized four systems: contract, share, lease, and ownership. By 1910, they owned or leased a total of 194,742 acres in California alone with that amount increasing to 458,056 a decade later (Takaki 1998, 188–89).

4. Most fruit and vegetable farmers were Japanese, producing 70 percent of California's strawberries in 1910, 95 percent of its fresh snap beans, 95 percent of its celery, 67 percent of its tomatoes, and 44 percent of its onions in 1940. Japanese production held a virtual monopoly in California by 1940 with its crops of snap beans, celery, pep-

High-boundedness and exhaustiveness factors extended to the residential sector, too, with Japanese being denied other potential residential areas and segregated into isolated ghettos dubbed "Little Tokyos" (see fig. 1). Many realtors discriminated against the Japanese, turning them away for fear that property values would decline. Japanese immigrants faced other forms of social discrimination—for example, being spat upon, segregated at schools and theaters, and turned away by white barbershop proprietors who did not "cut animal's hair." As a result, hotels, boarding houses, restaurants, shops, stores, and pool halls quickly sprung up in "Little Tokyos." These businesses catered to immigrants' needs while avoiding the direct racial discrimination of white-owned businesses. Despite the residential and economic containment of Japanese social space, prejudice nonetheless continued to target the Japanese. Businesses were vandalized with storefront windows being smashed and sidewalks smeared with horse manure.

Anti-Japanese polemics accompanied Japanese movement up the economic ladder (from laborers to landowners to entrepreneurs). Ronald Takaki notes, "white workers resented not only Japanese competition but

Figure 1. Homeowner Pointing to Anti-Japanese Sign © Bettmann/CORBIS.

pers, and strawberries, and half of the state's cauliflower, spinach, tomato, and garlic crops. Japanese farmers were generally small operators selling their crops to local markets in cities like Los Angeles, Sacramento, Fresno, and San Francisco. For example, the Japanese owned 120 of 180 of the produce stalls at the Los Angeles City Market in 1909 (Iiyama 1973, 26; Takaki 1998, 180–97).

their very presence in America" (1998, 198). In addition, the politics of prejudice exploited "yellow peril" fears, especially after Japanese success in the Russo-Japanese War (1904–1905), the first time in the modern era that a white nation had lost to a colored nation in war. Originally associated with the Chinese, "yellow peril" was widespread by 1905 among the American public to indicate an imminent invasion by the Japanese.[5] Several sources in particular fomented Japanese animus seeking their exclusion in California: California State Senator James Phelan, newspaper publisher William Randolph Hearst, and independent publisher V. S. McClatchy. First, California Senator Phelan wrote in a letter to the Chicago *Tribune* that California "would be an easy prey in case of attack," and that Japanese immigrants in California were an "enemy within our gates" (quoted in Daniels 1977, 70). He remained convinced of Japanese intentions to possess the West Coast, hence the necessity of their exclusion. "A Jap was a Jap," Phelan believed, with the natives being no less a threat than the immigrants. That position did not change when he sought re-election as a US Senator in 1919–1920 with his campaign slogan "Keep California White." Second, newspaper publisher William Randolph Hearst launched a thirty-five-year war against Japan in 1906 with headlines such as "JAPAN SOUNDS OUR COASTS: Brown Men Have Maps and Could Land Easily" and "JAPAN MAY SEIZE THE PACIFIC SLOPE." The January 1907 San Francisco *Examiner* also made the uncorroborated claim that Japanese immigrants were actually soldiers in disguise conducting midnight military maneuvers and stockpiling food in preparation for armed conflict. Third, independent publisher V. S. McClatchy claimed Japan to be the "Germany of Asia" who had come to America for the sole purpose of colonizing (US Congress 1924, 5–6):

> The Japanese are less assimilable and more dangerous as residents in this country than any other of the peoples ineligible under our laws.... With great pride of race, they have no idea of assimilating in the sense of amalgamation. They do not come here with any desire or any intent to lose

---

5. After the 1882 Exclusion Act put to rest the Chinese question, "the Chinese stereotype became the Japanese stereotype" (tenBroek, Barnhart, and Matson 1954, 22). The Japanese stereotype simply morphed from that of the "heathen Chinee" with exclusionary tactics directed against the Chinese eventually being directed against the Japanese. See the thorough treatment of the "yellow peril" stereotype in Okihiro (1994, 118–47).

their racial or national identity. They come here specifically and professedly for the purpose of colonizing...

McClatchy became extremely instrumental in rallying anti-Japanese pressure groups around the cause of Japanese exclusion in the 1920s. Some anti-Japanese groups in Los Angeles initiated a "Swat the Jap" campaign with leaflets to make Japanese lives there miserable.

> JAPS
> You came to care for lawns,
>   we stood for it
> You came to work in truck gardens,
>   we stood for it
> You sent your children to our public schools,
>   we stood for it
> You moved a few families in our midst,
>   we stood for it
> You proposed to build a church in our neighborhood,
>   BUT
> We DIDN'T and WE WON'T STAND FOR IT
> You impose more on us each day
>   until you have gone your limit
> WE DON'T WANT YOU WITH US
> SO GET BUSY, JAPS, AND
> GET OUT OF HOLLYWOOD. (quoted in Daniels 1977, 97)

McClatchy disapproved of the palpable vitriol within this "Swat the Jap" campaign leaflet viewing it as harmful to the exclusionist cause. Nonetheless, racial prejudice and "yellow peril" mutually influenced each other in pre-1924 anti-Japanese propaganda, betraying anxiety over colonization. But who really sought to colonize whom?

The answer to this question certainly does not remain in doubt with regard to interactions between Israelites and Gibeonites (Josh 9). Ethnic prejudices are indisputable so much so that the narrator makes the ethnic identity of Gibeonites as Hivites a point,[6] not once but twice (vv. 1, 7).

---

6. The biblical text associates the Gibeonites with both Hivites (Josh 9:7; 11:19) and Amorites (Josh 10:5), both groups doomed to extinction. Ascertaining the ethnic origins of the Gibeonites remains a speculative matter with no definitive conclusion in sight, but see the monograph of Blenkinsopp (1972), the essay by Day (2007), and discussions in Mitchell (1993, 175–76).

Why? Perhaps to distance the narrative character of the Gibeonites from that of the Hivites since the Hivites and other Canaanite groups clearly have violence in mind by preparing for armed conflict against Israel, whereas Gibeon sought terms of peace. From negotiations in which Gibeon represents itself as a distant country, their knowledge of Yahweh's acts in Israel's behalf raises the question in some interpreters' minds of how much, if any, of the legislation in Deut 20:10–18 did the Gibeonites know (Mitchell 1993, 85; Hawk 1999, 84). That legislation allowed for terms of peace and covenant treaties with distant nations, not Canaanite indigenes.

Or might the repetition of Gibeonites as Hivites serve to reinforce ethnic boundaries by demarcating Gibeon as "other?" The Gibeonites know that their only choice based on Israel's ethnic prejudicial terms was death. And their only fault?—being the wrong ethnicity in the right place. "They," who are clearly not "us," are "other," and the standard punishment for Otherness was death (Rowlett 1992, 17).[7] Reinforcing the boundaries of Gibeonites as "other" is the colonizer's representation of the Gibeonites as deceitful. Deceitfulness or death? The answer seems obvious in the interest of self-preservation. But deception, along with other *everyday* forms of passive noncompliance, is a form of resistance "intended to mitigate or deny claims made by superordinate classes or to advance claims vis-à-vis those superordinate classes" (Scott 1985, 32) in the struggle over, in this case, land rights.[8] The motif of Gibeonite deception marks Gibeonite social space as Israelite, though *not quite* Israelite. The Gibeonites threaten Israelite identity, not by their stature or might, but by their *difference*. Yet in spite of their *difference*, Gibeonite assimilation within Israel marks a significant ethnic boundary crossing that blurs the lines of demarcation.[9]

---

7. Lori Rowlett (1996) perceives the function for the book of Joshua's rhetoric of violence as "to make examples of Others while controlling the lines of authority within the community." The rhetoric becomes a means of self-reconstitution where outsiders can become insiders, and insiders can become outsiders just as easily, simply by failing to submit to the rules and norms of the king (identified as Josiah).

8. The object of struggle between those in power and those relatively powerless groups may vary (e.g. extraction of labor, rents, food, taxes, and interest) as may the weapons of resistance (e.g. foot dragging, dissimulation, feigned ignorance, slander, false compliance, subtle sabotage, evasion, and so forth), but they nonetheless signal the *everyday forms of resistance* in class struggle that, when reaching a crisis point, will explode into overt acts of rebellion (Scott 1985, 27–47).

9. The connotation of ethnic boundary crossing semantically links with the geographic boundary crossing earlier in the book, where the phrase וַיְהִי מִקְצֵה שְׁלֹשֶׁת

Despite exclusivist boundaries established in Deuteronomy, this particular story (and that of Rahab) where Canaanites as "other" who transform into marginal Israelites, outsiders becoming insiders, may "argue for flexibility in the determination of Israel's boundaries" though the boundaries, Hawk (1997, 154, 162) asserts, "must nevertheless be preserved." Yet how does the inclusion of Canaanites as part of the spoil along with goods devoted to the *ban* preserve boundaries? Gibeonite assimilation into Israelite culture would have resulted in a shared culture working and living among Israelites. Their physical presence within the symbolic center of Israelite identity, the temple complex, best emblematizes this paradoxical presence of "other" within Israel. Nevertheless, the high-boundedness and exhaustiveness factors for Gibeonites within the labor sector (as "wood cutters and water drawers" for temple functions) of Israelite society fix both social boundaries and identity: ethnically as Gibeonite/Hivite, sociologically as "other." Thus social boundaries still maintain à la Hawk's assertion despite the Gibeonites crossing ethnic boundaries.

Or perhaps the twice-repeated identification of Gibeonites as Hivites ideologically serves to displace the indigenous as indigenous? In other words, literature that justifies colonization includes efforts to discredit any genealogical claims to land. This ethnographic knowledge of the "other" also involves religious identity inter alia as part of a system of containment.[10] What we see in this narrative is not the Gibeonites but an Israelite perception of Gibeonites, or representation. Nonetheless, through this constructed knowledge of the "other," Israel sees its reflection clearly. In physical presence alone, the Gibeonites mock their colonizer with worn-out clothing, patched sandals, stale bread, and old wineskins, the migrant

---

יָמִים, introducing the Jordan crossing (3:2), reiterates that and is emphasized by thrice-repeated references to Gibeonites living "in the midst of" Israel (vv. 7, 16, 22; see Hawk 2000, 144).

10. David Chidester's (1996, 11–20) observations on the relationship between religion and colonization help illumine the colonizing impulses of this narrative. In tracing the colonization history of southern Africa, Chidester observed that the European colonizer customarily constructed a religious identity of the indigenous through discourses of denial and discovery, first denying that the indigenous had a religion or that it was somehow degenerate to the discovery of a religious system after all. And this identity construction worked in concert with contestations over land entitlements. Only once Africans came under colonial subjugation did they happen to have a religious system; prior to that point, they had no religion, and lack of religion entailed lack of "any recognizable human right or entitlement to the land in which they lived."

look Israel would have had sans Yahweh's provisions (Deut 29:5–6); their reference to "elders and inhabitants" bespeaks an ethnic affinity with Israel; they approach Israel with terms of peace as Israel had done with King Sihon (Deut 2:26–31); and they resort to deception though for purposes of self-preservation not self-aggrandizement.[11] The craftiness and savvy of the Gibeonites that should characterize Israel, according to its own story, does not (Hawk 2000, 141). Thus the anger directed toward the Gibeonites may reflect what Israel lacks but admires and wishes it possessed. Israel sees something of itself within Gibeon. The enemy is no longer simply "out there" but is now within (Israel).

While maintaining boundaries, the Joshua narrative simultaneously accounts for the presence of the "other" within those boundaries, especially in a postexilic milieu where a group migrating to Yehud would particularly be concerned about establishing ethnic identity.[12] As this group began reconstituting its identity, the virulence of difference precluded a trace of the indigenes remaining in proximity to Israel (Josh 7:1–26; cf. 8:19–20; 12:29–32), much less their entitlement to political control over the land and its resources. Regardless of the presence of outsiders, whether as pagans or illegal aliens, cementing social relations and forming a state identity necessitated the creation of "others." Ethnic border crossings and encounters with those of different ethnic backgrounds are experiences central to identity formation (Spencer 2006, 13–21). Despite the difference of *otherness*, Israel finds a reflection of its own image such

---

11. The narrative of Josh 9 assumes a comedic turn with Israel being duped by an unlikely tale followed by the irony of a people assured the fruit of the land sharing a meal of moldy bread instead. The Gibeonites single-minded purpose of making a covenant does not seem in doubt—the repetition of כרת־ברית (9:6, 7, 11, 15, 16), the repetition of עבד (9:8, 9, 11, 23, 24; 10:6), the ritual of a covenant meal, the reference to "shalom" (9:15), the oath sworn by Israel (9:15, 18–19, 20), the threat of divine wrath on those who break the covenant (9:20), and that the famine in 2 Sam 21:1–14 is understood as a covenant curse, altogether indicate a covenant. That representatives of a far-away nation should deem it necessary to travel such a great distance to negotiate a covenant with a rag-tag group of Hebrew ex-slaves, however, does seem to boggle the mind if not amuse because Israel cannot see through this ruse (see Mitchell 1993, 170–71).

12. The expression "to this day" (9:27), which appears quite frequently in the larger corpus of Joshua–2 Kings, suggests a postexilic era since that best fits the existence of a fully functioning temple system with Gibeonites present. See further details in section 2.1 of this essay.

that, up-close, *difference* really is not all that different. Ideological analysis exposes the chink in the textual armor donned by Israelite exclusivists in their anti-Canaanite propaganda with texts like this that emphasize the distinct message to the indigenes that the only way to save yourself is to be a traitor and a trickster, but you will "ultimately be found out, lose your land, and end up slaves" (Bailey 2005, 20). The designated status of Gibeonites and Japanese alike delimiting their social space simultaneously reinforced group boundaries and identity. For the Japanese, it was the agricultural sector; for the Gibeonites, it was the temple sector. When both boundedness and exhaustiveness factors are high, the residential boundary essentially coincides with the group boundary, thus reinforcing it. Colonizing the Gibeonites as a slave class by high boundedness and exhaustiveness within both labor and residential sectors of the larger Israelite community would certainly have disrupted their ethnic economy and solidarity as a result of their assimilation.

Legislative discrimination influenced by anti-Japanese prejudices posed the greatest threat and challenge to Issei ethnic economy and solidarity. The most notable was California's Alien Land Law in 1913. While not specifically referring to Japanese, the law basically targeted them by prohibiting "aliens ineligible to citizenship" from owning land. Similar land laws "were also enacted in Washington, Arizona, Oregon, Idaho, Nebraska, Texas, Kansas, Louisiana, Montana, New Mexico, Minnesota, and Missouri" (Takaki 1998, 206–7). Nevertheless, Japanese farmers found loopholes within such racially driven legislation either by leasing or owning land under the names of their American-born children, entering into unwritten arrangements with their white landlords, or borrowing the names of American citizens.

These restrictive land laws hinged on the ineligibility of the Japanese to naturalized citizenship. Although the 1790 Naturalization Law granted naturalized citizenship to "whites" and the 1882 Exclusion Act denied this privilege to Chinese immigrants, the laws did not specifically exclude the Japanese. Yet, the remarks of President Theodore Roosevelt that "American civilization" should be "filled" with a "white population," "a heritage for the white people," clearly reflected popular opinion on just who could be eligible for American citizenship and was later defined by the 1922 US Supreme Court *Ozawa* case. The court ruled that Takao Ozawa, who graduated high school in Berkeley, California, attended the University of California for three years, and worked for an American company in Honolulu, was ineligible for naturalized citizenship because "he was 'clearly' 'not

Caucasian.'" The decision shattered Issei dreams with some despairing of an inevitable deportation. Doomed to be strangers forever in America, their adopted country, the Issei placed their only one hope left for their future in their children—the Nisei.

Being born as Americans and educated in American schools would provide the Nisei with opportunities for success denied the Issei, or so the Issei thought. Issei stressed the importance of education and the need to excel, and they sacrificed comforts and necessities to ensure that goal. Nisei education would enable them to rise above the obstacles of discrimination as well as serve as a cultural bridge between the Issei and the larger American society. Issei farmer S. Nitta put it this way: "I think it is very good idea for Orientals and Occidentals to meet and exchange the good customs in each" (as quoted in Takaki 1998, 213). The Nisei became a model minority group with a low level of crime and strong upward mobility. They were diligent, ambitious, and determined to excel, and many did, graduating from high school with good grades, honors, and completing college—the average two years of college for the Nisei was well above the national average—only to face employment discrimination because of their race (of 161 Nisei 1925–1935 alumni from the University of California, 25 percent had professional vocations, 25 percent worked in family businesses/trades, and 40 percent had "blind alley" jobs; Takaki 1998, 218). As American citizens, however, the Nisei could work to effect change in ways their parents could not by voting and exercising power within the body politic to protect their rights. Various organizations began emerging (e.g., Japanese-American Democratic and Republican Clubs and American Loyalty Leagues)[13] to promote legislation to eliminate discrimination laws and to guarantee equal rights in employment, housing, and civil liberties all the while affirming their loyalty to America. Nevertheless, the Nisei could not escape the vicious social cycle of claims to their unassimilability amidst a politics of prejudice disallowing their assimilation. Nor could they avoid the high-boundedness factors that circumscribed their

---

13. As an outgrowth of the American Loyalty League, the Japanese American Citizens League (JACL), perhaps the most influential of all Japanese civil rights organizations prior to World War II, initially questioned the identity of "Japanese" in its very name. They kept the name "Japanese" but only as an adjective to modify "American." The JACL insisted that the Nisei demonstrate their American patriotism, and many did having renounced their Japanese citizenship with a conscious choice to be American citizens.

Figure 2. Japanese American storefront, Oakland, California. Courtesy of The Bancroft Library, University of California, Berkeley.

social space as American, though *not quite* American in spite of their affirmations (see fig. 2).

The Nisei struggle with identity would not easily be resolved because they embodied a culturally hybrid identity. They were both "Occident" and "Orient." They had cultivated an American cultural outlook speaking fluent English, adopting American slang, dress, and mannerisms, changing their names, and reading the *Saturday Evening Post* and *American Magazine*. And yet, theirs was a dual identity: Japanese New Year's Day and Christmas; Japanese love songs sung by their mothers and popular songs heard on the radio; banzai to the emperor's health and the pledge of allegiance to the flag of the United States. One Nisei described this odd mixture of the Occident and the Orient as follows:

> I sat down to American breakfasts and Japanese lunches. My palate developed a fondness for rice along with corned beef and cabbage. I became

equally adept with knife and fork and with chopsticks. I said grace at mealtimes in Japanese, and recited the Lord's prayer at night in English. I hung my stocking over the fireplace at Christmas, and toasted *mochi* at Japanese New Year.... I was spoken to by both parents in Japanese or in English. I answered in whichever was convenient or in a curious mixture of both. (quoted in Takaki 1998, 224–25)

Within the Nisei resided the "streams of two great civilizations." As Oriental they never desired to become completely and simply "American," while the racial prejudice of the Occident would never let them forget that they would forever remain Japanese. Anti-Japanese sentiments did not always remain vociferous, though after December 7, 1941, actions toward the Japanese by the US government would certainly bear out the undeniable truth of deep-seated Anglo prejudice and, ironically, the enemy "within."

1.2. INTERNAL COLONIZATION—DOMESTIC POLICY

Then all the congregation murmured against the leaders. (Josh 9:18)

Just who was responsible for the treatment of Japanese American citizens and their eventual internment? US historians continue to debate the question with no consensus in sight. Obviously, the Roosevelt administration, regardless of whether blame rests with the military, politicians, or the president, was ultimately responsible for implementing a domestic policy that officially incarcerated Japanese Americans. But the internal colonization of Japanese Americans had been well underway and for that, all Americans were to blame. EO 9066 simply manifested a pervasive politics of prejudice in US society that contributed to a confluence of factors driving the emergence of that order. We cannot dismiss those factors often cited— regional pressure, the military, and the president—though we will focus on the prejudicial politics prevalent within US intelligentsia.

In 1954 Jacobus tenBroek, Edward N. Barnhart, and Floyd Matson's *Prejudice, War, and the Constitution* first proposed military culpability, and this specifically in response to that of regional pressure espoused in Morton Grodzins's *Americans Betrayed* (1949).[14] Central to the military

---

14. The Japanese American Evacuation and Resettlement Study (JERS), comprised of social scientists, spawned both works by Grodzins and tenBroek. Grodzins

theory stands the figure of Lieutenant General John DeWitt, commander of the Western Defense Command, whose prejudice regarded Japanese presence in the US as an imminent threat, thus prompting the proposal of internment rationalized by colonization rhetoric like "military necessity." *Prejudice, War, and the Constitution*, however, took the claim of "military necessity" to task arguing instead the "yellow peril" redivivus. By the 1920s the Japanese stereotype had matured and, by the 1930s, with Japanese aggressions in Asia (specifically toward China) and the Great Depression within the US, had crystallized public perceptions of the Japanese as treacherous and disloyal. Oft-repeated fears of the "yellow peril" and rumors of espionage and sabotage firmly ensconced white suspicion and distrust along the West Coast by 1941.

General De Witt made his position on the Japanese clear at a January 4 conference:

> We are at war and this area—eight states—has been designated as a theater of operations.... I have little confidence that the enemy aliens are law-abiding or loyal in any sense of the word. Some of them yes; many, no. Particularly, the Japanese. I have no confidence in their loyalty whatsoever. I am speaking now of the native born Japanese—117,000—and 42,000 in California alone. (quoted in Daniels 1981, 45–46)

He was confident of a conspiracy afoot commenting to then Major Karl Bendetsen, "we know that they are communicating at sea" (though no such evidence existed) and insisting "the fact that we have had [not even] sporadic attempts at sabotage clearly means that control is being exercised somewhere" (though there was no real evidence of subversion or acts of sabotage; Daniels 1981, 49). Even after Japanese internment, his suspicion of Japanese loyalty remained resolute as he stated before a congressional committee in 1943, "A Jap's a Jap. You can't change him by giving him a piece of paper" (quoted in Dower 1993, 81).[15] Four days after De Witt's

---

began research for his work while a member of JERS in order to demonstrate causes for the decision to evacuate Japanese Americans from the Pacific Coast, whereas tenBroek's work was solicited by outgoing director Dorothy Thomas as a historical base for her studies in *The Salvage* (1952). See Okihiro (2001, 101, 103, 109).

15. Admiral William Halsey, commander of the South Pacific Force, spewed antiJapanese war propaganda that dehumanized Japanese as vermin and rodents. Marines at Iwo Jima had stenciled on their helmets, "Rodent Exterminator." Halsey called for the "almost total elimination of the Japanese as a race" on the grounds that this "was

evacuation recommendation, the long-awaited Roberts Commission Report (January 25, 1942) on the attack on Pearl Harbor reinforced De Witt's (and American) paranoia. It claimed that widespread espionage in Hawai'i by Japanese consular agents and residents greatly abetted the Pearl Harbor attack, a claim later proven false. By January 29 De Witt unqualifiedly supported the mass evacuation of Japanese despite self-exoneration attempts on February 3 to Assistant Secretary of War John McCloy: "Mr. Secretary ... I haven't taken any position" (quoted in Daniels 1981, 57). Japanese citizens were given the option of voluntary internment or forced exclusion from prohibited (militarization) zones; either way, they could not remain in the designated areas controlled by the military, though white citizens could (see the designated exclusion zone in fig. 3).

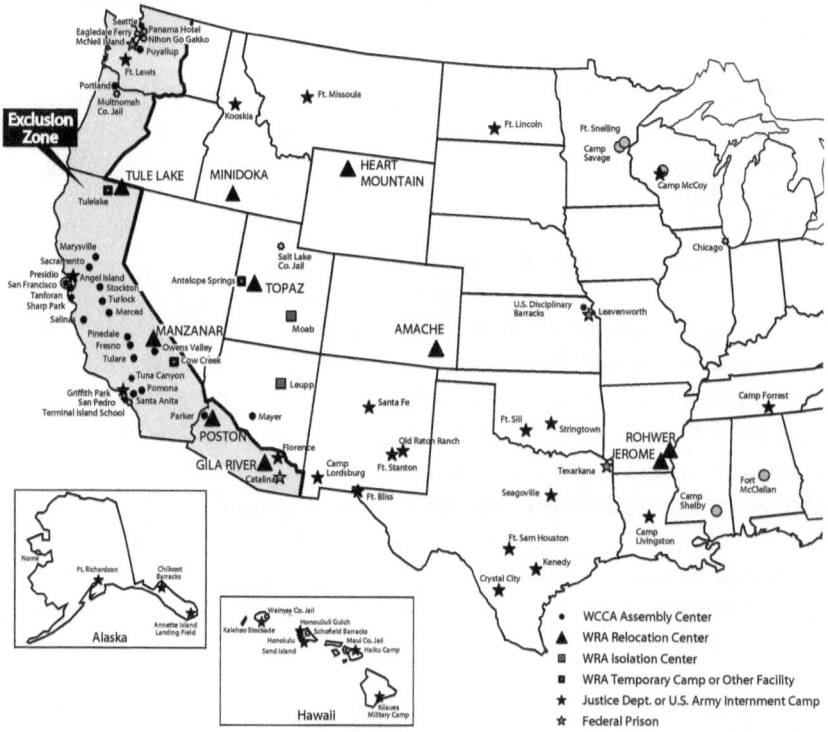

Figure 3. The designated exclusion zone. Courtesy of Manzanar National Historic Site.

---

a question of which race was to survive, and white civilization was at stake" (quoted in Dower 1993, 55).

Working from the same documents, Stetson Conn, Rose Engelman, and Byron Fairchild's *Guarding the United States and Its Outposts* (1964) espoused an alternative position that sought to exonerate General De Witt. These historians portrayed De Witt vacillating from one position to the other. At first, he responded to the Los Angeles Chamber of Commerce's report opposing their recommendation of Japanese evacuation. "An American citizen is, after all, an American citizen. And while they may not all be loyal, I think we can weed the disloyal out of the loyal and lock them up if necessary" (quoted in Conn, Engelman, and Fairchild 1964, 116–17). Then, after a meeting with Major Bendetsen (January 4–5, 1942), his concern over the alien problem, personal distrust of the Japanese, and the Robert's Commission findings prompted De Witt's unqualified acceptance of a mass internment plan and he recommended exclusion zones in California (January 21) and in Arizona, Oregon, and Washington (February 3). De Witt's vacillation coincided with his numerous correspondences with Major Bendetsen (promoted to Lieutenant Colonel on February 4). Bendetsen, from the Provost General Marshal's office, at times acted as a liaison between De Witt and the Justice Department, De Witt and politicians, and De Witt and the War Department. In a meeting with Justice Department officials and a congressional delegation on January 30, Bendetsen clearly presented his proposal for the mass evacuation of all Japanese to which De Witt had consented the day before. At a February 3 meeting with Secretary of War Henry Stimson, Assistant Secretary McCloy, Provost Marshal General Allen Gullion, and Bendetsen, Bendetsen recommended, on the advice of De Witt, the evacuation of unauthorized persons in military areas. By February 11 Gullion and Bendetsen had convinced McCloy, and soon Secretary Stimson and the President, of mass evacuation as a military necessity. With the President giving the War Department carte blanche on the matter, Bendetsen gave his assistance to De Witt in drafting recommendations to Stimson that appended the forced evacuation of Japanese American citizens to his earlier proposal to evacuate enemy aliens.

That the President green-lighted internment to Stimson and McCloy on February 11, thus prompting De Witt's formal recommendation, the basis of EO 9066, leads Roger Daniels, in *Concentration Camps* (1981), to place blame squarely on the president. Roosevelt had handed the decision-making power of mass internment over to two nonelected officials advising them to "go ahead and do anything you think necessary" so long as it was "dictated by military necessity," only "be as reasonable as you can" (quoted in Daniels 1981, 65). Eight days later EO 9066 clearly targeted the Japanese, aliens and citizens alike.

The question naturally follows, Why did Roosevelt acquiesce to the internal colonization of Japanese citizens? First, it was expedient. By early 1942, Japan had demonstrated itself as a formidable force having invaded Singapore (February 8), the last Allied stronghold on the mainland of Southeast Asia, New Britain (February 9), and having advanced rapidly against Burma. Conversely, the Allies were not faring well. Second, Roosevelt harbored "deeply felt anti-Japanese prejudices." He was no more immune to the racist paranoia of a Japanese fifth column element than any typical American. He remained convinced that the Japanese posed a real threat to American security. But did they? If the Japanese were indeed such a threat to American security, as Daniels astutely notes, then why was there no movement to incarcerate them in Hawai'i where they constituted more than a third of the population, instead of California where they comprised less than 2 percent of the population? The answer: logistics and economics. On the one hand, interning a tiny fragment of the population rather than a sizeable number is logistically more feasible. On the other hand, incarcerating the large Japanese population of Hawai'i would have severely disrupted the local economy (Daniels 1981, 72–73).

Economics that partly precluded the mass incarceration of Japanese in Hawai'i significantly contributed to its execution on the West Coast. Morton Grodzins's *Americans Betrayed* (1949) first advanced the theory of public pressure. Decades of anti-Asian sentiment easily shifted to open animus against the Japanese on racial and economic grounds. Even legislation clearly became racist (the common denominator of all proposed factors; see Hirabayashi and Hirabayashi): (1) the city of San Francisco segregated Asian students by 1906; (2) the state of California passed the Alien Land Law in 1913 prohibiting immigrant Asians from owning land; and (3) Congress passed the Oriental Exclusion Act in 1924. Anti-Japanese feelings ran deep despite improved relations from 1924 to 1941 as certain agricultural and business groups seized upon the attack on Pearl Harbor to expel Japanese from the agricultural sector. The Western Growers Protective Association especially recognized the economic benefits of such a move for white farmers though Japanese farmers only sold to local markets. The Grower-Shipper Vegetable Association of central California was more forthright about its motives: "We're charged with wanting to get rid of the Japs for selfish reasons. We might as well be honest. We do. It's a question of whether the white man lives on the Pacific Coast or the brown men" (quoted in Hirabayashi and Hirabayashi 1984, 106). Other pressure groups (e.g., American Legion, Native Sons of the Golden West, the Pacific League, labor unions) also remained unapologetic about the economic benefits gained by Japanese removal as they unabashedly publicized their positions.

But could such acrimony at the ground level actually affect federal government policy? The strongest critiques against Grodzins's theory are twofold: (1) the theory of regional pressure assumes public policy to emanate from the ground up, and (2) that the military shared the same racial attitudes as the public does not de facto suggest that their decisions were motivated by public attitude. Granting the theoretical value of both critiques, their contextualization does not render them ironclad. First, public policy develops from a rather complex process of interaction between politicians and their constituents; somewhere along this spectrum of the top down and the ground up, policies emerge. In addition, evidence bears out the fact of numerous letters to federal officials by regional pressure groups demanding Japanese removal. Second, General De Witt, headquartered in San Francisco, was not removed from public animus. Instead, he operated within the trenches of this clime in constant communication with the locals as well as Washington intelligentsia. On January 27 De Witt had a conference with California Governor Culbert Olson:

> There's a tremendous volume of public opinion now developing against the Japanese of all classes, that is aliens and non-aliens, to get them off the land, and in Southern California around Los Angeles—in that area too—they want and they are bringing pressure on the government to move all the Japanese out.... They don't trust the Japanese, none of them. (quoted in Hirabayashi and Hirabayashi 1984, 51)[16]

---

16. Governor Olson preyed upon the fears of Californians further inflaming public opinion in a February 4 speech: "it is known that there are Japanese residents of California who have sought to aid the Japanese enemy by way of communicating information, or have shown indications of preparation for fifth column activities." Los Angeles mayor Fletcher Bowron followed suit the next day: "Right here in our own city are those who may spring to action at an appointed time in accordance with a prearranged plan wherein each of our little Japanese friends will know his part in the event of any possible attempted invasion or air raid." He continued, "We cannot run the risk of another Pearl Harbor episode in Southern California" (quoted in Daniels 1981, 60–62).

It is completely inconceivable that De Witt, the "man on the ground" with his own racist prejudices against the Japanese, had no knowledge of public animus or remained uninfluenced by a growing movement calling for Japanese removal as he shaped what would become public domestic policy.

Similarly, Joshua and the Israelite political echelon were not that far removed from public opinion suspicious of the "other" within. Or were they? Having been sought out by the shrewd Gibeonite ambassadors, Joshua and the leaders conducted their own summit talks. They accepted the gifts of their newfound political friends, perhaps being impressed with the reputation of Yahweh that they assume as their own having preceded them (vv. 9–10), and established terms of peace and a covenant (vv. 6–7, 14–15), despite their failure to procure divine approval.[17] The Gibeonites acknowledge Yahweh and Yahweh's deeds having drawn them to Israel, whereas Israel seems to have forgotten Yahweh in a crucial moment. Nevertheless, the public intuits something askew from the outset with their initial query, "Perhaps you live among us…?" (v. 7). Only the tolerance of Israel's leaders trumps the intolerance of the public toward the Gibeonites. When the people find out the "immigrant" status of the Gibeonites, who indeed live among them, a social outcry permeates the community exacerbated further by a preexisting foreign policy that allowed Gibeonite presence within Israel all along. Swayed by public opinion the Israelite politicos cannot simply revoke their treaty. In an effort to reunify the community, the leadership does not turn to Yahweh for advice but relies on its own ingenuity engaging in damage control by spinning the situation as a boon to the community who will benefit from the labor and economic benefits derived from Gibeonite presence, that is, internal colonization (vv. 20–21). The leaders' quick response aborts sure social chaos wrought by mob vigilantism (vv. 18, 26). The propensity for wide-scale physical violence by the masses raises the likely probability of isolated hos-

---

17. The formal structure of vv. 14–15 with bracketing elements stresses their central emphasis:
    A   the leaders partook of their provisions
        B (the leaders) did not ask direction from Yahweh
    A'   Joshua made peace with them
Though the lexemes of A and A' are not identical, they nonetheless intimate the establishment of a covenant treaty since a meal was always a part of the diplomatic proceedings. Hawk (2000, 144) suggests a vassal treaty on the basis of the language employed and other elements in the encounter (cf. discussions in Grintz 1966; Fensham 1964).

tilities as having already occurred. What's more, that the Israelites could entertain the prospects of such violence bespeaks an ethos of prejudice requisite for the expression of such violence. The attitudes toward "them" within "us" enable "us" when felt threatened by the alien to justify violence against "them." Joshua and the political intelligentsia do just this, as do the *golah* leaders of Yehud, since "to this day" grounds the narrative conflict to a later era to justify the presence and treatment of the Gibeonites, not with the violence of bloodshed but with that of colonization (vv. 22–23). Only after the insistent pressure of public animus did Israelite intelligentsia implement the social institution of slavery that would mark Gibeonite social space within.

1.3. Internal Colonization—Language and Rhetoric

Why did you deceive us? (Josh 9:22)

When addressing the colonization of Japanese Americans and Gibeonites, we must attend to an integral though often overlooked matter in most histories—language. Why? Because language and reality mutually influence each other. Language of the intelligentsia conceals while it simultaneously reveals. Terms like "evacuation," "relocation," "assembly centers," "transit camps," "protective custody camps" dot the landscape of official memoranda that covered embarrassing and horrible truths. Such nomenclature filters through the ranks of government leaders, federal and state, to news outlets and eventually to the masses. Even scholars and historians since the ethnic awareness movements of the 1960s continue to use linguistic euphemisms that, in effect, influence modern perceptions of past events but also, perhaps more insidiously, perpetuate a positive, national image. Rather than allowing the rhetoric to deceive, we must examine it closely because the words that we use to depict an event are critical to our perception and understanding of that event. The linguistic philosopher Ludwig Wittgenstein struggled with this relationship between language and reality. Many no doubt assume, as did Wittgenstein in his early years, that reality dictates the language used to describe events. Thus language, the only means whereby we can picture the world, mirrors or corresponds to reality. Years after his *Tractatus Logico-Philosophicus*, Wittgenstein would revisit this relationship of language and reality in *Philosophical Investigations* to suggest a reverse order of influence. Social context, posited Wittgenstein, determines the meaning of the language used. Language, the vehicle utilized by humans for understanding reality, determines the way that people view reality. Language shapes reality, not the other way around, and our perceptions of reality. If we extrapolate these observations to the Japanese American experience, the language we use to describe their removal makes a big difference on how we construe that reality. Granted, "evacuation center" certainly sounds more palatable than "concentration camp." But the linguistic deception of such a euphemism fails to capture the reality of barbed wire compounds surrounded by guard towers and armed sentries in order to accurately shape that reality in the minds of casual observers.

Linguistic euphemisms in US propaganda ring eerily similar to those of the Third Reich. "Emigration," "evacuation," "relocation," "resettlement," "assembly centers," "protective custody camps," "reception centers," "transit camps," "special treatment," "final solution" were German code words to cover up what was actually happening to Jews, Gypsies, and many other "undesirables." Official literature described the prison city of Terezin, a way station to the gas chambers of Auschwitz, as a "paradise ghetto" and "retirement home" (Okamura 1982, 95). The linguistic propaganda deceived victims and general populace alike with a misapprehended reality corrected only later during the Nuremberg War Crimes Trial. The same was no different within the US where the effective employment of euphemistic language for propaganda purposes kept the general populace in the dark for many decades afterwards. Many at the time had no clue what happened to the Japanese, nor cared—a simple matter of "out of sight, out of mind."[18] Only years later did the revelation of the government's unlawful and unconstitutional actions come to light.

Therein becomes one reason for the American government's euphemistic language. It enabled them to sidestep any legal or constitutional challenges since two-thirds of Japanese detainees were American citizens.[19] Disguised language enabled officials to intern citizens, many being babies, children, and invalids, despite the lack of evidence that they could possibly be dangerous.

---

18. Okamura (1982, 108 n. 21) cites as example the White residents of Owens Valley, California, who seemed completely oblivious to the massive Manzanar Concentration Camp in their own backyard.

19. The unconstitutional convictions of Gordon Hirabayashi, Minoru Yasui, Fred Korematsu, and Mitsuye Endo upheld by the Supreme Court in 1943–1944 and later legally challenged by Peter Irons became the basis of his *Justice at War* (1983).

Second, the language co-opted the victims' willing participation. Japanese Americans complied with the round-up trusting the government's assurances that they were only being evacuated. The commonly used terms "evacuation" and "relocation" connote a movement "for the protection or safety of the affected people" (Okamura 1982, 97).[20] They do not suggest confinement or imprisonment as indicated by General De Witt's public proclamation: "all alien Japanese persons of Japanese ancestry who are within the limits of Military Area No. 1, be and they are hereby prohibited from leaving that area for any purpose until and to the extent that a future proclamation or order of this headquarters shall so permit or direct" (May 27, 1942; quoted in Okamura 1982, 99). Nor do they connote De Witt's policy concerning military police duties. "They will maintain periodic motor patrols around the boundaries of the center or area in order to guard against attempts by evacuees to leave the center without permission.... They shall apprehend and arrest evacuees who do leave the center or area without authority, using such force as is necessary to make the arrest" (September 17, 1942; US War Department 1943, 527). Perspectives of Japanese Americans quickly changed as they arrived at their detention camps. One anonymous detainee wrote, "This evacuation did not seem too unfair until we got right to the camp and were met by soldiers with guns and bayonets. Then I almost started screaming." Note Ted Nakashima's (1942, 822) similar description of the Puyallup Detention Camp:

> The resettlement center is actually a penitentiary—armed guards in towers with spotlights and deadly tommy guns, fifteen feet of barbed-wire fences, everyone confined to quarters at nine, lights out at ten o'clock. The guards are ordered to shoot anyone who approaches within twenty feet of the fences. No one is allowed to take the two-block hike to the latrines after nine, under any circumstances.

Third, the language enabled the government to ensure a decent public image. Intelligentsia went to great lengths to control language. De Witt instructed his subordinate commanders:

---

20. Continued use of the euphemistic terms "evacuation" and "relocation," albeit with capitals E and R, by former prisoners reveal the emotional scars left by their experience. Their continued usage of these terms becomes a self-defense mechanism against the outpouring of emotion (Okamura 1982, 104).

They have been moved from their homes and placed in camps under guard as a matter of military necessity. The camps are not "concentration camps" and the use of this term is considered objectionable. Evacuation Centers are not internment camps. Internment camps are established for another purpose and are not related to the evacuation program. (US War Department 1943, 216).

Similarly, Dillon Myer, the director of the War Relocation Authority, advised his civilian staff:

> The term "camp" when used to refer to a relocation center is likewise objectionable.... The evacuees are not "internees." They have not been "interned"…employees of the War Relocation Authority should refer to persons who have been evacuated from the West Coast as evacuees, and the projects as relocation centers. (October 2, 1942; quoted in Okamura 1982, 99–100)

Ironically, Myer did not find the term "colonists" objectionable.

"Military necessity" was perhaps the more pervasive of deceptive euphemisms. After assessing the West Coast situation, General Mark Clark disagreed with an evacuation plan on the basis of military necessity as did the army's G-2 (intelligence), which reported to Chief of Staff General George Marshall that its analysts believed that "mass evacuation [was] unnecessary" (quoted in Daniels 2004, 47). Nevertheless, the language of "military necessity" became part of the propaganda to accuse the victim of criminal activity and to justify the colonizer's victimization of the "other." It is the rhetoric of colonization as put simply by Jake Sully when describing the colonization efforts against the Na'vi in James Cameron's epic adventure *Avatar* (2009): "This is how it's done. When people are sitting on shit that you want, you make them your enemy. Then you're justified in taking it." The speech of the Israelite leaders presents themselves as *the* victims. Because the Gibeonites deceived Israel, the leaders' righteous indignation leads them to feel justified in enslaving the Gibeonites (9:19–20; note Bailey 2005, 19, who draws the conceptual parallel based on Howard Thurman's observations of the African American experience in his *Jesus and the Disinherited*). Likewise, the Japanese, represented as sneaky and deceitful, became likely targets facing accusations of fifth column activities on the West Coast contra the absence of proof of sabotage or espionage. In true-to-form fashion, Japanese victims received the blame from their victimizer. The Japanese became the face of white anxiety and fear run amok, especially that of a military feeling the inevitability of conflict, thus making the accessibility of local Japanese easy prey. Racial prejudice fueled incendiary acts and deceptive language by the victimizer cast in the role of victim, all part and parcel of an identity-shaping process.

Language is the essence of narrative, the heart of most ethnic identities and certainly that shaped by a colonizer. Narratives of ethnic identity have a subject, relate some central point or understanding concerning membership of a particular group, describe events, and attach value to their subject. Everything from white racist perceptions of Japanese to deceptive colonization rhetoric to justified treatment of the victim to blame, altogether these comprise the constructed narrative of Japanese identity by the US colonizer. Similarly, in assigning an identity to the Gibeonites vis-à-vis narrative, the Israelites justify their treatment of the Gibeonites by blaming them for having deceived them. The story becomes a means to bolster the presumed superiority of Israelite identity. But such narratives are never simply about either Japanese or Gibeonites, in this instance; they are also about those constructing the stories. The language that a society uses to describe a group not itself and the action that a society engages in due to that language signal primary clues about that society's self-understanding.[21] The "other" always bears some marker of "self" reflected back at "self." Thus, Gibeonite identity as migrant and deceitful reflects back that of Israelite identity as immigrant not indigenous in status, hybrid not homogeneous in identity, and colonized. The way that the Gibeonites become Israelites reflects back the constructed identity of "Israel" such that the story is not so much about Gibeonites as "hewers of wood and drawers of water," "but the Israelites, or rather the Gibeonites as Israelites as Gibeonites" (see Boer 2008, 109–34, who analyzes the motifs of deception and repetition in this story as traces of the social contradiction it attempts to resolve). Deception projected onto the "other" (Gibeonites/Japanese)

---

21. The "other" is always created, and in a social context of groups too much alike in close proximity to one another, hence the necessity to differentiate. When using a term to describe the "other" and to symbolize difference, a group has to reach deep within itself to find that quality that will induce a response, whether good or bad, admired or hated, to project onto the other (see Green 1985, 49–50). The act of projection becomes integral to the process of demonization whereby a group transfers some moral weakness to the outside to avoid any culpability. Demonizing the "other" preys on ethnocentrism in order to displace evil beyond group boundaries, an act that also encourages group narcissism and even killing, a far more unsettling enterprise if the "other" is considered human (Befu 1999).

154   POSTCOLONIALISM AND THE HEBREW BIBLE

is that of "self" (Israel/US) because the image of the "other" always originates within "self." Thus "deception by the Gibeonites is itself a deception over Israel's own origins" (Boer 2008, 128). In addition, ethnicity narratives imply "We are the people who..." in contrast to "...and you're not" (Cornell 2000, 50). Intriguingly, the shared story of Israelites–Gibeonites exclaims on the one hand, "we are not a people willing to resort to deception to obtain peace," while alternatively admitting on the other hand, but "we are a people capable of being deceived to ensure peace." The need to differentiate with the motif of deception underscores the reality that Israel and the US actively engaged in both deception and violence. The long campaign of prejudicial language and corresponding social action justifying the systematic demonization and victimization of Japanese Americans paved the way for their incarceration (see the intriguing exploration of Allied demonization of Japanese as "other" in Shillony, 293–308). Colonizer anxiety may have created the enemy without, but it was the enemy without whose presence unveiled the true enemy within.

2. A View from Within

2.1. Internment

> Now therefore you are cursed, and some of you shall always be slaves, hewers of wood and drawers of water for the house of my God…to continue to this day. (Josh 9:23, 27)

The expression "to this day" immediately shifts this narrative's contextualization to a later era to account for Gibeonite presence within Israel as slaves and the preoccupation with ethnic identity.[22] The Gibeonites refer to themselves as "servants" (4 times), generally regarded as deferential, if not fawning, language within the interpretive tradition. In the light of their subjugation to perform menial cultic tasks *in perpetua*, a status that did

---

22. Sutherland's (1992) redactional approach to Josh 9 posits three strata on the basis of Israelite principals in the negotiation processes with the Gibeonites: the אִישׁ יִשְׂרָאֵל, Joshua, and the נְשִׂיאֵי הָעֵדָה. Each strata reveals different leadership processes for a particular era, the most notable difference being between the אִישׁ יִשְׂרָאֵל passages of the premonarchic era (vv. 4–6, 7, 11–14, 16), where all adult males took part in the decision to make the treaty, and the נְשִׂיאֵי הָעֵדָה of the postexilic era (vv. 15b, 17–21), where an elite leadership cadre makes the decision.

not change with the postexilic period, their language may also reflect what James Scott (1985, 41) terms "onstage" acts, the language of false compliance in public contra "offstage" comments or perceptions of Gibeonites in private left unvoiced. References to Gibeonites in the postexilic literature of Chronicles, Ezra, and Nehemiah do appear with them listed among the *golah* community helping to rebuild the walls of Jerusalem (Neh 7:25; 3:7). By comparison, there are numerous references to the Nethinim, or "temple servants" (1 Chr 9:2; Ezra 2:43, 58, 70; 7:7, 24; 8:17, 20; Neh 3:26, 31; 7:46, 60, 73; 10:28 [MT 10:29]; 11:3, 21), thus eliciting speculation on their relationship to the Gibeonites.[23] Whatever that relationship, Gibeonite servant status in the temple "to this day" accounts for their presence within postexilic Yehud at a time of extreme ethnocentrism. Whether Nethinim, part of the Nethinim, or descendants of the "sons of Solomon's servants" ultimately matters not. The narrative lists clearly indicate a subordinate status. They always appear after the priests and Levites, and the singers and gatekeepers (1 Chr 9:2; Ezra 7:7; Neh 10:28 [MT 10:29]; 11:3; cf. the relative position of the Nethinim in Ezra 2 and Neh 7). In addition, the Nethinim assist the Levites (Ezra 8:20), subordinate cultic officials themselves. These factors altogether indicate just how low down the pecking order within the temple labor sector alone we find the Gibeonites. Relegated to menial temple service, their place in the Yehud labor market reveals high-boundedness and exhaustiveness factors. In addition, Gibeonite residential confinement to the Ophel ghetto district in Jerusalem, the designated living quarters for temple servants (Neh 3:26, 31; 11:21), clearly fixed their social space within Yehud. Gibeonite occupational and residential delimitations demarcated their colonized experience as "other," though certainly not in the same manner as that of Japanese Americans.

Japanese internment did not begin immediately upon issuance of EO 9066. Rather, hearings upon hearings were conducted as federal and

---

23. Jewish rabbis simply equated the two groups in the Talmud (b. Yebam. 71a, 78b–79a). Modern scholars, however, remain divided: Are the Gibeonites and Nethinim one and the same? Or were the Gibeonites one of several foreign ethnic groups absorbed within the Nethinim? Or do the Gibeonites bear no connection whatsoever to the Nethinim having been absorbed into the "sons of Solomon's servants," often listed immediately after the Nethinim and also comprising a significant foreign element (see Day 2007, 136–37)? The high plausibility of Day's alternative suggestion assumes the Gibeonites to belong to various Canaanite groups, including Hivites, enslaved by Solomon (1 Kgs 9:20–21), as well as the "sons of Solomon's servants" to be descendants of these Canaanite groups.

military authorities so long preoccupied with the idea of a "Jap-free" West Coast moved slowly. Authorities had no clear plans of what to do with the Japanese.[24] For all the proclamations and orders, none actually forced anyone to move or took anyone into custody. Until March 2 Japanese could freely leave the West Coast, and some did, only to return quickly after encountering frightening hostilities (e.g., being turned away at the Nevada border by armed posses, being thrown into jail by panicky local peace officers, and threatened with mob violence). Never forced into custody, the Japanese never contemplated open defiance or mass disobedience, rather, they appeared at designated assembly points at scheduled times in an orderly, civil manner. Like the Gibeonites, the Japanese offered no open resistance. But why not? The JACL leadership had encouraged a policy of compliance among the Japanese. Opposing the evacuation would have only (1) reinforced the existing disloyal stereotype of the Japanese and (2) incurred punitive actions against the hated Japanese enemy in wartime. Japanese Americans faced the dilemma of how to demonstrate their loyalty as citizens. JACL leadership chose to cooperate hoping that doing so might mitigate present circumstances and yield better treatment in the future.

First sight of the locations of the concentration camps to which the Japanese were sent quickly dashed any such hopes. The War Relocation Authority (WRA) had oversight of the ten concentration camps: Man-

---

24. A disorganized General De Witt began issuing a series of proclamations. Proclamation No. 1 (March 2) divided the states of Washington, Oregon, California, and Arizona into two military areas with Military Area No. 1 further subdivided into a "prohibited zone" (that strip of land on the shoreline) and a "restricted zone." (The Japanese living on Terminal Island, San Pedro, California, were actually the first Japanese forced to move feeling the capricious whims of the US Navy. The US Navy posted notices February 14 that the Japanese had until March 14 to leave, only to post new notices on February 25 demanding their eviction February 27.) Proclamation No. 2 (March 16) established four more military areas covering the states of Idaho, Montana, Nevada, and Utah with the ultimate intention to rid the Western Defense Command of Japanese. Proclamation No. 3 (March 27) instituted an 8 p.m. to 6 a.m. curfew in all prohibited areas for all enemy aliens. Proclamation No. 4 (effective midnight March 29) forbad all Japanese to leave Military Area No. 1. (Three days prior, De Witt had issued a "Civilian Exclusion Order" that followed Public Law No. 503, which "made it a criminal offense for anyone excluded from a military area to remain there." Daniels 1981, 85.) By June 5 all of Military Area No. 1 had been evacuated with supposedly safe Military Area No. 2 "Jap-free" by August 7.

zanar, California and Poston, Arizona (also Assembly Centers); Tule Lake, California, Minidoka, Idaho, and Heart Mountain, Wyoming (all undeveloped federal reclamation projects); and Gila River, Arizona, Granada (Amache), Colorado, Topaz, Utah, and Jerome and Rohwer, Arkansas (this list excludes Assembly Centers, Justice Department Internment Camps, and Citizen Isolation Camps; see Ng 2002, 31–54; and fig. 3, above). The weather conditions at some of the sites were brutally harsh with winter temperatures at Heart Mountain, Minidoka and Topaz commonly dipping as low as -30°F, and summer temperatures at Topaz easily reaching upwards of 106°F. All of these sites shared several qualities in common, including the fact that they were federal property, safely distant from strategic installations, and godforsaken. Surrounded with barbed wire and guarded by small detachments of military police, these camps existed in desolate, uninhabitable areas with dust all around that turned to mud after a rain, an ideal breeding ground for mosquitoes.

Living conditions at these camps matched their surroundings. Each family was assigned an "apartment," basically an 8 × 20-foot section in a long, barracks-like one-story building with the largest "apartment" being 20 × 24 feet for a family of six. Partitions that never extended to the ceiling separated these "apartments," none of which had running water (though all would eventually have electricity), furnishings (save army-style cots), and cooking facilities. Everybody ate in the mess hall where they received three meals a day, usually starchy, cheap food prepared in an unappetizing manner at a cost of 38.19 cents per day per detainee in comparison to 50 cents per day for each soldier. In addition, sanitation problems were a main concern. A woman prisoner at the Merced, California center wrote describing the deplorable conditions of toilet facilities (quoted in Daniels 2004, 65):

> The lavatories [are] not very sanitary.... The toilets are one big row of seats, that is, one straight board with holes out about a foot apart with no partitions at all and all the toilets flush together...about every five minutes. The younger girls couldn't go to them at first until they couldn't stand it any longer, which is really bad for them.

The equally deplorable improper sanitation conditions of the makeshift kitchens in the mess halls, erupting in mass outbreaks of diarrhea, further exacerbated conditions eliciting shock from a US Public Health Service report that more epidemics had not occurred.

To compound Japanese incarceration, the WRA circulated a questionnaire entitled "Application for Leave Clearance" to test loyalty in an effort to eventually move "loyal" Japanese out of the camps. The questionnaire, instead, created conflict within the Japanese community over two questions:

> 27. Are you willing to serve in the armed forces of the United States on combat duty, wherever ordered?
> 28. Will you swear unqualified allegiance to the United States of America and faithfully defend the United States from any or all attack by foreign or domestic forces, and foreswear any form of allegiance to the Japanese emperor, to any other foreign government, power or organization?

Aside from the inappropriateness of posing such questions to incarcerated citizens, how to answer these questions divided the community: the JACL urged the Japanese community to answer "yes"; some Nisei construed the phrase "foreswear allegiance" as a trap to admit to former allegiances; others qualified their response to question 27 with "Yes, if my rights as a citizen are restored"; and many Issei answered "no," fearing they would be removed from camp without resources if they answered otherwise.[25] The WRA questionnaire achieved nothing save further entrenching Issei feelings of strong loyalty to Japan while prompting many others to seek repatriation because of the strong prejudice in America (Daniels 2004, 68–70; 1977, 31).

Japanese life in these camps was virtually one of survival as they grappled with how to make their lives more bearable. They busied themselves with work—public work, agriculture, manufacturing, private employment (outside the camps), or self-supporting communities (similar to New Deal subsistence homesteads)—and were compensated according to two wage scales, one for work inside and one for work outside the camps. The top wage for the former never exceeded $19 per month (regardless of the work performed), whereas the top wage for the latter did not exceed the prevailing rate (Daniels 1981, 93). Work helped the daily life of the Japanese limp along as they contemplated circumstances of their liberation.

---

25. The WRA decided to move all the "disloyals" to the camp at Tule Lake, California and move "loyal" Tuleans to other camps. These moves coincided with WRA objectives in that they fractured the family, the basic cultural institution of Japanese ethnicity and solidarity.

2.2. RESISTANCE

No such hope existed for the Gibeonites circumscribed by a colonialist narrative representing their acquiescence to colonization with no possibility of open resistance. The same perspective toward Japanese American experiences in the concentration camps is maintained within sociological and historical studies where the issue of rhetoric surfaces once again. Interpretations of Japanese reaction to the camps basically reflect two dominant perspectives: the orthodox view (or the WRA-JACL perspective) and the revisionist view.

The orthodox view construes the Japanese as defenseless, dependent, abiding victims of circumstances totally compliant and submissive with their evacuation. Any resistance was sporadic and uncharacteristic. Various mass resistance movements were dismissed out of hand as mere "incidents" (note official documentation referring to the Manzanar "incident")[26] fomented simply by a small minority of pro-Japanese agitators. But the term "incident" trivializes the cultural significance of the event "by scaling down the affair to commonplace proportions" (Hansen and Hacker 1974, 116). "Normalization" followed these outbreaks with some amiable, yet sometimes uncertain, resolution resulting in a peaceful, "happy" camp.

The revisionist view basically posits that the near-century anti-Asian agitation and racial discrimination in America culminated with the concentration camps. Internee resistance, both active and passive, preceded evacuation and intensified within the camps. Internees were in conflict

---

26. The Manzanar event occurred December 6, 1942, after the assault of Fred Tayama, a well-known JACL leader and regarded *inu* ("dogs," a collaborator), by, it was assumed, Harry Ueno, president of the Kitchen Worker's Union and a Kibei (those Nisei who had been to Japan and returned to America), arrested the next day. A crowd of some 3,000 to 4,000 gathered to hear the demands for the release of the popular Kibei as well as investigations into camp conditions. Many felt Ueno was framed and called for a strike the next day if he was not released that night. Evacuee representatives followed by a crowd of about 1,000 went to the administration building on December 6 to meet with the project director only to be confronted by military police armed with submachine guns, rifles, and shotguns. Soldiers fired tear gas into the crowd to disperse it initially. But when the crowd reformed at 6 p.m. that evening, soldiers fired tear gas and bullets into the crowd, leaving one Nisei dead, another dying, and about a dozen wounded. That night the bells tolled continuously as the people held meetings and the soldiers patrolled the camp (Hansen and Hacker 1974, 113–15; Okihiro 1973, 24–25).

with their keepers and with each other.[27] Daniels (1981, 106–7, 118) further suggests that this conflict among the internees ran along lines of a split between Kibei and Nisei on the one hand (à la Manzanar) and between the "right opposition" (pro-Japan) and the "left opposition" (pro-American) on the other. Referring to the Manzanar event as "riot," as secondary works do, caution Hansen and Hacker (1974, 116), likewise trivializes the cultural significance of this event by construing it as merely episodic and parochial. Gary Okihiro augments the revisionist perspective throughout a series of articles where he identifies the result of the conflict, whether between generations, groups, or of politics expressed as pro-Japan or pro-American, as basically the struggle for civil liberties and human dignity (1973; 2001, 171). This was certainly the case with Japanese resistance at Tule Lake (1977).

Japanese resistance in American concentration camps did not principally manifest itself in overt acts of aggression, though the Manzanar revolt did result in numerous injuries and two deaths. Instead, resistance took on the quiet struggle for "possession of the children's minds and habits" (Okihiro 1973, 26, 31–32). In short, it became a struggle to resist the manipulation of Japanese lives and "the erasure of their ethnic identity" (Okihiro 2001, 172). Japanese religious belief played no small role, as Okihiro (1984, 233) notes: "religion and culture ... were both a vehicle for and an expression of the people's resistance." Religion formed the basis of this cultural resistance to "Americanize" (a process to alter the ethnic identity and culture of minority communities to Anglo-conformity) the Japanese and helped to preserve ethnic solidarity. The rise of Buddhism and increase in religious activity within the Japanese American community paralleled that of the camps. Religious activity tends to increase in relationship to stresses brought on by the uncontrollable, unknown, or threatening. Thus the psychological stresses of Japanese internment yielded responses at cross-purposes with the WRA "Americanization" program, which especially targeted filial piety by dislocating the family through evacuation. As time progressed in the camps, the Japanese block, consisting of fourteen barracks, took on the characteristics of the family to bolster ethnic solidarity. Block organizations such as the Young People's Association emerged and the slogan "Keep Children within the Block" widely circulated. As one

---

27. E.g. conflict occurred between newcomers from Sacramento, California and those from Washington and Oregon already at the Tule Lake camp over good jobs, scrap lumber, and various scarce resources (Okihiro 2001, 167).

internee commented, "It is not possible to be an informer as we are all Japanese. We should have loyalty to our own group. A Japanese cannot kick another Japanese" (quoted in Okihiro 1984, 228). In addition, aesthetic expressions such as landscape gardening, bonsai, *sumo*, art, music, drama, and poetry collectively created a common "Japanese spirit" whereby ethnic beliefs and practices, themselves acts of resistance, rechanneled the people's resistance away from open aggression (as representative examples of cultural resistance, see the collection of personal reminiscences in Lawson Inada's *Only What We Could Carry* (2000), the diverse artistry and crafts in Chiura Obata's *Topaz Moon* (2000), Delphine Hirasuna's *The Art of Gaman* (2005), and the Online Center for the Study of Japanese American Concentration Camp Art (http://www.lib.iastate.edu/internart-main/6786)).

But Japanese cultural resistance began prior to internment. The social prejudice behind each anti-Japanese attack precipitated Issei retreat further into traditional Japanese culture. And the high-boundedness and exhaustiveness factors in the labor and residential sectors together with incarceration faced by the Nisei undermined their growing Americanization as they returned to the Japanese American community. With the growing restoration of ethnicity and maintenance of group solidarity by the heightened determination to punish informers, boundary markers became more defined. Thus the Manzanar revolt reflects a "response to endangered ethnicity" (Hansen and Hacker 1974, 122, 133, 141) and highlights the deconstructive nature of colonization efforts to "Americanize" the Japanese. Similarly, Israelite colonization of the Canaanites (Judg 1), including Gibeonites, had the inverse effect than desired in that Canaanite religious practices proliferated in Israelite society, no doubt an indication of Canaanite cultural resistance.

2.3. REDRESS

Historians have observed that redress for the Japanese did not take place according to any systematic, deliberate plan though the benefits of certain developments here and there did eventually pave the way for monetary compensation. In addition, the high-boundedness and exhaustiveness factors marking Japanese ethnic identity prior to and during World War II diminished as more opportunities in the labor and residential sectors of American society became available. But I will only briefly touch on these developments and their concomitant benefits here (for a fuller discussion of each, see Daniels 2004, 88–106).

First, President Truman encouraged Congress to pass the Japanese American Claims Act (1948) after a ceremony awarding the Presidential Unit Citation to the Nisei 442nd Regimental Combat Team.[28] The Claims Act saw Congress appropriate $38 million to satisfy some 23,000 claims totaling $131 million. Obviously, this important symbolic gesture was just that since it was woefully inadequate as a financial settlement for losses of real property. Second, the McCarran–Walter Act (1952) began to erase ethnic and racial bars to immigration and naturalization by immediately naturalizing surviving Issei, and other Asians living in the US, as citizens. Third, the admittance of Hawai'i to statehood (1959) ensured a steady presence of Asian American legislation in Washington, D.C. that surely must have had some input and influence in the law passed that led to redress payments. Fourth, President Gerald Ford issued a proclamation that repealed EO 9066 as a part of the 1976 bicentennial celebrations. He acknowledged the "national mistake" of evacuating Japanese Americans and, on his last day of office, issued a presidential pardon to Tokyo Rose.

In 1980 redress began in earnest when President Jimmy Carter and Congress created the Commission on the Wartime Relocation and Internment of Civilians (CWRIC) for the purpose of investigating wrongs against the Japanese during World War II and recommending appropriate remedial action. With its investigations underway, the Japanese community remained divided on the matter of redress as did the nation. Many Japanese felt redress had been accomplished when President Ford repealed EO 9066 and lauded Japanese American loyalty; some wanted a formal apology from Congress; some wanted monetary compensation; others wanted both. In early 1983 the CWRIC issued its report *Personal Justice Denied* stating that EO 9066 "was not justified by military necessity" but rather by "race prejudice, war hysteria, and a failure of political leadership.... A grave injustice was done to Americans and resident aliens of Japanese ancestry ... excluded, removed and detained by the United States during World War II" (quoted in Daniels 2004, 97). In June of that same year the CWRIC made the following five recommendations: (1) a formal apology

---

28. The 442nd Regimental Combat Team became the most decorated unit in the entire American Army—18,143 individual decorations that included a Congressional Medal of Honor, 47 Distinguished Service Crosses, 350 Silver Stars, and more than 3,600 Purple Hearts. Their service also included the ironic liberation of the Nazi concentration camp at Dachau even as their parents and relatives remained in American concentration camps.

by Congress; (2) presidential pardons for those who violated the law while resisting wartime restraints upon Japanese Americans; (3) restoration of lost status and entitlements because of wartime injustices; (4) congressional establishment and funding of a special foundation whose research could illumine the causes and circumstances of such events; and (5) a one-time, tax-free payment of $20,000 to each survivor incarcerated because of ethnicity during World War II.

Constant budget struggles of the 1980s hampered congressional action to implement the CWRIC's recommendation. Only the Civil Liberties Act (1988), or Bill H.R. 442, enacted redress comprising all five recommendations of the CWRIC. Despite the bill's passage into law in 1988, Congress made no appropriations for financial redress for more than two years with the first checks being issued October 9, 1990. Until such time all that surviving Japanese had was a formal apology by the Congress and the president (US Congress 1988):

> The Congress recognizes that ... a grave injustice was done to both citizens and permanent resident aliens of Japanese ancestry by the evacuation, relocation, and internment of civilians during World War II.... The excluded individuals of Japanese ancestry suffered enormous damages, both material and intangible ... all of which resulted in significant human suffering for which appropriate compensation has not been made. For these fundamental violations of the basic civil liberties and constitutional rights of these individuals of Japanese ancestry, the Congress apologizes on behalf of the Nation.

According to Daniels, at least half of the victims of EO 9066 did not live to see vindication, collect their checks, and receive their letter of apology from President Reagan.

No such monetary redress or formal letter of apology could obviously be had for the Gibeonites. Their redress can only occur by resisting the resounding silence of history and refracting its colonizing language.

3. Conclusion

Japanese Nisei incarcerated in American concentration camps expressed concern that their incarceration wrought by racial prejudices and hysteria could happen again. Their concerns certainly bore merit when, even as the first redress checks were issued, some US government agencies began targeting Arab Americans re-presented as allies of Saddam Hussein on the basis of "national security." In the wake of 9/11, quite obvious racial and religious prejudices have targeted Arab Americans, most noticeably the illegal detainment of Muslims at Guantánamo Bay.[29] Unfortunately, nine years later that same prejudice remains as attested by recent anti-Muslim incidents nationwide sparked by the proposed construction of a Muslim cultural center at the 9/11 site. In 2010 a New York City Muslim cab driver had his face and throat slashed; a case of arson occurred at the site of a future mosque in Murfreesboro, Tennessee; the Dar El-Aman Islamic Center in Arlington, Texas was set on fire and marked with graffiti; and a Christian minister in Gainesville, Florida scheduled a burning of Quran copies for the anniversary of 9/11 before eventually canceling. Could something like the experience of the Japanese Americans indeed happen again, if it hasn't already?

With the known colonization of Japanese Americans, the admittedly modest objective of this essay has been to articulate the unknown colonization of the Gibeonites in Josh 9. Sociological insights have identified group dynamics at work between Israelites and Gibeonites on the social landscape with high-boundedness and exhaustiveness factors concurrently circumscribing the latter's social space and reinforcing their group identity, with rhetoric occupying a significant role. But for all the rhetoric about the Gibeonites and Japanese as "enemy" and the danger they posed, colonization ultimately deconstructs. Anglo-American prejudices toward the Japanese resulting in their limited opportunities in the labor and residential sectors only reinforced claims of Japanese non-assimilation, the very thing decried. Moreover, the social marginalization of the Japanese culminating in incarceration had the adverse effect than intended; it entrenched Japanese cultural traditions, including religion, thus reinforcing group solidarity and ethnic identity. But did the same maintain for the Gibeonites? The persistence of Gibeonite ethnic identity, their high-boundedness and exhaustiveness factors in both occupational and residential sectors, their close proximity to temple rituals, all well into the postexilic era, along with the overt influence and proliferation of Canaanite religion on Israelite practices throughout various periods of its history

---

29. Despite claims to the contrary by US government officials, interrogations and interviews have revealed that some 55 percent of detainees have had no terrorist ties. In addition, Pentagon officials indicate that only 50 to 75 percent of the detainees will ever actually be charged with a crime (Sutton 2006; see further the revealing research of Guantánamo lawyers Jonathan Hafetz and Mark Denbeaux 2009).

would seem to indicate Gibeonite cultural resistance to their colonization. The effect of colonization upon the Gibeonites most likely had the same less than desired effect—resistance, not in open acts of aggression, but resistance nonetheless. Colonization entrenched Gibeonite/Canaanite cultural traditions, including religion, thus reinforcing group solidarity and ethnic identity, albeit hybridized.

Colonization rhetoric distracts. The enemy is indeed a threat and does pose a danger. But the "enemy other" is neither "enemy" nor "other" who resides among, but rather resides "within." The enemy "within" incites the prejudices of one ethnic group toward another, and usually because of shared characteristics. The enemy "within" precipitates colonization efforts based on representations of the "other" as "deceitful," for example, and justifies those efforts with rhetoric like "military necessity" or "divine right." Exorcizing the enemy "within" establishes a sense of "self"-authentication within narratives of ethnic identity in American and Israelite history. Only then can the salient words of the Manzanar National Historic Site marker become the reality for ethnic identities in the US and Israelite national narratives:

> May the injustices and humiliation suffered here as a result of hysteria, racism, and economic exploitation never emerge again.

REFERENCES

Bailey, Randall. 2005. He Didn't Even Tell Us the Worst of It! *UQR* 59:15–24.
Befu, Harumi. 1999. Demonizing the "Other." Pages 17–30 in *Demonizing the Other: Antisemitism, Racism and Xenophobia*. Edited by Robert Wistrich. London: Routledge.
Blenkinsopp, Joseph. 1972. *Gibeon and Israel: The Role of Gibeon and the Gibeonites in the Political and Religious History of Early Israel*. Cambridge: Cambridge University Press.
Boer, Roland. 2008. *Last Stop Before Antarctica: The Bible and Postcolonialism in Australia*. Atlanta: Society of Biblical Literature.
Chidester, David. 1996. *Savage Systems: Colonialism and Comparative Religion in Southern Africa*. Charlottesville: University Press of Virginia.
Conn, Stetson, Rose C. Engelman, and Byron Fairchild. 1964. *Guarding the United States and Its Outposts*. Washington, D.C.: Center of Military History, United States Army.

Cornell, Stephen. 2000. That's the Story of Our Life. Pages 41–53 in *We Are a People: Narrative and Multiplicity in Constructing Ethnic Identities*. Edited by Paul Spickard and W. Jeffrey Burroughs. Philadelphia: Temple University Press.
Cornell, Stephen, and Douglas Hartmann. 2007. *Ethnicity and Race: Making Identities in a Changing World*. 2nd ed. Thousand Oaks: Pine Forge.
Daniels, Roger. 1977. *The Politics of Prejudice: The Anti-Japanese Movement in California and the Struggle for Japanese Exclusion*. 2nd ed. Berkeley: University of California Press.
———. 1981. *Concentration Camps: North America: Japanese in the United States and Canada During World War II*. Malabar: Robert E. Krieger.
———. 2004. *Prisoners without Trial: Japanese Americans in World War II*. Revised ed. New York: Hill & Wang.
Day, John. 2007. Gibeon and the Gibeonites in the Old Testament. Pages 113–37 in *Reflection and Refraction: Studies in Biblical Historiography in Honour of A. Graeme Auld*. Edited by Robert Rezetko, Timothy Lim, and W. Brian Aucker. VTSup 113. Leiden: Brill.
Dower, John. 1993. *War without Mercy: Race and Power in the Pacific War*. New York: Pantheon Books.
Fensham, F. Charles. 1964. The Treaty between Israel and the Gibeonites. *BA* 27:96–100.
Green, William Scott. 1985. Otherness within: Toward a Theory of Difference in Rabbinic Judaism. Pages 49–69 in *"To See Ourselves as Others See Us": Christians, Jews, "Others" in Late Antiquity*. Edited by Jacob Neusner and Ernest Frerichs. Chico: Scholars Press.
Grintz, Jehoshua M. 1966. The Treaty of Joshua with the Gibeonites. *JAOS* 86:113–26.
Grodzins, Morton. 1949. *Americans Betrayed: Politics and the Japanese Evacuation*. Chicago: University of Chicago Press.
Hafetz, Jonathan, and Mark Denbeaux. 2009. *The Guantánamo Lawyers: Inside a Prison outside the Law*. New York: New York University Press.
Hansen, Arthur, and David Hacker. 1974. The Manzanar Riot: An Ethnic Perspective. *Amerasia Journal* 2:112–57.
Hawk, L. Daniel. 1997. The Problem with Pagans. Pages 153–63 in *Reading Bibles, Writing Bodies: Identity and the Book*. Edited by Timothy K. Beal and David Gunn. New York: Routledge.
———. 1999. *Every Promise Fulfilled: Contesting Plots in Joshua*. Louisville: Westminster John Knox.

———. 2000. *Joshua*. Berit Olam. Collegeville: Liturgical Press.
Hirabayashi, Lane Ryo, and James Hirabayashi. 1984. A Reconsideration of the United States Military's Role in the Violation of Japanese-American Citizenship Rights. Pages 87–110 in *Ethnicity and War*. Edited by Winston Van Horne. Ethnicity and Public Policy. Madison: University of Wisconsin Press.
Hirasuna, Delphine. 2005. *The Art of Gaman: Arts and Crafts from the Japanese American Internment Camps, 1942–1946*. Berkeley: Ten Speed Press.
Iiyama, Patty. 1973. American Concentration Camps: Racism and Japanese-Americans during World War II. *ISR* 34:24–33.
Inada, Lawson. 2000. *Only What We Could Carry*. Berkeley: Heyday; San Francisco: California Historical Society.
Irons, Peter H. 1983. *Justice at War*. New York: Oxford University Press.
Ishigo, Estelle. 1972. *Lone Heart Mountain*. Los Angeles: Anderson, Ritchie & Simon.
Mitchell, Gordon. 1993. *Together in the Land: A Reading of the Book of Joshua*. JSOTSup 134. Sheffield: Sheffield Academic Press.
Nakashima, Ted. 1942. Concentration Camp: U.S. Style. *The New Republic*. June 15. 106:822–23.
Ng, Wendy. 2002. *Japanese American Internment during World War II: A History and Reference Guide*. Westport: Greenwood.
Obata, Chiura. 2000. *Topaz Moon*. Berkeley: Heyday.
Okamura, Raymond. 1982. The American Concentration Camps: A Cover-Up through Euphemistic Terminology. *JEtS* 10:95–109.
Okihiro, Gary Y. 1973. Japanese Resistance in America's Concentration Camps: A Re-evaluation. *Amerasia Journal* 2:20–34.
———. 1977. Tule Lake under Martial Law: A Study in Japanese Resistance. *JEtS* 5:71–85.
———. 1984. Religion and Resistance in America's Concentration Camps. *Phylon* 45:220–33.
———. 1994. *Margins and Mainstreams: Asians in American History and Culture*. Seattle: University of Washington Press.
———. 2001. *The Columbia Guide to Asian American History*. New York: Columbia University Press.
Rowlett, Lori. 1992. Inclusion, Exclusion and Marginality in the Book of Joshua. *JSOT* 55:15–23.
———. 1996. *Joshua and the Rhetoric of Violence: A New Historicist Analysis*. JSOTSup 226. Sheffield: Sheffield Academic Press.

Scott, James C. 1985. *Weapons of the Weak: Everyday Forms of Peasant Resistance*. New Haven: Yale University Press.

Shillony, Ben-Ami. 1999. The Flourishing Demon: Japan in the Role of the Jews? Pages 293–308 in *Demonizing the Other: Antisemitism, Racism and Xenophobia*. Edited by Robert Wistrich. London: Routledge.

Spencer, Stephen. 2006. *Race and Ethnicity: Culture, Identity and Representation*. New York: Routledge.

Sutherland, Ray. 1992. Israelite Political Theories in Joshua 9. *JSOT* 53:65–74.

Sutton, Jane. 2006. Many Guantanamo Prisoners Never Saw Battle—A Report. *CagePrisoners*. October 2. http://old.cageprisoners.com/articles.php?id= 12125 (accessed September 9, 2010).

Takaki, Ronald. 1998. *Strangers from a Different Shore: A History of Asian Americans*. Revised ed. New York: Little, Brown and Company.

tenBroek, Jacobus, Edward N. Barnhart, and Floyd W. Matson. 1954. *Prejudice, War and the Constitution*. Berkeley: University of California Press.

Thurman, Howard. 1949. *Jesus and the Disinherited*. New York: Abingdon-Cokesbury.

US Congress. Senate. 1924. *Japanese Immigration Hearings*. 68th Congress, 1st session. Washington, D.C.

———. 1988. *Civil Liberties Act of 1988*. Public Law 100–383. 100th Congress. August 10. http://www.internmentarchives.com/archimg/d00172p001.png (accessed August 6, 2008).

US War Department. 1943. *Final Report: Japanese Evacuation from the West Coast 1942*. Washington D.C.: U.S. Government Printing Office.

Zia, Helen. 2000. *Asian American Dreams: The Emergence of an American People*. New York: Farrar, Strauss & Giroux.

HOSEA AND THE EMPIRE

Leo Perdue

The most significant threat to Israel's and Judah's survival during the latter part of the eighth century B.C.E. was the powerful Assyrian empire.[1] This is reflected in Hosea's oracles that speak of Assyria's bringing to an end the nation of Israel and the foolishness of looking to this empire for support (5:13; 8:9; 10:6; 14:4 [14:3]).[2] The prophet Hosea, son of Beeri, was the single northern prophet whose prophecies were collected and redacted into a book. While the book was redacted in Judah, there is little to suggest that Hosea was a southern prophet who prophesied in Israel or that he represented a Judean point of view (cf. 5:14; 6:4). There are several passages which indicate that Judah and its traditions receive a reprieve from the condemnation of Judah, but these are likely from the hands of scribal redactors in the south (1:7; 3:1–5; 4:15; 6:11; 11:12) due to the fact that they are inconsistent with other texts that also direct Yahweh's judgment against the southern kingdom (Day 2010, 203–4 n. 3).[3] I would propose that while Judah does not stand at the center of his condemnation, this kingdom is not exempted from punishment for its crimes and moral and religious violations of the covenant. While he warns Israel not to make Judah a harlot, that is, a worshiper of the Canaanite gods (4:15), in another context he also indicates that Judah, like Ephraim, has become a worshiper of these gods (5:5). Another type of faithlessness is the dependence on a

---

1. For relevant literature, see Wolff 1974; Andersen and Freedman 1980; Jeremias 1983; Yee 1987, 1996; Neef 1987; Daniels 1990; Landy 1995; Macintosh 1997; Sweeney 2000; Trotter 2001; Kwakkel 2009; Dearman 2010.
2. When versification between the Hebrew text and English translations differs, the latter will be placed within brackets.
3. Wolff (1974, xxxi–xxxii) even maintains that the anti-Judean statements are likely later redactional insertions (4:15, 5:5, 6:11, 10:11; 12:3 [12:2]).

country's own military power and the seeking of alliances to oppose invasion, especially that of Assyria. Thus like its sister nation Judah also prepared defenses against invasion, depending on its own power instead of Yahweh (8:14). Judah, too, will plow the earth (10:11), likely a reference to military defeat likely from the Assyrians, and stands under divine indictment (12:2).

We know little about his family or life. We have him only indicating that Yahweh gave him the command to formalize marriage to an unchaste woman, Gomer, and the three children of "harlotry" which she bore (she is likely the same woman in both chs. 1 and 3). This designation does not necessarily mean Hosea is denying he is the father, but rather refers to the status he gives her as a practicing prostitute. He likely prophesied near the end of Jeroboam II's reign in 746 B.C.E. and concluded this activity before the fall of Israel to Sargon II in 722 B.C.E. The superscription (1:1) places his prophecies in the reigns of the Judean kings Uzziah, Jotham, Ahaz, and Hezekiah, but only Jeroboam II is mentioned among the northern rulers, a serious omission on behalf of later redactors to note the six kings of Israel who ruled from 746 to 722 B.C.E. During the reign of these six different kings following the death of Jeroboam II and the end of the dynasty of Jehu (Zechariah, Shallum, Menahem, Pekahiah, Pekah, and Hoshea), Israel experienced a growing instability (all but two died violently at the hands of their successors, save for Menahem and Hoshea). Several of Hosea's oracles reflect the unstable conditions of Israel's last years (5:1; 7:5–7; 8:4; 9:15; 13:10–11). Thus he was active when the state of Israel was still in existence and continued to be ruled by the northern kings (Hos 5:1; 7:1–7; 8:4; 10:7; 13:10–11). However, he either died or ceased his prophetic role prior to the fall of Samaria in 722 B.C.E. which he sees inevitably approaching with horrid descriptions of the death of its inhabitants (14:1). He was aware of a steady succession of rulers (7:1–7; 8:4) and came to the view that the king of Samaria was about to perish (10:7, 15). According to this prophet the northern kingdom was soon to fall (10:14; 13:9; 14:1 [13:16]), something yet impending. There may be a reference to Shalmaneser V's taking of Beth Arbel (10:14) when this Assyrian ruler began to invade the country (724–722 B.C.E.), if this is not the Moabite ally of Tiglath-pileser III.

In 745 B.C.E. Shallum assassinated Zechariah, likely to end Israel's position of serving as a client state in the Assyrian Empire and to establish an alliance with Aram to oppose the empire, but he ruled only for a month before Menahem murdered him. King Menahem (745–738 B.C.E.)

of Israel, recognizing the serious threat of Assyria's powerful empire when Tiglath-pileser III began his western campaign in 743 B.C.E. and the futility of attempting to resist, even with an alliance forged with neighboring states, willingly submitted to the empire and paid heavy tribute (1,000 talents of silver; 2 Kgs 15:19–21). As early as 738 B.C.E., a coalition of western states, which included the powerful state of Hamath, was defeated by the Assyrians. Once brought to its knees by Tiglath-pileser III during his first campaign into Palestine, Hamath was forced to relinquish nineteen provinces from the coast to the northern part of the Orontes Valley. By 720 B.C.E., Hamath was finally crushed, numerous people of the country were deported, and the nation was incorporated directly into the Assyrian empire. The Assyrians extracted a heavy tribute from the other defeated nations of the coalition.[4] During this time, Tiglath-pileser III received tribute from Sam'al, Byblos, Tyre, Damascus (Rezin), Samaria (Manahem), and a queen of Arabia (*ANET*, 282), but not from Uzziah or his son who served as co-regent (Jotham, 756–741 B.C.E.).

Tiglath-pileser III launched a second major campaign into Palestine in 735–732 B.C.E. to defeat the Syro-Ephraimitic coalition that included Israel, Kaspuna (a coastal city southwest of Hamath), Tyre, Ashkelon, and Damascus. Egypt was solicited to join as was Judah, now ruled by Ahaz (741–725 B.C.E.), although neither country participated. Also rejecting overtures to join the anti-Assyrian coalition were the nations of Moab and Ammon. Even the invasion of Judah by the armies of Israel and Syria to replace Ahaz, in spite of their attack of Jerusalem (2 Kgs 16:7; Isa 7:1) and the destruction of many of the towns of Judah (joined by Edom to retake Elath), eventually failed due to the second Assyrian campaign of major consequence. This resulted in the defeat of Israel, Damascus, Kaspuna, and Malahab (formerly ruled by Tyre). The Assyrians placed Mitini on the throne of Ashkelon, while Hanuna of Gaza was forced to flee to take refuge in Egypt. While Menahem of Israel paid heavy tribute to Tiglath-pileser III, a later successor, Pekah (735–732 B.C.E.), who came to the throne of Israel after assassinating his predecessor, Pekahijah (737–736 B.C.E.), joined with Rezin, king of Damascus in this unsuccessful attempt to force

---

4. The critical issue concerns whether Azriyau (also identified as Sam'al of the Annals of Tiglath-pileser III) or Ya'uda/Yaudi (lines 123 and 131) is the king of Judah (Uzziah) (see Tadmor 1961, 270) or possibly the king of Sam'al (Panammu II). The Akkadian spelling of Yaudi/Yaudah is identical. However, it is unlikely that Azria(u) is a northern Syrian name (Aramean), but rather is more probably Israelite.

neutral Judah to join their anti-Assyrian coalition. Once this coalition was defeated by the Assyrians and Damascus was sacked in 732 B.C.E., Pekah apparently was assassinated. The Assyrians then appointed as king of Samaria, Hoshea (732–723 B.C.E.). Initially loyal to the empire and prompt in his payment of tribute to the imperial court, Hoshea foolishly chose to rebel in 725 B.C.E., following the advice of an anti-Assyrian faction at court and relying on the promise of Egyptian aid which never materialized. This precipitated the eventual destruction of Samaria in 722. Shalmaneser V in some way managed to take Hoshea prisoner (2 Kgs 17:4). Sargon II speaks of his deporting of 27,290 Israelites (*ANET*, 284–85; Becking 1992). Yet, with the exception of Hezekiah's foolish decision to withhold tribute in 704 B.C.E., Judah was able during Assyrian sovereignty over Palestine to maintain for a century its own nation and traditions without serious interference from the Assyrian court.

During the prophet's activities, there were several encounters between the empire from the north and Judah. According to the Assyrian Annals, Tiglath-pileser III is said to have defeated a coalition of Hamath and northern coastal cities led by King Azriyau of Yaudi in 738 (*ANET*, 282).[5] Following this came the catastrophic loss by the Syro-Ephraimitic forces to the Assyrians, leading to the transformation of Damascus and much of Israel into Assyrian provinces. The city of Samaria was sacked by Sargon II, and many of its people were deported to elsewhere in the empire, leading to the end of Israel.

However, Pekah, dreaming of a free Israel, succeeded Pekahiah to the throne after a brief reign of two years. He was murdered by Pekah, likely one of his military officers, who declared himself king. In the effort to remove the Assyrian presence in Syria and Palestine, Pekah participated in the Syro-Ephraimitic war combining his forces with those of the Arameans and the Philistines against Judah in order to depose King Ahaz of Judah and thus force the southern kingdom to join the alliance of the mutinous states (735–733 B.C.E.). When the troops of Judah were being overpowered by the alliance, Ahaz, who had been a loyal client to the empire, warned his

---

5. While some historians have supposed that this ruler's name was corrupted or confused with Uzziah and that Yaudi was actually Judah, the rulers' nations are not mentioned. In all probability there were two separate fragments, the second one mentioning Azriau, king of Yaudi, which belongs to the time of Sennacherib and thus refers to Hezekiah, not Azariah (Na'aman 1974). The other, an earlier one, was perhaps a reference to Uzziah, the leper king.

liege, Tiglath-pileser III, of this threat to his expansion. This demonstrated his loyalty and thus saved his country from Assyrian destruction and the deportation of many of his people. He also preserved the nation from being placed into a province directly ruled by the empire. The Assyrian monarch marched southward to put down the rebellion. Defeating their combined armies, he dealt with their opposition brutally and destroyed much of Syro-Palestine in 733 and 732, laying waste to many of their cities and towns. "Breaking the bow" of Israel may refer, at least in the text produced by the Deuteronomistic Historian, to the final battle in the Valley of Jezreel that resulted in the submission of the Israelites to imperial sovereignty. This was followed by the deportation of many of its citizens to different regions of the empire, leaving behind them a ravaged kingdom, with the country being reduced to the northern hill country and the capital of Samaria. If this were accurate historically, the kingdom of Israel would have become a vassal with a serious reduction of land and deportation of large numbers of Israelites and their royal house to another region. In any case with the kingship of Pekah and Israel's next rebellion, the forces of Shalmaneser V invaded and destroyed much of Israel and sacked the capital of Samaria, although the campaign may have been concluded by Sargon II due to the possible death of his predecessor as the siege of the capital had already begun to unfold. There is the reference of Shalman's destroying Beth-arbella (Irgid?) on the day of battle; mothers of Israel were dashed in pieces with their children. Whether this is a reference to Shalmaneser V's invasion (724–722 B.C.E.) or the destruction of the site by a Moabite ruler known as Salamanu, a supporter of Tiglath-pileser, cannot be precisely determined (Andersen and Freedman 1980, 570–71).

The deportation of much of the population of Samaria and their scattering throughout the empire led to its final demise in 722 B.C.E., with its incorporation into Assyria as a conquered people. What happened to the northern kingdom afterwards is not known, but the lack of references to the people of Israel in either the cuneiform annals or in the Bible imply the likelihood of the nation's disappearance from history.

Hosea prophesied during this momentous time of internal instability and the approach of the Assyrian invasion under Shalmaneser V and Sargon II, likely in or near Samaria.[6] He functioned as a marginal prophet

---

6. The efforts by some recent scholars to attribute almost of the book to the postexile and later are not, in my estimation, convincing (see Lemche; Levin).

who did not have privileged access to the royal court. His proclamations may have been delivered at various sacred places, including those in Bethel and Gilgal which he mentions. Indeed the confrontation of Amos with Amaziah occurred at Bethel, the king's sanctuary. Cult prophets often spoke at such sanctuaries to worshipers who came to offer praise to the deity, but Hosea's message was not one of salvation, the usual type of discourse uttered by these prophets, but rather one of judgment and coming devastation. Hosea appears to have given voice to several oracles that allude to the capital city's final days, but he does not mention its fall (9:1–9; 10:3–10; 11:5–7; 14:1). As a subaltern, Hosea defended those who were the victims of oppressive political systems, including both those who were royalists in Israel and the Assyrian conquerors. Hosea's goal was to resist and subvert systems of oppression.

Hosea's contextualization strongly affects his interpretation and understanding of events that emerge from his own time for his own reality, consisting of culture, religious space and time, and sociopolitical institutions. If removed from this location, due to such things as shifting to a new worldview, the prior interpretation of reality becomes confusing, meaning that earlier knowledge has to be adapted to the new situation. This seems likely in the later Judean redaction of the prophetic book, following the fall of Israel and movement south to Judah by some of the refugees. For Hosea, however, his contextual interpretation sought to negate the present reality of imperial culture, its view of religion, and its interpretation of history under the leadership of the deity, Ashur. The prophet seeks to remove the elements of adaptation to and assimilation of the imperial metanarrative and especially the notion of Assyrian superiority in culture, religion, and knowledge. At the same time, his harsh criticism of kingship, both north and south, and his lack of interest in the temple of Yahweh in Jerusalem suggest he seeks to return to a golden age encompassed by the Mosaic tradition and especially the laws of covenant.

1. The Yahwistic Metanarrative of Hosea

In shaping his metanarrative to resist and subvert the imperial ideology of the Neo-Assyrians and the royal theology of Israel and Judah, Hosea speaks of Yahweh as the one who controls history, with the implication that it was not Ashur who had created and extended the empire. In addition, Yahweh controlled history, and the two nations should wait for his protection and not seek to survive by means of military alliances and the building up of their armies and defenses. This prophet is especially anti-Assyrian, for he sees any positive relation with this nation as a rejection of Yahweh (8:9; 10:6; 11:5, 11; 12:2 [11:12]; 14:4 [14:3]). Due to the disloyalty of Israel and its worship of other gods, Hosea stated that God will deport his own people. Disloyalty to Yahweh in worshiping Baal is also paralleled by the establishment of alliances, especially with Assyria, Egypt, and Aram (8:9). The design of alliances with foreign nations was to depend on them, instead of Yahweh, for protection (5:13; 8:9; 10:6; 11:5, 11; 12:2 [11:12]; 14:4 [14:3]; also see 5:12–13 and 7:11–12, which includes Egypt). These alliances represent for the prophet a lack of trust in Yahweh (5:8–7:16). Israel will soon be destroyed (5:9a). Indeed, Israel has forgotten his Maker, and built palaces, while Judah has constructed fortified cities, but to no avail, for fire will devour them (8:14). A fire will come upon Judah's cities and it shall devour its strongholds. Yahweh will not protect Israel and Judah due to the violation of the covenant (6:7–7:16).

The prophet makes important use of the Mosaic tradition as it had been formulated in northern Israel by the eighth century B.C.E., with the early stage of the Deuteronomistic History the likely representative of this theology. Important is the point that this covenant is conditional and depends on the faithfulness of the covenant partners. Drawing on the past, especially the traditions of Israel's early formation as a people, Hosea speaks of the patriarchal tradition of Jacob and of when Yahweh led Israel out of Egypt in the exodus (2:17 [2:15]; 11:1; 12:10, 14 [12:9, 13], and 13:14) and guided them through the Sinai (2:16 [2:14]) to enter the land of promise. Particularly important is his view that the wilderness was the pristine period in Israel's faithful bonding with Yahweh. It was only after the entrance into Canaan that apostasy and disloyalty to Yahweh, the God of the covenant, began and developed into full-blown apostasy. Israel's most significant sins were her rebellion against Yahweh (1:2, 2:4, 6 [2:6, 8]; 3:3; 4:10, 12–15, 18; 5:4, 7; 6:7; 7:1, 13, 14; 8:1–2; 9:15; 14:1) and the worship of other gods, in particular Baal (5:13; 7:8, 11; 8:9–10; 12:2 [12:1]; cf. esp. Baal-Peor in 9:10 at the time of the settlement in Canaan, Num 25:1–5), including their idols that its craftsmen had fashioned (8:4–5; 13:2). This judgment stands front and center in the book. The nation's transgressions against the commandments incorporated within the covenant (4:1–3; 6:7; 7:1; 8:1), the dependence on their own military strength, and the turning both to Assyria and Egypt, not Yahweh, for aid were additional violations of the covenant and also were seen as elements of apostasy. As a result, Yahweh has divorced her, as indicated by the divorce decree of Hosea issued to or about to be given to his wife Gomer, quoted in 2:4 ([2:2]: "I am not her husband, and she is not my wife"). Israel's apostasy began once the entry into Canaan had begun, but Yahweh will take Israel back into the wilderness where the faithful, loving relationship will be restored. However, even before the final end, if the nation will repent, they shall become as in the days of its youth when it came forth out of Egypt in the exodus (2:17 [2:15]). Thus, for Hosea, the sacred traditions include in particular God's leading them from Egypt to Canaan, during a time when the bond between Yahweh and his people was especially strong.

Yahweh indicts the people of Israel for their lack faithfulness and knowledge of God. Indeed, they violate the ethical commandments of the Mosaic covenant (Exod 20:13-19) in their swearing of false oaths, lying, stealing, and murder. These transgressions lead to mourning the land and all who dwell in it, including the perishing of the wild animals, the birds of the air, and the fish of the sea (Gen 1:20-25). Those responsible for leading people to violate the covenant's commandments are especially the northern priests and the prophets (4:4; 5:1). Thus God rejects them from being priests. Since they have forgotten the Torah, God shall forget their children. The priests' violation leads to Yahweh's contention against them for rejecting the divine knowledge found in the law of God. In addition to priests of Yahweh, there were also those who served Baal in Canaanite sanctuaries located in the capital city of Samaria, Bethel, and Gilgal. The prophet speaks of the calf being made by an artisan. Since it is not a god, the calf of Samaria will be broken to pieces (8:4-6), a fate similar to some of the idols of other nations conquered by Assyria.

Hosea's marriage, as he tells it, was his response to Yahweh's command to marry a promiscuous Gomer, either a prostitute or at least a woman prone to infidelity. If she were guilty of promiscuity and was unfaithful to her marriage partner, then the prophet's own personal experience enables him to understand Yahweh's relationship to Israel (14:8 [14:9]), for both involved a relationship of faithlessness. Of course this is the view of her husband, Hosea. How she would have described herself we have no way of knowing (Weems 1995). Was Hosea an abusive husband, a man who ignored his responsibilities of providing her with food, shelter, and sexual relations? Was he possibly one who ignored his responsibilities when it came to their children? Of course, without her voice, these questions remain unanswered. However, as the story is told, she is unfaithful and takes on lovers to provide for her even as Israel had abandoned Yahweh for other gods. Yet there was also the reconciliation in chapter 3 in which the prophet eventually took back his wife after a time that would allow her to experience remorse and to reject her former lovers. What becomes symbolically important is the naming of the three children of the marriage ("children of harlotry" which could suggest he rejected them as his own or that they were children born to a woman who was or became a prostitute). Their names illustrate the brokenness of the bond between Yahweh and Israel. The firstborn is a son named Jezreel ("God sows," Hos 1:4–5); the second child, a daughter who is given the name, "not pitied" (*lō' raḥûmâ*, a term that is especially used to speak of Yahweh's bonding with his people; Hos 1:6–7); and the third child, a second son, receives the name "not my people" (*lō' 'ammî*; contrast Lev 26:12). Yahweh shall no longer be the God of Israel (cf. Exod 3:14). Yet once the restoration is achieved, something for which Hosea argued, Israel shall once more be God's people (Hos 2:1 = 1:10).

Jezreel is the name of a city and that of the central plain of Israel which is on a west–east corridor that stretches from the "Way of the Sea" (an important trade route along the coastal cities of Israel and the major military route of armies from Mesopotamia to Egypt and vice versa) to the "King's Highway," the road that leads north from Egypt through the Transjordan to Syria. This valley was protected by two fortress cities, Megiddo and Taanach. Jezreel is a city located in the middle of this valley which was the location of many important battles, including Josiah's disastrous defeat and death in his unsuccessful efforts to block Necho II's Egyptian army from joining the Assyrians to resist the Babylonian invasion that was drawing to its final conclusion in the sacking of Harran, the last stronghold of the final Assyrian monarch, Ashur-uballit II. Hosea also uses the name Jezreel to refer to Jehu's bloody seizure of the throne of Israel, thus ending the Omride dynasty. The blood spilled in this *coup d'état* included Jehu's personal assassination of Joram, king of Israel, who was in the town, recovering from wounds suffered at the hands of the Syrian army in a battle at Ramoth-Gilead. The king of Judah, Ahaziah, who was present in Jezreel, attempted to escape the slaughter but was fatally wounded by one of the soldiers of Jehu. Jehu terminated the Phoenician alliance fashioned earlier by Omri and Ahab and ordered the death of Jezebel who at the time was living in Jezreel. The daughter of the king of Sidon and the wife of Ahab, she was hurled from the upper story to the street below by her own eunuchs according to Jehu's instructions. The royal assassinations were then followed by the murder of the northern kingdom's princes (Ahab's sons), whose seventy heads were brought and placed in two heaps before the new king in Jezreel. Some forty-two relatives of King Ahaziah were slaughtered by Jehu and his troops, because they were on their way to visit the royal princes at Samaria. This may have been designed to pave the way for Jehu's taking Judah and ending the Davidic dynasty. Then in Samaria he eliminated Ahab's remaining relatives. Hosea's naming of his firstborn, Jezreel, indicates that the house of Jehu will be repaid for this bloody slaughter and bring an end to the northern kingdom and its dynasty (Jeroboam II was the last descendant of Jehu and the dynasty he established). Jehu did not end entirely the worship of Baal in the north (2 Kgs 10:28–31; the golden calves at the royal sanctuaries in Dan and Bethel continued, 2 Kgs 12:26–33), and this is one factor in the naming of the firstborn. Jehu is presented in the "Black Obelisk" of Shalmaneser III following his defeat in 841 B.C.E., making Israel a client state of Assyria and requiring the state to sever alliances. Israel finally defeated Aram with Assyrian aid and controlled this country (2 Kgs 13:14–25; 14:23–29), although Assyrian weakness eventually allowed the Syrians to harass Israel. However, according to Hosea, Yahweh intended to bring the dynasty of Jehu to an end and to "break the bow of Israel" in the Jezreel Valley (1:5). Assyria's control of this valley would allow them to have control of commerce extending to the coastal plain and to have access to Egypt (Elat).

The names of the second and third children are symbolic and have no narrative explanations. The first means that Yahweh no longer has motherly compassion for Israel (lō' raḥûmâ) and the second (lō' 'ammî) declares that Israel is no longer the "people" of Yahweh (see Trible). In 1:7, however, a redactional insertion contrasts this rejection of Israel with the affirmation that Yahweh will pity Judah. However, he will not save them by bow, sword, war, horses, or horsemen. In this additional redaction, they shall go up from the land to the place where they were "not my people." These two nations shall be called "sons of the living God" (1:11) and will then possess the land, for great will be the "land of Jezreel," the location where Jehu ended the Omride dynasty in 845 B.C.E. and killed many of the princes of Judah. This reference likely speaks of the destruction of Israel's strongest dynasty, the killing of the Tyrian princess Jezebel (thus limiting the influence of Tyrian culture and Baalist religion), and the slaughter of forty-two royal members of the house of David, including eventually the fleeing King Ahaziah of Judah who had been in Jezreel. The goal of the Omride dynasty was to establish peaceful relations between the two major segments of population in Israel, the Israelites and the Canaanites, and seems to have been followed by some of the kings of Judah, including

Ahaziah who had been influenced by his mother, Athaliah, to permit the practice of Canaanite religion. This required granting religious privilege to the Canaanite population's worship of Baal religion.

Married to Jehoram, king of Judah, she was a daughter of the usurper Omri, who likely had been a mercenary who commanded the Israelite army. She was a powerful woman as Queen Mother in Judah, and, like her father, permitted and practiced the worship of Baal, even constructing for this god a temple in Judah. In order to consolidate her power as the ruler of Judah, she massacred most of the surviving male members of the house of Judah, save for the boy Joash. However, she incurred the wrath of the priests of the temple of Jerusalem, and, with their support she was assassinated in the royal palace and the temple of Baal was destroyed (2 Kgs 10:12–14). This bloodshed wrought especially by Jehu and then by Athaliah, and her assassination, brought to an end the alliance between Israel and Judah. Hosea alludes to the eschatological joining of the two nations into one, with one "head," likely a deliverer or judge comparable to the temporary leaders of a united Israel who fought against and defeated common enemies (2:1–11 [1:10–2:9]). Hosea, then, appears to have been disenchanted with not only the northern dynasties of Omri and Jehu, but also the house created by David who established the royal state of Israel and Judah following the death of Saul and who finally came to rule in his city, Jerusalem (5:10, 12, 14). If this is correct, then the redactional insertion of Israel in the future coming to worship Yahweh as their God (not Baal) and to accept "David their king" (3:1–5) will compare to Gomer, the adulteress, who shall return to Hosea, remaining as his wife for many days without conjugal relations, proving she no longer commits harlotry so Israel will worship without king or prince, sacrifice or pillar (*maṣṣebâ*, i.e., a cultic pillar), and ephod (sacred, priestly vestment, sometimes as here the clothing of an idol) or teraphim (household gods). A later redactional insertion by a scribe of Judah also mentions that Judah is still known by God and is faithful to the Holy One (11:11–12) and contrasts Judah's faithfulness in walking with God, while Ephraim has surrounded him with their lies (compare Andersen and Freedman 1980, 307–9). What is underlined by the prophet is that God prefers compassion and divine knowledge far more than sacrifices (6:4–6).

However, following the coming holocaust, there was still hope for a revival of the people. Due to Yahweh's grace and forgiveness, Israel one day will be taken back (2:22–23 [2:19–20]; 13:14), and the Valley of Achor (the valley just north of Jericho, which the Israelites had used to invade and conquer Canaan, Josh 7) shall become the door of hope (2:15). Then Yahweh shall once again become her husband (not Baal), and she will become his faithful wife. This divine love is exemplified by Hosea's own love for a repentant Gomer (2:7) whom he takes back as his wife who had forsaken him for other lovers, and Yahweh's redemption of the wayward son (2:16–23). Hosea continues to call for Israel to return. He pleads for his children to convince (or to contend, strive; plural of *ryb*, at times "to utter a legal complaint," i.e., a suit of divorce; cf. Deut 24:1–4) their mother to come back to him (Hos 2:4 [2:2–5]). To reverse the divorce proceeding in essence would necessitate that the mother recognize that she must abandon her faithless behavior with her lovers who provide her with bread, water, flax, oil, and drink (a husband is required to give to his wife food, clothing, and sexual relations, but now she is provided these necessities by her lovers; cf. Exod 21:10–11). Otherwise, Hosea will divorce her legally and end his support of her. For Israel, this is the removal of mirth, festival, new moon, Sabbath, and appointed feast, since they are polluted with sin and faithlessness. Yahweh, as Israel's husband will punish his people for serving other gods. He, not Baal, is her husband (*baʻal*). But, if she does not give up her lovers, he will divorce her by engaging in a lawsuit that will end the relationship (see 4:1–3). Baal's (or Hadad's) providing of rain, fertility, bread, wine, and oil are frequently mention in the Ugaritic Texts (KTU 1.19, III.6–7, 12–16). But Israel must know from the teaching of the Torah and its sacred history that Yahweh is the provider of what the nation needs.

Hosea's metanarrative placed Yahweh' power and punishment into the center of his story of Israel's final years, contrasting in particular his divine compassion and deliverance with his harsh punishment of Israel by means of the Assyrian invasion and destruction of the nation due to the violation of the Mosaic covenant. Indeed, Israel's end is near (10:14; 13:9; 14:1 [13:16]). However, it was Yahweh, not Ashur, who was the deity with whom to reckon. The prophet gives no credence to the religious ideology of Ashur. In spite of the powerful empire which appears unstoppable in its march to conquest, he maintains his faith that Yahweh is in control of history.

While Hosea appears opposed to kingship in Israel in particular, he also does not seem to advocate maintaining the house of David. It was at Gilgal, where Israel first encamped following its entrance into Canaan and where Saul was made king by the people that evil began (Hos 9:15–16; 11:14–15; cf. the larger unit of 1 Sam 8–12, which entwines the desire for kingship in a positive portrayal and its rejection not just of Samuel but of God). Hosea may be following his thesis of apostasy beginning after entrance into Canaan or more likely is alluding to the appointment of Saul as the first king. Both themes appear to be important ones in the book. Similar to the antikingship tradition embedded in parts of 1 Sam 8–12, Hosea also is especially critical of the priests and kings of Israel, including in particular the house of Jehu. "Gangs of priests" have not only failed to teach the commandments, but even engage in the murder of travelers to Shechem and in thievery (6:7–7:2). Instead of the sacred tradition of kingship in both north and south, Hosea speaks of the kings of Israel becoming a snare at Mizpah, a net spread on Tabor, and a deep pit at Shittim. Mizpah was an ancient assembly and cultic site of the tribes prior to pursuing holy war (Judg 20–21) and the place where the first king, Saul, was chosen by lot and elected to be king (1 Sam 10:17–25). Tabor is likely the site where an ancient sanctuary was located, where several tribes did not appear in the federation designed to defeat the Canaanites (Judg 4–5), while Shittim (5:2) was the location of an early rebellion of Israel against Yahweh (Num 25). These three references point to political rebellion in the selection of a king to rule instead of Yahweh, internecine warfare that continues to plague Israel throughout its history, and rebellion against Yahweh. Thus, judgment and chastisement are coming against Israel (5:1–2). Hosea in particular holds in contempt the dynasty of Jehu (842–815 B.C.E.), but he does not stop there. The entire institution is at fault for the nation's abandonment of God. Israel will turn again to the Assyrian king for assistance, but he will not save them. Even more, the prophet's strong attack on kingship is found throughout the collection. Yahweh becomes a lion who will devour Ephraim and a young lion to carry Judah away (5:14), for the "princes" ("officers" or "royal sons") of Judah illegally move the boundary stones marking the outlines of a farm's land. This suggests these officers or royal sons are also expanding their estates. Because the lion is a royal symbol in Syria and Judah may explain Hosea's metaphorical description of Yahweh's coming destruction of his own people. Following the invasion, presumably by Assyria, Israel's trust in its troops will come to an end. The nation will be rent apart and its population carried into exile. One day they will proclaim that they have no king (10:3). Prior to that time, Israel's king was gladdened by his people's wickedness, and his enemies, having made him drunk, were to assassinate him. This passage in Hosea indicates that the prophet is well aware of the numerous assassinations of kings (four of the last six) and the subsequent instability these bring to the nation (7:1–7; 8:4). What is particularly revealing is Yahweh's statement that Israel made kings, but not at his choosing (8:4). Hosea is portraying Yahweh as withdrawing from any responsibility for the selection of individual kings and perhaps even the entire institution. If the latter is true, this would be the case with both the house of David in Judah and the Israelite rulers. In 10:9 Israel began to sin against Yahweh in Gibeah. This anti-royal tradition also may be behind the mentioning of Gibeah, for this is the major city where Saul ruled for thirty-eight years (1 Sam 10:26; 11:4). This also could well be a rejection of kingship in general. Another possible interpretation is the internecine war initiated by the rape of the Levite's concubine that led to her death. When Benjamin refused to punish the people of the town of Gibeah for their heinous crime, a civil war ensued that almost led to the complete annihilation of the tribe (Hos 5:8; 10:9; see Judg 19–21; Andersen and Freedman 1980, 534). Thus, Gibeah may refer to both illicit leadership in the establishment of kings and internecine war.

Another type of unfaithfulness was the establishment of alliances with other nations to defeat especially the advancing Assyrian forces. For Hosea Israel made alliances, but for a time they did not anoint people as kings and princes (8:10). Indeed Israel is the one who wanted a king (13:10), a likely reference to 1 Sam 8, but he is not capable of saving them. Yahweh gave them a king and removed him due to his wrath (13:11). Finally, it is likely that during the invasion of the Assyrians, Israel concluded that they have no king, but rather will fear the Lord. They question what the king would do for his people (10:3). When Israel is taken into Assyrian exile, their golden calf will be taken with the conquerors to Assyria as booty (10:6). And the king of Samaria will perish, while the high places of Bethel will be destroyed (10:7). The king of Samaria is not identified in this text, but could likely be any one of the four who were assassinated. In 10:15 the king will be cut off in the storm of war. In 11:5 Egypt and Assyria will be their king. Metaphorically Israel will return to Egypt (presumably as slaves) in a reverse exodus, only now it is Assyria where they shall be deported and ruled by its king. Indeed, the people shall return from exile in Assyria and Egypt one day due to Yahweh's triumph, but only after he has destroyed them. Once more they shall settle upon the lands.

In contrasting this coming deportation, Hosea speaks of the ancient traditions of the patriarch Jacob (12:3–9 [12:2–8]), who strove with the angel at Bethel and spoke with God, the exodus from Egypt led by a prophet (12:13), the divine protection of Israel, the wandering in the Sinai wilderness, including their rebellion and desire to return to Egypt (11:1–9), and the conquest (Neef 1987).[7] Israel should return to God, hold fast to justice and love, and wait upon Yahweh who, when the people repent, will come to them like the reviving rains of spring (6:1–3). Alliances and kings are of no avail. Israel will go to the king of Assyria to seek support, but he will not save them. Israel's one hope is to reject the metanarrative of Assyria and its military power and to depend on Yahweh alone for survival.

2. Hybridity, Foreign Culture, and Religion in Israel

The prophet condemns the nation for mixing with the peoples who devour its strength (7:7–8).[8] In Israel hybridity, including the integration of Canaanite fertility cults into Yahwistic religion or the abandonment of the latter and its replacement with other cults, was well represented in state and private/family religions in Israel. This religious hybridity was also accompanied by a transition in culture. This is suggested by 7:8–12 where "Ephraim has mixed itself with peoples." The Samaritan ostraca contain a large number of theophoric names based on Baal. The ostraca of Samaria are inscribed with the names of persons or towns that delivered oil or wine to the king's palace, much of which was likely used for tribute to the empire. They are dated "in the ninth year," "in the tenth year," "in the seventeenth year" of the king, although the name of the king is not mentioned (Rollston 1999). Another key example of the adaption of Canaanite religion is Kuntillet 'Ajrud, a traveler's way station in the Sinai. The pithos that depicts a couple with bovine features points to the presence of a Yahwistic cult. The inscription on this pithos reads, "May you be blessed by YHWH of Samaria and by his Asherah." As noted below, this hybridity is well illustrated in the prophecies of Hosea who indicates that Yahweh on occasion is assimilated into Baal, but elsewhere is abandoned for the worship of this Canaanite deity.

Israel's prophets read the present through the lens of past traditions of salvation, including the Mosaic tradition and that of David and Zion. This

---

7. What is interesting is the positive portrayal of Jacob in order to portray Israel's Yahwistic roots in Aram and the covenant with Laban as a way of recalling Israel's former relationship with this nation during the prophet's own period. This nation was the early home of Abraham, Sarah, Rebekah, and the place where Jacob found his two brides, Leah and Rachel. This reference of Jacob and the other sacred traditions was a way of rejecting the relationship with Assyria.

8. For literature, consult McKay 1973; Cogan 1974, 1993; Spieckermann 1982.

conservative and reactionary enculturation of new elements taken from foreign religions and cultural expressions attempts to re-establish a romanticized past as the time of Yahweh's and the chosen's relationship. Hosea attempted to recall the Mosaic tradition that speaks of Israel's beginnings and especially the wilderness tradition. For Hosea the trouble for Israel began once they entered Canaan and identified Yahweh and Canaanite religion, especially focusing on Baal, that made Yahweh a member of the Canaanite pantheon. In 4:12 people seek oracles from "wood" (possibly the sacred tree that represents Asherah). Elsewhere they engage in the ritual of gashing themselves for the gifts of grain and wine (7:14). The calf of Samaria (8:5, Beth-aven, "house of iniquity," a pejorative term for Bethel in 10:5) is but one element of Canaanite religion, including the making of golden calves, and was understood by the prophet to have been incorporated into Israelite religious practices, and this religious aspect of hybridity was placed in motion (7:8). This is the process of Israel's enculturation into a land heavily permeated with the fertility religion of Canaan. In Israel's case Yahweh is identified with the Canaanite storm god Baal, and some Israelites even "gave" him Asherah as his consort. Assimilation or enculturation is common in the movements of people who come into contact with different cultures, and this would have been the case especially for the north, strongly influenced by Phoenicia and their worship of the god Baal. However, the Assyrians did not interfere in the religion of Israel. For Hosea the worship of Baal was tantamount to apostasy, for it was the people's and their leader's choice, not imposed from the outside, that is, by a superior military power. He included in his speeches of judgment directed against Israel the worship of the multiple locations of Baal (thus the "Baals"), sexual rites to Canaanite deities (2:7b–15 [2:5b–14]; cf. 1:2; 4:10–19; 7:4; 9:1), engaging in rituals at high places (4:15; 9:15), and Jeroboam's construction of golden calves which Israel continued to worship in Bethel (4:15; 10:5, 8) and Gilgal (4:15). To prove Baal and his symbol are not divine, the golden calf at Bethel will be carried as booty into exile (10:6). These sins of apostasy and the idolatrous worship of Baal led to Yahweh's lawsuit against his people (2:4 [2:2]; 4:1; 5:1; 2:10 [2:8]; 8:5–6; 10:5–6; 13:2; Day 2010). Indeed it is due to their worship of Baal that Israel's guilt was pronounced and led to Ephraim's death (13:1). The people of Israel failed to realize it was Yahweh, not Baal, who delivered them from Egyptian slavery and provided the fertility that enabled the land to prosper. The nation's punishment will be hunger (4:10; 9:2), the inability to produce offspring, and the horrors of invasion and destruction, a reference to the future destruction of the state which the prophet saw as inevitable. Israel's alliances with Egypt and its tribute to Assyria which was raised by taxing landholders (2 Kgs 15:19-20; *ANET*, 283) would not divert its eventual destruction (7:11-12, 16; 8:8-10; 12:2 [12:1]; 14:3).[9] It may have been that the large landowners in the business of expanding their estates by annexing the property of poor farmers were the ones most supportive of any king that opposed Assyrian control of the state. However, Hosea is much more passive. Instead of the royal efforts to build up its internal defenses, including the multiplication of fortified cities, they should have depended on Yahweh for deliverance and protection. The prophet proclaimed Yahweh's indictment and judgment that indicated Israel would be devastated by invasion: war would overtake them (5:8-12; 10:9, 14), cities would be destroyed by fire (8:14, 16), its people would die by the sword (7:16; 9:13; 11:6), children were to be dashed in pieces while pregnant women would be cut open (11:6; 14:11 [13:16]). In a reverse exodus, Israel would be brought back to Egypt (8:13; 9:3; 11:5) and go into Assyrian exile where they shall have to eat "unclean food" (9:3, 17; 11:5, 11). In Assyrian exile they will "wander among the nations." There they will remain without their false gods and idols, until Yahweh liberates them and allows them to return home (3:4-5; 11:11).

Judgment leads eventually to hope, for Yahweh will take Israel back (2:22-23 [2:19-20]). Divine forgiveness is exemplified in Hosea's willingness to accept once again his unfaithful wife, Gomer, and Yahweh's love for Israel as a child. Divine compassion would lead to Israel's restoration, even as Ephraim the child would be taken back by his parent (11:8-9); in the end the nation would be pitied (14:4 [14:3]), follow after Yahweh, and return home (11:10-11). Thus, they were implored to return to Yahweh (6:1; 12:7 [12:6]; 14:2-3 [14:1-2]), recognize their foolishness, and live again (6:1-2). They would be restored and healed (6:11). The exiles would return home again (11:10-11; 6:11; cf. 3:5) and be loved once more by their God (14:5, 8 [14:3, 7]). Subsequently, the past traditions of salvation, especially that of Moses (exodus, wilderness, Sinai and law, and conquest)

---

9. Perhaps Hosea made use of suzerainty treaties common to the empires of the ancient Near East to solidify its relationship to its vassals, although this appears unlikely. It is doubtful that the prophet knew of these treaties, since he gives no evidence of serving in the court where such treaties would have been known. Furthermore, there is no clear outline or features typical for this kind of treaty. See McCarthy 1978; Baltzer 1971.

are used by the prophet to provide hope to a people, soon to experience the ravages of conquest and the exile to different parts of the empire. However, this hoped-for deliverance never materialized, since Israel disappeared into the various Assyrian cultures.

Another element of Hosea's resistance is ambivalence, that is, the view that identity derives in part from differences with the "Other." It is impossible to enter the mind of the prophet to determine that he harbored the desire to become what those he condemned were, that is, a part of a people exalted and held supreme above the nations, but it is likely some of the poor did exactly that. The "Other," in the case the Assyrians and the practitioners of Canaanite religion, is the opposite of what Israel should be. For Hosea the identity of Israel is shaped by the conflict of traditional Yahwism with the religion of Canaan. This sharp dichotomy in this prophet's pronouncements is common throughout his collection. Israel can again become the chosen people by repudiating Canaanite religion and ceasing practice of many of its features. The prophet even makes an internal, political contrast. Kingship is also the "other." He condemns the acts of kings in the formulation of treaties with other nations and their quest for security by strengthening the state's military installations. He seems to suggest that Israel's true identity is not only in returning to the tradition of Moses and rejecting foreign religious incursions into their religion, but also in recognizing that their own kings were either not selected by Yahweh or were given them out of divine wrath. The implication is that they were leading the nation to its conquest and deportation. He may even be suggesting that kingship from its beginning was not established by Yahweh and that Israel's future governance should be that of tribal elders and charismatic leaders (Gelston). The only possible existence for a future Israel would be groups of tribes bonded by common interests and faith in one God.

3. Decolonizing the Mind

There is little doubt that the Assyrian invasions of Israel and other countries led to the transformation of some of their populace who adopted the imperial metanarrative. Three important elements of that metanarrative included, first, the recognition of the power of the Assyrian gods, in particular Ashur, who some of the Israelites likely came to believe possessed the divine power to control history, including that of Israel. The second, related to the first, was the invincibility of the Assyrian empire whose forces dominated large parts of the ancient Near East, including the Levant. The third was the power of the Assyrian ruler, beginning with Tiglath-pileser III (2 Kgs 15).

The powerful force of these three elements is found in the reigns of the last six kings. The Deuteronomistic History condemned these rulers especially for religious infidelity by worshiping other gods (especially Baal, Asherah, and foreign gods in general), building them high places and altars (8:11), and engaging in their sacred rituals (including the burning of their children to Molech). Idols, an asherah, and the two calves fashioned originally by Jeroboam I are mentioned. The Deuteronomistic History repeated the denunciation used of many of the northern kings: "he did not depart from the sins of Jerobo'am the son of Nebat, which he made Israel to sin" (2 Kgs 15:9, 18, 24, 28). Like Hosea, the Deuteronomistic History, as noted earlier, refers to both the exodus and the commandments of Yahweh in the covenant of Sinai as the two primary traditions which were violated by Israel and its rulers (2 Kgs 17:7–18). By this memory of its salvific past, Israel's bowing the knee to foreign gods would come to an end. At least this is the expectation.

Subsequently Hosea, who likely prophesied at the time of the early formation of the earliest form of the Deuteronomistic History, makes similar accusations. To decolonize the minds of the northern populace, he speaks of returning to the wilderness, before they yielded to the worship of foreign gods, to renew the binding relationship to Yahweh where it was first established and to repudiate the violation of divine commandments by religious duplicity. He also refers to the exodus in which Yahweh delivered his people from slavery (13:9, 13). The exodus and Sinai traditions become central to his theology by which he seeks to remind Israel of their earlier salvation (13:4, 5). The power of the Assyrians could not be denied, and he mentions the payment to them of tribute and costly oil to Egypt (12:1). Yet the prophet does promise the hope of divine deliverance of Israel from exile. Finally, depending on the support of the power of the Assyrians is a useless enterprise (5:13; 8:9; 9:6 [including Egypt]; 12:1; 14:3), while the build-up of their fortifications to resist invasion is a useless enterprise that will not succeed (8:14). In addition he rejects the efforts to establish treaties with other nations to build up their strength (8:10). Indeed, the population will be taken to Assyria and to Egypt (11:5). For the prophet it is Yahweh who controls history, not other gods (this would include especially Ashur), for he is the one who sends into exile his people and will return them to their homeland. Thus the prophet appears to anticipate that even this empire will fall.

It is also important to note that in decolonizing the mind of the population by denying the legitimation and power of their own rulers, the prophet rejects Israel's election of kings by either denying they were chosen by Yahweh (8:4) or indicating that they were given to them by Yahweh due to his wrath for their sins (13:11; 1 Sam 8–12). While this is likely a reference to the northern rulers and treaties, including that between Israel and Syria in the Syro-Ephraimitic war, it may be that the prophet intends to encompass in this oracle all rulers, including the house of David. It is likely that Hosea rejected the Davidic covenant and the Zion tradition. He certainly does not mention these sacred traditions of the selection of David and the establishment of Zion as the holy mountain. To decolonize the mind of the population of the North, the prophet repudiates the northern rulers, if not all rulers, for they led Israel into religious apostasy, the making of treaties with other nations, and the building of an army for conquest and defense. Yet they will not have the power to defend them from their enemies (13:10). It may well be that Hosea envisions a nation that does not have future kings, but, like the period of the judges, only charismatic leaders chosen by Yahweh through the prophets. He expressly mentions the violation of the protection of farms and their boundaries that, under Mosaic law, were to be household property handed down by the generations. More than likely those landowners who opposed Assyrian domination did so for the reason of having to endure high taxation to meet the annual tribute. Thus anti-Assyrian rulers were supported during the last years of Israel to advantage wealthy owners of expanding estates. Returning to sacred tradition prior to the evolving of the royal state would include the protection of the farms of small landowners. This prophet likely repudiated the class division developing during the monarchy and the increasing pauperization of the farmers.

Hosea's references to Assyria appear to allude to Israel's tribute gathered through the local payment of taxes in exchange for their favor and protection from invasion (5:13; 7:11; 8:9; 12:1; 14:3). Nevertheless, the nation (at least the upper class and skilled laborers) shall go into Assyrian captivity (9:3, 6; 10:6; 11:5). Among the losses endured by Israel for religious and political apostasy will be the lack of food and wine (9:2) endured by being a subject to Assyria and the heavy tribute required of them. In addition the Israelite families, the great of which consisted of farming households depending on the labor of offspring, will be punished by the loss of their children (9:12, 16). Indeed even the cattle that used to plow and thresh will be lost, resulting in the people themselves having to do the plowing and reaping by the labor of their own hands. Sciroccos, hot air from the desert filled with sand, will blow across the land, parching the soil of the nation (12:1; 13:15). Thus, farming was the major industry of the northern kingdom, but it shall be ravaged by desert winds, the loss of children, and the tribute paid to Assyria. Indeed, Assyria's poor farmland meant that they depended heavily on the food, wine, and oil produced by the nations they conquered.

4. Power, Discourse, and Knowledge in Hosea

Hosea's speeches suggest they are directed only to Israel, likely given in a royal sanctuary, and that he directed his verbal assault against the nation, its official state and various forms of religion.[10] Prophets believed that as the spokesperson for Yahweh their words were imbued with power for they contained what was revealed to them by the God of history. This means then that both oracles of judgment and salvation were powerful discourses that express Yahweh's power of ruling not only Israel, but the entire cosmos.

The knowledge of Yahweh is a major theme in Hosea. The verb *yâdâ'* indicated the intimate knowledge of partners in a covenant or marriage. Israel's relationship with Yahweh was once was one of faithfulness, for the nation knew no other God but Yahweh and he alone knew them (13:4). Yet it was the lack of knowledge, especially due to the abandonment of the commandments by the leaders and priests of the nation (4:1, 4–14; 5:4) that led to their devastation. This knowledge of God is found in the law of Moses (4:1–3, 6; 6:6; 8:12; 14:1 [13:16]). The priests are not fit for divine service, because they have not engaged Israel in following the Torah. In 4:1–19, he appears to confront a priest who demands that he no longer engage in disputation (v. 1). In response, Hosea indicates his dispute is with the priest, likely of a sanctuary where he was speaking, because the people perish for a lack of knowledge of Yahweh, likely a reference to the Torah. He rejects him and prevents others like him from being priests. Instead of teaching the Torah, the priests become drunken, promiscuous idolaters who lead the people into acts of idolatry and sacred prostitution, and who are present in northern sanctuaries (see 4:14). They offer sacrifice and burn incense on the mountains and engage in adultery with

---

10. For theoretical background, see Foucault 1973; Scott 1992.

sacred prostitutes, while their daughters and daughters-in-law engage in adultery beneath the trees in the forest. The emphasis of 4:15-19 stresses that Israel must leave the sanctuaries of Bethel (occasionally called Bethaven, "house of falsehood) and Gilgal (Dan is not mentioned for unknown reasons, since it too was a royal sanctuary) and return to Yahweh. Otherwise, both priests and people will be destroyed for a lack of knowledge. By implication this knowledge is not found in the sciences of the empire that include divination, omenology, augury, and astrology (Oppenheim 1977). This rejection of the validity of imperial knowledge was an important dimension of Hosea's efforts to subvert Assyrian culture and to decolonize the minds of the Israelites who had come under what appeared to be their dominant power based on superior knowledge. And the true knowledge found in the Torah is superior, but is flagrantly ignored or violated.

For this prophet of the north, the political, cultural, social, and religious changes taking place in the north as they developed were impossible to reverse. What he desired to achieve in the eighth century was impossible. His dream was to return the nation to faithfulness to Yahweh through the covenant by returning to a golden age prior to the entrance into Canaan and the establishment of the royal state. He continued to hope that Israel would rekindle its steadfast love and bonding to Yahweh (10:12) and would begin once more to practice a form of justice based on the Mosaic covenant that would end the oppression of the poor (12:7). If this occurred, God's judgment would end, and he would take Israel back as his bride in righteousness, justice, mercy, faithfulness, and loyalty. Then Israel will truly know Yahweh as its God (2:22-23 [2:19-20]).

REFERENCES

Andersen, Francis I., and David Noel Freedman. 1980. *Hosea*. AB 24. Garden City, N.Y.: Doubleday.
Baltzer, Klaus. 1971. *The Covenant Formulary: In Old Testament, Jewish and Early Christian Writings*. Philadelphia: Fortress.
Becking, Bob. 1992. *The Fall of Samaria: An Historical and Archaeological Study*. Leiden: Brill.
Cogan, Mordecai. 1974. *Imperialism and Religion: Assyria, Israel and Judah in the Eighth and Seventh Centuries B.C.E.* Missoula: Scholars Press.
―――. 1993. Judah under Assyrian Hegemony: A Reexamination of Imperialism and Religion. *JBL* 112:403-14.

Daniels, Dwight. 1990. *Hosea and Salvation History: The Early Traditions of Israel in the Prophecy of Hosea*. BZAW 191. Berlin: de Gruyter.
Day, John. 2010. Hosea and the Baal Cult. Pages 202–24 in *Prophecy and the Prophets in Ancient Israel*. Edited by John Day. LHBOTS 531. London: T&T Clark.
Dearman, J. Andrew. 2010. *Hosea*. NICOT. Grand Rapids: Eerdmans.
Foucault, Michel. 1973. *The Order of Things: An Archaeology of the Human Sciences*. New York: Vintage.
Jeremias, Jörg. 1983. *Der Prophet Hosea*. ATD 24. Göttingen: Vandehoeck & Ruprecht.
Kwakkel, Gert. 2009. The Land in the Book of Hosea. Pages 167–81 in *Land of Israel in Bible, History, and Theology*. Edited by Jacques van Ruiten and J. Cornelis de Vos. Leiden: Brill.
Landy, Francis. 1995. *Hosea*. Sheffield: Sheffield Academic Press.
Macintosh, A. A. 1997. *A Critical and Exegetical Commentary on Hosea*. ICC. Edinburgh: T&T Clark.
McCarthy, Dennis J. 1978. *Treaty and Covenant: A Study in Form in the Ancient Oriental Documents and in the Old Testament*. 2nd ed. Rome: Biblical Institute Press.
McKay, John W. 1973. *Religion in Judah under the Assyrians 732–609 B.C.* London: SCM.
Na'aman, Nadav. 1974. Sennacherib's "Letter to God" on His Campaign to Judah. *BASOR* 214:25–39.
Neef, Heinz-Dieter. 1987. *Die Helstraditionen Israels in ihrer Verkündigung des Propheten Hosea*. BZAW 169. Berlin: de Gruyter.
Oppenheim, Leo. 1977. *Mesopotamia: Portrait of a Dead Civilization*. Revised ed. Chicago: University of Chicago Press.
Rollston, Chris A. 1999. The Script of Hebrew Ostraca of the Iron Age 8th–6th Centuries BCE. Doctoral thesis, Johns Hopkins University.
Scott, James C. 1992. *Domination and the Arts of Resistance: Hidden Transcripts*. New Haven: Yale University Press.
Spieckermann, Hermann, 1982. *Juda unter Assur in der Sargonidenzeit*. FRLANT 129. Gottingen: Vandenhoeck & Ruprecht.
Sweeney, Marvin A. 2000. *The Twelve Prophets*. Collegeville, Minn.: Liturgical Press.
Tadmor, Hayim. 1961. Azriyau of Yaudi. *ScrHier* 8:232–71.
Trotter, James A. 2001. *Reading Hosea in Achaemenid Yehud*. Sheffield: Sheffield Academic Press.

Weems, Renita. 1995. *Battered Love: Marriage, Sex, and Violence in the Hebrew Prophets*. Minneapolis: Fortress.
Wolff, Hans Walter. 1974. *Hosea: A Commentary on the Book of the Prophet Hosea*. Hermeneia. Philadelphia: Fortress, 1974.
Yee, Gale A. 1987. *Composition and Tradition in the Book of Hosea: A Redactional-Critical Investigation*. Atlanta: Scholars Press.
———. 1996. The Book of Hosea: Introduction, Commentary and Reflections. *NIB* 7:195–297.

African Culture as *Praeparatio Evangelica*: The Old Testament as Preparation of the African Post-colonial

Gerald West

1. Introduction

There has been plenty of discussion about African culture (and/as religion) as a preparation for the gospel and so as the bedrock of African Christianity/Christianities, with African culture (and/as religion) functioning as Africa's "Old Testament,"[1] preparing the way for the gospel/New Testament. There has been an even more abundant conversation about the related topic of the resonances between African culture (and/as religion) and the Old Testament. In both cases the Old Testament hovers in the background, much like "the spirit of God" in Gen 1:2, as the prelude to "the real thing," the gospel/New Testament.

Both discourses assume, at least, and often presuppose, a post-colonial stance. Here I deliberately reintroduce the hyphen in "post-colonial" to signify the long, tensive, and resistant transactions that take place from the moment, different in different African contexts, that the missionary-colonial package shifts from an exploratory to an exploitative enterprise. In many parts of Africa, particularly in the African interior, at some remove from the more militant presence of empire on the coastal peripheries, Africans remained in control long after the edges of their continent had come under imperial mastery. But in most cases, and this was certainly the case in southern Africa, the missionary-colonial presence on the coast reverberated across the hinterland, placing increasing pressure on spaces and peoples, and escalating conflict. Yet even in these decades of social

---

1. My use of the term "Old Testament" in this essay is therefore deliberate.

flux, Africans controlled their territories and those missionary-colonial agents who ventured into them. It was only when diamonds (1867) and gold (1886) were discovered in the interior of southern Africa that the interior itself became of significance to imperial powers (Beck 1997, 114). What had been a slow creep of cautious, even fearful, encroachment into the African interior, now became a covetous rush to control these lands and minerals. Now we can properly speak of conquest and colonialism. And it was precisely at this time, in the mid-1800s, in southern Africa that the Bible became available in local languages (Lubbe 2009), providing one more site of post-colonial contestation.

So I pause here to remind the reader of that under-theorized period of European presence in the African interior in which they were not in control, but were under the territorial and psychosocial control of Africans (West 2004). But, unfortunately, we cannot linger too long here. For we must push on, along with the advancing missionary-colonial forces, to colonialism "proper," and so to the post-colonial response of Africans. For the focus of my essay is on what resources the Old Testament offered in the forging of the post-colonial African.[2]

We must push on also because it is colonialism proper that is foregrounded in African reflections on the role of the Bible and the formation of the post-colonial African. As part of the imperial project of taking hold, quite literally, of African territories and resources, the colonial-missionary enterprise set about, as soon as it could, to prepare Africans for their entry into the Christian commonwealth, which included being inducted into God's economic order. "Saving the savage meant teaching the savage to save" (Comaroff and Comaroff 1997, 166). Africans must be taught to turn away from their inefficient mode of production so that, using God's talents, they might bring forth the greatest possible abundance. "Only then would black communities be animated by the spirit of commerce that—along with the Gospel of Christ—promoted exchange on a worldwide scale. Only then might they be part of the sacred economy of civilized society" (166). For many a missionary, even the Non-Conformist missionary in the interior of southern Africa, the political economy was a form of "secular theology" (166), and so the missionaries set out to establish economic reform with religious zeal, persuading with word and deed the

---

2. I gratefully acknowledge the financial support of the National Research Foundation toward this research.

Africans "to accept the currency of salvation, a task involving the introduction, along with the gospel, of market exchange, wage work, sometimes even a specially minted coinage" (168).

It was the regimes and routines of the missionary-colonial order of things that was most persistently resisted by Africans for as long as they could. As an old man from the BaTlhaping clan, located in the interior of southern Africa, told the missionary John Campbell in June 1813, "if they were to attend to instructions, they would have no time to hunt or to do any thing" (Campbell 1815, 193). He clearly understood that allowing the missionaries "to instruct them" would immerse them in the time schedules and modes of production of the established mission stations, churches, and schools to the south (in the Colony), whose "notions of time, work, and self-discipline were drawn from the natural lineaments of the industrial capitalist world" (Comaroff and Comaroff 1997, 179).

It was also this order of things that, when eventually implemented under colonial control, did the most damage, denigrating and destroying significant dimensions of African life. It is this recognition that haunts almost all African Christian theological and biblical discourse. Oddly, however, it is the Bible that is credited by a significant strand within African theology with restoring what had been damaged. But before we consider this contribution, there is a prior move that this strand of African theology makes, namely that the very African culture (and/as religion) that missionary-colonial forces denigrated and destroyed is the vehicle for God's revelation of the gospel to Africans.

2. Decoding African Religious Instincts

The African theological trajectory that considers African culture (and/as religion) as "a preparation for the gospel" owes its impetus to John Mbiti, the Kenyan biblical scholar and theologian. Mbiti has been at the forefront of discussions about the continuities and discontinuities between "African Religion"—he prefers the singular though acknowledges that "it is not uniform throughout the continent"—and "Christian Faith" (Mbiti 1978a, 309). In a section entitled "African Religion as a Preparation for the Gospel" of his 1976 address to the Pan African Christian Leadership Assembly (PACLA) in Nairobi, Mbiti argues that "African Religion made people to be disposed towards the Christian Faith." He continues:

It is African Religion which has produced the religious values, insights, practices and vocabulary on which the Christian Faith has been planted and is thriving so well today. The points of continuity between Biblical faith and culture and African Religion have been sufficiently strong for the Gospel to establish a strong footing among African peoples. (1978a, 311)

Mbiti acknowledges the integrity of African religion in its own right (but see Opoku 1993, 69) but stresses its preparatory role. "Although African Religion has been self-sufficient for many generations, it has nevertheless kept itself open enough to absorb and benefit from the new elements that the Christian Faith brings." Indeed, he continues, it is African religion that "has created a spiritual yearning, spiritual insights and sensitivities, which receive their ultimate satisfaction in the Gospel scheme." And while "African Religion could not produce that which the Gospel now offers to African peoples," yet, he argues, "it tutored them so that they could find genuine fulfillment in the Gospel" (Mbiti 1978a, 311). The allusion here to the apostle Paul's argument in Gal 3:24–25 is clear, though the weight placed on the second part of Paul's formulation in its application to African culture (and/as religion) is debated within this African theological trajectory: "Therefore the Law has become our tutor to lead us to Christ, so that we may be justified by faith. But now that faith has come, we are no longer under a tutor" (NASB).

Drawing on Paul in another way, the West African theologian Lamin Sanneh uses the story of Paul's proclamation of a correlation between the Athenian "unknown god" (Acts 17:23) and "the God of the risen Christ" (Sanneh 1989, 157), to argue that the proclamation of the missionary "gospel," notwithstanding the damage its missionary-colonial incarnation had done, enabled Africans "to decode" their "religious instincts" (157). In other words, "the truth" of "the gospel" was already within African culture (and/as religion), and had preceded the missionaries who proclaimed it (157).

While it is clear that Mbiti understands "the Gospel" (always with a capital "g") as having an "essence" (Mbiti 1968; cited in Bediako 1993, 379–80), it is not always clear to what extent Sanneh and those who have followed his theological logic understand "the gospel" to have a fixed content, activated and incarnated in a host of receptor cultures; what is clear in this strand of African theology is that "God was not disdainful of Africans" (Sanneh 1983, 166; cited in Bediako 1995, 120). Building on

Sanneh's work, Kwame Bediako, another West African theologian, argues that this recognition

> carried two far-reaching consequences for how one may view the African cultural world. First, [quoting Sanneh] "This imbued local cultures with eternal significance and endowed African languages [as the vehicles of this recognition] with a transcendent range." And second, it also "presumed that the God of the Bible had preceded the missionary into the receptor-culture." (Bediako 1995, 120)

It is important to note the centrality of the Bible in this process. But before we probe this central presence more fully, both Sanneh and Bediako are making a prior claim. Prior to the Bible's presence, God was/is present in African culture (and/as religion). So while, according to Sanneh, "It is the hidden reality of this divine presence that both validates external mission and requires translation as a *sine qua non* of witness" (Sanneh 1983, 166; cited in Bediako 1995, 120), Sanneh is concerned, insists Bediako, "to show not only that the crucial factors involved in the Gospel communication do not require the Western missionary transmitter to be at the center of the picture, but also that African pre-Christian religions have had a theological significance in the whole process" (Bediako 1995, 120).

3. Revitalizing African Culture

The Bible plays such a prominent role in this process because the "enterprise of Scriptural translation, with its far-reaching assumptions about traditional religious categories and ideas as a valid carriage for the revelation and divine that precedes and anticipates historical mission, concedes the salvific value of local religions" (Sanneh 1983, 170; cited in Bediako 1995, 120). "Vernacular agency," according to Sanneh, "became the preponderant medium for the assimilation of Christianity," pushing missionaries into "a secondary position," though this was certainly not their intention (Sanneh 1989, 162). However, because most missionaries, like Robert Moffat the translator of the first full Bible into a southern African language, believed that "the simple reading and study of the Bible alone will convert the world" and that the task of the missionary therefore was "to gain for it [the Bible] admission and attention, and then let it speak for itself" (Moffat 1842, 618), the missionary's "subordinate" position was "necessary and inevitable," says Sanneh (1989, 162).

A dimension of subordination the missionaries might have expected was their subordination to the word of God, the Bible; the messengers should be secondary to the message. What would have been hard to come to terms with, however, was their increasingly secondary role to those they came to instruct with the message. But because the Bible was both produced by and its texts located within what Bediako refers to as "a primal world-view," there was a substantial resonance between large parts of the Bible and the primal worldviews of Africans. Drawing on Harold Turner's characterization of a primal worldview—including a recognition that humanity has a kinship with nature, a recognition of humanity's finitude and creaturehood, a recognition of a spiritual world of powers and beings more powerful than humanity, a recognition that humanity can enter into relationships with the spiritual world, a recognition that there is continuity between this life and the afterlife, and a recognition that there is no boundary between the physical and the spiritual—Bediako argues that Africans shared a phenomenological relationship with the biblical worldview (1995, 91–108).

And while some African theologians have argued that this primal worldview was primarily preparatory, preparing Africans for "the gospel"/ Christianity, others like Bediako have argued that this primal worldview was/is also constitutive of African Christianity. John Mbiti, for example, made a distinction between "Christianity," which "results from the encounter of the Gospel with any given local society" and so is always indigenous and culture-bound, on the one hand, and the gospel, which is "God-given, eternal and does not change," on the other (cited in Bediako 1995, 117). "We can add nothing to the Gospel, for it is an eternal gift of God," writes Mbiti (1970a, 438). In other words, for Mbiti "the gospel" apprehended by Africans is substantially the same as that transmitted by the missionaries (Bediako 1995, 118). But for Bediako and Sanneh, the contribution of the African soil/soul is more distinctive. While not disputing significant continuity between what the missionaries proclaimed and what Africans appropriated, Sanneh asserts that "the God of the Bible had preceded the missionary into the receptor-culture—so the missionary needs to discover Him in the new culture" (Sanneh 1983, 166). In other words, for Sanneh "the gospel" is not fully understood until African voices have spoken.

Because, argues Sanneh, "language is the intimate, articulate expression of culture," the missionary decision to render the Bible in African vernaculars "was tantamount to adopting indigenous cultural criteria for the message, a piece of radical indigenization far greater than the standard portrayal of mission as Western cultural imperialism" (Sanneh 1989, 3). Sanneh sees "translation as a fundamental concession to the vernacular, and an inevitable weakening of the forces of uniformity and centralization"; translation introduces "a dynamic and pluralist factor into questions of the essence of the religion." So, says Sanneh,

> if we ask the question about the essence of Christianity, whatever the final answer, we would be forced to reckon with what the fresh medium reveals to us in feedback. It may thus happen that our own earlier understanding of the message will be challenged and even overturned by the force of the new experience. Translation would consequently help to bring us to new ways of viewing the world, commencing a process of revitalization that reaches into both the personal and cultural spheres. (1989, 53)

Sanneh's emphasis here is on the agency of Africans as they engage with the Bible (and go on to engage with missionary Christianity), both in terms of the content of the gospel, but more significantly in "the shape" of the gospel (Nolan 1988, 14–17). We may discern two dimensions to this central argument of Sanneh's. The first dimension is the revitalization of indigenous religion and culture. This occurs when the technical process of translation pushes indigenous respondents to reexamine their culture in order to assist the translators with appropriate language with which to translate biblical texts. This re-turn to local culture, a culture of which it has often been said by missionaries and other "civilizing" forces is inadequate at best and demonic at worst, revitalizes the culture, as local respondents in the translation process reclaim aspects of their culture in order to provide a language for translation that is true to both the biblical text and their culture. And because there is so much resonance between African culture (and/as religion) and the culture (and/as religion) of biblical communities and the texts they produced (Bediako 1997), the scope for potential "revitalization" is substantial.

The second dimension is the potential of the receptor culture to now add their own voice to the voices of the many other communities of faith that have interpreted the Bible before them. If God really does speak the vernacular, then what is it that God is saying as understood by this new community of faith? The very act of making the Bible available in the language of the indigenous people causes it to slip from or be prised from the grasp of the missionaries who brought it. "If hearers of the Word of God in their own languages may then be presumed to respond in their own terms," argues Bediako, "this is another way of saying that it is not others' but their own questions which they would bring to the Bible, taking from it what they would consider to be *its* answers to their questions" (Bediako 1995, 63). To put it provocatively, what "the gospel" is is yet to be determined, for not all indigenous voices have yet been heard speaking for themselves.

We could go further, saying that what the Bible is is yet to be determined by reflecting more carefully on what Africans actually do with the Bible. Bediako comes close to considering this question in his discussion of West African William Wade "Prophet" Harris (1865–1929) of Liberia, "a trail-blazer and a new kind of religious personage on the African scene, the first independent African Christian prophet" (Bediako 1995, 91). Prophet Harris is significant for Bediako because he is "a paradigm of both a non-Western and essentially *primal* apprehension of the Gospel and also of a settled self-consciousness as African Christian, which is uncluttered by Western missionary controls" (Bediako 1995, 91–92). Speaking of Prophet Harris's appropriation of the Bible, Bediako draws on the work of David Shank, who suggests that Prophet Harris was not so much interested in "belief in" the truth of the Bible but "participation in" the truth of the Bible. It was not so much "a question of what Moses saw, or what Elijah did, or the words and works of Jesus as reported in the Bible"; it was more "a question of involvement—as with the ancestors, the living dead—with Moses, with Elijah, with the Archangel Gabriel, and supremely with Jesus Christ" (Bediako 1995, 104; citing Shank 1980, 466).

Quite what the Bible *is* has changed with translation into African vernaculars. This recognition has not received enough attention by African biblical and theological reflection, which has been dominated by content-based discussions. Even the shift within South African liberation biblical and theological analysis from "the content" of the gospel to "the shape" of the gospel (Nolan 1988, 14–17) does not move sufficiently in the direction suggested by the case of Prophet Harris.

4. Engaging with Modernity

By considering another late nineteenth-century African Christian prophet, Isaiah Shembe, we can probe more carefully not only what the Bible is for African Christians, particularly those who appropriated the Bible outside the control of missionary and settler Christianity in southern Africa, but also what role the Bible played in preparing the post-colonial African.

I begin, however, by returning to West Africa and the work of Lamin Sanneh. The theological trajectory founded by Mbiti (1970b, 36), given its "translation" shape by Sanneh (Maluleke 1997, 19–20),[3] theoretically elaborated by Kwame Bediako, and consolidated by Ogbu Kalu, emphasizes that African Christianity "should be read as part and parcel of the organic growth and development of Africa's religious quest" (Clarke 2010, 109), and so emphasizes the "'native' agency" of African Christianity (Kalu 2005, 36). But this African theological strand also adopts a more positive assessment of missionaries under the notion of "reciprocity." "We may characterize the ... interrelationship between missionaries and Africans as reciprocity," says Sanneh.

> Missionaries paid huge "vernacular" compliments to Africans, enabling many peoples to acquire pride and dignity about themselves in the modern world, and thus opening up the whole social system to equal access. For their part Africans returned the compliment by coupling a faith forged in the Scriptures with a commitment to social and political issues. Missionaries as vernacular agents thus helped Africans to become modernizing agents. (Sanneh 1989, 172–73)[4]

While there is no doubt that the translation of the Bible into a local African language, even today, recovers and codifies many aspects of that local African culture, some of which was in danger of being forgotten in the face of modernity (Sanneh 1989, 181; Yorke 2004), and enables local African communities to engage with the Bible on/in their own terms, the claim that vernacular Bible translation opens up "the whole social system to equal access" rings rather hollow in a context like South Africa, where African social systems remain severely damaged by apartheid colonialism. But what I want to probe more fully in the remainder of this essay is the contribution of local African biblical appropriation to the emergence of African post-colonial engagement with modernity in the guise of British colonial and racial capitalism (1795–1890) and a related system of British colonial and mineral capitalism (1890–1948) (Terreblanche 2002, 15) in South Africa.

---

3. Mbiti recognizes the importance of African vernacular translation but does not develop this aspect as fully as Sanneh and Bediako (Bediako 1995, 116–19).
4. A similar assertion is made by Cherif Keita (2009) in his film on the relationship between the American missionary William Wilcox and the South African religious and political leader John Langalibalele Dube.

What is quite different about Isaiah Shembe is that he is from the beginning and remains throughout his life independent of missionary-colonialists and is wary of their *kholwa* (missionary "converted" and educated Africans)[5] offspring. While for Mbiti African Christianity is fundamentally a biblical theology, he also considered it essential that African Christianity must remain in continuity with "the major traditions of Christendom" so that it was linked into "the mainstream of ecumenical and apostolic heritage" (Mbiti 1978b; cited in Bediako 1993, 372). By contrast, Shembe deliberately locates his religion outside of missionary-colonial (*kholwa*) control, but firmly within the Bible, which results, ironically, in a far more "biblical" theology than that of Mbiti. As we will see, the Old Testament is foundational to Shembe's construction of his "Christian" community.

Born in the increasingly unstable southern African interior on a farm to a Zulu polygamous family who were probably tenant farmers (Gunner 2002, 17), Isaiah Shembe was baptized in July 1906 by Rev. William Leshega, a Baptist minister who was affiliated to the Baptist Union and the African Baptist Native Association (18). At this time Shembe was already "healing and preaching in the Harrismith district and in the adjoining Witzieshoek without attachment to any church" (19). Indeed, it seems that Leshega was drawn to Shembe at least partially in order "to baptize those to whom Shembe had preached and in many cases healed" (19–20), for Shembe showed no interested in establishing his own church.

Perhaps part of the reason for Shembe's wariness of institutionalized religion was what he witnessed happening to his mentor, Leshega. Though clearly a *kholwa* Christian, Leshega was something of a dissident (Gunner 2002, 18), regularly contending with both the British colonial establishment and the Baptist Union, primarily about access to land (18–19). As Elizabeth Gunner notes, though Leshega attempted to locate himself within the imperial British infrastructure, he was marginalized "by a social and religious order that blocked him many times in his efforts to gain legitimacy as an ordained minister and in his efforts to gain land for his church" (20). Among the many things Shembe may have learned from his association with Leshega were perhaps the limits of *kholwa* Christianity in general and both the limits and potential of writing in contending with modernity, for Leshega was "a tireless writer of letters and user of print," across several languages (20).

---

5. I place "converted" in quotation marks to problematize the notion of what we might understand by African "conversion" to Christianity; see Peel 2000, 3–4.

In her study of Isaiah Shembe Gunner emphasizes the role literacy plays "in negotiating various forms of modernity and in attempting to counter the power of the state's writing"; but she also recognizes that Shembe would also have understood the limits of literacy and how "writing" must "also need to co-exist alongside and to intersect with other forms of experience, such as the visionary and the revelatory dream," key features of Shembe's "making of his church" (Gunner 2002, 22). Indeed Shembe did go on to establish "a church" or, more precisely, a community when he "returned" to his family's home region of KwaZulu-Natal in the early 1900s, a time of considerable sociopolitical flux, impacted by the Anglo-Zulu War, the Anglo-Boer War, the Bambatha Rebellion, and the formation of the Union of South Africa.

So while writing "was always a critical element in Shembe's enterprise," this writing "existed outside the ambit of the new [kholwa-schooled] African elite" (Gunner 2002, 26–27). As Joel Cabrita notes in her recent study of "Texts, Authority, and Community in the South Africa 'Ibandla lamaNazaretha' (Church of the Nazaretha) 1910–1976," Shembe both "affirms the value of writing and alludes to the capacity of texts to create and shape human communities" and reconfigures the very notion of "writing" and "text" (2010, 60). In a parable told by Shembe, recorded by Petros Dhlomo, who gathered such material from Shembe's community when he became the archivist of the Nazaretha church in the 1940s until his death in the 1990s, and cited by Cabrita (2010, 60), he draws on a biblical image from the apostle Paul, who writes to the church in Corinth, saying "You are our letter, written in our hearts, known and read by all men; being manifested that you are a letter of Christ, cared for by us, written not with ink but with the Spirit of the living God, not on tablets of stone but on tablets of human hearts" (2 Cor 3:2–3, NASB). Rewriting Paul, Shembe tells the following parable:

> The lord [Shembe] said these words in the village of Ekuphakameni [the sacred place of the amaNazaretha]. You are a letter which is not written with ink but with diamonds which cannot be erased and is read by all people (II Cor. 5:1-3) [sic]. It is not written on flat stones. Rather it is written in your hearts. When the people of the system will come and take these letters of which the children here at Ekuphakameni are singing and when they will say: "You see all that Shembe was preaching has come to an end then even a child of Ekuphakameni could say: 'We greet you, Kuphakama; we greet you, Judia'" (No. 6 in the *Hymn Book of the amaNazaretha*). These things which were spoken at Ekuphakameni

are written in the hearts of the people who love God (Malachi 4:2, 3). (Hexham and Oosthuizen 1996, 211, §143)

Cabrita does not probe the biblical citations and other possible biblical allusions, but she does capture rather well the import of this parable with respect to writing.

> In Dhlomo's text Isaiah [Shembe] speaks of the threat of the European state, the "people of the system," destroying the church's texts and in particular the body of hymns that were circulating in both oral and written form by the mid-1920s—"the books from which the children at Ekuphakameni are singing." Yet Isaiah affirms that if this were to happen, the true book of the church would be the Nazaretha community itself. The power of the written word can conjure up communities of people as enduring records; Isaiah tells the congregation at Ekuphakameni that a virtuous Nazaretha life is itself a written record for posterity. Isaiah presents Nazaretha lives as an enduring text written in "diamonds," not written on a physical surface but "in your hearts." Dhlomo's text suggests that Nazaretha writing creates a group of people connected by the common inscription of Isaiah's words on their hearts. Both Isaiah's spoken words and Dhlomo's recording of the parable affirm the power of writing to create enduring memory. This presents writing not only as a rational technology of pen and paper, but ultimately as a spiritual inscription "in the hearts of the people who love God." Writing, then, for both Isaiah Shembe and Dhlomo as archivist, proclaims the power of texts to generate cohesive communities that are able to withstand the incursion of the state. (Cabrita 2010, 61)

But my focus is on a particular text, the Bible, and its place in Shembe's reformation of "institutions of memory" as he "provided multiple means to 'practise' memory" and "set up the cultural means and the institutions through which specific practices of memory were mediated" (Gunner 2002, 22). As Gunner argues, Shembe's (successful) attempt "to constitute a theatre of memory" was "his response on one level to the radical dislocation of the early twentieth-century city, from which many [mainly women; cf. Muller 2003][6] who joined his church in the second decade of the century were seeking respite." Shembe's answer, continues Gunner, "was to recreate the social group and to resituate its mental and material spaces" (Gunner 2002, 23).

---

6. A 1921 report on Shembe estimated that 95 percent of his followers were female (Cabrita 2009, 618 n. 58).

More theologically, in the words of Carol Muller, Shembe's "mission was to preach the word of God, as he found it in the mission Bible, to the traditional peoples, whom Western missionaries had had little success in convincing." Shembe believed, Muller continues, "that these people could be converted to Christianity and still retain their own cultural ways, many of which were reflected in the narratives of the Old Testament" (Muller 1999, 25). Shembe saturated his social project in the biblical text, having seized it from the colonial agents who brought it, recounting in another parable how this was accomplished.

Again, Petros Dhlomo, the great collector and historian of Isaiah Shembe's life and ministry (Papini 2002, xiii–xiv), tells the story of Shembe's sermon in the home of Nldlovu, "the headman of Zibula at Lenge, in the year 1933" (Hexham and Oosthuizen 1996, 224), in which Shembe tells the story or "the parable of the liberating Bible" (224, §152). "In olden times there were two might[y] nations who were fighting over a certain issue. In their war the one conquered the other one and took all their cattle away. They took even their children captive and put them into the school of the victorious nation" (224–25). The story continues with a focus on three of these children, "three sons of the same mother." Among the tasks given to these children was that they "had to sweep the houses of their teachers and the house of the Pope" (225).

Shembe goes on to tell that "All these children made good progress in school and passed their examinations well. Then they were trained as bishops." However, Shembe goes on immediately to recount how there was a certain book that was locked away from them. The implication is clear. Children of the conquered nation had limited access to the texts of the victorious nation, thereby allowing them to rise to a level no higher than that of bishops. The Pope alone had access to one special text. This was the Bible: "In the house of the Pope there was a Bible which was kept under lock by him and only read by himself" (Hexham and Oosthuizen 1996, 225).[7] However, Shembe goes on to relate,

> On a certain day he [the Pope] had to go for a few weeks to another place and he forgot to lock the Bible up at home. When the boys were sweeping his home they found the Bible unlocked. When they began to read it they discovered that their nation which had been demolished so badly by the

---

7. There is no evidence that Shembe had a particular problem with the Roman Catholic Church, so this church probably represents all of *kholwa* Christianity.

war could never be restored unless they would get a book like this one and they considered what to do.

When they came back from school they bought a copybook and copied the whole Bible. When they had finished their work, they returned the Bible to its place. Thereafter the Pope came back and saw that he forgot to lock his Bible in. He called the boys who worked in his house and asked them whether they had opened this book. They denied it and said that they did not see that it had not been locked up. Then he forgot about it. The boys considered how they could bring this book to their parents at home.

At another day, they went and asked permission to visit their parents at home. They were permitted to go and they were given a time by which they must be back. When they came home, they did not stay there, rather they went from home to home and preached about this book until their time of leave was over and policemen were sent to look for these boys. Then they left this book there and returned to school. (Hexham and Oosthuizen 1996, 225)

Shembe's parable now shifts to what appears to be a catechetical exercise to which the boys are subjected on their return to school. "They were asked, 'Do you believe that Thixo [God] can only be found in the Roman Catholic Church?'" Shembe makes it clear that "It was expected that all of them should say so" (Hexham and Oosthuizen 1996, 225–26). However, "the oldest boy did not. Rather he said: 'I believe that Thixo can be found in all beings on earth.'" The questioners were "greatly startled by these words," and he and the other boys, who answer similarly, are threatened with death by burning if they persist in "contradicting this our doctrine, in which you have been instructed" (226). But the following day the first boy refuses again to follow what he has been taught, repeating "what he had said on the previous day." And when faced with "the fire," he sang a hymn and "went into the flames and was burned." The second boy met a similar fate, but when the third boy was questioned his mother intervened, persuading him that it would not be so wrong "to say that Thixo belongs to the Roman Catholics, so that your life may be spared and that I may retain you on earth." He follows her advice, saying what is required of him. But the Pope demands more, requiring not only oral but written assent, saying "that they should bring a book where he should write these words down and make an affidavit," which he did (226–27).

That night, when he slept, "his spirit was taken up and brought to the joyful place of the elected ones. He heard a wonderful singing from a certain place and when he looked there he saw a large crowd of people who were clad in white gowns, on the other side of the river," where "he saw his two brothers." But when he "wanted to go to them," a voice said to him, "You cannot go to your brothers. Because they died for a promise while you did not die for it" (Hexham and Oosthuizen 1996, 227). Distraught, the boy weeps all night, then goes to the Pope to recant, and finally rekindles the fire in which his brothers died and "burned himself to death." But even then he has no peace, for even this does not unite him with his brothers. Breaking out of the parabolic form, "The lord of Ekuphakameni [Shembe] said: 'The death of the young man did not help him in any way. He did not go to the place where his brothers were because he did not die for the promise" (227). Shifting from narration to proclamation, Shembe then says,

> Now I speak no longer of these people. Rather I speak today to you people of Ekuphakameni. You have been told that a young man of Ekuphakameni should never write a letter to a maiden of Ekuphakameni and a maiden of Ekuphakameni is not allowed to write to a young man of Ekuphakameni. I ask you: what kind of a Bible do you write? Because you will suffer very much on the Last Day. And when you will then come to me and say: "Our father, I wish to enter the Kingdom." Then I shall be unable to do anything because you have broken the law of which you were told not to break it. (Hexham and Oosthuizen 1996, 227–28)

A remarkable parable becomes an even more remarkable sermon. The Bible is clearly targeted by Shembe as a text of power, which is why it must be stolen. But once stolen, copied, and shared with the community its message is quite different from "the instruction" of missionary-*kholwa* Christianity. And yet Shembe requires of his followers a similar obedience to "the law" as that demanded by the Pope. Indeed, law is a key feature of Shembe's new community, and laws on the relationship between men and women, alluded to in the sermon, are central tenets of "the law."

5. Interpreting "The Law"

If recognizing the power of the Bible is a first move in Shembe's biblical hermeneutics, and seizing it by stealth his second move, then the third distinctive move (reminiscent of Prophet Harris) Shembe makes is his engagement and participation with the major characters of the Bible, especially Moses. Among the "texts" associated with Isaiah Shembe are a genre known as *imithetho*/laws. The "laws" form a considerable part of the corpus of Shembe's "writings,"[8] and may well allude to "the law of Moses."

Significantly, those sections in one of the notebooks whose use was encouraged by Shembe among his followers that include the word "law" are about marriage and adultery; indeed, many of Shembe's instructions are about the relations between men and women (West 2006). So the shift in Shembe's story about the stolen Bible from the three young boys who stole the Bible to the issue of young men and women writing to each other is not so strange. The Bible is for Shembe extensively about law, and law is primarily about how the community should govern the relationships between men and women.

While the oral record indicates that Shembe did not intend to start a church, "his growing following of women, young girls, and orphans persuaded him to provide a space of sanctuary for them" (Muller 1999, 19). His first response was to purchase land, in 1915 or 1916, "using money given to him by those he had healed." On this site, called Ekuphakameni, says Carol Muller,

> Shembe established what became the headquarters of a large and powerful religious community. Combining his deep knowledge of the mission Bible with his respect for Nguni traditional ways, and with some knowledge of commodity capitalism, he constituted a new and hybrid regime of religious truth … in competition with ideologies of the state and the Christian mission. (Muller 1999, 19)

Shembe's law relocates African women in a new "moral" community.

From Muller's analysis we can discern at least three narratives which Shembe reconstituted into a fourth, dealing directly with the female body. The first is the narrative of Zulu traditional religion and life. In the African precolonial homestead economy women played a central but highly circumscribed role (Guy 1990, 34). As Muller notes, marriage was the most important social institution in this economy (Muller 1999, 27). Marriage enabled "both the productive and reproductive units of the homestead, and facilitated the transfer of property from the household of the man's family to that of the women's," usually through the system of the exchange of cattle (known as *lobola*) (27). In Jeff Guy's analysis, accepted by Muller,

---

8. It is not clear to what extent Shembe was literate (see West 2006, 163–65), and his "writings" are all produced by his followers, much like "the writings" of Jesus!

he suggests that "The object of accumulation in southern Africa's precapitalist societies was indeed cattle, but cattle as the means by which men acquired and accumulated the labor power of women" (Guy 1990, 40). Muller elaborates, saying,

> A man's wealth was, therefore, determined by his accumulation of women, their labor, and children. For this he required cattle, which in turn created surplus through reproduction of the species. Since marriage was the institution that legitimated the sexual relations of the man and woman, and thus the birth of children, the fertility of women was crucial to the productive and reproductive capacities of the structures of the precapitalist African homestead. (1999, 28)

The second narrative is of Shembe's particular context in the early 1900s, a context in which African women were particularly at risk. The African homestead economy came under massive pressures, brought about both by the colonial encounter and by internal conflicts within African chiefdoms (Muller 1999, 32). From the "concubinage" of individual European traders to the more systematic colonial devastation of the African homestead through annexation of African land (in 1844), the removal of Africans from their land (between 1846 and 1847) to demarcated Reserves, their subjugation to unwritten customary "Native Law" under the control of colonial agents, and the colonial surveillance and taxation of the African population in the reserves, colonial forces combined in the destruction of this precolonial socioeconomic form (38). The pressures on the homestead economy were just too great; taxation eroded the cattle-centered economy, forcing young men to the mines and cities into order to earn the money to pay these taxes, and colonial and Union legislation removed more and more land from the African populations, keeping women on increasingly barren reserve land (38–39). The result of the collapse of the homestead economy for many women, whether from the direct consequences of colonial policy or from the indirect consequences of internal African interclan conflict (usually exacerbated by colonial encroachment), was migration, following their men, to the cities, where wage labor, domestic service in white homes, or prostitution were the most viable options.

Within this mix, mission Christianity made its own contribution, and so added a third narrative. While conversion to missionary Christianity was slow in the mid-1870s, there were a number of factors that led local Zulu people to the mission stations. Missions were allocated large pieces of land in the Native Reserves, where they "encouraged the formation of self-sufficient, petty commodity-producing units based in the nuclear household and on family labor" (Meintjes 1990, 132). Mission stations, therefore, offered an alternative economic base to those who had been driven off their land, either through direct colonial intervention or through more local upheavals. Mission land was offered for agricultural production. Furthermore, missionaries received and welcomed all those "who had been ostracized or marginalized by their own communities. This was particularly important," Muller argues, "for women who wished to escape arranged marriages or to acquire land" (1999, 40; see also Etherington 1989). However, for African women, Muller argues, "conversion to Christianity offered a contradictory package. It created a dialectical tension between breaking free of precolonial traditions and courting the patriarchy and domesticity of colonial Christianity" (1999, 41; referring to Gaitsgill 1990, 254). Missionary Christianity offered a place to African women, but drastically reconfigured this place, discouraging African women from their accustomed agricultural production (insisting that it was more appropriate for the men to till and plough the fields), and undermining (in alliance with the state) polygamy and *lobola* (Muller 1999, 41).

This brings us to a fourth narrative, a hybrid narrative constructed by Shembe from elements of each of the three narratives. As Muller argues, "Deeply disturbed by these events, Isaiah Shembe established a place of spiritual and economic refuge for widows, orphans, and those women previously in polygamous marriages whose husbands had converted to mission Christianity, a belief system that insisted on monogamous alliances." "Shembe created," she continues,

> this hybrid religious community from the substance of archaic Nguni and biblical beliefs about women, virgin girls, and their bodies. In so doing, he reconstituted a sense of order, religious sanctuary, and ritual power by reinventing the feminized notion of cyclicity, a central principle of traditional performance, agricultural method, and cosmological understanding. (1999, xix)

Put differently, the Nazaretha's "distinctive social grammar" rested "on idioms of health, healing, and ritual performance" and drew heavily "on the symbolic capital gained from attracting female adherents" (Cabrita 2009, 624).

Shembe "authorized these practices" by appropriating biblical narrative, particularly the prominent biblical figures like Moses and Paul.

Having stolen the Bible from missionary-*kholwa* Christianity, Shembe used it to harness "the mythical power of virgin girls to win his battles against the racist state" (Muller 1999, xix). One of the ways in which Shembe instituted and annexed the power of the female body was through the ritual appropriation of particular biblical narratives, such as the story of Jephthah's daughter in Judg 11 (West 2007). Another was through "the law" of the Moses-like Shembe.

As Gunner notes, "the voice" that one encounters in reading those sections in the notebooks on "the law" is quite different from the more narrative sections. "It is the speech of authority, of a leader and law-maker. It shows Shembe setting out marriage regulations for his church and for those who lived on church land." Shembe's pronouncement, continues Gunner, "on marriage, divorce, on adultery and remarriage shows a path that is neither true to [African] customary law nor to Roman Dutch Law. Rather, Shembe looked to Biblical precedents and statements" (2002, 35). This is clear when we consider Shembe's teaching recorded simply as "the law" (70/71).[9]

"The law" is entirely about adultery (71) and begins unambiguously with a focus on the male: "I have placed the weight of the law on adultery on the man's shoulders, as it is he who ought to use most control in that matter because woman is but a child in bodily strength compared to a man" (71). After this introductory instructional statement, the remainder of the instruction provides a detailed elaboration and application, in a style strongly reminiscent of the Pastoral Epistles (1 Timothy, 2 Timothy, and Titus), but within a Mosaic rhetorical framework. However, nowhere in "the law" is there any overt reference to these biblical texts, though there is reference to other biblical texts, as we will see. Biblical texts are often alluded to without being actually cited. While it is clear that "the law" is heavily dependent on 1 Timothy, the citations Shembe makes are to Moses.

Having declared his emphasis on "the man," Shembe now turns to the woman (following the format of Gen 3), saying,

> But in the case of woman, woman was created from man therefore a woman lacks the strength to hold herself back if she is assailed by a man's weakness because she herself is formed from man. If a man lures her through the tricks of love she will succumb quickly because man is the

---

9. Gunner has served us well by placing the isiZulu version on one page and her English translation on the facing page. In my analysis I will refer to both.

father of woman. When woman was created man suckled her, she grew, she was nurtured through the expertise of the man (Genesis 2 v 21). (71)

This paragraph—and I am following the paragraphs as presented by Gunner, who follows the paragraph layout of the original notebook—points to two recurring elements of Shembe's perspective on these matters. First, unlike so much patriarchal literature, including much of the Bible and African oral tradition *on adultery*, the woman is passive and is "assailed by a man's weakness" (*ehlelwa ubuthakathaka bendoda*) (70/71). She is acted upon, and "lacks the strength to hold herself back" (*akamandla ukuzimbamba*) (70/71), but only "if [or when, *uma* (70)]" (71) the man succumbs to his (and, in Shembe's opinion, the primary) weakness.

It is the next sentence, however, which situates Shembe's instruction in its biblical frame. The conditional clause, "because man is the father of woman" (*ngokuba indoda inguyise womfazi*) (70/71), alludes, in my opinion, to 1 Timothy, even though the citation that follows the next sentence refers to Genesis. This is not that strange when we remember that 1 Tim 2:13–15, which Shembe's text echoes, is itself an exegesis of the Genesis text to which Shembe explicitly refers. Shembe cites the primary text, not the secondary text (1 Timothy), though both are present in his argument.

Indeed, it is the argumentative form itself that Shembe borrows from 1 Tim 2:13–15, though the terms of the argument are recast. Like the "Paul" of 1 Timothy, Shembe begins his argument by establishing a hierarchy, both in terms of time and substance, with the latter having the priority in Shembe's argument, while the former takes precedence in Paul's argument:

> I permit no woman to teach or to have authority over a man; she is to keep silent. For Adam was formed first, then Eve; and Adam was not deceived, but the woman was deceived and became a transgressor. Yet she will be saved through childbearing, provided they continue in faith and love and holiness, with modesty. (1 Tim 2:12–15)

As with so many other biblical texts, Shembe draws on elements of this text, recasting them for his own purposes. In this case, he retains the interest in the male–female relationship, the first-person form of address, and the argumentative style. He shifts the focus, however, from issues of female and male roles in worship to issues of marriage and adultery. What allows Shembe to make this shift is the dependency of 1 Tim 2:13–15 on Gen

2:21-25, which for Shembe is clearly about marriage, and his prioritizing of "the voice" of the primary biblical lawgiver, Moses.

As I have said, Shembe emphasizes that "woman was created from man" rather than that "Adam was formed first." Shembe, like the Genesis text, wants to foreground connections between the man and the woman, rather than the oppositions between the man and the woman, as does the 1 Timothy text. Both, however, retain the man–woman hierarchy. Shembe is also alluding here to Gen 3, which is part of the larger literary unit that has its beginning in Gen 2. In approaching the man and the woman in the garden, after they have disobeyed, God addresses the man first (3:9), and only then turns to the woman (3:13). Shembe, it seems, follows this ordering, addressing the man first and then the woman. Like God/Moses and unlike Paul in 1 Timothy, Shembe refuses to isolate the man and the woman from each other. The man is "the father of woman," who "suckled her," causing her to grow; "she was nurtured through the expertise of the man (Genesis 2 v 21)" (71). Remarkably, though there remains a clear sense of male-female hierarchy, the male's role includes that of suckling and nurturing; the male, it would seem, is also a mother. This becomes explicit in the next paragraph.

Shembe continues with the man's nurturing role in the next paragraph, incrementally elaborating his argument:

> Man has been twice responsible for woman, he has been both father and mother, and this is how it still is. If a man feels tempted by a certain woman, the woman will quickly be tempted too. The strength to stand fast in the face of that temptation is the man's. That is why I say that the law concerning adultery rests most heavily on the man. It is he who most needs to control himself. Adam was superior to his wife because from the beginning woman came from below man's head (Genesis 2 v 22). (71)

Man as the nurturer of woman is "both father and mother," an interpretation that is unique to Shembe (in that it is not overtly indicated in either of his source texts), and an interpretation that certainly emphasizes Shembe's dual instructing and nurturing role towards women.

According to Shembe's interpretation, it is precisely the "strength" of the man that makes him both the usual perpetrator who "lures her through the tricks of love," the one who "feels tempted" first (followed by the woman who subsequently "will quickly be tempted too"), and who has the "strength to stand fast in the face of that temptation." It is the man's responsibility to resist his own impulses. There is no sign here of the woman as temptress, a figure implicit in 1 Timothy and explicit in the traditions of the Christian church's reading of 1 Timothy. Here the man is tempter. "It is he who most needs to control himself." Shembe does not deny that the woman must exercise self-control, but in his opinion it is the man who "most needs" to exert self-control.

The paragraph ends with an overt reference to Gen 2:22, as Shembe uses the biblical text to buttress his argument. The frame remains that of the 1 Timothy text, but Shembe now moves into an extended exegesis of the Genesis text, beginning here and continuing into the next paragraph:

> Coming from the rib of man, woman is the flesh of man, if a man says to any woman, "Come flesh of my flesh return from whence you came," the woman will quickly be overcome. So the man must realise this: that very rib that was taken from Adam and formed into a woman was not the only rib, the Almighty caused it to increase and he gave Adam's stock rib upon rib, so it is not for any Adam to say to a rib that is not his, "Come flesh of my flesh, come to me," just because Eve was created from Adam when he was already full grown. (71)

This is quite a complex argument and represents Shembe's commentary on Gen 2:21–23. Like many commentators before him, Shembe "re-members" this text in order to address the matter at hand—adultery. The notion that "Adam was superior to his wife because from the beginning woman came from below man's head" has been argued before, and almost certainly draws on another biblical text, Eph 5:21–33, a text which has the same instructional tone and structure as 1 Timothy, which deals with marriage, and which also explicitly cites Gen 2:23. The resonances between this text and Shembe's are striking, but so too are the differences. Both Paul and Shembe position the woman below the man's head and both expect the man to exercise considerable responsibility for the well-being of the marriage, using the language of nurturing and nourishing. But whereas Paul, here and in 1 Timothy (though I must stress that I am making no claims here to Pauline authorship of either of these texts), begins with the woman, Shembe, like Moses, begins with and remains focused on the man.

In this paragraph Shembe seems to be arguing that the act of creation is repeated with each man, God having given "Adam's stock rib upon rib" (*uNkulunkulu sewalwandisa wabanika oAdam ubambo ngobamo*) (70/71). The implication of this, it would seem, is that each man must be content with his own rib and must not "say to a rib that is not his, 'Come flesh of my flesh, come to me.'" My reading here of Shembe's somewhat awkward argument is supported in the next paragraph.

> Eve did not know for herself that she was formed from Adam. She was told, "You, woman, you were taken from Adam's flesh," she did not see the scar showing her origin. Eve was simply told, and even to this day it is so. If a man says, "Come, my flesh," the woman rushes fascinated to him as if created from that very man. I am speaking, indeed pleading with you men, a calf has very tender flesh (Genesis 18 v 17). A woman's body, her shape, her softness is very appealing to you men. Men love saying, "Come flesh of my flesh." I beg you, men, you really must control yourselves. (71)

The woman, Shembe seems to be arguing, is not able to detect which man she is the rib of, unless she is explicitly told. So again, Shembe reiterates the woman's passivity and the man's agency. Given her inability to know to whom she belongs, she is susceptible to the man who beckons her *as if* she were his rib. The responsibility, he states again, is the man's. It is men who must control themselves. The woman's body, her shape, and her softness are not declared to be a problem—an occasion for sin, as they are in so many patriarchal texts, including the Bible. The problem is the man's inability to control his adulterous nature, calling to women who are not his rib.

The Genesis reference in this paragraph is illuminating, because it reveals other elements of Shembe's biblical hermeneutics. The actual verse cited says, "The Lord said, 'Shall I hide from Abraham what I am about to do...?,'" so obviously the verse itself is not what is being referred to. Shembe often uses chapter and verse references to point to a larger textual unit. In this case the textual unit is the story of God's dialogue with Abraham about the injustice of Sodom, and God's decision to take Abraham, the man, into his confidence, "since Abraham will surely become a great and mighty nation, and in him all the nations of the earth will be blessed? For I have chosen him, so that he may command his children and his household after him to keep the way of the LORD by doing righteousness and justice" (Gen 18:18–19a, NASB). But quite what this has to do with the woman, like the calf (*ithole lenkomo*, 70), having tender flesh is not immediately clear. Perhaps Shembe is simply making the point that women, like the calf, require protection, and that this protection cannot come without the man being attentive to the voice of God/Moses.

Shembe concludes this instruction on adultery with the following final paragraph:

> Keep hold of yourself so that if [God] has already given the rib to another of your spiritual brethren, don't trouble it by saying, "Come my flesh," don't cause that rib to sin before God (1 Corinthians 7 v 39). The law should be obeyed (Romans 7 v 4). (71)

Here it is explicit that particular women (as he says earlier and as is alluded to in the "flesh of my flesh" reference (Gen 2:23) in the paragraph above) are "given" to particular men. The social fabric is sustained by God, Shembe argues, and men must abide by God's giving of a woman to a man. When men step out of God's order (as declared here by Shembe), they threaten their "spiritual brethren." They also "trouble" (-*hlupha*, 70) the woman and "cause … [her] to sin before God." Clearly, it is not the woman who is the cause of either congregational/social strife or sin, but the man. The cost, of course, is substantial, for in Shembe's view women remain passive. In his zeal to construct a society that would protect the vulnerable women of his world he summons men to relational responsibility, but at the cost of relegating women to passive respondents.

In the final paragraph of Shembe's instruction the focus shifts to Paul (West 2009), but the Romans reference, with its overt reference to "the law," may be Shembe's way of bringing Paul and his own teaching within the ambit of the great ancestral lawgiver, Moses. Romans 7:4, it seems to me, has very little to do with Shembe's instruction in "the law," but serves as a general pointer to a whole range of associations Shembe wants to make, some of which may not be apparent to the uninitiated. To those of us not steeped in the traditions of the Ibandla lamaNazaretha what is apparent is Shembe's close association of his teachings and those of Paul and Moses. He adopts Paul's literary mannerisms, Paul's authority, Paul's position as leader of God's people. He also adopts some of Paul's theological perspectives, though he often adapts them, "re-membering" them for his context, often by subordinating them to the rhetoric of the primary lawgiver, Moses.

6. Conclusion

But I do not want to set up too hard a distinction between Shembe's appropriation of Moses and Paul. Both are important in Shembe's project of community construction. In these teachings Shembe appropriates the authority and rhetoric of Moses the lawgiver addressing the people of "Israel" (in the Pentateuch) and the authority and rhetoric of Paul the apostle addressing his churches (in the Epistles). In each case Shembe, like Prophet Harris, engages with those ancestors with whom he shares the task of building community. Neither traditional tribal authorities nor missionary-*kholwa* Christianity were able to construct a "moral ethnicity" (Cabrita 2008), but the Bible and its ancestral figures provide Shembe with plenty of potential for both a "virtuous polity" and a "theological nationalism," "a discourse that, to legitimate itself, posited national unity on ideas of virtue, healing, peacefulness, repentance and submission to Jehovah's dictates" (Cabrita 2009, 618, 609). As Joel Cabrita argues, "Shembe's ministry was preoccupied with both 'mourning for [his] scattered nation' [with a particular concern for the plight of African women] and working tirelessly to re-found it upon the new social possibilities exemplified by his Nazaretha communities, some of which endure to this day" (625).

This is a quite different "gospel" from that envisaged by the Mbiti, Sanneh, Bediako, Kalu trajectory of African Christianity; but the African "Christianity" of Isaiah Shembe is a powerful example of African agency and how the Bible, particularly the Old Testament, apprehends and is apprehended in the struggle of a particular post-colonial African.

REFERENCES

Beck, Roger B. 1997. Monarchs and Missionaries among the Tswana and Sotho. In *Christianity in South Africa: A Political, Social, and Cultural History*. Edited by R. Elphick and R. Davenport. Berkeley and Los Angeles: University of California Press.

Bediako, Kwame. 1993. John Mbiti's Contribution to African Theology. Pages 367–90 in *Religious Plurality in Africa: Essays in Honour of John S. Mbiti*. Edited by K. Olupona and S. S. Nyang. Berlin and New York: Mouton de Gruyter.

———. 1995. *Christianity in Africa: The Renewal of a Non-Western Religion*. Edinburgh: Edinburgh University Press; Maryknoll: Orbis.

Cabrita, Joel. 2008. A Theological Biography of Isaiah Shembe, c.1870–1935. Doctoral thesis, Faculty of Divinity, Cambridge University.

———. 2009. Isaiah Shembe's Theological Nationalism, 1920s–1935. *Journal of Southern African Studies* 35.3:609–25.

———. 2010. Texts, Authority, and Community in the South African "Ibandla lamaNazaretha" (Church of the Nazaretha), 1910–1976. *JRA* 40:60–95.

Campbell, John. 1815. *Travels in South Africa: Undertaken at the Request of the Missionary Society*. 3rd ed. London: Black, Parry, & Co.
Clarke, Clifton R. 2010. Ogbu Kalu and Africa's Christianity: A Tribute. *Pneuma* 32:107–20.
Comaroff, John L., and Jean Comaroff. 1997. *Of Revelation and Revolution: The Dialectics of Modernity on a South African Frontier*. Vol. 2. Chicago: University of Chicago Press.
Etherington, Norman. 1989. Christianity and African Society in Nineteenth Century Natal. In *Natal and Zululand from Early Times to 1910: A New History*. Edited by A. Duminy and B. Guest. Pietermaritzburg: University of Natal Press and Shuter & Shooter.
Gaitsgill, Deborah. 1990. Devout Domesticity? A Century of African Women's Christianity in South Africa. Pages 251–72 in *Women and Gender in Southern Africa until 1945*. Edited by C. Walker. Cape Town: David Philip.
Gunner, Elizabeth. 2002. *The Man of Heaven and the Beautiful Ones of God: Writings from Ibandla lamaNazaretha, a South African Church*. Leiden: Brill.
Guy, Jeff. 1990. Gender Oppression in Southern Africa's Precapitalist Societies. Pages 34–45 in *Women and Gender in Southern Africa until 1945*. Edited by C. Walker. Cape Town: David Philip.
Hexham, Irving, and G.C. Oosthuizen, eds. 1996. *The Story of Isaiah Shembe: History and Traditions Centered on Ekuphakameni and Mount Nhlangakazi*. Vol. 1 of *Sacred History and Traditions of the Amanazaretha*. Lewiston: Edwin Mellen.
Kalu, Ogbu U. 2005. African Christianity: An Overview. Pages 23–39 in *African Christianity*. Edited by Ogbu U. Kalu and J. W. Hofmeyer. Pretoria: University of Pretoria.
Keita, Cherif. 2009. *Cemetery Stories: A Rebel Missionary in South Africa*. Film. Mogoya Productions.
Lubbe, J. J. 2009. "By Patience, Labour and Prayer. The Voice of the Unseen God in the Language of Bechuana Nation": A Reflection on the History of Robert Moffat's Setswana Bible (1857). *AcT* 12:33–47.
Maluleke, Tinyiko S. 1997. Half a Century of African Christian Theologies: Elements of the Emerging Agenda for the Twenty-First Century. *JTSA* 99:4–23.
Mbiti, John. 1968. Christianity and East African Culture and Religion. *Dini na Mila* 3:1–6.

———. 1970a. Christianity and Traditional Religions in Africa. *IRM* 59.236:438.
———. 1970b. *Concepts of God in Africa*. London: SPCK.
———. 1978a. Christianity and African Religion. Pages 308-13 in *Facing the New Challenges: The Message of PACLA (Pan African Christian Leadership Assembly): December 9-19, 1976, Nairobi*. Edited by M. Cassidy and L. Verlinden. Kisumu, Kenya: Evangel Publishing House.
———. 1978b. *Prayer and Spirituality in African Religion*. Bedford Park: Australian Association for the Study of Religions.
Meintjes, Sheila. 1990. Family and Gender in the Christian Community at Edendale, Natal, in Colonial Times. Pages 125-45 in *Women and Gender in Southern Africa until 1945*. Edited by C. Walker. Cape Town: David Philip.
Moffat, Robert. 1842. *Missionary Labours and Scenes in Southern Africa*. London: John Snow.
Muller, Carol Ann. 1999. *Rituals of Fertility and the Sacrifice of Desire: Nazarite Women's Performance in South Africa*. Chicago: University of Chicago Press.
———. 2003. Making the Book, Performing the Words of *Izihlabelelo ZamaNazaretha*. Pages 91-110 in *Orality, Literacy and Colonialism in Southern Africa*. Edited by J. A. Draper. Atlanta: Society of Biblical Literature; Pietermaritzburg: Cluster; Leiden: Brill.
Nolan, Albert. 1988. *God in South Africa: The Challenge of the Gospel*. Cape Town: David Philip.
Opoku, Kofi Asare. 1993. African Traditional Religion: An Enduring Heritage. Pages 67-82 in *Religious Plurality in Africa: Essays in Honour of John S. Mbiti*. Edited by K. Olupona and S. S. Nyang. Berlin and New York: Mouton de Gruyter.
Papini, Robert. 2002. Introduction. In *The Catechism of the Nazarites and Related Writings*. Edited by R. Papini and I. Hexham. Lewiston: Edwin Mellen.
Peel, J. D. Y. 2000. *Religious Encounter and the Making of the Yoruba*. Bloomington: Indiana University Press.
Sanneh, Lamin. 1983. The Horizontal and the Vertical in Mission: An African Perspective. *IBMR* 7.4:165-71.
———. 1989. *Translating the Message: The Missionary Impact on Culture*. Maryknoll, N.Y.: Orbis.
Shank, David. 1980. A Prophet for Modern Times—The Thought of Wil-

liam Wade Harris, West African Precursor of the Reign of Christ. Doctoral thesis, University of Aberdeen.

Terreblanche, Sampie. 2002. *A History of Inequality in South Africa, 1652-2002*. Pietermaritzburg: University of Natal Press.

West, Gerald O. 2004. Early Encounters with the Bible among the BaTlhaping: Historical and Hermeneutical Signs. *BibInt* 12:251–81.

———. 2006. Reading Shembe "Re-membering" the Bible: Isaiah Shembe's Instructions on Adultery. *Neot* 40.1:157–84.

———. 2007. The Bible and the Female Body in Ibandla lamaNazaretha: Isaiah Shembe and Jephthah's Daughter. *OTE* 20.2:489–509.

———. 2009. Constructing African Christianity: The Voice of Paul in the Formative Teachings of Isaiah Shembe. Pages 130–44 in *Paul, Grace and Freedom: Essays in Honour of John K. Riches*. Edited by P. Middleton, A. Paddison, and K. Wenell. London: T&T Clark.

Yorke, Gosnell. 2004. Bible Translation in Anglophone Africa and Her Diaspora: A Postcolonial Agenda. *BTIJ* 2.2:153–66.

THUS I CLEANSED THEM FROM EVERYTHING FOREIGN: THE SEARCH FOR SUBJECTIVITY IN EZRA–NEHEMIAH

Roland Boer

I approach the texts of Ezra and Nehemiah, or parts thereof, with a specific concern, that of subjectivity, specifically political subjectivity. How is a subject constructed? What process leads to the identification of a political subject? Who or indeed what is such a subject? Subjectivity may have become a vital topic in political debates today, with both Alain Badiou (2009b, 2006, 2009a) and Slavoj Žižek (1999, 2006) (following on from Louis Althusser and Jacques Lacan) insisting in the central importance of the Cartesian subject in political discourse, over against the criticisms if not dismissals of Heidegger, Derrida, or Agamben. Postcolonial critics have mounted their own attacks on the subject, asking who is included and excluded within the category of the subject (Loomba 2005, 104–83; Spivak 1999). But the subject has not as yet made any significant inroads into biblical criticism, except perhaps where a biblical critic responds to the aforesaid philosophers (Blanton 2007; Karlsen 2010). So my topic is the subject, which may well be collective rather than the default assumption of the individual that so affects our mental associations with words. Why Ezra–Nehemiah? It is a text brimming with a desire for and questions concerning political subjectivity. Ostensibly narrating the repeated return to Judah and Jerusalem and the reestablishment of a people and a state, the subject is never far from the surface, as recent work by Blenkinsopp (2009) and Washington (2003) make abundantly clear.[1] However, instead

---

1. Blenkinsopp's essentially historical study focuses on the emergence of a distinctive group identity in the aftermath of the fall of the Judean state, the degree of continuity–discontinuity between national identity before the Babylonian exile and the competition among a distinct group for legitimacy after it. By contrast, my study focuses on the text and its dynamics. In order to come up to speed on the usual criti-

of a massive wad of theory before we actually get to the text, I prefer to work with the text first, allowing the issues to arise from that analysis; only then will some of the theoretical issues appear on the printed page.

The discussion has four overlapping phases, the first three of which begin by seeking some clarity in terms of the formation of the subject. It begins with a treatment of the obvious text for treatments of the subject in these texts, namely, Neh 9. Here we find the well-worn narrative of the people being led out of slavery into the wilderness by a God who comes into his own with such a feat; in that process the people are constituted as a political subject. However, soon enough the story troubles this process of subjectification, pointing to a repeated pattern of disobedience that threatens their very identity as a people. The second effort at clarity regarding the subject concerns the text's effort to demarcate an identifiable subject by creating a series of outsiders. The problem with this process of differentiation is that once begun, the process seems unstoppable, carving up what initially appears as a stable in-group. From there I move to a third phase, assuming now the conflicted nature of the text but asking whether class identification is the key to subjectivity. Again we will be disappointed, as multiple conflicts overlay that of class, all of which has the effect of thoroughly undermining any clear idea of a political subject. Finally, in light the conclusion that the very effort at subjectification is an internal, conflicted one, I ask, What is a subject in Ezra–Nehemiah?[2]

1. Classic and Cliché

The obvious point to begin an analysis of political subjectivity must be Neh 9, with its ritual recitation of the political myth of Israel's origins.[3] The story is known well enough, but let us revisit the text in its context

---

cal questions surrounding Ezra–Nehemiah—textual, historical, theological, especially burning issues such as the "Nehemiah Memoir" (the first-person sections)—the reader may fruitfully consult Batten (1913), Blenkinsopp's commentary (1998), Myers (1995), and Clines (1990, 124–64). Of far less worth is Grabbe's effort (1998) and the commentary by Williamson (1985)—the latter revealing all the blind spots of traditional historic-theological commentaries. For an entirely different angle, but one that appeals to my own exegetical proclivities, see Bishku's article on "Operation Ezra and Nehemiah" (1991).

2. This paper picks up and develops much further the closing observations of my "No Road: On the Absence of Feminist Criticism of Ezra–Nehemiah" (2005).

3. On political myth see Lincoln 2000; Boer 2009.

(Neh 8-9) to identify its specific features: the people gather at the Water Gate and pressure Ezra into reading from this new-fangled thing called the Book of the Law of Moses. Slow realization as to what they really should be doing according to this book—a festival here, a prayer there, some contrite observance elsewhere—leads to the climax of chapter 9 in which Ezra (still not hoarse from all his reading thus far) retells the narrative from creation to the present, with a distinct focus on the wilderness wanderings between Egypt and Canaan. There is no need to offer a paraphrase of the text here, for it can easily be read; so I prefer to pick out the main points.

It is, as I have mentioned above, a complex political myth, one that moves from creation to the establishment of a people—as subject. The people are called out of Egypt by a relatively unknown god and thereby become a political subject—easy, direct, momentous. The crucial moment of that subjective formation comes after the creation of the world and the mention of Abram/Abraham (although he is, as usual, important to establish the claim to the land): affliction in Egypt is met by signs and wonders and release, division of the Reed Sea, guidance by pillars of cloud and fire, the laws on fiery Sinai, including the Sabbath, vital food and water, and then the land promised (vv. 9-15). By the end of the reworking of this canonical story, Israel is thoroughly constituted as a subject: a state-in-waiting with its deliverance, god, laws, religious perimeters, and a land awaiting them. (Of course, this state never existed as depicted—hence the description as political myth.)

But now two disruptions creep into the narrative. To begin with, as Yahweh was busy bestowing the Egyptians with sundry itches, boils, parasites, and plagues, the text observes, "thou didst get thee a name, as it is to this day" (Neh 9:10). Yahweh's own subjectivity emerges along with the Israelites. As their subjectivity clarifies, so does his. Further, the subjectivity of the people is chronically unstable—a theme that will recur throughout my analysis. After the fifteenth verse we now enter into the cyclic pattern in which the people threaten to surrender that subjectivity, although the text puts it in terms of disobedience and rebellion. The first cycle of wilderness rebellion rolls out slowly (Neh 9:16-25), with Yahweh acting like an indulgent parent, continuing to bestow goodness upon this wayward subject, but then as the literary present looms, the cycles of rebellion and indulgence run into one another ever more rapidly. Except that now resignation on Yahweh's part creeps in, allowing the people to be overrun by their enemies.

All of which suggests that the political subject of Israel is less certain and stable than it at first appeared to be. It wavers at the edges, threatens to dissipate. Only in this sense can we understand the curious close to ch. 9: Ezra makes an appeal to Yahweh for mercy, assistance and the renewal of subjective identity as a people through another covenant (Neh 9:32–38). In other words, political subjectivity must be maintained with due diligence, less it melt away in the noonday heat.

2. The Spiral of Exclusion

That initial search for subjectivity has been less than successful, so let us begin again, for perhaps another mechanism in Ezra–Nehemiah will provide a clearer narrative of subjective formation. A second possibility is through the tried and true mechanism of inclusion and exclusion, a delineation of who does not count as insider and who does. So we find phrases such as the title of this essay, "Thus I cleansed them from everything foreign" (Neh 13:30);[4] or in the stunning account of enforced marriage break-up in Ezra, "separate yourselves from the peoples of the land and from the foreign wives" (Ezra 10:11), as also in Nehemiah, which speaks of those "separated from Israel all those of foreign descent" (Neh 13:3); or, as Nehemiah narrates, "the Israelites separated themselves from all foreigners, and stood and confessed their sins and the iniquities of their fathers" (Neh 9:2); and finally, "the priests and the Levites purified themselves; and they purified the people and the gates and the wall" (Neh 12:30).

It is hardly necessary to elaborate on this initial point: subjectivity seems to require a world in which we can distinguish between us and them, between the impure and ignorant foreigner—Arab, Chinese, Afghan, Muslim, Jew, Hindu, atheist, Ammonite, Moabite, woman, child, indeed anyone—and the clean, purified in-group of one's own (see Douglas). But now matters become less clear and pure, especially when we look more closely at the terms used to designate insiders and outsiders in the text. Most obviously they include "members of the people of Israel" (Ezra 2:2), those who "belonged to Israel" (Ezra 2:59; Neh 7:61), "all Israel" (Ezra 2:70), and so on (Ezra 3:1; 6:16–17, 21; 8:25, 35; 9:1; 10:5, 25; Neh 1:6; 2:10; 7:7, 73; 8:1, 7, 14; 9:1–2; 10:30/29; 12:47; 13:2,

---

4. Unable to contemplate Nehemiah uttering such words, Batten opines (without any support whatsoever) that it was "added by a well-meaning scholiast" (1913, 301).

26). Israel is of course the crucial term used in the phrases of separation I noted earlier: "separated from Israel all those of foreign descent" (Neh 13:3); "the Israelites separated themselves from all foreigners, and stood and confessed their sins and the iniquities of their fathers" (Neh 9:2). Less commonly they are also called "Jews" (*yĕhûdîm*), a term that can be used in much the same way as "Israel," such as the "Jews who were in Judah and Jerusalem" (Ezra 5:1; Neh 5:1). However, this usage of "Jew" soon turns out to be an anomaly, for in the majority of cases "Jew" is used in association with foreignness and outsiders. Thus, Cyrus uses the term (Ezra 6:7–8), it applies to Jews in a foreign location (Neh 1:2), and above all, it appears again and again in opposition to often hostile "outsiders" (Ezra 4:12, 23; 5:5; 6:14; Neh 4:12; 6:6; 13:23). In sum, there is a clear pattern in the use of "Jew": in contrast to the internal designator Israel, with its focus on the in-group, Jew is usually used in demarcating difference from outsiders, at times in the mouths of outsiders, often hostile, with a clear sense of distinction.

Standard group dynamics, is it not? Create a category of outsider, however artificial, and use it to define yourself through differentiation. At last, we have a clear subject! Unfortunately that clarity of subjectification does not last long, for in a few key verses the process of differentiation continues, but now in an internally divisive fashion. Once begun, that differentiation is impossible to stop. I list those verses first (a process not unknown to the biblical text in question) and then analyses:

> Moreover there were at my table a hundred and fifty men, Jews and officials [*wĕhayyĕhûdîm wĕhassĕgānîm*], besides those who came to us from the nations which were about us. (Neh 5:17)

> And there went up also to Jerusalem, in the seventh year of Ar-ta-xerx'es the king, some of the people of Israel, and some of the priests and Levites, the singers and gatekeepers, and the temple servants. (Ezra 7:7)

> And the officials did not know where I had gone or what I was doing; and I had not yet told the Jews, the priests, the nobles, the officials, and the rest that were to do the work. (Neh 2:16)

> These are the chiefs of the province who lived in Jerusalem; but in the towns of Judah every one lived on his property in their towns: Israel, the priests, the Levites, the temple servants, and the descendants of Solomon's servants. (Neh 11:3)

The first text may well refer to Jews and non-Jewish officials (so Blenkinsopp 1998, 265), imperial or whatever, although the context suggests not.[5] The next three verses are much more intriguing: in Ezra 7:7, the people of Israel are distinguished from the priests, Levites, singers, gatekeepers, and temple servants. And in Neh 2:16 the Jews are one in a list that includes priests, nobles, officials and the rest that were to do the work. I will have more to say about those who do not work in a moment, but do these two texts mean that the Israelites and Jews are to be distinguished from the rest? Or do these terms function as generic markers for the rest of the lists, a first inclusive term that is then differentiated?[6] Or do the categories leak into one another? A similar effect is achieved by the fourth verse, for here Israel is distinguished from priests, Levites, temple servants and descendants of Solomon's servants. Rather than a quick effort to paper over a contradiction, I prefer to let the contradiction stand, for it points to a central issue concerning the subject. It seems as though the text is uncertain as to who precisely Israel is, or who the Jews are. Do the terms designate the people as a whole, perhaps in opposition to constructed outside groups, or do they refer to *internal* divisions, Israel/Jew designating one among a number of internal groups?

Before we answer that question, let us consider one other instance of "outsiders" who seem to offer a clear demarcation. In this case, it involves the people left in the land who oppose the repair of the walls of Jerusalem by these recent arrivals. As far as the returnees are concerned, this riffraff is to be avoided and denied. The people of the land respond in kind, pursuing legal channels, furiously sending endless letters in a process that outlasts various Persian kings, generating decrees that in one instance stop the temple building (Ezra 4:6–24) and then allow it to resume until completion (Ezra 5:3–6:15). In the Book of Nehemiah the opposition from Sanballat and Tobiah is more direct, sneering, and military. Here the issue is not so much the rebuilding of the temple but of the walls of the city, which then requires armed guards for the builders (Neh 3:33–4:17// Ezra 4:1–23; 6:1–19). Often read as opposition from the people of the land

---

5. Batten finds this verse sufficiently troubling, so he simply deletes "and officials" (1913, 246).

6. Blenkinsopp lamely suggests that in Ezra 7:7 "Israelites" refers to the "laity" (1998, 138). By the time he gets to Neh 2:16 he is genuinely confused and increasingly tentative (1985, 223–24). So also Batten, who, for all his deft confidence, runs into the mud eventually with Neh 11:3.

left behind during the exile (the lack of identity of these dissenters in Ezra until 5:3 hints in this direction), in Ezra-Nehemiah the opposition seems to come primarily from the governors of the province "Beyond the River." Yet clarity is again elusive, for the indistinctness of these opponents, as well as the sheer range of methods used—methods legal, literate and military, along with subterfuge, insult, and drawn-out harassment—suggest a lack of a clear sense of inside and outside, so much so that it too seems like an internal conflict. All of which comes to a head in the opening of the conflict itself in Ezra 4:1-3. The text itself is caught in a bind. On the one hand, it begins with the "adversaries of Judah and Benjamin" (4:1), yet they are the ones who approach the returned exiles and say without guile, "Let us build with you; for we worship your God as you do, and we have been sacrificing to him ever since the days of E'sar-had'don King of Assyria who brought us here" (Ezra 4:2). Then comes the response from Zerub'babel, Jeshua, and the rest of the heads of fathers' houses: "You have nothing to do with us in building a house to our God" (Ezra 4:3). In other words, "bugger off: you might count yourselves as Judeans, but we don't." The people of the land certainly do not feel as though they were distinct, so the ruling class among the returnees attempts to tell them they are.

In these cases—the use of terms for Israel and Jew and then the effort to designate the people of the land as outsiders—the attempt at differentiation backfires, for it spills over into internal differences. We may view this process in at least three ways: the process of differentiation has an internal component, needed to weed out those who are not genuinely one of "us"; once begun, the need to identify a subject through differentiation cannot be halted, thereby continuing its inexorable path from outside to inside; or the whole process is in fact an inside job. Each possibility has some truth, although I have pursued the second here and will eventually move to the third as the most persuasive option—a position hinted at in one more text in which "Jew" is used, once again as a designator of hostile opposition, but now internally: "Now there arose a great outcry of the people and of their wives against their Jewish brethren" (Neh 5:1; see also v. 8).

3. CLASS CONFLICT

On two occasions now I have sought after a stable political subject only to be frustrated by a text that refuses such stability. But now, with the spiral of exclusion continuing its path inward, I shall focus on those internal dynamics. For a third time, I ask the question, Is a clear political subject able to be located, perhaps now through the prism of class?

Let us begin with class struggle. The verse with which I ended the previous section actually introduces a narrative of explicit class conflict that runs through Neh 5. The situation is one of exploitation and debt: in the face of famine, the nobles and officials have been all too ready to make a killing, charging exorbitant rates for rare grain and food. The people cry in a literary sequence of three (Neh 5:1–5): fields, vineyards, houses, sons, and daughters have all been lost through debt.[7] So Nehemiah confronts the nobles and officials and instructs them to return the items seized in lieu of unpaid debts, including also the interest of money, grain, oil, and wine—although not the debt-slaves themselves.[8] They do so with alacrity, while Nehemiah curses any who would likewise exploit the people. He then observes that unlike the former governors and their officials, who laid heavy burdens on the people, took their food and wine, and even the silver (forty shekels) of the governor's allowance, he does not: "But I did not do so, because of the fear of God. I also ... acquired no land" (Neh 5:15–16; but compare Neh 5:10).

All very admirable, but before we are persuaded by Nehemiah's sense of justice, benevolence and frugality, note that he insists that only the interest and security for defaulted debts (property but not people) be returned, not that the debts themselves should be forgiven. The sacred economy must remain intact![9] Indeed, the reason for curbing the excesses by the nobles is

---

7. Only Davies gives some attention to literary matters, although his commentary fails to deliver despite occasional flashes of brilliance (1999). Otherwise, commentators simply fail to notice the literary device here, asking in all seriousness what the different social groups in the first verses might be (Blenkinsopp 1998, 255–57; Batten 1913, 238–39; Williamson 1985, 216–19).

8. Here the text reads *mĕ'at hakkesep*, a hundredth part of, which puzzles most commentators, since that would be a mere 1 percent. Some suggest 1 percent per month, while others, still unhappy, prefer to read *mē'āh* in the general sense of interest (Blenkinsopp 1998, 255, 259–60; Batten 1913, 243). Even if we stay with the 1 percent, the text exhibits an abhorrence of interest.

9. Blenkinsopp's detailed and occasionally useful commentary, which is very good at outlining the economic issues, simply misses this point (1998, 253–65). A case of the proverbial forest and trees. Of the commentators I have consulted, only Davies notes the conservative nature of the intervention: "He never deals with the root cause," but then he too misses the point, observing that the cause was "land ownership" (1999, 101).

that they threaten the system itself with collapse, as well as the vital task of repairing the walls (that task itself is a symbol of the need to shore up the economic and social system). In short, the intervention with the nobles and officials is hardly revolutionary, opting, as he does, for a trickle-down social justice; as long as the nobles do the right thing, then the economic and social system will keep going. The protests against the actions of the nobles result in band-aid measures that ensure nothing changes.

Here at last it appears that we have subjective clarity, now through class, for surely here we can identify various oppositional subjects clearly. Let us begin with the literary presence of ruling classes, identified with a congeries of terms, such as "nobles" (*haḥōrîm*), "mighty ones" (*'addîrîm*; Neh 10:30/29), "officials" (*hassĕgānîm*),[10] or "leaders" (*haśśārîm*). Separated from everyone else and named in Neh 10:2–28/1–27, the rulers both do not actually work (Neh 4:16–17) and are followed by those who do, the

> rest [*šĕ'ār*] of the people, the priests, the Levites, the gatekeepers, the singers, the temple servants, and *all who have separated themselves* from the peoples of the land to the law of God, their wives, their sons, their daughters, all who have knowledge and understanding, join with their brethren, their mighty ones.... (Neh 10:29–30/28–29)

This ragtag collection of unnamed individuals just make it in after their rulers, a remainder, a leftover like the dags on a sheep's ass—or perhaps like an "under-arse" fly, as the Serbs like to call it, a fly that tries to tag along with the big boss, seeking to be part of the action, but all they get is a pile of shit. And yet, at least they are better than the "peoples of the land" (*'amê hā'āreṣ*).

However, just when it looks as though we have three levels in the text—rulers, sundry hangers-on and the riff-raff beyond any recognizable status—the second and third levels start to collapse into each other. Of all people, the singers open the gates for all those "outsiders," who now begin to stream into the text—quite literally, for they are part of the story itself.

---

10. This term, cognate with Babylonian *shaknu* and Assyrian *saknu*, appears only in Ezra–Nehemiah (Ezra 9:2; Neh 2:16; 4:8, 13; 5:7, 17; 7:5; 12:40; 13:11); Isa 41:25; Jer 51:23, 28, 57; Ezek 23:6, 12, 23. In the prophetic texts the reference is directly to Babylonian and Assyrian officials, which indicates a similar usage in Ezra–Nehemiah.

So, towards the end of the litany of men and their sons in the long census-like genealogy in Ezra 2 and Neh 7, we find the following:

> The whole assembly [*kol-haqqāhāl*] together was forty-two thousand three hundred and sixty, *besides* their menservants and maidservants, of whom there were seven thousand three hundred and thirty-seven; and they had two hundred male and female singers. Their horses were seven hundred and thirty-six, their mules were two hundred and forty-five, their camels were four hundred and thirty-five, and their asses were six thousand seven hundred and twenty. (Ezra 2:64–67; cf. Neh 7:66–69)

Why do I pick on the singers? Elsewhere they are part of the in-group, second-class citizens to be sure, but still inside (Ezra 2:41 and so on). But not here, for now they join slaves, horses, mules, camels, and asses. Along with the people of the land, they too do not count; they are nonsubjects. Nor, in light of the passages I discussed earlier, do the following: late arrivals at assemblies (Ezra 10:8), sabbath traders, people who were not in exile and are now opposed to rebuilding Jerusalem, debt-slaves (for they are slaves too), tithe avoiders, false prophets, and, of course, the "foreign" women and their children. Or rather, the singers are responsible for muddying the clarity of class distinctions and thereby subject positions, for they constitute the passage from outside to inside: as both nonsubjects and subjects, they enable all these other denizens to come streaming back into the text, the story, the city, and thereby subjectivity.

The subjective stability of class conflict is eroded further by the myriad overlays of other struggles, which in their own way fracture the subject position of the people. So let us trace this fracturing in some detail, especially in a text that embarrasses most commentators, Neh 13.[11] The text exhibits a whole series of tensions and oppositions: Eliashib the priest allows Tobiah the Ammonite in the temple during Nehemiah's absence,

---

11. Again and again, commentators voice their disappointment with Neh 13, some drastically rearranging the text so that it is not the conclusion (Batten 1913, 286–302), others offering as few comments as possible in downplayed conclusions (Davies 1999, 127–34), and others valiantly defending desperate and xenophobic measures as necessary for survival (Blenkinsopp 1998, 363) or even as a revolutionary purge (Davies 1999, 129). Blenkinsopp suns up the general feeling with, "The conclusion of this section, and of the book, will generally leave the reader disappointed" (Blenkinsopp 1998, 366). As will become clear, Nehemiah is a vital part of the book—and, of course, my argument.

much to the latter's disapproval (Neh 13:4–8); the people stop paying taxes (tithes), so priests and Levites abandon their temple posts (Neh 13:10–14); merchants from Judah and Tyre arrive in Jerusalem to sell a whole range of wares on the Sabbath (Neh 13:15–18). Nehemiah will have none of it, so he prevents them from entering by closing the town gates; in response they calmly set up shop outside the gates until told to get lost (Neh 13:19–23). Nor should we forget the "false prophets," of whom the prophetess Noadiah is the only one named (Neh 6:14).

The text is beginning to reveal a political subject split along multiple and overlapping lines, full of dissent, civil disobedience, and open confrontation.[12] It is in this context of opposition and conflict across the social spectrum that the stories of "foreign wives" in Ezra 9–10 and Neh 13:23–27 should be understood.[13] Of the two, Neh 13 is the more curious and thereby intriguing. Rather than a stand-alone moment, the expulsion of women from "mixed" marriages is the last in the series of conflictual stories in Neh 13. It is worth noting how the mad governor responds to the situation. Upon hearing the languages of Ashdod, Ammon, and Moab spoken by the children of mixed marriages, our narrator (really a ghostwriter) writes on behalf of Nehemiah: "I contended with them and cursed them and beat some of them and pulled out their hair" (Neh 13:25). Picture the scene for a moment: in the midst of the rubble of a ruined town, with widespread hunger, dissatisfaction, and opposition, the crazy governor rushes about, screaming and punching and pulling people's hair. (To his credit, in Ezra 9:3 he is more disciplined, merely pulling out his own hair and beard.) The scene is more at home in one of those mad, marginal religious experiments, a community of zealots with a leader who claims to speak on God's behalf. But the story also suggests that the enforced oath—"I made them take an oath in the name of God" (Neh 13:25)—is exacted with rough frontier violence.[14] It would be tempting to make a standard feminist and indeed postcolonial point that the only subjects in these texts

---

12. The connections made with the wayward past practices of the Israelites exacerbate the picture (see Neh 1:6–9; 9; 13:18).

13. For problematic discussions of these texts, see Eskenazi 1994 and Eskenazi and Judd 1994, along with my sustained criticisms of these arguments (Boer 2005). The reading by Washington is far more productive (2003).

14. So also with the son of Eliashib the high priest, who seems to have married a daughter of the loathed Sanballat the Horonite (although she is not in fact mentioned), whom Nehemiah chases out of town (Neh 13:28).

are adult males, indeed that the women are "subjects-on-trial" in the midst of an effort to produce a Judean subjectivity (so Washington 2003),[15] but that is to simplify matters too much. The telling moment of that indeterminacy comes with the question, Who is the "them" with whom Nehemiah contends? Whose hair does he pull? If we consider the preceding v. 24, it may be the sons, half of whom speak the language of Ashdod. Or is it perhaps the women of Ashdod, Ammon, and Moab themselves (Neh 13:23)?[16] Or is it the men who are punched, beaten, given a rough haircut, and then forced to take an oath, while being admonished not to be like Solomon by doing "all this great evil" or acting "treacherously" against God by marrying foreign women (Neh 13:25–27). Yet it is not entirely clear whom Nehemiah addresses in his rage, for even the gender distinctions become murky.

All of these episodes have now become part of a pattern: foreign women and their children, stallholders inside and then outside the walls, the son-in-law of Sanballat, the people refusing to pay tithes for priests, Levites and singers, the rebuffed offer for assistance with the temple and then the opposition to the rebuilding of the walls, and the protests against the exploitation that is enacted by that ever-present yet unclear group of "nobles." In short, the text of Ezra–Nehemiah seethes with dissent and opposition.

4. Conclusion: An Inside Job

My exegesis has been moving toward two conclusions: first, that the manifold oppositions are part of an inside job; second, that the unresolved pattern of conflict has profound implications for understanding the political subject in Ezra–Nehemiah. They are of course related, but let us take each in turn. Thus far I have argued that what appear to be external elements are actually internal, that the efforts to differentiate Israel or the Jews from

---

15. A position supported by the comparable story in Ezra, where "all the returned exiles" (Ezra 10:7) who are called to meet in an assembly to deal with the question of "foreign women"—on pain of dispossession of property and banishment from the community—turn out to be "all the men of Judah and Benjamin" (Ezra 10:9).

16. In the comparable story in Ezra 10:18–44 we find not merely a few Ashdodian, Ammonite, and Moabite women but now women from just about everywhere: Canaanites, Hittites, Perizzites, Jebusites, Ammonites, Moabites, Egyptians, and Amorites, in a direct echo of peoples of the land mentioned in Ezra 9:1.

outsiders fails, that the text itself presents the people of the land as merely constructed outsiders, that the spiral of exclusion soon becomes an internal dynamic. But now let me introduce another feature of the text that exhibits its internal nature. Throughout the books of Ezra–Nehemiah we have constant references to, even a celebration of, writing and reading. The text is full of almost endless lists, whether of the numbers of returnees, the temple vessels, the perpetual concern with money for rebuilding the walls and temple, the organization of temple duties, and so on. The people stand for an interminably long period, listening to the Torah read and interpreted for them, so much that one must wonder if they can understand what it is like to read the lists, again and again. Above all, we have the perpetual interplay of letters and decrees, some of which are "reproduced" in the text. Writing, reading, hearing, and interpretation—it is as though the text wishes to tell us that the word itself is all powerful, or rather that the real conflict is always with words (note that the people of the land never actually *attack* Jerusalem). That is to say, not only do the anonymous scribes write themselves into the text, a thoroughly self-indulgent exercise in which they foreground themselves (see Boer 2010), but the text itself becomes the all-encompassing "reality" within which everything must fit. So also with the various struggles: the outsiders are really in the text, the people of the land as well, even Cyrus and the Persians. And the text reveals this in the way these distinctions, at the level of the content of the stories, are unsustainable and break down.

This insider job also affects the process of subjectification, for in the chronic inability to distinguish insider and outsider, the text constantly undermines its own efforts to make the distinctions needed for subject formation.[17] One last example of this process, now drawn from one of those items that highlight scribal activity—the lists: in this case, it is not merely the uncertainty of the lists themselves but the fact that they are needed at all, repeated again and again in a desperate effort to assert what cannot be asserted—clear identity.[18] The uncertainties show up soon enough, such

---

17. A point that Esler's (2003) rather flat reading misses. See the withering critique by Thompson against those who would use the Bible for securing national identity (2008).

18. The list of returnees especially (Ezra 2:1–67; Neh 7:5–69) has been a cornerstone in historical reconstructions of the Persian-period province of Yehud. The problem, as Finkelstein has shown recently (2008), is that archaeological evidence suggests that the places mentioned have little connection with the Persian period.

as the observation concerning those who came back to Judah anyway even though they "could not prove their fathers' houses or their descent, whether they belonged to Israel" (Ezra 2:59; Neh 7:61), or the opposition to the banishment of the women from some of the supposedly genuine, genealogically verified, members, namely Jonathan the son of As'ahel and Jahzei'ah the son of Tikvah, along with Meshul'lum and Shab'bethai (Ezra 10:15), a rare and precious Levite (see Ezra 8:15-18). But it is the need, repeatedly, to produce these lists, with their genealogical clutter, that suggests a deep aporia over who is who: we find them in Ezra 2:1-67; 7:1-5 (a mini one for Ezra that traces his lineage back to the mythical Aaron); 8:1-21; 10:18-44; Neh 3 (the "roster" of wall repairs, all made by card-carrying Israelites); 7:5-69 (an almost identical text to Ezra 2); 10:2-28/1-27 (those who put their seal on the newly struck covenant); 11:1-36 (now for the sake of living allocation); 12:1-26 (now for those who came to Jerusalem with Zerub'babel et al.); 12:27-43 (to celebrate the completion of the wall). An extraordinary collection, is it not? Almost like a nervous twitch that betrays a much deeper problem. Far from ensuring clarity over the identity of the collective subject, these very lists obscure and fudge.

I have been singularly unable to identify a clear subject in Ezra–Nehemiah. Every effort, whether in terms of the narrative of Israel's wilderness call to subjectivity, or the effort to demarcate outsiders and insiders, or to specify who is an opponent, or even to engage in bitter class conflict, ends up in a state of indistinctness. My conclusion can only be that none of these are subjects, not Israel, not the nobles or rulers, not the common people, not the foreigners expelled or those suddenly and to their great surprise identified as outsiders. But what, then, is subjectivity in the text? One path would be to follow Heidegger, Agamben, or even Adorno and use this argument to show that the subject is a useless category, destined for such an undoing every time it is examined closely. Or I may take a much more dialectical path, following Lacan through to Žižek, arguing that the subject is not a self, an ego, or the symbolic entity produced through various processes of subjectification. No, the subject is the unstable process and unrealizable search itself. In other words, the subject is not centered but split—Lacan's famous $ for the subject of the unconscious.

Indeed, archaeological data indicates that the list came from the late Hellenistic (Hasmonaean) period. In short, they are thoroughly literary products.

For this analysis of Ezra–Nehemiah, then, the split between subject and nonsubject, between Israel and non-Israelite, between insider and outsider, ruling class and the rest, is the point of subjectification. It is a little like the proverbial onion: I have attempted to peel the texts back, layer after layer, and all I have found is a void, a point of pure negativity. That is, the "subject proper is empty, a kind of formal function, a void which remains after I sacrifice my ego (the wealth that constitutes my 'person')" (Žižek 2006, 150). But we need to go one step further, for not only is the subject a negativity or void, but it is also the process in which we come to the void, that, is the failure of symbolization that is supposed to produce the subject. So the subject emerges as a negativity or void that both forecloses the totality of the process of subjectification and simultaneously fuels this process. In other words,

> what drives the process of subjectification is the attempt to fill the void, which emerges as the failure of this very process. The subject is thus at once its own impetus and obstacle, it is what both drives and hinders the process of subjectification, both its condition of possibility and its condition of impossibility. (Karlsen 2010, 147)

Now, one may well read Žižek's theory as a complex reflection upon and response to the break-up of Yugoslavia, in which he played his guilty part. By a curious congruence, and since Žižek and his able interpreter Karlsen have lain behind this paper from its beginning, I have found a very similar pattern in my reflection on and response to Ezra–Nehemiah. To sum up: the political subject appears to be constructed through a perpetual spiral in which the impure element is sought out, but the catch is that the subject is not the final, unattainable product but the internalization of the endless process itself. Thus, Ezra–Nehemiah is the perfect example of subjectification.

References

Badiou, Alain. 2006. *Being and Event*. Translated by O. Feltham. London: Continuum.

———. 2009a. *Logics of Worlds, Being and Event, 2*. Translated by A. Toscano. London: Continuum.

———. 2009b. *Theory of the Subject*. Translated by B. Bosteels. London: Continuum.

Batten, Loring W. 1913. *A Critical and Exegetical Commentary on the Books of Ezra and Nehemiah*. The International Critical Commentary. Edinburgh: T&T Clark.

Bishku, Michael B. 1991. The Other Side of the Arab–Israeli Conflict: Great Britain and the Issue of Iraqi Jewry Prior to "Operation Ezra and Nehemiah." *JIH* 12:29–41.

Blanton, Ward. 2007. Disturbing Politics: Neo-Paulinism and the Scrambling of Religious and Secular Identities. *Dialog* 46:3–13.

Blenkinsopp, Joseph. 1998. *Ezra–Nehemiah: A Commentary*, Old Testament Library. Louisville: Westminster John Knox.

———. 2009. *Judaism, the First Phase: The Place of Ezra and Nehemiah in the Origins of Judaism*. Grand Rapids: Eerdmans.

Boer, Roland. 2005. No Road: On the Absence of Feminist Criticism of Ezra–Nehemiah. Pages 233–52 in *Her Master's Tools: Feminist and Postcolonial Engagements of Historical-Critical Discourse*. Edited by C. Vander Stichele and T. Penner. Atlanta: Society of Biblical Literature.

———. 2009. *Political Myth: On the Use and Abuse of Biblical Themes*. Durham, N.C.: Duke University Press.

———. 2010. Too Many Dicks at the Writing Desk, or, How to Organise a Prophetic Sausage-Fest. *Theology and Sexuality* 16:95–108.

Clines, David. 1990. *What Does Eve Do to Help? And Other Readerly Questions to the Old Testament*. Sheffield: JSOT Press.

Davies, Gordon F. 1999. *Ezra–Nehemiah*. Berit Olam. Collegeville, Minn.: Liturgical Press.

Eskenazi, Tamara C. 1994. Out from the Shadows: Biblical Women in the Post-Exilic Era. Pages 252–71 in *A Feminist Companion to Samuel–Kings*. Edited by A. Brenner. Sheffield: Sheffield Academic Press.

Eskenazi, Tamara C., and Eleanore P. Judd. 1994. Marriage to a Stranger in Ezra 9–10. Pages 266–87 in *Second Temple Studies 2. Temple Community in the Persian Period*. Edited by T. C. Eskenazi and K. H. Richards. Sheffield: Sheffield Academic Press.

Esler, Philip. 2003. Ezra–Nehemiah as a Narrative of (Re-invented) Israelite Identity. *BibInt* 11:413–26.

Finkelstein, Israel. 2008. Archaeology and the List of Returnees in the Books of Ezra and Nehemiah. *PEQ* 140:7–16.

Grabbe, Lester. 1998. *Ezra-Nehemiah*. London: Routledge.

Karlsen, Mads-Peter. 2010. The Grace of Materialism: Theology with Alain Badiou and Slavoj Žižek. Doctoral thesis, Faculty of Theology, University of Copenhagen.

Lincoln, Bruce. 2000. *Theorizing Myth: Narrative, Ideology, and Scholarship*. Chicago: University of Chicago Press.
Loomba, Ania. 2005. *Colonial/Postcolonial*. 2nd ed. London: Routledge.
Myers, Jacob M. 1995. *Ezra, Nehemiah*. AB 14. New Haven: Yale University Press.
Spivak, Gayatri Chakravorty. 1999. *A Critique of Postcolonial Reason: Towards a History of the Vanishing Present*. Cambridge: Harvard University Press.
Thompson, Thomas L. 2008. The Politics of Reading the Bible in Israel. *HLS* 7:1–15.
Washington, Harold C. 2003. Israel's Holy Seed and the Foreign Women of Ezra–Nehemiah: A Kristevan Reading. *BibInt* 11:427–37.
Williamson, H. G. M. 1985. *Ezra–Nehemiah*. WBC. Nashville: Thomas Nelson.
Žižek, Slavoj. 1999. *The Ticklish Subject: The Absent Centre of Political Ontology*. London: Verso.
———. 2006. *The Parallax View*. Cambridge, Maine: MIT.

Responses

"It Is More Complicated":
Reflections on Some Suggestive Essays

Richard Horsley

The observance of the four hundredth anniversary of the King James Version of the Holy Bible was barely noticeable compared with the celebration of its three hundredth anniversary. In the United States it involved high-profile public readings and fanfare, as both former President Theodore Roosevelt and President Woodrow Wilson proclaimed it America's "national book." Before that of course it was the British national book and was distributed, read, and preached everywhere in the British Empire.

Twenty-some years ago, when I was a visiting faculty member at Harvard Divinity School, many students from (previously) colonized countries enrolled in my courses—from Burma, Nicaragua, the Philippines, South Africa, and others. I still have vivid memories of the two Zulus, Purity Malinga and Michael Mkize, a Methodist minister and a Catholic priest who became special friends. Both were graduates of quality theological schools in South Africa and had thus acquired the standard assumptions, procedures, knowledge, and interpretive discourse of European (British) theological education. Several weeks along, as the class began discussing the Gospel of Mark, Malinga and Mkize still understood the Gospel as a European text. But of course. The Bible, along with theological education for ministers and priests, had been brought from Europe. After a week or so of class discussion, however, Malinga and Mkize suddenly began speaking of Mark not as a European text but as *their* story, a story about, by, and for people like them and their newfound Burmese, Filipino, and Nicaraguan friends.

Discontented biblical interpreters have been smuggling postcolonial criticism into biblical studies for only the last couple of decades. It is still not clear what postcolonial biblical criticism is or can be. So far it has focused mainly on what the Bible became under and as part of the cultural archive of European colonialism. In some discussions it seems that the Bible *is* what became the dominant reading operative in Western imperial hegemony. As texts carrying or justifying European colonizing and imposed on African, Asian, and other peoples as the word of God, the means of their salvation, this is indeed what the Bible *was* and perhaps still *is*, and it will take a long time and exhaustive energy to work through the effects of the Bible as colonial text.

In coping with the European and North American colonial Bible, however, several questions arise about the scope of postcolonial criticism. The "post-" suggests "after," but we are still living with the effects of colonialism and anticolonialism, and imperial domination has only been intensified. Postcolonial criticism, nourished from its roots in Fanon, Cesaire, and C. L. R. James and their connection with anticolonial struggles, can include continuing analysis and critique of colonialism and its legacy.

Much of the postcolonial criticism from which biblical scholars are borrowing is focused mainly on culture, without attention to its political-economic conditions. But this perpetuates the division that Western culture has made between the real world of politics and economics (colonial wars, industrialization, displacement of peoples) and the separate spheres of culture and religion, which can heal the pain or provide an inner life (Said 1993; Asad). At least some have sounded a critical note, insisting that by confining its concerns to the cultural (analysis mainly of texts), postcolonial criticism may even be "complicitous in the consecration of hegemony" (Shohat 1992, 110; Dirlik 1995, 331; 1995; Ahmad 1992). Postcolonial criticism in biblical studies has so far focused mainly on texts of the Bible as colonial. Yet it is possible to consider also the direct relationship between colonial practices and the colonial Bible and/or to consider the political-economic as well as cultural effects of the colonial Bible.

Another set of questions focuses on what the Bible is or has become. Has the European colonial Bible's hegemony over the last few centuries been so overwhelmingly effective that the Bible *is* now (by definition) the Western colonial/imperial Bible? Is there anything else, more or less, in the Bible? There was previously. Part of the agenda of postcolonial criticism is to bring to light the previously submerged histories and identities of colonized peoples (on whom the Bible was imposed) and reveal the contingencies of their life in the postcolonial world. At times and places in the past, however, the Bible became a factor in such largely submerged histories, sometimes in resistance to domination. When Bible stories and prophecies were translated into the vernacular and heard by late medieval peasants, it became one of the motivating factors in movements of resistance and liberation (Lollards, Hussites, etc.). Again under European colonialism, when the Bible was translated into indigenous languages, for example in Central America or areas of Africa, indigenous peoples heard stories, songs, prophecies, and laws with which they could identify, that could even lead them to form communities of resistance.

In their origins as well as in their effects, moreover, books included in the Bible were not what they became in the European colonial Bible. Ironically perhaps, one of the results of established biblical studies developed in the Western imperial metropoles is the recognition that the Gospels and Paul's letters were texts of peoples subjected to a previous Western empire, texts that proclaimed that history was moving through one of those subject peoples, not the imperial metropolis, and that an alternative society was now forming in local communities. Similarly in the Hebrew Bible, texts such as the Song of Deborah (Judg 5) and many prophetic oracles can hardly be characterized as colonial. It may be possible that postcolonial criticism, availing itself of previous historical criticism, can help open access to people's histories that became submerged in the scribal development of texts that were later included in the Bible.

At least part of the agenda of postcolonial studies is to expose or subvert the Western colonial Bible, with or without attention to its effects. Previous modes of biblical criticism have already developed certain exposés and subversions of biblical books. Historical criticism has shown that certain books later included in the Hebrew Bible were composed to legitimate the Judean monarchy or temple-state. Such historical studies can be pressed into service for a postcolonial agenda that aims to undermine the authority of "the dominant reading" of the Bible.

Finally, an important part of the agenda of postcolonial studies is to give voice to previously colonized but now postcolonial people who may critically subvert and/or creatively appropriate and/or deepen the various modes of biblical criticism.

The essays in this volume exemplify, explicitly or implicitly, a number of the issues and complications that postcolonial criticism encounters. They are not heavy on theory and the jargon often encountered in postcolonial criticism, and they give little attention to the roots or the accumulating archive of the enterprise. The authors plunge right into their chosen text or critique or situation. In contrast with some previous exercises in postcolonial criticism of biblical texts that focus more narrowly on the colonial text/dominant reading itself, these essays include attention to related matters such as historical effects of texts, comparisons with historical critical readings, and the difference between the political economy in which the dominant reading developed and that in which the composition of the text was rooted. All of this invites us as readers to recognize and explore the ways postcolonial criticism is or can be related to other modes of biblical criticism, some of which have seemed problematic.

In her postcolonial criticism, Judith McKinlay, as a New Zealander still grappling with a legacy of issues of power from her colonial past, is concerned primarily with the Bible as it has functioned in the cultural archive of the colonial West and its colonies, "the dominant reading." Because of her feminist concerns, her attention is drawn to the daughters of Zelophehad, some of the few women given voice in the Hebrew Bible. Her suggestive creation of a periodic conversation with those daughters is only a thinly veiled conversation of a feminist postcolonial New Zealander with other New Zealanders whose understanding of life has been shaped by the book of Numbers as part of their social memory. Taking a cue from Edward Said, she does a contrapuntal exploration of the parallel between Moses' allocation of land to the Israelites before they entered the land and Edward Gibbon Wakefield's mapping of land for the settlers he was sending to Aotearoa (to displace the Maori).

McKinlay's training in the more standard modes of biblical criticism, however, has her explaining that "it is more complicated," "there is more to it," and wondering if the story (of Moses, and of the daughters) is "fact or fiction" and if "these figures ever existed." She repeatedly cites and builds on previous historical-critical analyses of Numbers and related texts and recent feminist criticism, and draws on an important anthropological study and recent studies of cultural memory. The previous historical criticism of Numbers, moreover, has her repeatedly qualifying the parallels she finds between Moses' allocation of land and Wakefield's mapping of land. While the latter was a real historical figure, Moses was a character in plotted story.

If part of the agenda of postcolonial criticism is to expose the dominant reading of the Bible that became central to the cultural archive of Western colonizing, then other modes of biblical criticism can be pressed into service. Previous historical-literary criticism has shown that purportedly historical accounts of historical figures and events have been shaped to justify Jerusalem rule. Recent study of the role of scribal circles in composition and cultivation of texts and manuscripts that turned up in the

Dead Sea Scrolls, moreover, is only compounding questions about the origins of "biblical" texts.

McKinlay herself is the composer of the (hi)story of Wakefield's colonial allocation of land in Aotearoa and is frank about her agenda. Her periodic references to historical criticism of Numbers only whets our appetite for a fuller explanation of how the biblical text is not really all that parallel to what she lays out about Wakefield. Biblical scholars have slipped into the habit of referring to "Israel's narrative of origins" or "Israel telling its story." McKinlay offers leads to other modes of biblical criticism that attempt to sort out the origins of the books of the Pentateuch (and of the Deuteronomic History). The narrative from Genesis to Joshua surely includes legends and laws that originated with Israelites. But these "books" were developed in scribal circles to authorize/legitimate the Jerusalem monarchy and/or temple-state and the allocation of land among the people over whom it ruled. "Moses" was the authority figure from the hoary past of "Israel's" origin to whose mediation with God they attributed the customs, rulings, and land-allotments that they continued to develop in their service of the monarch or temple-state. In her historical account McKinlay makes Wakefield's motive and actions directly visible. In the "constitutional" texts developed to authorize Jerusalem rule, the scribal composers make their role invisible behind the lawgiving of Moses in hoary antiquity.

In contrast to Wakefield's allocation of land from a distance before the settlement, however, the scribes working in the service of the Jerusalem state were drawing upon oral tradition of customs and lineages and their ancestral land that they were reshaping in the interests of the state. As McKinlay mentions, for example, it is possible that the names of Zelophehad's daughters and their story were derived from or served as an etiology for certain villages. Might some of the lineages and clans to whom land is allotted in Numbers have been people living in territory taken over by rulers of Israel and fitted into the traditional list of tribes and clans? From several other traditions included in law codes of the Pentateuch it is clear that, ideally at least, land was allocated to and was to remain an inalienable inheritance of particular lineages (as the basis of their livelihood). McKinlay's "daughters of Zelophehad" point out that the concern about possible women's rights or inheritance is a distinctly modern one. In Num 27:1–11 their concern appears rather to be for the survival of their father's "name," that is, his lineage on its land. Might delving further into anthropological studies (such as Carol Delaney's) suggest that Yahweh's legislation in response to the daughters' appeal addressed the problem of how a patriarchal lineage could survive in the absence of a son, through the next-of-kin, starting with his daughter, then (failing that) his brother, and so on (Num 27:1–4, 5–7, 8–11)? To keep the land in that lineage's clan and tribe, however, further legislation would be necessary, again in the tradition occasioned by the daughters of Zelophehad: the daughter who inherited would have to marry a man from the clan of her father's tribe (Num 36:8).

So when and how did these books (as distinct from many other written and/or oral versions of some of their component legends, laws, and incidents) become identified as "Israel's narrative of origin"? Or, more precisely, when and how did they become (the key books of) the Bible and the dominant reading develop? Keeping ancient political-economic structure in mind, it may help to remind ourselves that, contrary to common presumption in scholarly discourse, it would be hard to identify a "nation" of Israel. Nationalism is a modern European invention (Anderson 1991), a major precondition of which was the invention of the printing press (Eisenstein 1979). A monarchic state had developed at some point in Jerusalem, which ruled over people living in villages who may have identified themselves as some of the clans of Israel. The temple-state, moreover, was sponsored by and subject to one imperial regime after another. As Boer points out, the books of Ezra–Nehemiah speak of the *yĕhûdîm*, among other identifiers, but who comprised *Yehud* is elusive.

Furthermore, the Bible, in which "Israel's narrative of origins" is supposedly found, did not yet exist in "biblical" times. The diversity of texts and manuscripts of texts found among the Dead Sea Scrolls indicate that the Hebrew text of the books "of Moses" later included in the Bible were still developing in multiple versions (Ulrich 1999). Their authority at the time was only relative to other texts of Torah such as the book of Jubilees and the Temple Scroll. Insofar as the great scrolls on which these texts were inscribed were expensive and cumbersome, they were confined mainly to the temple and scribal circles, such as the Qumran community. Literacy was limited mainly to scribal circles, moreover, and authoritative texts were in the archaic language of Hebrew, whereas the people spoke Aramaic. It thus seems doubtful that during the Second Temple period ordinary Judeans (and later Galileans) had direct contact with the scrolls on which the "constitutional" texts of Torah were inscribed and laid up in the temple. They cultivated their own popular Israelite tradition (of stories, songs, covenant commandments, and customs) orally in their village communities. It was important for ethnic elites in the Roman Empire to have a history reaching back as far as possible, which the historian Josephus, client of the Flavian emperors, attempted to supply for the Jews in his *Antiquities*. But the Hellenistic Jewish elite in Alexandria were more interested in spiritual allegorical interpretation of the Jewish Scriptures in Greek. It is thus difficult to identify a historical "Israel" with an identifiable "Bible" with a story of origin in which an imperial allocation of land was for them a key feature.[1]

Once "Christianity" was established in the late Roman Empire, the intellectual elite were more interested in allegorical interpretation than in narration of history. Studies of rabbinic and Christian clerical practice in the Middle Ages indicate that they continued to learn and recite texts orally, and usually in fragments such as laws and sayings. In medieval Europe the Bible was in Latin, not the vernacular. Ordinary people knew some of its contents primarily from their own storytelling and paintings, sculptures, and reliefs on the walls and doors of churches. The friezes on the last of these were the steps in the story of sin and salvation.

More promising for the origin of the dominant reading is the invention of the printing press, which prepared the way for nationalism and led to the translation of the Bible into European people's languages and widespread reading and knowledge of its contents. The King James Version, which became the Bible of the British Empire, was sponsored by the English monarchy and shaped in its interest. A crucial component in the translation was the rendering of "those who sit in (the fortified cities of) Canaan" as "inhabitants," so that key passages read as genocide and not people's battles against kings. European monarchs and their bishops found narratives, and the royal psalms, to authorize their empire building. And the English Puritans and others (Dutch settlers in South Africa) found in the narratives of exodus and "conquest" a charter for their flight from Pharaoh-like monarchs and their colonization of new lands.

The narratives in both the Pentateuch and Deuteronomic History, however, portray Israel and Judah and even their monarchies as relatively

---

1. If we want to speculate on who might have had interest in Judean/Israelite traditions of claims to land in Palestine, the likely suspects would have to be the early temple-state regime in Jerusalem and the rival regime in Samaria, the expansionist Hasmonean high priesthood that conquered Idumea and Samaria and took over Galilee, and Herod, to whom the Romans granted control of more and more territories. Did church intellectuals supply justification for the Crusades from passages in the Bible?

backward, insignificant, and under regular threat from the surrounding empires. How could those biblical narratives have become components of the Western imperial archive in which Wakefield worked from the common conviction that the British were "the superior race" and "the most civilized people in the world" bringing their language, customs, and religion to lands without civilization? In the development of American exceptionalism, the sense that America was the new Rome preceded and incorporated the sense of mission derived from the chosen people of the biblical narrative: contradictory as it was, the New Rome became fused with "God's New Israel." The biblical narrative was subsumed and transformed by America's Manifest Destiny as the mission to civilize, and perhaps evangelize, other peoples.

One wonders whether Wakefield was influenced by British Evangelicalism, as were other British colonial ventures. Wakefield's allocation makes one think of that later and far more official and, for later history, far more ominous mapping of Palestine carried out under Lloyd George and Lord Balfour (both good evangelicals with a sense of mission) and the British Mandate. In India the British had surveyed the length and breadth of the land to make their domesticating colonial maps. No need in Palestine, the "Holy Land," for which they already had their maps, or the information for them, in biblical books such as Numbers and Joshua, presumably including the allocation for the daughters of Zelophehad. (These maps of the British Mandate are still being used today by the State of Israel; see Whitelam 2007; Quiquivix 2012.)

McKinlay provides yet another lead to how the dominant reading developed. Wakefield, like the English settlers in North America, understood the land in New Zealand as there for the taking. In that "uncivilized" territory, the land was "wilderness" or "waste," inhabited but not owned, fenced, plowed, and planted. The developing dominant reading corresponded to the developing capitalist system and its transforming of land into private property. The intensive and revealing study of the Comaroffs cited by West in this volume shows this fusion of the Bible-based mission with emerging capitalist economic life. Joining the Christian commonwealth required induction into God's economic order. "Saving the savage meant teaching the savage to save" (Comaroff and Comaroff 1997, 166). Only by turning away from their inefficient mode of production to commerce could Africans join the sacred economy of civilized society. In Africa as well as earlier in Western Europe and North America, as Max Weber discussed, the Bible had become a source of "the Protestant ethic and the spirit of capitalism."

McKinlay's recognition that "it is more complicated" and her acquaintance with previous historical-literary criticism of the origins of texts that were later included in the Hebrew Bible, thus lead well beyond a literary analysis of narratives and laws in "the Bible" to a complex analysis of the origins of texts later included in the Bible (in an ancient tributary society) and the translation of the Bible into European national languages that were widely distributed and read in print (becoming the prime culture text that corresponded to nascent capitalism and European colonialism). In their origins the texts later included in the Bible, drawing on oral traditions of local clans or tribes' claims to land, were combined and developed to authorize the rule and claims of regimes in Jerusalem. After the modern translation and printing of the Bible, however, not just monarchs and prime ministers, but dissenting and evangelical religious groups and ambitious colonial politicians and missionaries of the salvation to be found in the capitalist social-economic order as well, could all participate in creating the European colonial Bible.

Christina Petterson's discussion of Solomon's throne focuses on one of the many ways in which the biblical portrayal of Solomon became the scriptural paradigm and justification for European monarchs' lavish courts and ostentatious displays of wealth and luxury. It thus also indirectly helped legitimate nascent imperial European mercantilism and pillage of oceans, forests, and peoples. Petterson notes also that in coronation ceremonies the Bishop of Copenhagen articulated the ideology of kingship focused on the Danish monarch as standing in the line of David's son Solomon, with his wisdom and peaceable reign. Recitation of (royal) psalms and Rom 13 also figured in the coronation. This look at the biblical representation of Solomon and the royal psalms in the coronation of the Danish kings helps us realize just how pervasive the use of the Bible was in the ideology and legitimation of European (divine right) monarchy in general. It had deep roots in medieval European political theology (she mentions the important study of Kantorowicz 1957). And this biblically based theology that revolves around imperial kingship survives in many areas of Western culture. One example that I cannot help thinking of is the annual performance of Handel's Messiah during Advent (or "Holy Days") and even "sing-alongs" in many mainline churches. Arias and choruses celebrate the imperial king (of the royal Pss 2 and 110) "dashing them in pieces" and the enthronement of the victorious imperial figure in the book of Revelation.

Petterson picks up on the concern that postcolonial criticism should include attention to the political economy that corresponds to cultural expressions and, in that connection, the difference between the political-economic system that corresponded to (presupposed by/attested in) biblical narratives, psalms, and prophecies and the later political-economic context in which they were/are used. While our standard training in biblical interpretation has not included competence in this area, prominent European intellectuals of recent generations, notably Marx and Weber, carried out what have become enduring studies of "pre-capitalist economic formations" that others have built upon since (Petterson mentions Polanyi 2001, who also saw that the economy of the ancient Near East was "pre-market," precapitalist). Well-known European intellectuals such as Eric Hobsbawm and Erich Fromm were involved in (accessible) discussions of precapitalist formations in the 1960s and 1970s. Even more accessible are the discussions of "the sociology of the monarchy" in a program unit of the Society of Biblical Literature two decades ago. Norman Gottwald and others outlined what appears to be the "tributary" political economy presupposed and attested in the Deuteronomic History and the Prophets.

In such a political economy, as Marx had discerned, God and/or the king was understood as the head of the whole, hence his "servants" owed tribute (tithes, offerings, taxes, labor, etc.). The king built the temple as the "house of God" and was the pivotal mediator between God and the people. Huge "surplus" accumulated from the tithes, offerings, and taxes—and was "transubstantiated" into palaces and precious metals such as gold, which was used in the lavish décor (gold leaf) and golden vessels, and otherwise "stored" in temple and palace. Appropriately, Roland Boer has explained this as a "sacred economy." All of this is recognizable in the narrative of Solomon in 1 Kgs 3–10 (and the parallel in Chronicles). But Solomon's was no mere petty monarchy with a merely local tributary political economy. Petterson calls attention to the gold, spices, and precious stones brought or sent to Solomon by the Queen of Sheba and the kings of Arabia as well as those brought by traders. Solomon headed an imperial political economy in which other monarchs, receiving tribute from their people, in turn sent tribute to him (as "gifts") and in which the regime had its own traders and fleet to handle the largely luxury trade.

It would make a fascinating study to examine how the ideology of imperial kingship that authorized the ancient Near Eastern tributary economy headed by the divine cosmic powers and their regents, the kings, was adapted into the divine-right monarchy that emerged from the more complex medieval feudal system. According to the research cited by Petterson, the "demand" for and import of ivory escalated in

Western Europe imperial countries as the importance of monarchies and their ivory or narwhal thrones faded in importance. With the rise of capitalist economy, ivory, no longer just a form in which wealth was displayed in royal palaces, became a commodity as well, in the products of industrial workshops "consumed" by bourgeois households in drawing rooms (pianos and decor) and dressing rooms (combs and mirrors). Whether biblical images or narratives were useful in the marketing of ivory remains unclear.

Postcolonial criticism, availing itself of other lines of biblical criticism, might also inquire if the Deuteronomic History offers anything other than the ideology of imperial kingship, with Solomon's throne and other excessive accumulation of wealth? Petterson provides an important opening: 1 Sam 8:9–17, which Bishop Wandall read as royal law of the king's rights and the people's duties, was rather Samuel's warnings to the people (who were demanding a human king when they already had God as their king) of how a king would expropriate their resources, labor, and family members to enhance his own wealth and power. Solomon was the fulfillment of all that Samuel had warned about and more, as in his extensive use of forced labor. The Deuteronomic History is ambivalent about monarchy, to say the least. Kings who were less oppressive than Solomon are condemned. It is not clear what the "ideal internal economics" might be in the Solomon narrative, but it includes virtually no suggestion that Israel as a whole prospered from his excessive wealth (cf. only 1 Kgs 4:20; otherwise Israel is *dependent* on his mediation with God, e.g. 8:65–66). He is censured only because his many "foreign wives" turned his head. But it is clear that he came to power via a palace coup and that his forced labor was what led to his dynasty's loss of the northern ten tribes.

Uriah Kim's essay leads quickly to the sense that there is something more in the Bible than what became the colonial Bible that legitimates conquest. After summarizing his chosen section of text, Jephthah's speech to the king of the Ammonites in Judges 11:12–28, he applies Musa Dube's postcolonial reading of Exodus and Joshua as "anticonquest ideology" parallel to European colonial "travel narratives." Dube sees in these key biblical narratives "the literary strategies of representation by which the colonizers secure their innocence while asserting their right to travel to, enter, and possess resources and lands that belong to foreign nations" (2000, 58). (As Kim explains in n. 3, this is not an ideology that opposes conquest but rather one that masks colonial conquest.) Among the four key literary-rhetorical strategies of the ideology is a positive representation of the targeted land but a negative representation of its people in order to claim that the latter do not deserve to occupy the land, therefore the Israelites are vindicated in displacing them.

In Jephthah's speech and the rest of the book of Judges, however, Kim finds something more than or different from the key rhetorical strategies. Even though Judges represents the people of the land as incompetent and sinful, for example, it depicts them as formidable oppressors and the Israelites as tricksters—virtually reversing the colonizers' view of themselves as strong and the others as weak. Kim had anticipated his closer examination of Jephthah's speech and Judges in noting the different voices or layers in the Exodus–Joshua narrative. It does exhibit colonial/imperial discourse that the West used in its conquest of the Rest, as Dube lays out in her focus on Africa—and as many of us are acutely aware of in the colonization and conquest (and extermination of indigenous peoples) of North America. Yet the Exodus–Joshua (and the Deuteronomic History) narrative emerged from imperial/colonial contexts in which the Israelites were subjected by ancient empires. Thus Israelites (again that collective authorship) had an ambivalence about using imperial ideology to justify their domination of others. Kim points briefly to the (successive) contexts in which the Deuteronomic History was probably composed and further developed as under the Neo-Assyrian, Neo-Babylonian, and Persian Empires in which Israel was dominated by an empire, on the one hand, and concerned to secure territory (perhaps already occupied under the Persians), on the other.

Kim thus recognizes that the narratives of the Hebrew Bible are more complex than the colonial Bible of Europe or the Scriptures from which colonial powers and missions derived much of their self-justifying ideology. He could further avail himself of other aspects of the biblical criticism that was developed (mostly ironically and not self-critically) by critics in the imperial metropolis and he could draw upon what some of those critics and certainly subject peoples have found in the Hebrew Bible over the generations. Two kinds of illustration must suffice.

Many biblical scholars (as noted above) write as if (an essentialist) "Israel" collectively composed the Pentateuch or the Deuteronomic History or collectively was ambivalent. But literacy in the ancient Near East was limited to the tiny circles of professional scribes who served monarchies and temple-states. Thus what we have in the texts that were much later included in the Hebrew Bible was composed by scribes in service of the Davidic monarchy in Judah or, closer to the forms in which we have them, by scribes in the service of the temple-state in Jerusalem. As has been discussed for some time in biblical scholarship, those scribes included (composed with) traditional (orally cultivated) songs, legends, laws, stories and, in some cases, "royal archives" in plotting a history with a purpose or agenda (support/authorization of the monarchy or temple-state). Thus Kim could get more specific, for example, about the composition of the Deuteronomic History. It would have been ambivalent if it began under Josiah, whose monarchy was eager to take over land previously under the monarchy in Samaria but operating under the shadow of the Neo-Assyrian empire. The Neo-Babylonians did not just threaten conquest, but conquered and deported the elite of the monarchy. Under the Persian regime, however, descendants of the Jerusalem elite previously exiled to Babylon were sent as a colony to form a temple-state in Jerusalem and its environs. As some Hebrew biblical scholars have been saying in the last few decades, in its origins the temple-state involved "colonization."

Among the different "voices" that many Bible readers or listeners have discerned and the traditional materials that scholars have discerned included in the Deuteronomic History are songs, stories, and leaders that stand in tension, even conflict and contradiction, with the dominant overall narrative. The people who were ruled by the Davidic monarchy in Jerusalem and the monarchic state of Israel cultivated such customs, songs, and stories of leaders and struggles. Especially interesting in the book of Judges, as poetry in very early northern Israelite Hebrew, is the "Song of Deborah," which celebrates the northern tribes' victory in guerrilla warfare against "the kings" and their general Sisera, with their war-chariots. This was the people's song celebrating their struggle to stay independent of those kings. But this is just the most striking example of many tensions and conflicts in the books of Joshua and Judges. Joshua 1 and 10:40–43, and 11:16–20 portray the Israelites taking possession of the whole land in a Blitzkrieg. But Judg 1 indicates that the Israelites lived only in the hills and were for some time unable to take control of the (fortified) cities, especially in the plains. Many biblical scholars still write as if the Israelites were fighting against other peoples (e.g., Canaanites). But most of the narratives say explicitly that they were fighting against kings of those peoples and their warriors, not against the other peoples.[2] Two of the stories in

---

2. It must be noted in this connection that the Western colonial Bible lives on in

Joshua, the attacks on the fortified cities of Ai and Hazor (Josh 8:10–23; 11:1–9), are accounts of guerrilla warfare similar to any number of fights in the anticolonial struggles of the twentieth century.

Thus as he moves to complicate previous postcolonial criticism, Kim could more fully explain the ambivalence of the Deuteronomic History and offer examples of antimonarchic and, in the case of the Philistines, anticolonial stories and songs embedded in the overall narrative.

Althea Spencer-Miller joins, and offers to broaden and deepen, the small circles of interpreters who have attempted to appreciate the vitality of psalms sung, prophecies pronounced, and stories told and heard in committed communities of predominantly oral cultures. She brings her ethnographic experience as an oral-literate Jamaican to exploration of the oral communication and oral performance involved in the origins of the Gospels and other texts. She thus joins, and brings important new experience-based insight to, fledgling explorations that, especially if they conspire with separate but related lines of recent research, are undermining not just the colonial Bible but the basic assumptions of the established biblical studies that has been "establishing" the text.

Just as postmodernism is embedded in modernism and postcolonialism presupposes colonialism and both are limited by the very discourse and practices they are criticizing, so scholars in academic fields embedded in modern print culture (i.e. all of them) are limited by their typographic assumptions and discourse. Bourgeois scholars such as the brothers Grimm "recovered" some of their ("national") folklore from villagers and cleaned it up, not to re-*tell* but to put in print. It was more the "discovery" of the "savage" peoples of Europeans' colonies who appeared to have no writing that led to their rediscovery of orality. And of course Westerners of the nineteenth and twentieth centuries thought in terms of progress and evolution. Early explorers of "orality" in contrast to "literacy" such as Jack Goody (Goody and Watt 1963) claimed, on the basis

---

recent translations, with its disastrous consequences, for example, in the European settlers killing the indigenous peoples in North America. Even though scholars have recognized that the Hebrew construct (participle-like) *yōšĕbê-X* (city), that is, "those who sit in X (fortified city)," means "rulers" (with their "warriors") in poetic parallelism with "kings" in the prophets, both RSV and NRSV still perpetuate the old KJV (colonial/imperial) translation of "those who sit in (the cities of) Canaan" etc. as "inhabitants." The accounts in Joshua are indeed violent. But they portray the people killing the kings, and not genocide.

of the fragmentary evidence from ancient Greece, that orality led to but was displaced by literacy, with (superior) attendant effects such as "democracy." Although Walter Ong (2002) knew better than that, he constructed a dichotomy between orality and literacy as two distinctive mentalities, the limitations and implications of which Spencer-Miller criticizes sharply. Ong and Werner Kelber (1983), the pioneer of the exploration of orality in New Testament studies, were attempting to lead other scholars still imprisoned in print culture to discern the vibrant life of oral communication, in contrast to the fixity of words and the death of sound in written texts. Kelber paved the way in showing that form criticism had seriously misconstrued oral tradition in terms of written texts.[3] Oral tradition's life depended rather on its resonance with hearers, which meant of course that oral tradition adapted to its reception in life-situations.

Those exploring oral communication and recitation quickly learned that there was no dichotomy between orality and literacy in historical societies and that as writing developed it was embedded in oral communication as its matrix, points that Spencer-Miller strongly affirms. They also learned that there were different kinds and functions of writing, and that what at first appeared as a dichotomy of orality and literacy was more the difference between the features/habits of oral communication and the assumptions and habits of print culture in which scholarly thinking was embedded (some might say "imprisoned").

They also realized that investigators in other fields, including those in direct contact with oral communication and performance, might offer considerable help dealing with written texts that were "oral-derived" (originally orally performed but now accessible only in ancient manuscripts or modern print; see esp. Hymes, Tedlock). From sociolinguistics, folklore studies, ethnography of performance, and ethnopoetics, and by way of theorists of oral performance such as John Miles Foley (1991, 1995, 2002), they learned that appreciation of oral performance of texts (whether or not they also existed in writing)[4] involves consideration of the many fac-

---

3. The "Lego-like" "clastic topography" image is more applicable to what Kelber is criticizing in the form critics' and redaction critics' imagining words and phrases being mechanically reconfigured, like broken pieces of rock.

4. The concept of "text" has been reduced in print-cultural literary criticism and biblical studies to "literature," i.e. something printed (or handwritten) in letters. Etymologically, however, "text" comes from a root meaning "to weave," which is the way certain forms of oral discourse were understood in an oral culture, as in "weaving

tors involved in communication. Oral communication involves interaction, tone of voice, body language, gestures that might be distinctive to particular cultures, and the mood and life circumstances of those communicating. Oral performance, say of a cycle of stories already known and revered by a people, happens in a community gathering, involves interaction of performer and hearers, and the life-situation of the people (Horsley and Draper; Draper 2006; Horsley 2006; Rhoads 2006). Of particular importance in appreciating oral performance is the whole wider common cultural heritage in which both speaker and audience are embedded, what Kelber termed the "biosphere" in which the performed text resonates with the audience by "metonymically referencing" that heritage (Kelber 1983; Foley 1991; Horsley 2006). Spencer-Miller is reaffirming all of these recognitions and more from her auto/ethnographical experience, making them all the more poignant. And, as she argues, she and others who are oral-literate, experienced in orality as a cultural mode, can deepen and broaden the exploration of oral performance of texts in the oral cultural mode of the ancient audiences.

As Spencer-Miller states repeatedly, it is especially important for biblical studies to recognize that writing was embedded in oral communication, which was its matrix. This embeddedness of writing was particularly determinative prior to the printing press. Two separate (but related) lines of recent research have explained this for communication in Second Temple Judea, where most of the books later included in the Hebrew Bible reached roughly the form in which we have them. First, research on literacy(ies) has documented that reading and writing were limited basically to the professional scribes who served the temple-state (Hezser 2001). Writing was used mainly as an instrument of power by the wealthy and powerful. Writing was of different kinds, some mundane such as records of debts, but some more monumental, such as inscriptions on Roman arches. Since writing was so rare in predominantly oral societies, some writing had a

---

a tale" or "spinning a yarn" (as might still be suggested by the term "texture"). The Greek root of "rhapsodize" meant to weave songs together. Since there is really no more apt term, therefore, I am using "text" for any configured message such as a song, epic, story, prophetic oracle, drama, etc., whether it is oral or written or both. In many, perhaps most, contexts in scholarly discourse, therefore, it would be important to specify. Psalms are oral texts, but in the book of Psalms they are written (printed). Beowulf was an oral text, but the text was also (in different versions) written on manuscripts (chirographs).

numinous aura to it: what stood written on a monument or a scroll laid up in a temple had elevated authority (Niditch 1996; Horsley 2007).

Second, research on scribal practice has shown that, while scribes inscribed texts on new scrolls, they learned the texts by repeated recitation so that they became "written on the tablet of their heart" (Carr 2005; Horsley 2007).[5] Like the later rabbis and their students, they did not so much "study" and "interpret" texts (like modern scholars, as it were) as recite them ("by heart," only not verbatim, as in the print culture). In the scribal community at Qumran, for example, at the evening gatherings they would not read but orally *recite the writing* (*lqrw' bspr*) and offer communal blessings (1QS 6:6–8; Jaffee 2001). This intimate interaction between orally recited text and written text suggests that what we know as the texts of the Hebrew Bible derived in many ways from oral communication and performance.

Caribbean scholars such as Spencer-Miller will bring the personal and ethnobiograpical experience that has previously been missing to further explorations of oral communication and oral performance. It is also quite conceivable, moreover, that the experience in the oral cultural mode of Caribbean scholars in particular can deepen and broaden appreciation of the oral-performative register of Hebrew Bible texts through just such linguistic links as she traces toward the end of her article. She refers to the "linguistic land bridge" that Edwina Wright finds in the Afro-Asiatic phylum that connects the African continent to ancient Middle Eastern languages. In particular there are significant similarities between ancient Hebrew and African languages in vocabulary, sound patterns, and some grammatical forms. And of course a high percentage of the slaves in the Caribbean were taken from Africa at the western end of that phylum.

While they have hardly gained a toehold in the field, explorations of oral communication and oral performance, especially if they were to be coordinated with separate but related researches, threaten to undermine basic assumptions and procedures of established biblical studies. Working on the assumptions of the print culture in which it developed, biblical studies sought to "establish" a stable "original," "early," or "best" text of each verse and chapter and book of the Bible, the words of the Word of

---

5. In ancient Judean scribal practice, and other societies where the literate elite produced chirographs, the learning and reciting of texts did not involve verbatim memorization and recall. The latter evolved in modern print culture as the oral counterpart of a fixed printed text.

God visible in print—with an apparatus just in case of scribal errors or deviations in copying. Oral tradition was deemed unreliable, but once the wording was stabilized in writing, the manuscripts supposedly provided a secure basis for establishing a reliable early text. This quest for security in the words was a symptom of print culture, however, just as the established text was the product of modern scholarship. As text critics are now finding, in the earliest manuscripts and fragments of the texts included in both the Hebrew Bible and the New Testament, the manuscripts have great variation; they are still-developing different versions of the texts. The chirographs closest to (contemporary with) continuing oral performance of the texts are themselves multiform. The relation of this variation to the variation in oral performances has yet to be investigated. But the destabilization of the established printed text does seem to offer an opening to further exploration of how oral-derived texts may have resonated with their hearers in more holistic contexts of communication.

These suggestive essays in postcolonial criticism of texts in/from the Hebrew Bible lead well beyond a focus mainly on biblical texts that became components of the Western colonial Bible, but further to their political-economic roots and enduring effects in postcolonial life. And they lead to more comprehensive exposure and subversion of the dominant reading as well as to opening access to people's histories submerged either in the development of texts later included in the Bible or in the development of the dominant reading of the Bible.

References

Ahmad, Aijaz, 1992. *In Theory: Classes, Nations, Literatures*. London: Verso.
Anderson, Benedict. 1991. *Imagined Communities: Reflections on the Origins and Spread of Nationalism*. London: Verso.
Asad, Talal. 1993. *Genealogies of Religion*. Baltimore: Johns Hopkins University Press.
Carr, David. 2005. *Writing on the Tablet of the Heart*. Oxford: Oxford University Press.
Cesaire, Aime. 2000. *Discourse on Colonialism*. New York: Monthly Review Press.
Comaroff, John L., and Jean Comaroff. 1997. *Of Revelation and Revolution: The Dialectics of Modernity on a South African Frontier*. Vol. 2. Chicago: University of Chicago Press.

Dirlik, Arif. 1995. *The Postcolonial Aura*. Durham, N.C.: Duke University Press.
Draper, Jonathan, 2006. Jesus' "Covenantal Discourse" on the Plain (Luke 6:12–7:17) as Oral Performance: Pointers to "Q" as Multiple Oral Performance. Pages 71–98 in *Oral Performance, Popular Tradition, and Hidden Transcript in Q*. Edited by Richard A. Horsley. SemeiaSt 60. Atlanta: Society of Biblical Literature.
Dube, Musa W. 2000. *Postcolonial Feminist Interpretation of the Bible*. St. Louis: Chalice.
Eisenstein, Elizabeth L. 1979. *The Printing Press as an Agent of Change: Communications and Cultural Transformations in Early Modern Europe*. Cambridge: Cambridge University Press.
Fanon, Frantz. 1963. *The Wretched of the Earth*. Translated by Constance Farrington. New York: Grove.
———. 1965. *A Dying Colonialism*. Translated by Haakon Chevalier. New York: Grove.
———. 2008. *Black Skin, White Masks*. Translated by Richard Philcox. New York: Grove.
Foley, John Miles. 1991. *Immanent Art*. Bloomington: Indiana University Press.
———. 1995. *Singer of Tales in Performance*. Bloomington: Indiana University Press.
———. 2002. *How to Read an Oral Poem*. Urbana: University of Illinois Press.
Goody, Jack, and Ian Watt. 1963. The Consequences of Literacy. *CSSH* 5:304–45.
Hezser, Catherine. 2001. *Jewish Literacy in Roman Palestine*. Tübingen: Mohr Siebeck.
Horsley, Richard A. 2006. Performance and Tradition. Pp. 43–70 in *Oral Performance, Popular Tradition, and Hidden Transcript in Q*. Edited by Richard A. Horsley. SemeiaSt 60. Atlanta: Society of Biblical Literature.
———. 2007. *Scribes, Visionaries, and the Politics of Second Temple Judea*. Louisville: Westminster John Knox.
Horsley, Richard A., with Jonathan A. Draper. 1999. *Whoever Hears You Hears Me: Prophets, Performance and Tradition in Q*. Harrisburg, Pa.: Trinity Press International.
Hymes, Dell. 1981. *"In Vain I Tried to Tell You": Essays in Native American Ethnopoetics*. Philadelphia: University of Pennsylvania Press.

Jaffee, Martin. 2001. *Torah in the Mouth*. Oxford: Oxford University Press.
James, C. L. R. 1977. *The Future in the Present: Selected Writings, Vol. 1*. London: Allison & Busby.
———. 1980. *Spheres of Existence: Selected Writings, Vol. 2*. London: Allison & Busby.
———. 1984. *At the Rendezvous of Victory: Selected Writings, Vol. 3*. London: Allison & Busby.
Kantorowicz, Ernst H. 1957. *The King's Two Bodies: A Study in Medieval Political Theology*. Princeton: Princeton University Press.
Kelber, Werner. 1983. *The Oral and the Written Gospel: The Hermeneutics of Speaking and Writing in the Synoptic Tradition, Mark, Paul, and Q*. Philadelphia: Fortress.
Niditch, Susan. 1996. *Oral World and Written Word: Ancient Israelite Literature*. Louisville: Westminster John Knox.
Ong, Walter. 2002 (1982). *Orality and Literacy: The Technologizing of the Word*. 2nd ed. New York: Routledge.
Polanyi, Karl. 2001 (1944). *The Great Transformation: The Political and Economic Origins of our Time*. Boston: Beacon.
Quiquivix, Linda. 2012. The Political Mapping of Palestine. Doctoral thesis, University of North Carolina at Chapel Hill.
Rhoads, David. 2006. "Performance Criticism: An Emerging Methodology in Second Testament Studies, Parts I and II." *BTB* 36:1–16, 164–84.
Said, Edward W. 1978. *Orientalism*. New York: Pantheon Books.
———. 1993. *Culture and Imperialism*. London: Chatto & Windsor.
Shohat, Ella. 1992. Notes on the Postcolonial. *SocT* 31:99–113.
Tedlock, Dennis. The Spoken Word and the Work of Interpretation. Philadelphia: University of Pennsylvania Press, 1983
Ulrich, Eugene. 1999. *The Dead Sea Scrolls and the Origins of the Bible*. Grand Rapids: Eerdmans.
Whitelam, Keith W. 2007. Lines of Power: Mapping Ancient Israel. Pp. 40–79 in *To Break Every Yoke: Essays in Honor of Marvin Chaney*. Edited by Robert Coote and Norman Gottwald. Sheffield: Sheffield Phoenix Press.

Responses to Miles, Perdue, West, and Boer

Joerg Rieger

This set of postcolonial readings of the Hebrew Bible is a welcome addition not only to more established efforts at postcolonial readings of the New Testament but also to emerging efforts at reading theological texts in postcolonial perspective.[1]

More postcolonial readings are welcome, first of all, because they help us interpret a set of ancient texts at new levels and with new intensity. The tensions between empire, colonialism, and various forms of resistance are so deeply engrained in many of these texts that one wonders how we were able to interpret them for so long without noticing those tensions. In other words, because they resonate with dynamics that are clearly visible in the texts themselves, postcolonial readings can no longer be considered as merely optional.

Second, postcolonial interpretations of ancient biblical texts are welcome and necessary because they also invite an account from the interpreters about the tensions of empire, colonialism, and various forms of resistance in their own contexts. Postcolonial interpretations do not allow for the safe distance of the interpreter that was practiced in modern exegetical methods, particularly in the methods of historical criticism. The challenge in this regard is, of course, to develop postcolonial interpretations in a comparative frame, distinguishing the various historical forms of empire and colonialism in different times. Merely identifying empires and colonialisms today with empires and colonialisms in the past without a comparative framework is not only inadequate but also misleading.

Third, postcolonial interpretations have the potential to bring together both scholars from different fields in the academy in general and scholars

---

1. Examples of emerging postcolonial theological efforts include Keller, Nausner, and Rivera 2004; Kwok Pui-lan 2005; and Rieger 2007.

from different fields in the realms of religious studies and theology in particular. It is for this reason, I assume, that I was invited to write a response to some of the texts in this volume, although I am not a biblical scholar by trade but a theologian and scholar of religion, and it is for this reason that I was very happy to accept the challenge.

The great merit of this interdisciplinary work is that it helps us to redraw some of the established lines between the disciplines and to create a critical mass of scholarly work that produces new bodies of knowledge that are bound to make a difference not only in our fields but also in the practice of religion and in the world. In other words, a biblical scholar working in a postcolonial paradigm may have more in common with a historian of religion or a theologian working in a postcolonial paradigm than with other biblical scholars who have not yet developed the deepened and broadened critical awareness that postcolonial thought demands of us.

Several important insights can be gained from a constellation that allows for such cross-fertilization. First, and most important, is the realization that our interpretive work is never done in a vacuum. We are always working in contexts of power and power differentials, which need to be accounted for. The topics of colonialism and empire are, therefore, not optional but mandatory, since this is where we find ourselves, whether we like it or not, and this is the context in which our texts, whether ancient or modern, have developed as well. Second, the now widely accepted insight that we need to account for the contexts of both the interpreter and the texts is no longer sufficient. Much talk of context or social location does not yet sufficiently account for the flows of power. As the emerging field of cultural studies reminds us, we need to study not just context but context plus power.[2] Postcolonial studies take up this insight and develop it in greater historical detail. Finally, postcolonial interpretations require deep historical readings. Colonialism and empire take on very different forms and shapes in different times and places. Orientalism, as Edward Said has explained (1978), is a particular Western way of interpreting the East in such a way that it shapes the West in turn. Yet this is only one part of the history of colonialism as it forms the West, and even here there are significant differences between different nations and contexts. In order to come to a fuller understanding of colonialism, we also need to take into account

---

2. This is the key difference between H. Richard Niebuhr's famous book *Christ and Culture* (1951) and my *Christ and Empire*. See my account in the latter, 2007, vii.

what Walter Mignolo (2000) has called Occidentalism, which refers to the way the West has been shaped in regard to the conquest and the subsequent colonization of Latin America. In addition, Africa and Oceania also need to be studied in this light.

In conclusion, the cross-fertilization that postcolonial perspectives call for leads to major methodological shifts and developments. We are only at the very beginning of this work, and so we are yet to find out where it all leads. In addition to the analytical work, postcolonial perspectives point beyond the study of empire and colonialism to the alternatives that empire and colonialism seek to rule out. Postcolonial interpretations, when done successfully, point us towards new worlds that are emerging in the midst of the old.

1. Refracting Colonizing Rhetoric in Narratives of Gibeonite and Japanese Identity

The first chapter to which I would like to respond along these lines is the one by Johnny Miles. Miles's interpretation of the situation of Japanese Americans in the United States helpfully demonstrates the substantial insights that can be gained from what I would call a self-critical investigation of the context of the interpreter. At this juncture, historical critical work turns into historical self-critical work (Rieger 2007, 8–9). Miles demonstrates that developing a sense of colonial tensions as they take shape at home is a helpful hermeneutical tool, which is essential for a successful postcolonial critique. As this hermeneutical tool is used in the interpretation of both recent and distant historical events, the question emerges: Can this sort of thing happen again today?

Of course, one could imagine other investigations of recent manifestations of colonialism and empire that do the same kind of work as Miles's investigation of the situation of Japanese Americans during World War II, but one should not overlook the value of the self-critical element. For a German American like myself, for instance, an analysis of German fascism and the Holocaust is a required self-critical exercise. This is all the more true as such an analysis has a deeply personal component, due to the fact that one of my grandfathers fought in Hitler's armies and that my religious community, the German United Methodist Church, also had a role to play in the German Third Reich, however small. By the same token, for Caucasian residents of the United States, an analysis of racism as it affects our families and communities is not optional, especially if it is cloaked in the sort of all-American respectability that Miles portrays as a factor in the way Japanese Americans were treated. In the United States, it is simply too easy to point fingers at German fascism without analyzing the manifestations of colonialism in a liberal democratic society, which Miles describes.

The results prove Miles's approach right. As we begin to understand ourselves better in relation to the history of Japanese Americans in our midst, our understanding of the relation of the Israelites and the Gibeonites in Josh 9 gains depth. Furthermore, developing a sense for the situation of the Gibeonites helps us develop an understanding for the genesis of Israel at a certain moment in its history. In addition, we also learn that power, oppression, and resistance can take various forms that are not always easily discerned. In this connection, understanding the relation of the Israelites and the Gibeonites teaches us something about our own situation, as some of these dynamics can also be observed in the present.

Miles reminds us that each of these cases of colonization, no matter how harmless they may seem on the surface, are ultimately matters of life and death. Lives are taken not only in gas chambers and ovens, as he notes, but also by forms of internal colonization that are much more subtle. This is an insight that often escapes us, as we evaluate both ancient empires and present ones. One of the factors in this internal colonization concerns ethnic prejudices, both in the case of the Gibeonites and the Hivites. Of course, things get more complex when it becomes clear that the other of the empire is not just "out there" but within, so that the identity of the colonizers is inextricably connected with the colonized. This is another key insight in postcolonial studies that has been pointed out early on by Frantz Fanon (1963), Albert Memmi (1991), and others.

One of the most interesting questions in Miles's interpretation is who is responsible for colonization. In response to this question, he focuses on the intelligentsia in the various different contexts. This brings the matter close to home, as this is the place where biblical and other postcolonial scholars are located as well. Here language plays a crucial role, and the language of the intelligentsia, as Miles reminds us, conceals while it simultaneously reveals. Furthermore, language shapes reality more deeply than we commonly realize. These dynamics remind us of the importance of self-critical reflection and the fact that scholars are in particular need to undergo this kind of critique.

Important in postcolonial reading is, of course, not just an analysis of how colonialism works but also an understanding of how resistance takes shape. In this regard, Miles explains the Gibeonites' deceit of the Israelites as a strategy for survival that can be compared to other forms of resistance by passive noncompliance. The reference to James Scott's study of everyday forms of resistance is very important here and ties together the chapters of Miles and Gerald West, whose work has also been influenced by Scott, although he does not mention Scott in his chapter.

Of interest to scholars of religion is that religion plays an important role in resistance. For the Japanese, this meant that Buddhism gained new significance; in the case of Israel, traditional Canaanite practices were reinforced as a response to oppression and in order to keep resistance alive by strengthening group solidarity and ethnic identity. While Miles examines the parallels between the resistance of Japanese Americans and of Canaanites, the question that is unfortunately left open in this regard is where such resistance can be found in our own time. Miles's wish that these things will never happen again depends on identifying such resistance here and now.

2. Hosea and Empire

Leo Perdue presents another perspective on Israel's and Judah's identity that emerges not from a position of dominance but from a position of being the underdog in the world of the Assyrian Empire of the eighth century B.C.E., which is the historical setting of the book of Hosea. The prophet Hosea, who prophesied during a time of internal instability which culminated in the Assyrian invasions under Shalmaneser V and Sargon II, plays an important role as the colonial/postcolonial drama unfolds. In order to develop a sense for what is going on, it is important to keep in mind that Hosea is not part of the ruling class. Unlike the cult prophets, he has no privileged access to the powers that be.

There is an advantage to this underdog perspective, as from this vantage point reality can be seen in a new light. Unlike the message of the cult prophets who prophesy salvation, Hosea's message is not encouraging, as he announces that doom and destruction are looming. Nevertheless, this announcement is also the location of hope, which is found not by closing one's eyes to reality and wishing for the best, but in the theological expectation that even in the midst of destruction Yahweh's grace is at work. Rather than the imperial divinity Ashur, Hosea notes that Yahweh is in control of history.

But what are we to make of the fact that this is an odd sort of control if the Assyrians indeed invade and destroy Israel? During Hosea's life, there are several successful military expeditions by the Assyrians against Israel. Eventually, Israel is conquered by Sargon II in 722 B.C.E., shortly after Hosea's activity had ended, resulting in the nation's disappearance from history. A postcolonial interpretation needs to wrestle deeply with this tension.

Another question is what we make of the strong attacks on kingship in the book of Hosea—a recurring theme in the Hebrew Bible. Kingship presents us with a social problem, as it exacerbates class divisions and the growing gap between the rich and the poor. But there is also a theological problem, as Yahweh apparently wants nothing to do with kings. What is the reason for this problem? Is it that Yahweh wants to be king, or is it possible that Yahweh rejects certain forms of monarchical rule altogether? Postcolonial theologians, myself included, might argue that there is a deeper rejection of the institution of the monarchy and of empire that ultimately leads to a rethinking of the place of Yahweh himself. When Hosea points out that Yahweh prefers compassion and knowledge of Yahweh to sacrifice, does this not point to a different conception of the divine?

Key postcolonial terms emerge as Perdue develops Hosea's story. For instance, hybridity, including religious hybridity, was a common way of life in Israel, especially after the arrival in Canaan. Perdue discerns a certain romanticism in prophets like Hosea for a time when this sort of hybridity did not yet exist. While in postcolonial discourse ambivalence is usually a term which describes resistance to the empire that seeks a totality,[3] Perdue describes Hosea's resistance to ambivalence in terms of purity. This raises the interesting question, not often discussed in postcolonial theory, in which sense a resistance to ambivalence might be seen as a resistance to empire. Perhaps a struggle for purity has a role to play not only in oppression—ethnic cleansing comes to mind—but also in resistance, through the formation of communities of resistance.

Let us take a closer look at how resistance takes shape in the book of Hosea. "Hosea's goal was to resist and subvert systems of oppression," says Perdue. He does so by challenging elements of assimilation to the imperial metanarrative. This challenge includes resistance to the idea that the

---

3. This is the way in which Homi Bhabha uses the term in *The Location of Culture* (1994). See the same text for his treatment of hybridity.

Assyrians are superior in the realm of culture and religion, as well as resistance to the institution of kingship within Judah and Israel, which seeks to make common cause with the enemy. Hosea's prophecy incudes symbolic acts, like his marriage to an unfaithful wife and the naming of his children (naming his first son Jezreel, for instance, is a reference to the judgment of Israel). God's judgment can be reversed, according to Hosea, by abandoning efforts to assimilate to the Assyrian Empire.

Resistance can also be described in terms of a process of decolonization of the mind. This form of decolonization includes a refusal to recognize the power of Assyrian gods and a refusal to believe in the invincibility of the Assyrian Empire and the power of its rulers. Hosea resists these colonial beliefs by talking about a return to the wilderness experience of Israel after the exodus. Perhaps the most powerful tool of resistance here is the expectation that even the Assyrian Empire will eventually fall.

Perdue as interpreter never steps outside the text, and so we are left to wonder how these reflections might work in terms of a self-critical reflection and what might be learned here for the present. This question needs to be raised not for the sake of being "relevant" but rather to complete the hermeneutical task. Perdue's location in Texas might give us some interesting clues, as Christianity in Texas faces challenges similar to the people of Israel and Judah, like assimilation to the status quo and to the powers that be. What about images of the divine that portray God more as an emperor, who demands sacrifice[4] (like the sacrifice of soldiers in war or the workers in low-wage jobs), than as one who seeks mercy? Presumably questions like those are not foreign to Perdue, but if he were to put them on the table, this might benefit the overall trajectory of his work.

3. The Old Testament as Preparation of the African Postcolonial

Gerald West addresses the crucial role of the Old Testament in his native South Africa. As a white South African, West is particularly sensitive to the colonial and postcolonial situations in Africa. Readers might be surprised to learn that the Old Testament has played a substantial role in both colo-

---

4. The topic of sacrifice and oppression is worked out in a conversation of René Girard with Latin American liberation theologians. See Assmann 1996.

nial and postcolonial settings, but these settings in turn throw new light on how we interpret these texts not just in Africa but in other contexts as well.

The focal point of West's study is a particular religious group, Ibandla lamaNazaretha (the Congregation/Community of the Nazarites), an African Independent/Initiated Church founded in the early 1900s by Isaiah Shembe. This is a church that is thriving today in a post-Apartheid context, but West understands it as a postcolonial community from its very beginnings, resisting colonialism long before the end of Apartheid in South Africa.

West helps us understand why the Bible as a whole needs to be seen as part of the conflict between colonialism and the postcolonial. Although it is part of colonial history, as soon as the Bible became available in local languages in the mid-1800s in southern Africa, it also provides a site of postcolonial contestation. In this context, Shembe plays an important role, as he maintains a distance from the missionaries and the African elites trained by them. He recognizes the power of the text to generate communities of resistance, West notes. These communities work with the biblical texts but maintain their own cultural ways, many of which appeared to be reflected in the Old Testament. Moreover, these communities support women, who suffer especially from a collapse of the traditional African economies, being forced into the cities. The symbolic capital of these communities develops in relation to the struggles of women, with a grammar related to notions of health, healing, and ritual performance.

One of the theological questions that emerges at this juncture is how the God of the Bible is related to African culture. Some African theologians, like John Mbiti, have argued that African culture was preparatory for the God of the Bible, while others like Kwame Bediako and Lamin Sanneh argue that the God of the Bible was already at work in African culture before the Bible arrived. This means that God cannot be fully understood without African voices. For biblical studies, this means that what the Bible says is not yet understood fully, because we need to continue to listen to what African and other voices have to contribute. Ultimately, it seems to me that what follows from this theological argument is a broader hermeneutical question, as dominant biblical scholarship is reminded of the open-endedness of all scholarship.

West notes, in conclusion, the differences between Shembe's approach and that of Mbiti, Sanneh, and Bediako. Nevertheless, he finds in Shembe another particular African form of resistance to the colonial spirit. This is what West considers the postcolonial, and it moves through various struggles and hybridizations of various discourses and practices. Nevertheless, the question that is left open by West is what we make of the complexity of it all. Shembe's concern for women creates a safe space for women who otherwise have no choice but to sell out to colonialism by moving into the cities and perhaps ending up in prostitution. Yet, as West himself notes, there are limits when it comes to the role of women. Shembe maintains a strict hierarchy of male and female, and colonial stereotypes of women as passive and men as active remain. Thus, Shembe's postcolonial effort compromises traditional African settings where women are more active in everyday work. This serves as a reminder that postcolonial agency must never be idealized and needs to come to terms with its own limitations.

The struggle for the formation of postcolonial identities is an ongoing one, as the colonial system seems to have influenced Shembe more strongly than West acknowledges, especially in his rather authoritarian leadership style. Of course, we are still at the beginning of exploring which role the Old Testament can play in the formation of postcolonial identities. To be sure, West himself in his writings and in his praxis has made significant contributions to the development of such identities.

4. The Search for Subjectivity in Ezra–Nehemiah

Lastly, Roland Boer considers the notion of subjectivity as it unfolds in the texts of Ezra and Nehemiah. From a postcolonial perspective, subjectivity has undergone various critiques.[5] As a result, subjectivity appears in a new light, no longer merely as a characteristic of individuals but also of collectives.

In this framework, the subjectivity of Israel can be discussed. The texts of Ezra–Nehemiah are particularly fruitful for such an investigation, as the desire for political subjectivity is a key topic. After all, the challenges to subjectivity during the Babylonian exile loom in the background. Interesting for the theologically interested reader is that the subjectivity of Yahweh emerges together with the subjectivity of the people, with both ups and downs, as subjectivity is never stable.

---

5. Perhaps the strongest challenge to subjectivity comes from Gayatri Spivak's famous question whether the subaltern can speak, which she addresses in various ways throughout her career (1988, 1999). The importance of this question is the reminder that subaltern subjectivities are fragile at best and cannot easily be addressed in terms of dominant subjectivities.

One of the key insights of postcolonial studies is that subjectivity takes shape as dominant groups struggle for hegemony, seeking to establish themselves on the backs of the others. Class conflict is another issue at the core of the book of Nehemiah, and Boer points out the ambiguous position of Nehemiah, which insists on return of interest and security for defaulted debts, but not that the debts themselves should be forgiven. The result is that the excesses of what we today would call the "1 percent" are curbed in order to maintain the status quo, rather than in order to challenge the status quo.

The fact, noted in Boer's conclusion, that no clear subject emerges in Ezra–Nehemiah is significant. The subject positions presented are complex and cross the lines of power in various different directions. All this gets worked out in the text itself, which seeks to create a reality but is far from stable. This instability, reflected in the inability to distinguish insider and outsider, undermines the success of subject formation. In this context, Boer introduces the work of a number of theorists of recent memory, in particular Martin Heidegger, Giorgio Agamben, Theodore Adorno, Jacques Lacan, and Slavoj Žižek. These theorists have developed differing accounts of the formation of subjectivity, with the former three rejecting the subject as a useless category, and the latter two arguing that the formation of the subject exposes a constant split and void. Boer pushes beyond these thinkers and concludes that the production of the subject is without end, and that this is precisely what Ezra–Nehemiah teaches us.

Given these results, however, I wonder whether historicizing the various positions might give us some further clues. Lacan, for instance, is not merely talking about the subject in general, but about the subject in what he calls the "era of the 'ego,'" that is, the world of modern capitalism (1977, 77). In other words, Lacan is addressing particular tensions that arise at a particular moment in the struggle of the colonial and the postcolonial. If we understand our own subjectivity in terms of the complexity of life under the conditions of late capitalism, what might this tell us about Ezra–Nehemiah?

In this context, the fact that Boer introduces the notion of class is important, since this notion is too often overlooked. There is a class struggle going on in Ezra–Nehemiah and, despite the complexity that Boer presents, I would argue that some benefit more from it than others. This is clearly the case under the conditions of contemporary capitalism, where a few at the very top are doing well, while all others—including the middle class—are increasingly forced to deal with loss of power and financial security. If we compare this situation with Ezra–Nehemiah, we arrive at two contradictory possibilities. One is that there are some in this context who are indeed benefiting from all the confusion, and we need to find out who that might be. Could it be the nobles of the people after all, an option which Boer dismisses, or is it the Persians? The other conclusion is that indeed no one benefits. In this scenario, the challenge would be how to understand such a situation that is very different from ours, and what it might teach us for the present.

In any case, the realization that class is a factor in biblical texts is an important step in the right direction. Mainline biblical scholarship has never really paid attention to this point, a problem that is particularly pronounced in the United States, where there is little history of class analysis. Moreover, Boer's account reminds us that class is not merely a matter of social stratification but rather of tension between the classes. Learning more about these particular tensions—Who benefits at whose expense? How does resistance manifest itself?—would help us understand not only Ezra–Nehemiah better but also ourselves.

5. Conclusions

Each of these readings of Old Testament/Hebrew Bible texts with a postcolonial lens is fruitful in its own way. Each interpretation makes me want to read these texts again with new eyes, which is not an insignificant matter for a theologian to confess.

One lesson that has been with me since my seminary days is the appreciation for the material quality of thought processes and theologies found in the Hebrew Bible. This is particularly important for Christians and religious scholars who have moved on from a concern for the material to a concern for a narrowly constructed otherworldly spirituality or world of ideas. In this regard, postcolonial readings are a godsend, for they contribute to a fresh awareness of these material qualities, in all their complexity and ambiguity, and push us to the next step in taking them seriously and addressing them.

At the same time, the concern for the material that develops here is no flat emphasis on the importance of the material realm over against the realm of ideas and spirituality. The postcolonial contributions in this volume are aware of the dialectic that emerges as these realms encounter each other and interact with each other. Language and ideas, for instance, are not merely part of some ideal realm but are connected to material developments and have direct material consequences so that they might be understood as material players that shape our lives. This broader horizon not only allows for but ultimately demands fresh theological reflections as well, because the divine cannot be relegated to the ideal realm either.

Finally, postcolonial readings of the Old Testament can help us identify strategies of resistance both then and now. Even the term postcolonial itself serves as a reminder that colonial systems, as powerful as they may be, can never have the last word.

REFERENCES

Assmann, Hugo, ed. 1996. *Götzenbilder und Opfer: René Girard im Gespräch mit der Befreiungstheologie*. BZMT. Translated by Horst Goldstein. Thaur: Verlagshaus Thaur; Münster: LIT Verlag.
Bhabha, Homi. 1994. *The Location of Culture*. London: Routledge.
Fanon, Frantz. 1963. *The Wretched of the Earth*. Translated by Constance Farrington. New York: Grove.
Keller, Catherine, Michael Nausner, and Mayra Rivera, eds. 2004. *Postcolonial Theologies: Divinity and Empire*. St. Louis: Chalice.
Kwok Pui-lan. 2005. *Postcolonial Imagination and Feminist Theology* Louisville: Westminster John Knox.
Lacan, Jacques. 1977. The Function and Field of Speech and Language in Psycho-analysis. Pages 23–86 in Jacques Lacan, *Écrits: A Selection*. Translated by Alan Sheridan. New York: W. W. Norton, 1977.
Memmi, Albert. 1991. *The Colonizers and the Colonized*. Expanded ed. Translated by Howard Greenfeld. Boston: Beacon.
Mignolo, Walter. 2000. *Local Histories/Global Design: Coloniality, Subaltern Knowledges, and Border Thinking*. Princeton: Princeton University Press.
Niebuhr, H. Richard. 1951. *Christ and Culture*. New York: Harper.
Rieger, Joerg. 2007. *Christ and Empire: From Paul to Postcolonial Times*. Minneapolis: Fortress.
Said, Edward W. 1978. *Orientalism*. New York: Pantheon Books.
Spivak, Gayatri Chakravorty. 1988. Can the Subaltern Speak? Pages 271–313 in *Marxism and the Interpretation of Culture*. Edited by C. Nelson and L. Grossberg. London: Macmillan.
———. 1999. *A Critique of Postcolonial Reason: Towards a History of the Vanishing Present*. Cambridge: Harvard University Press.

Contributors

Roland Boer is Xin Ao Professor of Literature at Renmin University of China, Beijing. His main research area is the intersection of Marxism and religion, and among numerous works he has published recently *In the Vale of Tears: On Marxism and Theology V* (Brill, 2013), *Lenin, Religion, and Theology* (Palgrave Macmillan, 2013), and edited, with Fernando Segovia, *The Future of the Biblical Past: Envisioning Biblical Studies on a Global Key* (Society of Biblical Literature, 2012)

Steed Vernyl Davidson is Associate Professor at the Pacific Lutheran Theological Seminary and the Graduate Theological Union in Berkeley California. He also teaches courses at the Church Divinity School of the Pacific in Berkeley. He research centers on the intersection of empire, gender, and marginality in biblical literature with particular emphases on prophetic literature.

Richard Horsley, Professor of Study of Religion Emeritus at the University of Massachusetts, Boston, has written widely on the social-political context and implications of biblical tests and history, for example, in *Jesus and Empire* (Fortress, 2003), *Jesus and the Powers* (Fortress, 2011), *Scribes, Visionaries, and the Politics of Second Temple Judea* (Westminster John Knox, 2007), and *Revolt of the Scribes* (Fortress, 2009).

Uriah Y. Kim is the academic dean and associate professor of Hebrew Bible at Hartford Seminary. He is the author of *Decolonizing Josiah: Toward a Postcolonial Reading of the Deuteronomistic History* (Sheffield, 2005) and *Identity and Loyalty in the David Story: A Postcolonial Reading* (Sheffield, 2008). He also has written several articles on the book of Judges from a postcolonial perspective, including "The Politics of Othering in North America and in the Book of Judges" (*Concilium*), "More to the Eye Than Meets the Eye: A Protest against the Empire in Samson's

Death" (*Biblical Interpretation*), and "Where Is the Home for the Man of Luz?" (*Interpretation*).

Judith E. McKinlay was formerly a senior lecturer in biblical studies in the Department of Theology and Religion at the University of Otago, New Zealand.

Johnny Miles teaches at Texas Christian University, Fort Worth, Texas. His research interests focus on the intersections between the Hebrew Bible and contemporary literary theory, postcolonialism, and mythic studies. He has published *Wise King—Royal Fool: Semiotics, Satire, and Proverbs 1-9* (T&T Clark, 2004), and his *Constructing the Other in Ancient Israel and the US* is in press.

Althea Spencer-Miller is Assistant Professor of New Testament at Drew Theological School, Drew University. A graduate of Claremont Graduate University (2008), her interest in liberative hermeneutics dates to her earliest seminary training at the United Theological College of the West Indies as an inspiration for Caribbean theology. Spencer Miller's current research advances an anticolonial posture as she explores orality as an alternative epistemology lived and expressed in oral-literate cultures such as the Caribbean. Recent publications include *Feminist New Testament Studies: Global and Future Perspectives,* co-edited with Kathleen O'Brien Wicker and Musa Dube; "Women and Christianity in the Caribbean: Living Past the Colonial Legacy," an essay in *Women and Christianity,* co-edited by Cheryl A. Kirk-Duggan and Karen Jo Torjesen; and "Chiefs, Female" in *The Oxford Encyclopedia of Women in World History.*

Leo G. Perdue is Professor Emeritus of Hebrew Bible, Brite Divinity School, Texas Christian University. A graduate of Vanderbilt University, he taught previously at Radford University, Indiana University, and Phillips University. He is the author of numerous books, including *Wisdom and Creation* (Abingdon, 1994) and *Wisdom in Revolt* (Almond, 1991). He retired in August 2012.

Christina Petterson is a postdoctoral research fellow in the postgraduate research group "Gender as a Category of Knowledge" at Humboldt University, Berlin. Her research focuses on the role of Protestant Christianity in the formation of modern Europe and its colonial enterprises, with special focus on gender, race, and class. She has recently published *Acts of Empire: The Acts of the Apostles and Imperial Ideology* (Chung Yuan Christian University, 2012); her next book, to be published in 2013, is *The Missionary, the Catechist and the Hunter: Foucault, Protestantism and Colonialism*.

Joerg Rieger is Wendland-Cook Professor of Constructive Theology at Perkins School of Theology, SMU. He is the author of numerous books, most recently *Occupy Religion: Theology of the Multitude* (co-authored with Kwok Pui-lan, 2012), *Traveling* (2011), *Grace under Pressure* (2011), *Globalization and Theology* (2010), *No Rising Tide: Theology, Economics, and the Future* (2009), *Beyond the Spirit of Empire: Theology and Politics in a New Key* (co-authored with Jung Mo Sung and Néstor Miguez, 2009), and *Christ and Empire: From Paul to Postcolonial Times* (2007).

Gerald O. West is Professor of Old Testament and African Biblical Hermeneutics in the School of Religion, Philosophy and Classics at the University of KwaZulu-Natal, South Africa. He also works within one of the School's community engagement projects, the Ujamaa Centre for Community Development and Research.

Index of Ancient Texts

Bible		Joshua	
		2	74, 82
Genesis		2:1	81, 86
3:15	77 n. 9	2:3	81
2:20–25	176	2:2–4	79
15:19	89 n. 21	2:4	81
		2:9–13	83
Exodus		2	123
1–2	12	3:2	137 n. 9
3:14	177	3:31	123
20:13–19	176	4:17	123
		4:20	89
Leviticus		6	82
26:12	177	6:17	81
		6:22	81
Numbers		6:23	81
14	20	6:25	76, 81
16	24	7	180
25:1–5	175	7:1–26	138
25:6	25	7:13–14	123
27	2, 12, 14, 18, 25, 26	8:19–20	138
27:4, 7	17	9	5, 135
32:33	16	9:1	135
32:39–40	16	9:4–6	154 n. 22
34	20	9:6	138 n. 11
36	2, 18, 26	9:6–7	148
36:10–12	16	9:7	135 n. 6, 137 n. 9, 138 n. 11, 148, 154 n. 22
Deuteronomy		9:8	138 n. 11
2:26–31	138	9:9	138 n. 11
6:10–11	23	9:9–10	148
20:10–18	136	9:11	138 n. 11
24:1–4	180	9:11–14	154 n. 22
29:5–6	138	9:14–15	148

Joshua (cont.)		1:27–30	121
9:15	138 n. 11, 154 n. 22	1:28	121
9:16	131, 137 n. 9, 138 n. 11,	1:30	121
154 n. 22		1:33	121
9:17–21	154 n. 22	1:34	116
9:18	142, 148	1:35	121
9:18–19	138 n. 11	2:1	115
9:20	138 n. 11	2:2	121
9:20–21	148	2:3	121
9:22	137 n. 9, 149	2:6	115
9:22–23	149	2:6–3:6	115, 121
9:23	138 n. 11, 154	2:11	121
9:24	138 n. 11	2:12	116, 121
9:26	148	2:13	121
9:27	138 n. 12, 154	2:14	118
10:5	135 n. 6	2:17	121
10:6	138 n. 11	2:18	118
11:19	135 n. 6	2:19	121
12:29–32	138	3:5	118
16:1–16	16	3:6	121, 126
17:3–6	23	3:7	115, 121
		3:7–11	119
Judges		3:7–16:31	119
1	74 n. 7, 89 n. 21, 161	3:8	119
1:1	74 n. 7	3:12	119, 121
1:1–2:5	115, 121	3:12–30	119
1:2	115	3:17	119
1:3	115	3:19	119, 122
1:4–7	120	3:20	119
1:6	120	3:21	122
1:6–7	120	3:22	119
1:8	115	3:25	120
1:10	117	3:26	119
1:11	117	3:28	115, 118
1:12	125	3:29	122
1:12–15	115	3:30	120
1:13	125	3:31	122
1:17	115, 117	4	74, 83
1:19	115, 122	4–5	181
1:20	115	14:1	121
1:22	115	4:1–5:31	119
1:22–26	123	4:2	119
1:23	117	4:3	119, 122

4:4	83	7:25	121
4:7	83, 119	8:1	124
4:9	83, 120	8:12	120
4:11	84, 89	8:20	121
4:14	115	8:21	121
4:15	120	8:28	120
4:17	83, 84	8:34	118
4:17–22	119	9	124
4:18	77–78 n. 13, 86, 89	9:53–54	126
4:18–19	77	10:6	121
4:19	77–78 n. 13	10:6–16	115, 116, 121
4:21	79	10:6–18	5
4:22	78 n. 13, 121	10:6–11:11	110
4:24	85	10:7	119
4:23–24	74	10:8	110, 116, 117, 121
4:23–25	120	10:9	110, 121
4–5	74 n. 7	10:12	121
5	74, 84	10:13	121
5:7	84	10:16	121
5:8	122	10:17–18	122
5:24	76, 84, 85	11:1–11	5
5:26	84, 121	11:12	109
5:27	121	11:12–28	4, 109, 115, 116, 121
5:28	122	11:13	109
5:30	85	11:14	109
5:31	85, 118	11:15	109
6:1	119, 121	11:17	109, 110
6:3–4	119	11:18	109, 110
6:3–6	118	11:19	109, 110
6:5–7	119	11:20	110
6:6	122	11:21	110
6:7–10	115, 116, 121	11:21–22	109
6:8–9	116	11:23	110, 116
6:9	121	11:24	110
6:10	116, 121	11:26	110
6:12	122	11:27	111
6:15	122	11:28	111
6:16	120	11:29	110, 122
6:33	119	11:29–33	110
7:1–7	120	11:29–40	5
7:3–6	122	11:32	110, 115, 122
7:12	119	11:34–40	126
7:21–22	120	11:35	126

Judges (cont.)

11:36	118	21:8–24	126
12:1–6	124	1 Samuel	
12:1–7	5	8	97, 98
12:3	115	8–12	180, 181,188
13:1	119, 120, 121	8:9–17	97
13:5	120	8:11–18	96
14:3	124	15:16	89 n. 21
14:4	120	27:10	89 n. 21
14:15–17	126		
15:5	118	2 Samuel	
15:11	120	7:13	99
15:14–15	122	7:16	99
15:20	120	21:1–14	138 n. 11
16	189 n. 21, 126		
16:1–3	120	1 Kings	
16:24	120, 126	3:16–28	97 n. 6
16:25–26	126	4:1–19	96
16:30	120	5:13–18	96
16:31	115	5:15	95
17:1–21:25	115	9:20–21	155 n. 23
18:1	116	10:9	95 n. 3
18:2	116	10:10	95
18:5	116	10:13	95 n. 3
18:6	116	10:14–29	93
18:7	116	10:15	93,94
18:9	118	10:18–20	4, 93, 98, 99
18:10	116, 117, 118	10:22	95
18:24	118	10:25	95
18:27–29	117	14:17	13
18:29	117	19:16	13
19	126		
19–21	182	2 Kings	
19:12	123	6:4	169
19:14–15	123	6: 11	169
19:22–30	123	8:9	169
19:23–24	123	10:6	169
19:29	126	10:12–14	179
19:30	123	11:12	169
20–21	124	12:26–33	178
20:1	126	13:14–25	178
20:5	127	14:4	169
20:6	123, 126	14:23–29	178

INDEX OF ANCIENT TEXTS

15:9	187	7:1–5	234
15:18	187	7:7	155, 225–26
15:19–20	185	7:24	155
15:24	187	8:1–21	234
15:28	187	8:15–18	234
17:7–18	187	8:17	155
		8:20	155
1 Chronicles		8:25	224
9:2	155	8:35	224
		9–10	231
2 Chronicles		9:1	224, 225, 232 n. 16
9:13–28	93	9:2	229 n. 10
9:14	93, 94	9:3	231
9:17–19	93	10:5	224
		10:8	230
Ezra		10:7	232 n. 15
2	155	10:11	224
2:1–67	233 n. 18, 234	10:15	234
2:2	224	10:18–44	232 n. 16, 234
2:41	230	10:25	224
2:43	155		
2:58	155	Nehemiah	
2:59	224, 234	1:2	225
2:64–67	230	1:6	224
2:65	230	1:6–9	231 n. 12
2:70	155, 224	2:10	224
3:1	224	2:16	225–26, 229 n. 10
4:1	227	3	234
4:1–3	227	3:7	155
4:1–23	226	3:26	155
4:2	227	3:31	155
4:3	227	3:33–4:17	226
4:6–24	226	4:8	229 n. 10
4:12	225	4:12	225
4:23	225	4:13	229 n. 10
5:3	227	4:16–17	229
5:3–6:15	226	5	228
5:5	225	5:1	225, 227
6:1–19	226	5:1–5	228
6:7–8	225	5:7	229 n. 10
6:14	225	5:8	227
6:16–17	224	5:10	228
6:21	224	5:15–16	228

Nehemiah (cont.)		13:15-18	231
5:17	225, 229 n. 10	13:18	231 n. 12
6:6	225	13:19-23	231
6:14	231	13:23	225, 232
7	155	13:23-27	231
7:5	229 n. 10	13:24	232
7:6-68	233 n. 18	13:25	231
7:7	224	13:25-27	232
7:25	155	13:26	225
7:46	155	13:28	231 n. 14
7:60	155	13:30	224
7:61	224, 234		
7:66-69	230	Psalms	
7:73	155, 224	54:8	95 n. 4
8-9	223		
8:1	224	Song of Songs	
8:7	224	5:14	95 n. 4
9	222-24, 231 n. 12	6:4	13
9:1-2	224	7:4	95 n. 4
9:2	225		
9:3	224	Isaiah	
9:9-15	223	7:1	171
9:10	223	41:25	229 n. 10
9:16-25	223		
9:32-38	224	Jeremiah	
10:2-28/1-27	229, 234	51:23	229 n. 10
10:28	155	51:28	229 n. 10
10:29-30/28-29	229	51:57	229 n. 10
10:30/29	224, 229		
11:1-36	234	Ezekiel	
11:3	155, 225, 226	23:6	229 n. 10
12:1-26	234	23:12	229 n. 10
11:21	155	23:23	229 n. 10
12:27-43	234		
12:30	224	Hosea	
12:40	229 n. 10	1:1	170
12:47	224	1:1-11	184
13	2331	1:2	175, 184
13:2	224	1:4-5	178
13:3	224, 225	1:6-7	178
13:4-8	231	1:7	178
13:10-14	231	1:11	178
13:11	229 n. 10	2:1-11	179

2:4	175–76, 180, 184	8:1–2	175
2:6	175	8:4	170, 181, 182, 188
2:7	180	8:4–5	175
2:7b–15	184	8:4–6	176
2:10	184	8:5–6	184
2:14	176	8:9	175, 187, 188
2:15	180	8:10	182
2:16–17	175	8:12	189
2:26–23	180	8:13	185
2:22–23	179, 185, 190	8:14	170, 175, 185
3	176–77	8:16	185
3:1–5	179, 184	9:1	184
3:3	175	9:1–9	174
3:4–5	185	9:2	184
4:1–3	175, 180, 189	9:3	185, 188
4:4–14	189	9:6	187, 188
4:6	189	9:10	175
4:10	175, 184	9:12	188
4:12–15	175	9:13	185
4:15–19	190	9:14	184
5:1	170	9:15	175
5:1–2	180	9:15–16	180
5:4	189	9:16	188
5:8	182	9:17	185
5:8–12	185	10:3	181
5:12–13	175	10:3–10	174
5:13	187, 188	10:5	184
6:1	185	10:6	175, 182, 188
6:1–3	173	10:7	170, 182
6:4–6	179, 184	10:9	182, 185
6:6	189	10:11	170, 185
6:7–7:2	181	10:12	190
6:7–7:16	175	10:14	180, 185
7:1	175	10:15	182
7:1–7	170, 181	11:1	175
7:4	184	11:1–9	182
7:7–8	182	11:5	175, 185, 187, 188
7:8	184	11:5–7	174
7:8–12	182	11:6	185
7:11	188	11:8–9	185
7:11–12	175	11:10	185
7:14	175	11:11	175
7:16	185	11:11–12	179, 184

Hosea (cont.)		14:11	185
11:14–15	180		
12:1	187, 188, 189	Amos	
12:2	170	3:15	95 n. 4
12:3–9	182	6:4	95 n. 4
12:7	190		
12:13	182	Romans	
12:24	175	13	97
13:1	184		
13:2	175, 184	Hebrews	
13:4	189	11:31	76
13:4–5	187		
13:9	187	James	
13:10	182, 188	2:25	76
13:10–11	170		
13:11	188	Revelation	
13:13	187	18:12	95 n. 4
13:14	179	20:11	99
13:15	189		
14:1	170, 174, 189	OTHER ANCIENT SOURCES	
14:3	187, 188		
14:4	185	b. Yebamot	155 n. 23
14:5	185	*Odyssey*	39
14:8	176, 185		

Index of Modern Authors

Adams, L. Emilie	62, 63	Bos, Johanna	74
Adorno, Theodor W.	234, 270	Bradley, Richard	29
Agamben, Giorgio	221, 234, 270	Braithwaite, Edward Kamau	49, 55, 58, 59, 60
Aichele, George	27		
Alcock, Susan E.	13, 14, 17, 28	Brett, Marc C.	112, 113
Alexander, Loveday	41	Brueggeman, Walther	93–94, 96
Althaus-Reid, Marcella	83, 88, 89	Budd, Philip J.	18
Amit, Yairah	77	Burns, Patricia	22, 25
Assis, Elie	71, 79, 114, 123	Byrskog, Samuel	40
Assmann, Hugo	267	Cabrita, Joel	203–4, 210, 217
Badiou, Alain	221	Campbell, John	195
Bailey, R.	139, 152, 165	Campbell, K. M.	88
Bal, Mieke	77, 89, 123	Carby, Hazel	71, 79
Barnhart, E.	134, 142, 168	Carden, Michael	15
Batten, Loring W.	222, 224, 226, 228, 230	Césaire, Aime	50
		Chatterjee, Partha	75, 87
Bauckham, Richard	38, 42–3	Chidester, D.	137, 165
Bauer, Uwe F. W.	117	Chow, Rey	70, 86, 88
Beck, Roger B.	194	Clarke, Clifton R.	201
Bediako, Kwame	196–97, 198, 200, 201, 202, 217, 268	Clines, David	222
		Comaroff, Jean	194–95, 248
Befu, H.	153, 165	Comaroff, John L.	194–95, 248
Ben-Barak, Zafrira	13	Conn, S.	145, 165
Bennett, Milton J.	48, 49	Conway, Colleen	28, 29
Bhabha, Homi	5, 80, 81, 82, 88, 90, 266	Coote, Robert	73
		Cornell, S.	132, 154, 166
Bird, Phyllis	81, 82	Cross, Frank M.	113
Bishku, Michael B.	222	Crossan, Dominic	40, 43
Blanton, Ward	221	D'Costa, Jean	53, 54
Blenkinsopp, Joseph	135, 165, 221, 226, 228, 230	Dalziel, Raewyn	26
		Daniels, R.	131, 134–35, 143–47, 152, 156–58, 160–62, 166
Boer, Roland	15, 17, 24, 25, 93, 94, 105, 124, 153–54, 165, 222, 231, 233, 269–61	Davies, Gordon F.	228, 230
		Day, J.	135, 155, 166

Delaney, Carol	15	Heidegger, Martin	221, 234, 270
Denbeaux, M.	164, 166	Hexham, Irving	204–7
Dewey, Joanna	36, 53	Hirabayashi, J.	146–47, 167
Dijkstra, Meindert	5	Hirabayashi, L.	146–47, 167
Douglas, Mary	224	Hirasuna, D.	161, 167
Dower, J.	143–44, 166	Horsley, Richard	3, 7, 36, 39, 40, 52, 54
Draper, Jonathan	36, 40, 46, 48, 49, 52, 53, 55	Hyldahl, Jesper	37, 45, 55
		Iiyama, P.	133, 167
Dube, Musa	2, 20, 72, 73, 87, 111–13, 126–127	Ilan, Tal	15
		Inada, L.	161, 167
Elwell, Sue Levi	14	Irons, P.	150, 167
Engelman, R.	145, 165	Ishigo, E.	129, 167
Eskenazi, Tamara	12, 13, 14, 17, 231	Jackson, Michael	47
Esler, Philip	233	Jobling, David	29, 94, 95, 105
Etherington, Norman	210	John, Catherine	49
Exum, J. Cheryl	26	Kalu, Ogbu U.	201, 217
Fairchild, B.	145, 165	Kantorowicz, Ernst H.	99, 100
Fanon, Frantz	75, 80, 82, 83, 85, 86, 87, 264	Karlsen, Mads-Peter	221, 235
		Keita, Cherif	201
Fensham, C.	148, 166	Kelber, Werner	36, 40, 41, 44, 45, 55
Finkelstein, Israel	233	Keller, Catherine	261
Fleras, Augie	19	Kim, Uriah	4–5, 114, 118
Foley, John Miles	40, 53	Kirk, Alan	41
Gaitsgill, Deborah	210	Kloppenborg, John S.	52
Gillmayr-Bucher, Susanne	81	Kramer, Phyllis	76
Girard, René	267	Kuan, Kah-Jin Jeffrey	88
Glissant, Èdouard	50	Kwok Pui-lan	25, 28, 261
Gottwald, Norman	73	Lacan, Jacques	234, 270
Grabbe, Lester	222	Lalla, Barbara	53, 54
Green, W.	153, 166	Liew, Tat-siong Benny	2, 29
Grintz, J.	148, 166	Lemos, T. M.	120
Grodzins, M.	142, 146, 166	Lerner, Berel	76, 89
Guillaume, Philippe	113	Le Tran, Mai-Anh	88
Gunkel, Hermann	35, 39, 43	Levine, Baruch	14, 16, 18, 24
Gunn, David	77	Lincoln, Bruce	222
Gunner, Elizabeth	211–12	Loomba, Ania	221
Guy, Jeff	208–9	Lord, Albert	40
Hacker, D.	159–61, 166	Love, Ngatata	21, 30
Hafetz, J.	164, 166	Lowenthal, David	19
Hansen, A.	159–61, 166	Lubbe, J. J.	194
Hardy, Linda	22	Maluleke, Tinyiko S.	201
Hartmann, D.	132, 166	Marcus, David	78
Hawk, D.	136–38, 148, 166–67	Matson, F.	134, 142, 168

INDEX OF MODERN AUTHORS 287

Mbiti, John	195-96, 198 201-2, 268	Rivera, Mayra	261
McCann, J. Clinton	118	Römer, Thomas	18, 113
McIver, Robert	41	Rogers, J. W.	118
McKinlay, Judith	2-3	Robinson, Bernard	76
Meintjes, Sheila	210	Rowlett, Lori	72, 73, 136, 167
Memmi, Albert	264	Russell, Heather	49
Mignolo, Walter	263	Russell, Letty	11
Miles, Johnny	5, 263-65	Ryan, Roger	119
Miscall, Peter	27	Said, Edward	20, 262
Mitchell, G.	135-36, 138, 167	Sakenfeld, Katherine Doob	11, 15, 16, 27, 30
Moffat, Robert	197		
Mohanty, Chandra	71	Sanneh, Lamin	196-99, 201, 217, 268
Montrose, Louise	72, 73, 76, 78, 88	Schwartz, Regina M.	125
Moon, Paul	22	Scott, James	136, 155, 168, 265
Muller, Carol Ann	204-5, 208-11	Segovia, Fernando F.	19
Myers, Jacob M.	222	Shank, David	200
Nakashima, T.	151, 167	Sharp, Carolyn	80, 82
Nausner, Michael	261	Shembe, Isaiah	7, 201-8, 210-17, 268-69
Nelson, Richard	74, 79		
Ng, W.	157, 167	Shemesh, Yael	13, 26, 30
Niditch, Susan	35, 74, 89, 122	Shillony, B.	154, 168
Niebuhr, H. Richard	262	Silberman, Lou	42
Nolan, Albert	199, 200	Simkins, Ronald A.	18
Noth, Martin	113	Smend, Rudolf	113
Obata, C.	161, 167	Smith, Andrea	88
Okamura, R.	150-52, 167	Snaith, N. H.	16, 18
Okihiro, G.	134, 143, 159-161, 167	Soares, Judith	50
Ong, Walter	35, 36, 37, 38, 39, 40, 41, 42, 43, 44, 45, 48, 53	Spencer, S.	132, 138, 168
		Spencer-Miller, Althea	3, 49
Oosthuizen, G. C.	204-7	Spivak, Gayatri	70, 80, 221, 269
Opoku, Kofi Asare	196	Spoonley, Paul	19
Papini, Robert	205	Stager, Lawrence	73
Parry, Milman	40	Sterring, Ankie	23
Patterson, Brad	20	Stewart, Edward C.	48, 49
Peel, J. D. Y.	202	Suárez, Margarita M. W.	47
Petterson, Christina	4	Sugirtharajah, R. S.	18, 19
Patte, Daniel	12, 30	Sutherland, R.	154, 168
Polayni, Karl	94, 95, 102	Sutton, J.	164, 168
Polzin, Robert	113	Takaki, R.	132-33, 139-40, 142, 168
Pratt, Mary Louis	111	tenBroek, J.	134, 142, 168
Purdue, Leo	5-6, 265-67	Temple, Philip	20, 21, 22, 23, 24, 26, 27
Reis, Pamela	78		
Rieger, Joerg	7, 261, 262, 263	Terreblanche, Sampie	201

Thompson, Thomas L.	233	West, Gerald O.	6–7, 194, 208, 211, 216, 248 252, 265, 267–69
Thurmond, H.	152, 168		
Tonks, Rosemarie	21, 24	Wevers, Lydia	21
Tucker, Dennis	12	Whitelam, Keith	73
Ulrich, Dean R.	15	Williamson, H. G. M.	222, 228
US Congress	134, 163, 168	Wolde, Ellen van	77
US War Department	151–52, 168	Wright, Edwina	58, 59, 60, 61, 64
Van Dyke, Ruth M.	13, 14, 17, 28	Yee, Gale	79
Walsh, Richard	27	Yorke, Gosnell	201
Warner-Lewis, Maureen	49–50, 59, 60, 64	Young, Robert	72
		Zia, H.	129, 168
Washington, Harold C.	221, 231, 232	Žižek, Slavoj	221, 234–35, 270
Wedde, Ian	23		

www.ingramcontent.com/pod-product-compliance
Lightning Source LLC
Chambersburg PA
CBHW031707230426
43668CB00006B/144